DEEP COSMOPOLITANISM

Activist Encounters in Folklore and Ethnomusicology

David A. McDonald, editor

DEEP COSMOPOLITANISM

KUTIYATTAM, DYNAMIC TRADITION, AND GLOBALIZING HERITAGE IN KERALA, INDIA

Leah Lowthorp

INDIANA UNIVERSITY PRESS

This book is a publication of

Indiana University Press
Herman B Wells Library
1320 East 10th Street
Bloomington, Indiana 47405 USA

iupress.org

First printing 2025

Library of Congress Cataloging-in-Publication Data
Names: Lowthorp, Leah K. author
Title: Deep cosmopolitanism : Kutiyattam, dynamic tradition, and globalizing heritage in Kerala, India / Leah Lowthorp.
Description: Bloomington : Indiana University Press, 2025. | Series: Activist encounters in folklore and ethnomusicology | Includes bibliographical references and index.
Identifiers: LCCN 2025001503 (print) | LCCN 2025001504 (ebook) | ISBN 9780253073587 hardback | ISBN 9780253073594 paperback | ISBN 9780253073617 ebook | ISBN 9780253073600 adobe pdf
Subjects: LCSH: Kūḍiyāṭṭam | Sanskrit drama—India—Kerala—History and criticism | Performing arts—India—Kerala—History and criticism | Cultural property—India—Kerala | Postcolonialism
Classification: LCC PN2884.5.K83 L69 2025 (print) | LCC PN2884.5.K83 (ebook) | DDC 792.0954/83—dc23/eng/20250414
LC record available at https://lccn.loc.gov/2025001503
LC ebook record available at https://lccn.loc.gov/2025001504

For my mother,
dear Margi Usha-teacher,
beloved Guru Padmashree P.K. Narayanan Nambiar,
and all of the Kutiyattam artists
who so generously welcomed me into their lives

എൻറെ അമ്മയ്ക്കും,
സ്നേഹംനിറഞ്ഞ മാർഗി ഉഷ ടീച്ചർക്കും,
ഹൃദയംനിറഞ്ഞ പത്മശ്രീ പി. കെ. നാരായണൻ
നമ്പ്യാർ ആശാനും,
എന്നെ അവരുടെ ലോകത്തേക്ക് ഹാർദ്ദമായി സ്വാഗതം ചെയ്ത
എല്ലാ കൂടിയാട്ട കലാകാരന്മാർക്കും

CONTENTS

ACKNOWLEDGMENTS

I would like to express my boundless gratitude to the Kutiyattam community, who have opened their homes, hearts, and lives to me over the past seventeen years. You are what made this project possible. To Usha-teacher (Margi Usha), I can never truly express how grateful I am. Thank you for your laughter, friendship, mentorship, and generous research assistance all these years. This book could not have happened without you. To Joby-chetan (K. R. Joby), thank you for your wonderful logistical support and never-ending humor. To Unni-ashan (Kalamandalam Unnikrishnan Nambiar), thank you for your playful joking nature and instruction. To Sindhu-chechi (Kalamandalam Sindhu), thank you for your insight and friendship. To Sajeev-ashan (Margi Sajeev Narayana Chakyar), thank you for sharing your deep knowledge of Kutiyattam. To Kalamandalam Sajikumar, thank you for the frequent rides! To all of the artists at Margi, thank you for your incredible generosity and support. Padmasree P. K. Narayanan Nambiar-ashan and his family were particularly generous with me, opening their home and giving me special perspective into Kutiyattam as a familial way of life. I am so grateful. Special thanks also go to Painkulam Narayana Chakyar for spending thirteen hours interviewing with me, a testament to his great enthusiasm for and knowledge of the art. For providing me institutional homes in Kerala, I'd like to deeply thank both Margi and Kerala Kalamandalam.

To all of the Kutiyattam scholars and fellow enthusiasts I have met along the way, thank you for the supportive community surrounding this incredible art. I would especially like to thank Killimangalam Vasudevan Namboodiripad, C. K. Jayanthi, G. Venu, Sudha Gopalakrishnan, Clifford Jones, Krzysztof

Byrski, Heike Oberlin, Virginie Johan, John Sowle, Diane Daugherty, V. Kaladharan, Coralie Casassas, Milena Salvini, Pragna Enros, Bruce Sullivan, Graeme Vanderstoel, Aparna Nangiar, Ammannur Rajaneesh Chakyar, Salini Harikrishnan, Frank Korom, M. D. Muthukumaraswamy, Valdimar Hafstein, Regina Bendix, Andrew Ollett, J. Devika, Adheesh Sathaye, and Richard Schechner for their scholarly and personal generosity. Particular thanks go to those who read drafts—Krzysztof Byrski, Bruce Sullivan, and Finnian Moore-Gerety—and especially to Diane Daugherty, who generously read and commented on every chapter! I am very appreciative of my anonymous reviewers, who helped make this a better book. I'd also like to thank Ullattil Manmadhan for his insight, assistance, and translation suggestions and Bindu-teacher (V. K. Bindu) for her transcription assistance and patience while helping me learn the unbelievably difficult language that is Malayalam. To Mike Murashige, thank you for your invaluable editing suggestions. To my sister Jessica, thank you for your Photoshop expertise. To Regie-auntie, Prasannan-uncle, Rimi-chechi, and Mr. Pathros Matthai, thank you for your hospitality and support. To Gautam-chetan (Gautama Thirthas), thank you for your laughter, incredible generosity, and unwavering friendship. To Abril Gomez, thank you for our long evenings in Kerala of good food, laughter, and discussion, and to Unni-attan (Jayachandran Vellodi), thank you for your quiet friendship. To my aunt Veena Paulson, thank you for your warmth, laughter, and endless enthusiasm for my research and for offering me a familial home in Kerala. It meant the world.

This book began during my graduate studies in folklore and anthropology at the University of Pennsylvania. I'd like to express my deepest appreciation for the support and encouragement of my advisers Deborah Thomas and Mary Hufford and additional committee members Dan Ben-Amos and Lisa Mitchell. I'd also like to thank Alan Dundes and Roger Abrahams for their important early mentorship and encouragement. Special thanks go to Charles Briggs, who generously offered me an academic home at the University of California, Berkeley, and provided me with critical insight that inspired me to rethink and ultimately shift the theoretical moorings of my work. My gratitude also goes to my folklore and anthropology colleagues at the University of Oregon, as well as the Center on Diversity and Community (CoDaC) caregivers writing group that helped keep me on track.

This book was made possible through generous financial support from a number of sources over the years. I would like to thank the Wenner-Gren Foundation for Anthropological Research, the American Institute of Indian Studies, the Zwicker Memorial Fund, the Kenneth Goldstein Summer Research Fund, the Foreign Language and Area Studies Fellowship program,

Rotary International, the University of Pennsylvania, Harvard University, and the Philadelphia Folk Society. I would also like to thank generous funders at the University of Oregon, including the Office of the Provost, the Office of the Vice President for Research and Innovation, the College of Arts and Sciences, the Oregon Humanities Center, the Center for Asian and Pacific Studies, the Center for the Study of Women in Society, the Department of Anthropology, and the Folklore and Public Culture Program.

To my parents, thank you for always believing in me. Mom, it has meant so much that you support me in all that I do, wherever in the world I happen to be. Thank you for patiently reading and editing my full manuscript. Dad, thank you for always offering your love above all else. To Dana Hercbergs, your wacky sense of humor has often carried me through. To Kevin Durkin, thank you for your friendship and steady encouragement. To my son Tao, thank you for your sweetness, laughter, curiosity, and love. And last but not least, to my husband Terry, I am eternally grateful for your unwavering love and support on this journey and for taking the leap to walk alongside me in India.

NOTE ON TRANSLITERATION

I transliterate Malayalam and Sanskrit terms the first time they appear in the text according to ISO 15919: Transliteration of Devanagari and related Indic scripts into Latin characters.

LIST OF ILLUSTRATIONS

LIST OF ABBREVIATIONS

BJP: Bharatiya Janata Party
CPI: Communist Party of India
CPI(M): Communist Party of India (Marxist)
EMS: EMS Namboodiripad
ICH: Intangible Cultural Heritage
ICH Convention: UNESCO's 2003 Convention for the Safeguarding of the Intangible Cultural Heritage
ICOMOS: International Council on Monuments and Sites
SNA: Sangeet Natak Akademi
UNESCO: United Nations Educational, Scientific and Cultural Organization
UNESCO/JFIT: UNESCO/Japan Funds-in-Trust
WIPO: World Intellectual Property Organization
World Heritage Convention: UNESCO's 1972 Convention concerning the Protection of the World Cultural and Natural Heritage

DEEP COSMOPOLITANISM

INTRODUCTION

Figure 1. *Antakawadham* Kutiyattam at Padmasree Mani Madhava Chakyar Smaraka Gurukulam with (*left to right*) Vinayakan Namboothiri and Sarath Narayanan. Photo by author.

Kūṭiyāṭṭam Sanskrit theater is an illustrious art with a deep cosmopolitan past. Part of the larger phenomenon of Sanskrit drama performed across the Indian subcontinent long ago, this art form hails from the historically cosmopolitan region of Kerala, now a coastal state in southwestern India. Those intimately familiar with Kutiyattam (pronounced *koodiyaattam*) know it to be an art like no other. Performed on Kerala stages for around one thousand years, Kutiyattam is a feast for the senses. Spectators have long enjoyed its vibrantly painted faces that convey exquisite emotional nuance, its vivid costumes with gold-laden ornaments, and a rich soundscape of sharp, rhythmic beats emanating from the *mizhavu* (*milāvŭ*) copper drum.[1] One of the art's most striking features is the important role women have played alongside men onstage since its earliest days, a rare phenomenon in the wider South Asian theaterscape.

I still remember the first time I saw Nangiarkoothu (Naṅṅyārkūttu), Kutiyattam's solo women's performance, during my first summer of Malayalam language immersion in Kerala's capital city of Trivandrum (Thiruvananthapuram). With her elaborate makeup, vibrant expressions, and control over the audience's predominantly male gaze, the actress was both beautiful and powerful. Portraying gods and goddesses, heroes and heroines, and even plants and animals, the actress as omnipotent narrator moved her body across the stage in feats of strength, an interplay of emotions washing over her expressive face: anger, sorrow, wonderment, joy. I was mesmerized. My host-father, vice president of a prominent local arts organization, later asked me: "Did you enjoy the show? The actress is Margi Usha, a friend of mine. I can invite her over for chai one day if you'd like to meet her."

When the day finally came for Margi Usha's visit, I was both excited and apprehensive. After only one year of study, my Malayalam was not nearly good enough to speak with her as I wanted. She arrived in a flash, descending sidesaddle from the back of her husband's motor scooter. As she greeted me with a warm smile, I felt an immediate connection, as I often do when I meet people who will impact my life in a significant way. She sat down next to her husband, and we smiled across at each other, peppering our silence with short sentences and sips of chai. She laughed often, displaying a wide row of gleaming white teeth, and her carefree, welcoming nature made me feel completely at ease. When the time came for her departure, she took my hand and gazed into my eyes with a smile, inviting me to train with her the next time I came to Kerala. I planned to explore the impact of Kutiyattam's recognition by the United Nations Educational, Scientific and Cultural Organization (UNESCO) as an intangible heritage of humanity. I had not anticipated training in the art, but Margi Usha inspired me to put my own body on the line as part of this process.

~

As India's first UNESCO Masterpiece of the Oral and Intangible Heritage of Humanity, Kutiyattam was inscribed in 2001 alongside other "endangered" art forms from around the world. This achievement was celebrated by the Indian government and across Kerala state. A decision made by a distant intergovernmental body in Paris elevated an ancient art, performed in an ancient language, to a heritage of humanity. With a stroke of the director general's pen, the elite matrilineal temple art—today performed by caste-diverse and economically marginalized artists in a communist Indian state—no longer belonged only to the artists, Kerala, or India but also to the world. For Kutiyattam artists today, UNESCO's inscription has had a lasting impact, but despite all of the fanfare, they do not see it as the pinnacle of their art's history or even as its defining moment. For artists, this cosmopolitan heritage recognition is simply the most recent act of a much longer play that began roughly one thousand years ago.

Deep Cosmopolitanism: Kutiyattam, Dynamic Tradition, and Globalizing Heritage in Kerala, India is an ethnographic study of the world's oldest continuously performed theater—Kutiyattam Sanskrit theater of Kerala, India—that offers a unique perspective on cosmopolitanism, heritage, and tradition over the *longue durée*. Investigating Kutiyattam's UNESCO designation in the context of the art's deep history, I explore how the many roles Kutiyattam has played in various cosmopolitan formations over time challenge Eurocentric cosmopolitan genealogies and assumptions about cosmopolitanism, tradition, and modernity and prompt new ideas about what these might mean today. In the process, through a combination of postcolonial and decolonial approaches, I fundamentally rethink the notion of cosmopolitanism from a non-Western perspective with premodern roots and offer a critique of the colonialist undertones of how international heritage regimes conceptualize peoples and traditions around the world today.[2]

Deep Cosmopolitanism begins by positioning Kutiyattam in one such heritage regime, via its 2001 UNESCO Intangible Cultural Heritage (ICH) designation as a heritage of humanity. UNESCO's ICH program evidenced an organizational shift from tangible to intangible heritage that was the culmination of a decades-long movement by the Global South for greater equity in international heritage recognition. Here I argue that, despite UNESCO's best intentions, the endangered-local to safeguarded-global trajectory evidenced in its ICH program problematically reproduces cultural hierarchies rooted in colonialist ideologies of white supremacy. By framing expressive forms primarily from the Global South as endangered—outmoded, hearkening from another time, and unable to adapt to the contemporary world—we see the UNESCO ICH program reify colonialist paradigms that have long framed non-Western/nonwhite peoples, societies, and cultures as backward, ahistorical, and premodern.[3]

Anthropologist Johannes Fabian (1983) has aptly termed this a "denial of coevalness," a discourse central to colonialism and early anthropology that conceptualizes non-Western Others as inhabiting a different time than the Western, white, modern subject. In a model whereby the spatial ordering of the world is equated with a temporal ordering, traveling from Europe elsewhere was experienced not only as movement across space but as movement backward in time. Rooted in nineteenth-century ideologies of racialized difference, colonial paradigms thereby mapped the world into racialized regions designated as modern or premodern, with only white Europe conceptualized as the former (Mignolo 2011). Through its discourse of endangerment concentrated in the Global South, I argue that UNESCO's ICH program problematically reproduces a colonialist map of the world that relegates non-Western/nonwhite peoples and their "endangered" traditions to a premodern past. In so doing, I challenge the taken-for-granted reproduction of colonialist binaries today, disentangling one in particular: the binary of tradition and modernity.

Deep Cosmopolitanism presents an alternative narrative that tells the story of a UNESCO ICH form on its own terms. Rejecting the universality of UNESCO's endangered-local to safeguarded-global trajectory, I explore the global-to-global trajectory of Kutiyattam Sanskrit theater. Tracing Kutiyattam's cosmopolitan engagements with the early Sanskrit cosmopolis of the first millennium CE (Pollock 2006) through UNESCO's Intangible Cultural Heritage of Humanity, I position the elite matrilineal temple art within a South Asian cosmopolitan trajectory that reaches much further back than European eighteenth- and nineteenth-century local-national-global projections.

Here I challenge UNESCO's Eurocentric trajectory by exploring what I term the *deep cosmopolitanism* of Kutiyattam. Adopting Breckenridge, Bhabha, Pollock, and Chakrabarty's (2002) definition of cosmopolitanism as "multiple ways of thinking and acting beyond the local," the concept of *deep cosmopolitanism* allows us to consider what it means to be cosmopolitan in the world in multiple ways across a temporal depth that moves beyond the "abbreviated time" of colonial modernity (Menon 2018, 69).[4] Locating Kutiyattam's origins in the Sanskrit cosmopolis—the circulation of Sanskrit poetry across South and Southeast Asia from approximately 300 to 1300 CE (Pollock 1996, 2006)—I chart multiple episodes of the art's larger-than-local engagements to the present day. I situate

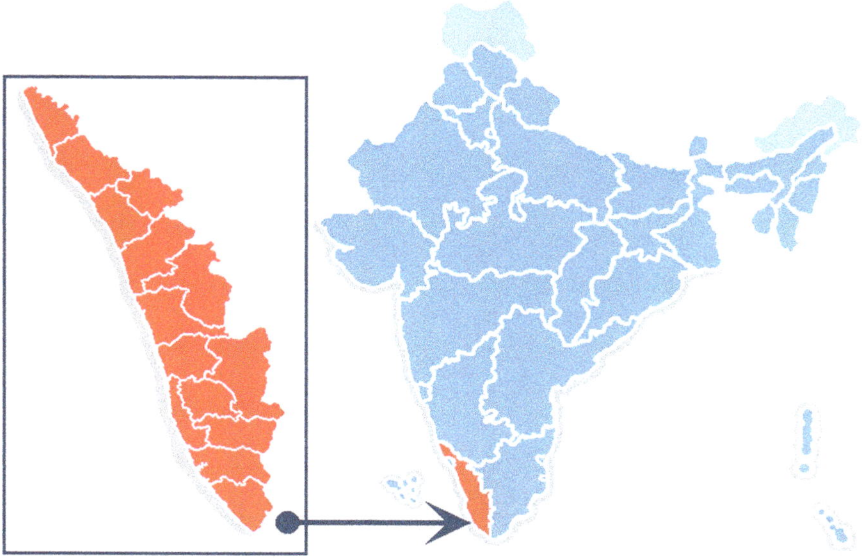

Figure 2. Map of Kerala. Image courtesy of Wikimedia Commons.

Kutiyattam in the region of Kerala, famed for its spice trade across much of the known world—from ancient Rome to China and the Middle East—since ancient times. Known as the land of pepper, Kerala's Malabar Coast was the halfway point between Middle Eastern and East Asian trading routes, where ships stopped to refresh their provisions at vibrantly international ports. Kerala's renowned religious diversity today—with its Hindu, Christian, Muslim, and Jewish communities—is a result of its positioning within the larger social geography of the Indian Ocean (Arunima 2006).[5] Against this rich historical backdrop, I trace how Kutiyattam has regularly traversed borders, encountered cultural Others, and, more recently, been reimagined as heritage and embraced as part of the distinct national narratives of a communist Kerala, a Hinduizing India, and a globalizing world. In the process, I explore how the art has dynamically adapted to shifting power centers and audience tastes over time.

Deep Cosmopolitanism: Reassessing Tradition and Modernity

The United Nations system to which UNESCO belongs was founded on an idea of cosmopolitanism conceived in a particular time and place: late eighteenth-century Western Europe. From his vantage point in the European Enlightenment, German philosopher Immanuel Kant imagined a cosmopolitanism based on the peaceful freedom of individual movement between nation-states ([1795] 1917). This concept of cosmopolitanism and an accompanying nation-centric world order have come to dominate global modernity. Kant's trajectory of nation-centric cosmopolitan movement—from local to national to global—forms the backbone of UNESCO's ICH program and its "triangulation between local, national, and global levels" (Hafstein 2018, 165). The organization's foundational Masterpieces of the Oral and Intangible Heritage of Humanity program envisioned "endangered" local expressive forms, mediated through the nation-states that submit ICH applications to UNESCO, transformed into cosmopolitan, "safeguarded" heritages of humanity. This endangered-local to safeguarded-global trajectory reveals a worldview that sees expressive forms endangered in local contexts, their only hope of survival a global intervention by an organization with headquarters in Western Europe.

In *Deep Cosmopolitanism,* I argue against UNESCO's local-to-global trajectory and associated colonialist ideologies to propose an approach that considers a UNESCO ICH form on its own terms. What follows is an explanation of Kutiyattam's *deep cosmopolitanism,* rooted in non-Western experiences spanning the premodern and modern periods. By exploring the global-to-global trajectory of Kutiyattam Sanskrit theater—from the premodern Sanskrit cosmopolis to the contemporary UNESCO intangible heritage of humanity—I locate the elite temple art within a South Asian cosmopolitan trajectory that reaches into a much deeper past than European eighteenth- and nineteenth-century cosmopolitan imaginings. In so doing, *Deep Cosmopolitanism* prompts reflection on contemporary understandings of cosmopolitanism, traditionality, and modernity and reveals the artificial nature of UNESCO's categories.

This book fundamentally expands the anthropology of cosmopolitanism. Urging a postcolonial perspective, Arjun Appadurai (1996, 49) called for the study of cosmopolitan cultural forms of the contemporary world "without logically or chronologically presupposing either the authority of the Western experience or the models derived from that experience."[6] This spurred a robust body of work known as the new cosmopolitanism in anthropology, which has largely concentrated on exploring the cosmopolitics of increasingly democratized postcolonies (Werbner 2008). This has involved democratizing the cosmopolitan and expanding "membership in the once exclusively Western, exclusively upper-class club . . . [to] confer honor on unrecorded lives, especially non-Western lives, which, as was now noticed, had not merely stayed in place in order to be studied by visiting cosmopolitan westerners but were themselves mobile and cross-cultural" (Robbins 2012, 11). Anthropologists have contributed to our growing understanding of contemporary forms of cosmopolitanism in the Global South through ethnographic research that traces relations between elite and nonelite perspectives.[7] Through an ethnographic exploration of the multiple cosmopolitanisms of an elite yet economically marginalized South Asian theater form, my study broadens this approach by complicating elite/vernacular binaries and pluralizing experiences of cosmopolitanism over time. In the process, I align with postcolonial scholars to call out the European origins of concepts assumed to be universal within a capitalist modernity, thereby "provincializing" widely universalized European genealogies of cosmopolitanism (Chakrabarty 2000). As most of the broader scholarship examining cosmopolitanism in South Asia tends to be purely historical in nature, Kutiyattam's thousand years of continuous performance uniquely positions the art to connect cosmopolitan pasts and presents.

Deep Cosmopolitanism likewise unsettles binaries of colonial modernity that are still pervasive today, including those of tradition/modernity and parochial/cosmopolitan. The binary between tradition and modernity in particular plays a key role in the cultural-cum-racial hierarchies and spatiotemporal mapping of past or presentness onto racialized regions that are the hallmark of the modern/colonial world (Mignolo 2011). Habermas (1989, 48) describes modernity as "the epochal new beginning that marked the modern world's break with the world of the Christian Middle Ages and antiquity." The perception of rupture inherent in modernity notably sparked the conceptualization of tradition and traditional practitioners as part of a premodern past. As Menon notes (2006, 120), "It is in the space of modernity, hyper-modernity even, that the discovery of 'tradition' becomes possible." Conceived within the local context of Western European Enlightenment thought, these ideas were imposed on the rest of the world as "global designs" through the power imbalances and accompanying violence of colonialism (Mignolo 2000). This originally localized history thereby became "world-encompassing" (Habermas 1989). As Mignolo (2011, 174) states, "The distinction between modernity/tradition is part of the larger strategy of the denial of coevalness, the creation and reproduction of colonial and imperial differences, and, more generally, of building and maintaining the colonial matrix of power."

Mignolo's perspective melds especially well with the work of folklorists who have problematized the tradition/modernity binary as Eurocentric, including Charles Briggs, Richard Bauman, and Sadhana Naithani. Bauman and Briggs (2003, 17) examine the role that the discourses of language and tradition in seventeenth- to nineteenth-century Europe played in symbolically coconstructing modernity and contributing to "economies of social inequality." Like Mignolo, they recognize that "the logic of temporality continues to structure imaginations of difference and social inequality" today (2003, 307). Naithani (2010) makes a strong case for colonial folkloristics as the antecedent of contemporary international folkloristics.[8] As she points out, current histories of the field privilege European Romantic nationalism without acknowledging the parallel colonial folklore enterprise and associated power imbalances it depended on. Briggs and Naithani (2012) extend this by arguing that the Eurocentrism of folklore theory evidences Mignolo's (2000) "coloniality of power," and call for a wider recognition that colonialism continues to impact the field of folkloristics in myriad ways today. Building on Mignolo's work, they propose the term *traditionality/coloniality* to describe traditionality's fundamental relationship with colonialism.

Deep Cosmopolitanism gets to the heart of both international folkloristic and anthropological inquiry, whose intertwined origins were built on the colonialist binary of tradition/modernity part of a modernizing world. In so doing, both fields often defined ethnographic subjects as non-Western/nonwhite, conceptualizing them as spatiotemporal Others living premodern lives. This book evidences how entrenched the binary of tradition/modernity is in international heritage regimes today by demonstrating how the paradigm of colonial modernity and its accompanying cultural hierarchies rooted in white supremacy still dominate at UNESCO. Drawing on decolonial and postcolonial perspectives, I seek to push the conversation to consider how Eurocentrism in this context is really about centering whiteness. In the process, the book advances a growing body of critical scholarship by folklorists and anthropologists on the UNESCO ICH program as the first ethnography of UNESCO ICH in India. It likewise fulfills multiple calls for folklorists to embrace postcolonial and decolonial studies.[9] Through an ethnographic exploration of unprecedented temporal depth—considering Kutiyattam Sanskrit theater's multiple cosmopolitanisms over a period of one thousand years—*Deep Cosmopolitanism* offers a model for decolonizing modernity and invites us to reconsider what it means to be cosmopolitan, traditional, and modern in the world today.

Decolonizing Global Heritage

Global heritage discourse in recent years has increasingly focused on the intangible, part of a movement led by the Global South to decenter the hegemony of Eurocentric, materialist conceptions of heritage at international organizations such as the International Council on Monuments and Sites (ICOMOS) and

UNESCO.[10] These critiques have questioned the global dominance of what Smith (2006) has famously called an "authorized heritage discourse"—a Eurocentric heritage discourse facilitated by underlying colonialist power structures that has served to naturalize particular ways of thinking about heritage that privilege materiality, expert knowledge, monumentality, and aesthetics.[11] Accompanied by calls for greater global equity in the arena of international heritage recognition, these critiques inspired a shift in focus within global heritage policy from tangible to intangible heritage forms. This shift is most evident at UNESCO, with the development of the organization's ICH program beginning in the 1980s, closely intertwined with folklore and the work of folklorists (Foster 2015a; Noyes 2015). Despite UNESCO's move toward a more equitable system of recognition, this pivot toward intangibility still, ultimately, reified troubling hierarchies rooted in nineteenth-century ideologies of racialized difference. Despite the widespread characterization of the ICH program as a decolonizing project, the decolonization of heritage at UNESCO is far from complete.

UNESCO's conceptual shift from the tangible to intangible was part of a conscious decolonizing push. As de Jong (2022, 27) writes, "Conceiving globalization as a threat to human diversity, UNESCO has opted to support local identities by adopting a whole range of conventions that have aimed to diversify the concept of heritage and to decolonize the notion of heritage itself." Sponsored by Japan, Korea, and a coalition of African states, UNESCO's 2003 Convention for the Safeguarding of the Intangible Cultural Heritage (hereafter ICH Convention) carried "the hope that the Global South would receive its due once performative arts, ritual practices, and skills were also taken into focus" (de Jong 2022, 27). De Jong (2022) observes that the ICH Convention emerged from dissatisfaction with UNESCO's 1972 Convention concerning the Protection of the World Cultural and Natural Heritage (hereafter World Heritage Convention). Bortolotto (2015, 255) clarifies this dissatisfaction, specifying that many member states regard the World Heritage program as a "colonialist" and "Eurocentric" apparatus that "globally legitimises and disseminates methods of cultural preservation and representation that were established in European contexts and that rest on the exclusive authority of heritage experts."

This questioning of hegemonic heritage structures has led to an increased awareness of intangibility that emphasizes that heritage encompasses not only material objects but also the knowledge and intangible processes of meaning-making and maintenance of cultural knowledge that surround them (Hemme, Bendix, and Tauschek 2007). Bortolotto (2015, 255) writes that decolonizing claims inspired the ICH Convention, highlighting that an important part of the "decolonising model" that the convention champions is the accompanying idea that "communities, groups and individuals have a right to heritage self-determination" rather than having to depend on "expert" intermediaries. Other important changes—hard-won negotiations by folklorists, anthropologists, and ethnomusicologists—included discarding the notion of authenticity (Hafstein 2018; Seeger 2015). States from the Global South, many of which were still colonized in the 1960s when the World Heritage Convention was developed, have heralded the ICH Convention as a challenge to Western hegemony in international heritage policy, a welcome attempt to refashion and provincialize "universal" categories (Hafstein 2018).

UNESCO's ICH program originated with a 1973 letter to the director general of UNESCO from the minister of foreign affairs and religion of the Republic of Bolivia (Hafstein 2018).[12] In light of the previous year's World Heritage Convention and the controversy surrounding folk-rock duo Simon & Garfunkel's appropriation of the Andean folk song "El Cóndor Pasa," the Bolivian minister called for an international instrument to protect "forms of expression such as music and dance" that he observed undergoing a "process of commercially oriented transculturation destructive of the traditional cultures" (UNESCO 1977). Bolivia's call for the recognition and legal protection of folklore first materialized through a joint effort between the World Intellectual Property Organization (WIPO) and UNESCO. This led to the development of the 1982 Model Provisions for National Laws on the Protection of Folklore against Illicit and Other Prejudicial Actions (UNESCO and WIPO 1985).[13] This collaboration divided the work of folklore protection between the two organizations, with WIPO focusing on the intellectual property aspects of protection and UNESCO on the work of safeguarding.[14] After the failure of the Model Provisions, UNESCO continued its work on the safeguarding and promotion of folklore through several programs and nonbinding legal instruments that ultimately culminated in the 2003 ICH Convention.[15] In the process, UNESCO moved away from the term *folklore*, which it viewed as having significant colonial baggage, toward the more neutral term *intangible cultural heritage* (van Zanten 2004).[16]

ICH initiatives begun in the 1990s—in which Japan and the Republic of Korea played a foundational role—focused preservation efforts for the first time on skills and knowledge, indicating a major shift in UNESCO's discourses of authenticity, representation, and membership since the World Heritage Convention (Blake 2001).[17] These initiatives were widely seen as a triumph for non-Western conceptions of heritage and a means of correcting a global imbalance that located only 4 percent of all UNESCO World Heritage sites in sub-Saharan Africa and 55 percent in Europe by the early 1990s (Meyer-Rath 2007). UNESCO's first large-scale recognition of ICH came with its Proclamation of Masterpieces of the Oral and Intangible Heritage of Humanity program and associated 2001, 2003, and 2005 lists.[18] Characterizing ICH as "by nature fragile and perishable," the Masterpieces program depicted globalization as a destructive force endangering ICH forms around the world (UNESCO 2003a). Consequently, one of the six criteria for inscription was that a form "risks disappearing due to a lack of means for safeguarding and protecting it or to processes of rapid change or to urbanization or to acculturation" (UNESCO 2003a, 6). The Masterpieces program's three proclamations recognized a total of ninety cultural expressions and spaces worldwide, mostly from the Global South: fourteen from Africa, eight from the Arab states, thirty from the Asia-Pacific region, twenty-one from Europe (primarily Eastern), and seventeen from Latin America and the Caribbean. UNESCO inscribed Kutiyattam as India's first Masterpiece of the Oral and Intangible Heritage of Humanity in 2001.

UNESCO member states adopted the ICH Convention in 2003, intending it as a counterpart to the World Heritage Convention. The convention entered into force in 2006 with the ratification of its thirtieth member state. This created two lists: a Representative List of the Intangible Cultural Heritage of Humanity that incorporated the three previous proclamations and a List of Intangible Cultural Heritage in Need of Urgent Safeguarding. Seitel and Early (2002, 13), who participated in the development of the ICH program, expressed disappointment that the convention continued the Masterpieces program's focus on listing. They asserted that by doing so, UNESCO ICH became simply an "arena for the agency of national governments to proclaim the richness of their cultural heritage." The ICH Convention also problematically continued the Masterpieces program's narrative of ICH as endangered by globalization, warning that "the processes of globalization and social transformation, alongside the conditions they create for renewed dialogue among communities, also give rise, as does the phenomenon of intolerance, to grave threats of deterioration, disappearance and destruction of the intangible cultural heritage" (UNESCO 2003b, 1). Valdimar Hafstein (2004, 36) observes that the threat of globalization is fundamental to UNESCO's concept of ICH and "so centrally involved in its discursive construction, that the two cannot be disentangled." He further notes that as part of this, the organization foregrounds "the vulnerability of intangible heritage [as] the basis of a moral imperative to intervene . . . before it is too late" (2018, 163).

Some might recognize this as a new iteration of the "saved-from-the-fire" narrative of early salvage anthropology and folkloristics that decried traditional cultures as threatened by modernity, calling on anthropologists and folklorists to document these cultures for posterity before they disappeared forever (Abrahams 1993). UNESCO has clearly refashioned this familiar narrative, pitting "endangered" culture no longer against the threat of modernity alone but also against a new enemy—capitalist globalization. UNESCO envisions a global cultural diversity under threat from a cultural standardization driven by neoliberal globalization, with its ICH program vital to the preservation of cultural diversity worldwide (UNESCO 2001a).

By conceptualizing ICH as endangered by globalization, UNESCO troublingly maps this endangerment onto a particular area of the world. The organization explicitly acknowledges that ICH "often belong(s) to the countries of the (Global) 'South'" (UNESCO 2001b). The global distribution of UNESCO ICH evidences this. By framing expressive forms primarily from the Global South as outmoded and unable to adapt to the contemporary world, we see the UNESCO ICH program echo colonial paradigms that framed non-Western peoples, societies, and cultures as backward, ahistorical, and premodern. In so doing, UNESCO problematically creates a spatiotemporal map of the world that equates the nonwhite Global South with the nonmodern.

The work of Walter Mignolo, a leading theorist of decoloniality, resonates here. The decolonial school of thought, led by Latin American scholars, asserts the interdependence of modernity and coloniality—that modernity emerged in the context of colonialism and cannot be conceived independently from it—and questions Western universalism by seeking alternative histories and futures. Mignolo's robust history of scholarship explores what he terms the "modern/colonial world" with its associated "colonial matrix of power." As he describes in *The Darker Side of Western Modernity* (2011), the modern/colonial world mapped the globe into racial hierarchies of difference associated with space—a geographical location—and time—modern or premodern. In this model, which continues to influence contemporary conceptions of the world, white Europeans in Europe were classified as modern, whereas nonwhite non-Europeans throughout the rest of the world were classified as premodern or backward. This is, in effect, exactly what we see happening with UNESCO's ICH program.

Mignolo lists a number of what he calls "historico-structural nodes" associated with this mapping, which permeated all aspects of life and culture. I include a few particularly relevant ones here.

> A global racial/ethnic hierarchy that privileged European people over non-European people . . .;
>
> An aesthetic hierarchy that . . . establish[ed] norms of the beautiful and the sublime, of what art is and what it is not, what shall be included and what shall be excluded, what shall be awarded and what shall be ignored . . .;

> An epistemic hierarchy that privileged Western knowledge and cosmology over non-Western knowledge and cosmologies . . .;
>
> A linguistic hierarchy between European languages and non-European languages [that] privileged communication and knowledge/theoretical production in the former and subalternized the latter as sole producers of folklore or culture, but not of knowledge/theory . . ., and;
>
> A particular conception of the "modern subject," an idea of Man, introduced in the European Renaissance, [that] became the model for the Human and for Humanity, and the point of reference for racial classification and global racism. (Mignolo 2011, 18–19)

Here we see modernity and coloniality inextricably intertwined with the ideology of white supremacy, which pervaded the realms of knowledge, language, the arts, and the very idea of what it means to be human. Along these lines, folklorist Barbara Kirshenblatt-Gimblett (2006, 170) makes an apt critique of the UNESCO ICH program. Observing that the program propagates racialized geographic-aesthetic hierarchies, she states: "By admitting cultural forms associated with royal courts and state-sponsored temples, as long as they are not European, the intangible heritage list preserves the division between the West and the rest and produces a phantom list of intangible heritage, a list of that which is not indigenous, not minority, and not non-Western, though no less tangible."

Viewed through a decolonial lens, UNESCO ICH is very much a product of the modern/colonial world. As we have seen, the ICH program is part of a conscious decolonizing push by UNESCO away from its Eurocentric World Heritage program. Yet, through its narrative of endangerment directed primarily toward non-European expressive forms, the ICH program problematically reproduces cultural hierarchies rooted in colonialist ideologies of white supremacy. It is, in effect, a project of salvage anthropology and folkloristics in the present day, plagued by unsettling echoes of Social Darwinism, an ideology that centered around the idea that racialized cultural groups follow an evolutionary progression from "savage" to "civilized," with white Europeans and their descendants setting the civilized standard the rest of the world was often violently made to follow. Anthropologists Gupta and Stoolman (2022, 790) observe that Social Darwinism "continues to be reinvented under different guises in the contemporary world."

To be clear, I am not decrying the entire ICH project, and I recognize that it remains important in terms of international heritage recognition for the previously ignored Global South. My point is that the decolonization of heritage at UNESCO is an unfinished project. I urge UNESCO to undertake additional efforts to decolonize their intangible cultural heritage enterprise and to consider what global heritage without reproducing cultural-cum-racial hierarchies might look like. I also call upon folklorists and anthropologists working with UNESCO and other international organizations in the field of culture to consider how they might actively contribute to the process of decolonization at an international level.

Kutiyattam Sanskrit Theater

Kutiyattam, meaning "combined performance" (*kūṭi* + *āṭṭam*), is a theater of the imagination that requires fifteen years of intense training.[19] Actors and actresses have the power to spend hours improvising a single line of text, to embody heroes and heroines, demons and goddesses, and plants and animals, and to move backward and forward through time, millennia even, in a single sitting.[20] Recognizable by its rich narrative expression through mudra hand gestures, highly emotive facial expressions, stylized movements, and sparse dialogue of chanted Sanskrit, Kutiyattam has been described as an "art of elaboration (that) extends the performance score to unbelievable heights of imaginative fancy" (Gopalakrishnan 2000).[21] Composed by classical Sanskrit playwrights such as Bhasa, Shaktibhadra, and Harsha, Kutiyattam presents plays dating from approximately the second to tenth centuries CE. These plays portray episodes from the *Rāmāyana* and *Mahābhārata* epics, although a few address Buddhist themes.[22] Widely known as the world's oldest continuously performed theater, Kutiyattam has been performed since the ninth or tenth century CE in what is now the southwestern Indian state of Kerala (Raja [1958] 1980). In the thirteenth or fourteenth century, the art was integrated into Kerala's upper-caste temples, with theaters called *koothambalams* (*kūttampalaṃ*) built specifically for its performance, where it remained exclusively until 1949 (Narayanan 2006).[23]

Notably, a play in Kutiyattam is never performed in its entirety. Instead, only one act at a time is performed over multiple days. Kutiyattam's focus on the aesthetic elaboration and extension of each moment, with several days of opening rituals and elaboration of previous acts, means that a Kutiyattam performance lasts anywhere from five to forty-one days on the temple stage.[24] These extended performances consist of three parts: (1) the *purappad* (*puṟappāṭŭ*), or solo entry of a character, (2) several days of each character's solo *nirvahanam* (*nirvvahaṇam*), a flashback sequence that constitutes the bulk of performance, and (3) one to three days of combined *kutiyattam* performance with multiple actors/actresses onstage (see fig. 4).[25] As Kutiyattam performs individual acts

Figure 3. (*Left to right*) Kalamandalam Reshmi, Kalamandalam Shivan Namboodiri, and Kalamandalam Krishnakumar in *Jaṭāyuvadham*. Photo by author.

as self-contained performances, the purpose of the *nirvahanam* flashback is to bring the audience up to speed by recounting events that occurred in previous acts as well as earlier in a character's life. Multiple *nirvahanams* thereby provide audiences with different characters' perspectives. While this unabridged model is still the norm on hereditary temple stages, Kutiyattam performance on contemporary public stages, which forms the majority of performances today, is usually restricted to an abridged single night of combined kutiyattam performance lasting approximately three hours.

Kutiyattam's alternative approach to time is recognized alongside other premodern South Asian classical and vernacular genres for its ability to highlight the modern regime of time (Kaul 2022).[26] As David Shulman (2022b, 24) describes, "Kutiyattam de-linearizes sequence at every point . . . its unique temporal mode operates through non-sequential flares, irregular, dizzying journeys into the depths of time." Actors create a universe onstage where time is something they "actively make," creating that universe at the beginning of a performance and tearing it down at the end (2022b, 25). Kutiyattam engages in nonlinear narration in multiple ways. An actor or actress generally begins in the play's present moment, and then, through the *nirvahanam* flashback, travels increasingly farther

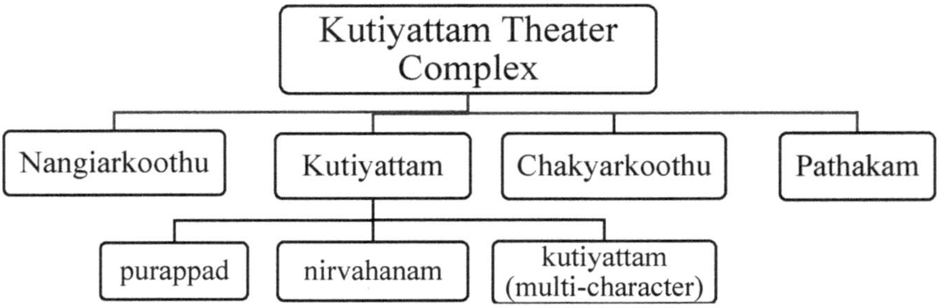

Figure 4. The Kutiyattam theater complex as emically categorized today. Image by author. (Technically a Kutiyattam *nirvahanam* solo, Nangiarkoothu is today considered a separate, allied form.)

back in time before narrating forward to the present once again. Another nonlinear convention is that of *vistara* (extension), whereby artists expand moments of performance, connecting them to tangential narratives in other temporalities belonging to Kutiyattam's wider "fictional and epic universe" before circling back to rejoin the narrative at hand (Johan 2011a).[27] As Shulman (2022b, 39) generalizes, in Kutiyattam performance, "it is always the present that brings pastness to the past and futurity to the future, by inventing them."

The term *Kutiyattam* encompasses a larger theater complex that includes Kutiyattam (Kūṭiyāṭṭam), Nangiarkoothu (Naṅṅyārkūttu), Chakyarkoothu (Cākyārkūttu), and Pathakam (Pāṭhakaṃ) (see fig. 4). Kutiyattam is the enactment of Sanskrit drama. This begins with play preliminaries and the entry and flashback sequences of each character and culminates in combined performance. An important feature of Kutiyattam is its *vidushaka* (*vidūṣaka*) jester figure, or Brahmin fool, that humorously translates the hero's Sanskrit dialogue into Malayalam for local audiences. While the vidushaka is a common character in wider Sanskrit drama, in Kutiyattam, his satirical musings uniquely deviate from the dramatic text, regularly incorporating folktales or descriptions of daily life in Kerala.[28] The Kutiyattam vidushaka also significantly breaks the fourth wall of performance by speaking directly to the audience, occasionally asking them questions or poking fun at them. Many attribute the art's survival over such a long period to the vidushaka, whose comical interactions in the local language gave Kutiyattam an adaptability and enduring appeal over time.

Nangiarkoothu is a women's acting solo whereby the actress, in Kutiyattam's female costume, takes the role of an omniscient storyteller who alternately narrates and embodies multiple characters in her enactment of the story of Lord Krishna (*Śrīkṛṣṇacaritam*). Although technically the *nirvahanam* flashback sequence of the character Kalpalathika in Kulashekhara's play *Subhadrādhanañjaya*, Nangiarkoothu today is considered a related yet distinct form.[29] Chakyarkoothu is the male actor's verbal solo performance, wherein he demonstrates verbal prowess by cleverly interpreting Sanskrit verses from the *Purāṇas* and Hindu epics while in the costume of Kutiyattam's vidushaka.[30] During his extended monologue to occasional mizhavu accompaniment, the actor humorously relates these stories to contemporary events as a form of contemporary social critique while actively interacting with audience members.[31] The improvisatory nature of the performance, combined with its humorous audience interaction, has led some to liken Chakyarkoothu to stand-up comedy. As in Kutiyattam, Nangiarkoothu and Chakyarkoothu are traditionally performed inside the temple accompanied by the mizhavu drum and *kuzhithalam* (*kuḻitāḷam*) cymbals. In contrast, Pathakam, the drummer's verbal solo performance with its own distinct costume, has no musical accompaniment and was historically permitted outside of the temple.[32] Akin to Chakyarkoothu in narrative style, Pathakam also narrates Puranic lore but does not allow social critique.

Passed down as palm-leaf manuscripts within hereditary Kutiyattam families, stage manuals called *āṭṭaprakārams* and *kramadīpikas* guide Kutiyattam performances. *Attaprakarams* explain the methods of acting out meanings embedded in the text and how they should be portrayed according to each mood and character onstage. *Kramadeepikas* explain the logistics of the stage, including the opening rituals, stage decoration, and remuneration for the actors and musicians. Absent from the manuals are the techniques passed down orally and mimetically from teacher to student in a training process that lasts up to fifteen years—of rendering the text through bodily movement, vocal melodies, and facial expressions as well as corresponding percussive rhythms. As the manuals leave much room for improvisation and alternate interpretations by the actor, Kutiyattam has been described as a "theatre of the actor" (Gopalakrishnan 2011a). In fact, as many of the *Ramayana* and *Mahabharata* episodes performed onstage are already familiar to audiences; it is not the story itself but the skill of the actor or actress in interpreting or elaborating their role that is most important.

Until the latter half of the twentieth century, Kutiyattam remained an exclusively hereditary, caste-based occupation (*kulattoḻil*) performed by upper-caste Chakyar (Cākyār) actors, Nambiar (Nambyār) drummers, and Nangiar (Naṅṅyār) actresses under temple and royal patronage.[33] In exchange for land, food, and clothing, they performed in Kerala's elite upper-caste Hindu temples that barred all other groups from entry. Following the *marumakkathayam* (*marumakattāyam*) matrilineal kinship system for which Kerala is renowned, traditional Kutiyattam families today still determine their caste membership and hereditary profession through their mother's line. While they all belong to the larger category of upper-caste *ambalavasi* (*aṃpalavāsi*) temple servants, Chakyars have a higher status than Nambiars/Nangiars as "half-Brahmins," with the right to wear the sacred thread that signifies Brahminical identity. Prior to the art's temple exit in the mid-twentieth century, Kutiyattam was performed in three different temple-associated contexts—as yearly performance cycles (*aṭiyantirakūttu*) often corresponding with a temple's annual festival, as privately sponsored theatrical events (*kāḻchakūttu*), or as either temple-sponsored or privately sponsored rituals (*vaḻivāṭakūttu*), generally for the benefit of childless couples desiring children.

In the course of the twentieth century, the system that had sustained Kutiyattam as an elite, temple-based occupation for nearly one thousand years crumbled beneath the artists' feet in a dramatic tide of change that swept over Kerala and the emerging Indian nation. The Kutiyattam community was deeply impacted by the loss of royal patronage and associated decrease in temple patronage, communist land redistribution legislation that deprived artists of their lands, and state legislation that dismantled the legal structures of matrilineal inheritance. Amid extreme social, political, and economic upheavals, Kutiyattam families found themselves deprived of income and socially stigmatized for practicing what became seen as a "backward-looking" hereditary occupation inside the temple. Like many others at the time, members of Kutiyattam families began leaving their traditional occupation in droves. For those who remained, pressure mounted to adapt the art to keep up with the times, particularly to bring it outside of the temple.

Painkulam Rama Chakyar was the first artist to perform outside of the temple shortly after Indian independence. This paved the way for the widespread democratization of the art's performance space. He would later play a major role as the head of the Kutiyattam department at Kerala state's performing arts institution, Kerala Kalamandalam, democratizing performers' bodies by training the art's first nonhereditary professional actors and actresses. This was done alongside P. K. Narayanan Nambiar, who trained the art's first nonhereditary mizhavu players. As a result, contemporary Kutiyattam is characterized by two overlapping spheres of performance—a temple sphere of hereditary performance inhabited exclusively by hereditary performers and a public sphere of democratized performance inhabited by both hereditary and nonhereditary performers (see fig. 5). With these changes, the art as a locus of group identity has shifted from one in which family, ethnicity/caste, occupational, and performance identities merged in the exclusively caste-based performance of the art to one of a primarily professionalized, occupational identity in which family and caste identifications are largely absent from the equation.[34]

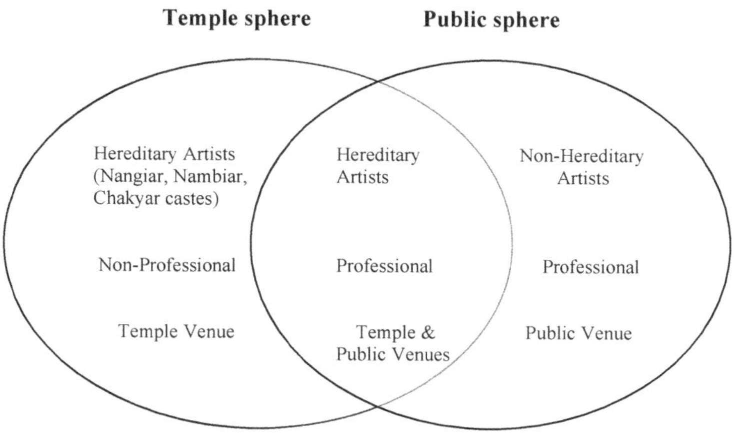

Figure 5. Venn diagram of contemporary Kutiyattam artists' identities with respect to caste and professional status. Image by author.

In the temple sphere shown in figure 5, we see hereditary nonprofessional artists who perform Kutiyattam exclusively in temples out of a sense of familial, caste, and/or community duty, in exchange for remuneration that often does not cover the basic costs of performance (Chakyar 2011).[35] In the public sphere, nonhereditary professional artists of a democratized Kutiyattam perform exclusively in nonhereditary contexts. In the overlapping space in between, we see hereditary professional artists who perform in both hereditary and nonhereditary contexts, thereby actively negotiating between two simultaneous worlds of "traditional" and "modern" performance that coexist in present-day Kutiyattam. The twentieth-century fracturing of the art into temple and public spheres has led to changing conceptions of identity and belonging in Kutiyattam, and is closely associated with the blurred dichotomies of private/public, traditional/modern, religious/secular, and orthodox/progressive.

Despite its dynamic processes of contemporary change, Kutiyattam has been depicted as a static marginal survival of an ancient, Sanskritic, pan-Indian past since it first came to wider public attention. In 1909, Ganapati Shastri "discovered" the so-called Trivandum Bhasa plays in Kerala. These palm-leaf dramatic manuscripts found preserved in performance in Kerala's Kutiyattam community were attributed to famed Sanskrit playwright Bhasa, whose plays had "long since been given up for lost" (Sastri 1915).[36] Since then, Kutiyattam has been characterized as the "only surviving link with the ancient Sanskrit theatre," a window onto the past of ancient Sanskrit dramatic performance (SNA 1995a). While artists themselves often claim that the art is two thousand years old, they nevertheless struggle against common media representations of themselves as remnants of an ancient past by virtue of being performers of an "ancient" art. I witnessed several attempts by artists to contemporize themselves through asserting their subjectivity as contemporary artists practicing a contemporary art. I observed one young nonhereditary artist once tell an audience of university students from across India: "I am just like you. I also like to go to the cinema and spend time with my friends." A newspaper article about this artist depicted her as a "time traveler" who "straddles two worlds," that of "the global village of mobile phones, e-mails, televisions and automobiles . . . [and] the other . . . peopled by mythical, larger-than-life characters who come alive on stages lit by the flickering golden light of traditional lamps" (Nagarajan 2009). In *Deep Cosmopolitanism*, I explore how Kutiyattam resists these types of temporalizing practices as a self-reflexively modern art.

Methodology

This book is the result of twenty-eight months of ethnographic research that I began in 2006, the summer I first met Usha-teacher (Margi Usha). My main period of research with Kutiyattam artists and institutional administrators across Kerala and Delhi, India, took place in 2008–2010, with follow-up visits in 2014, 2016, 2017, and 2020. I began my primary research period with several months of training under Usha-teacher and subsequent stage debut (*araṅṅēṭṭaṃ*) in Nangiarkoothu, as described in chapter 1. This gave me a unique embodied perspective that has deeply enriched my understanding of the art and my relationships with Kutiyattam artists. Looking back, my own training was necessary to understand the embodied experience of artists as well as the fundamental relationship students develop with their gurus. It was likewise critical to my credibility, situating me within local community hierarchies.

The broader ethnographic research methods I draw on include participant observation of artists on- and offstage, my training and performance, and semi-structured and informal interviews with a wide range of individuals. I conducted approximately one hundred and fifty interviews with Kutiyattam actors, actresses, percussionists, makeup artists, costume makers, students, scholars, and institutional administrators as well as Indian government, Kerala government, and UNESCO officials. These methods, alongside the archival research I describe below, helped me understand the wider picture of contemporary artists' on and offstage lives and gather a diverse set of perspectives on the art and its wider political positioning as regional, national, and global heritage.

I supplemented my ethnographic methodology with archival research and analysis of oral and historical texts, which provided necessary historical context. The analysis of different versions of oral texts circulated today revealed how community members engage in memory work and interpretation in divergent ways. In the following chapters, I examine second- to sixteenth-century CE Sanskrit texts-in-translation, contemporary texts-in-performance of sixteenth- to nineteenth-century Malayalam legends, twentieth-century communist writings on classical art, and twenty-first-century artist and administrative perspectives on history, heritage, and tradition. My archival research took place in India and the United States. In Kerala, I was granted access to private archives, most notably those of Killimangalam Vasudevan Namboodiripad and the Margi institution. In Delhi, I visited the archives of the Sangeet Natak Akademi, the Indian Ministry of Culture, the Indira Gandhi National Centre for the Arts, and the UNESCO Delhi field office. In the United States, I was granted access to the archives of the Smithsonian Center for Folklife and Cultural Heritage in Washington, DC, specifically those of Dr. Richard Kurin, who served on the jury for UNESCO's Proclamation of Masterpieces and codrafted the ICH Convention, and the private collections of Dr. Richard Schechner and Dr. Clifford R. Jones. Through this comprehensive ethnographic, archival, and textual work, *Deep Cosmopolitanism* reveals a detailed picture of the compelling story of Kutiyattam's multiple cosmopolitanisms over time.

Reflexivity: The Ethnographer's Lens

My introduction to India goes back to the day I was born, making my entrance into the world in an India-themed room at a birthing clinic in California. My mother had wanted colonial America; she got India. Half a world away, the experience still somehow embodied India, despite the essentialized room with its pillows and tapestries. You arrive expecting one thing and end up with another. Not better or worse, just different, in a go-with-the-flow mentality that happens to stereotype both California and India. A few years later, I met my childhood best friend Meera. With a shock of closely cropped black curls and an infectious laugh, she lived just up the street from me. Born in London to parents born in East Africa to grandparents from Gujarat, India, Meera befriended me—a shy, blonde girl, a head taller than her even then—on the first day of preschool. I spent a large part of my childhood at her home, greeting her *ba* (grandmother) with "Jaya Shri Krishna," drinking chai before it was readily available in American coffee shops, becoming Leah-*ben* (big sister) to her younger siblings, and attending community Garba dances in beautiful outfits she loaned me. This early friendship sparked a lifelong interest in Indian culture.

As both a folklorist and an anthropologist, I initially came to Kutiyattam through my fascination with the UNESCO ICH program that combined my interests in folklore and notions of global citizenship. I wanted to explore how such global recognition affected communities on the ground, and India appealed to me because of my childhood affinities. It was ultimately a number of serendipitous coincidences that brought me to Kerala and Kutiyattam. First, a fellow folklore graduate student from Kerala, Rajalakshmi Nayar, encouraged me to do research there. She intrigued me with tales of the state's widespread matrilineal kinship, telling me: "We value the birth of girls more than boys, because it is the girls who pass on the family line." Second, my maternal aunt Veena lives in Kerala as part of a spiritual community, and I was eager to learn more about her life there. Third, when I switched my intended research site to Kerala, I was fortunately already attending one of only three universities in the US to offer Malayalam language instruction at the time. Finally, as a musician and dancer myself, I had long fostered a deep curiosity about theater. Upon learning that India's first UNESCO ICH was the world's oldest continuously performed theater—and one in which women have always had a place onstage—I decided to embark on my research journey with the extraordinary art of Kutiyattam.

During my research in Kerala, I was keenly aware of my own power and privilege as a white woman from a prestigious American university with a scholarship that was generous by local standards. I knew that my positionality provided greater research access, with people from all walks of life more open to sharing their stories with me than they might have otherwise been. I recognized that my fast-tracked artistic training and subsequent stage debut was a privilege inaccessible to local students, as was the media attention I often received in Kerala as a white Malayalam-speaking foreigner. Throughout my research, the power imbalances and inequities that generally characterize relationships between ethnographers and their interlocutors were in the forefront of my mind.

In particular, I was conscious of receiving more from Kutiyattam artists than I was giving back. Artists lamented a general lack of reciprocity with previous researchers, especially with researchers documenting and not providing copies to the community. They helped me understand my role in and responsibility to the Kutiyattam community. As a result, I decided not to film performances to prevent any perception that I might seek to monetize the recordings. I instead focused on photographic documentation, using my talent as an amateur photographer to produce beautiful images that I could give back to the artists. In addition to approaching photography as a way of giving back to the people who were so generously sharing their lives with me, it was also a way to contribute to the public promotion of Kutiyattam in Kerala. At the end of my main research period in 2010, I held public photography exhibitions of my fieldwork photos in the capital city of Trivandrum and at Kerala Kalamandalam that were featured in several newspapers and television broadcasts. I view my photographs as another ethnographic vehicle for conveying the humanity, both on- and offstage, of Kutiyattam artists. I therefore place them throughout the book sometimes independently of the text. They offer a secondary visual narrative that draws the reader closer to Kutiyattam than can text alone.

My aim in *Deep Cosmopolitanism* is to present contemporary Kutiyattam artists in a way that resonates meaningfully for readers regardless of their cultural background. In so doing, I build on the legacy of humanistic anthropology and folkloristics, both of which foreground the humanity of their interlocutors. Folklorists have especially done so through their focus on the individual's role in expressive culture.[37] I have found that my favorite ethnographies are those where I am able to connect with human experiences across cultural and linguistic boundaries. It is my hope, despite the number of Kutiyattam artists I present here, that this book successfully conveys their humanity, individuality, and diversity. While readers will meet different Kutiyattam personalities, they will come to know one artist in particular—my wonderful teacher Margi Usha.

As often happens in ethnographic fieldwork, the questions and theoretical frameworks with which we begin are not always the most meaningful for the people and communities with whom we work. When I first arrived in Kerala, my research questions centered around the impact of the UNESCO ICH program on Kutiyattam artists' lives. I quickly discovered, however, that I was more interested in these questions than the artists, who perceived Kutiyattam's UNESCO inscription as but one moment in the art's millennial history. With this in mind, *Deep Cosmopolitanism* decenters this moment within the art's longer historical trajectory in order to better reflect how Kutiyattam artists conceive of their UNESCO status in relation to the art's past and present. In telling this story, I made the choice to focus on Kutiyattam's cosmopolitan encounters over time, recognizing Kutiyattam's potential to fundamentally challenge our thinking about cosmopolitanism. And yet, the cosmopolitan moments described here emerged from my conversations and lived experiences with artists, evidencing their continued meaning in the present day.

Outline of the Book

In *Deep Cosmopolitanism*, I combine historical analysis with ethnographic insight on memory, identity, and contemporary meaning-making to narrate Kutiyattam's multiple cosmopolitanisms over time. In so doing, I offer an alternative version of the story of UNESCO ICH, which, as mentioned above, is pervaded by colonialist models of racialized cultural hierarchies. With each core chapter considering a different cosmopolitan engagement in Kutiyattam's history, the structure of the book loosely models the art's characteristic circular storytelling.

An important part of Kutiyattam's storytelling strategy is the *nirvahanam* flashback sequence, or narration of a tale's background story, which takes audiences back in time and then forward again. As Kutiyattam performs only one act of a play at a time, these flashbacks remind audiences of important events from preceding acts and beyond. Each performance radically departs from the dramatic text through three flashback narrative strategies. The first, *anukramam,* begins with the first line of the act's dramatic text before questioning its way backward in time. While repeatedly asking the question "And before that?" the solo actor outlines important events preceding the action of the current act. Directly thereafter, as part of the *samkshepam* (*saṃkṣēpaṃ*), the actor jumps abruptly back to the creation of the world or another foundational mythological event and then narrates forward in time, briefly summarizing events that occurred up until the point where the *anukramam* left off. In the third strategy, the *nirvahanam* proper, the solo actor elaborately narrates and acts out events forward through time, starting where the *samkshepam* left off and ending back at the beginning of the whole sequence—the beginning of the dramatic act itself that brings together multiple actors. Heike Moser (1999/2000) has charted this complicated narrative process (see fig. 6).

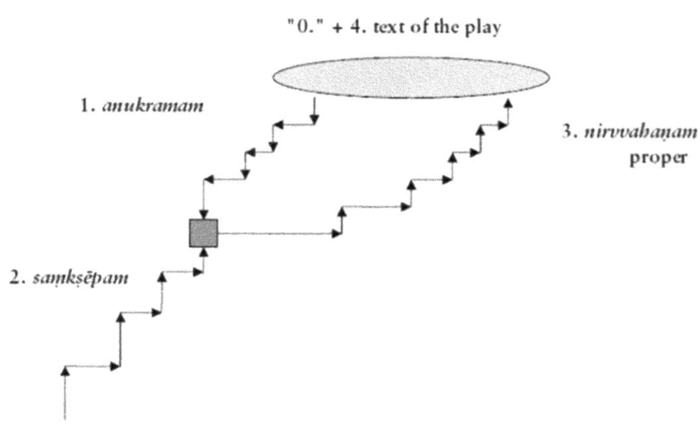

Figure 6. Insertion of a *nirvahanam* flashback in Kutiyattam's dramatic text. Image courtesy of Heike Oberlin.

Although my storytelling strategy is not nearly as elaborate, I have loosely modeled the story arc of *Deep Cosmopolitanism* on Kutiyattam to give the reader a sense of the art's temporal fluidity as well as its sheer scope and time depth. While this book encompasses a single millennium, Kutiyattam artists regularly time travel through multiple millennia in the stories they richly evoke onstage. Through its alternative time-telling strategies, the art of Kutiyattam might even be said to decolonize the notion of time itself. *Deep Cosmopolitanism* thus begins with the first line of dramatic text, so to speak, of an act in which I—a young, white female ethnographer from the United States—am initiated into the art and community. The book then jumps back one millennium to the creation of the world of Kutiyattam and then narrates chronologically forward in time through the art's cosmopolitan encounters with the Sanskrit cosmopolis, rulers of disparate kingdoms, colonial powers, international communism, an emerging nation claiming the Sanskrit cosmopolis as its own, and UNESCO intangible cultural heritage.

In chapter 1, "Getting into the Kutiyattam Body," I set the ethnographic stage of the book through an exploration of my own training and stage debut in Nangiarkoothu, the female solo form of Kutiyattam. Offering my body in an act of "kinesthetic empathy" (Sklar 1994), of learning to move with Kutiyattam artists as a way of understanding their embodied experience, I detail my process of getting into the Kutiyattam body, both physically and emotionally, under the guidance of my teacher Margi Usha. In so doing, I provide a window onto the embodied practice and performance of the art.

In chapter 2, "Contemporary Kutiyattam," I introduce the world of Kutiyattam through the ethnographic lens of the style- and caste-diverse Margi institution in Trivandrum. Meeting Margi's artists individually, we get a sense of the institution as a microcosm of the larger world of a diverse Kutiyattam and learn how artists actively negotiate this diversity. I consider several issues relevant to contemporary Kutiyattam—intersections between the stage and everyday life, the contested terrain of caste versus artistic titles, temple versus public performance, and the discourse of style—by exploring how they play out in the lives of Margi artists.

In chapter 3, "The Sanskrit Cosmopolis and Embodied Cosmopolitanism," I locate Kutiyattam's ninth- or tenth-century origins in the Sanskrit cosmopolis of the first millennium CE (Pollock 2006). In the world of the Sanskrit cosmopolis, rather than penning plays in local languages strictly for local audiences, playwrights composed in Sanskrit and the related Prakrit for wider audiences across the Indian subcontinent and beyond. As Sanskrit drama adapted to the Kerala stage, Kutiyattam epitomized the cosmopolitan circulation of Sanskrit poetry across South and Southeast Asia happening at the time. Connecting this multilingual phenomenon to present-day performance, I make a case for Kutiyattam's embodied cosmopolitanism through exploring how artists experience performing in multiple languages—Sanskrit, Prakrit, Malayalam, Manipravalam, Tamil, and mudra hand gestures—while considering the changing relationships between language and power over time.

In chapter 4, "Kings, Sultans, and Colonialists: Legendary Circulation and Encounters with the Other," I explore three legends of historical cosmopolitanism told by the Kutiyattam community today: of an invading Muslim sultan, an English colonialist made a fool, and the cross-border circulation of artists in the centuries before Kerala statehood. Delving into the meanings these legends hold for the artists who tell them, I consider how their narration and interpretation reveal undertones of resistance to authority and reflect the art's relationship to Kerala's medieval and colonial past, reimagined with each telling today. Placing the legends in historical contexts spanning the sixteenth through nineteenth centuries, I consider each a lens onto Kerala's fascinating cosmopolitan history. In so doing, I draw on recent South Asian historiography that rejects hegemonic, Eurocentric conceptualizations of history by turning to written folk narratives as a serious form of inquiry into Indian regional history. I expand this approach by prompting the consideration of contemporary orally circulated narratives such as those we encounter here.

In chapter 5, "Kerala, Communism, and Heritage: Reinventing Tradition at Kerala Kalamandalam," I explore the relationship between Kutiyattam and the cosmopolitan imaginary of international communism. With Kerala welcoming the world's first large-scale democratically elected government in 1957, I examine how an elite temple art paradoxically became the heritage of a communist state. Focusing on the establishment of a Kutiyattam department at the Kerala Kalamandalam state performing arts institution, I consider the caste and gender dynamics of the art's reinvention for local communist audiences. I highlight the pivotal role of Guru Painkulam Rama Chakyar and his efforts to make Kutiyattam simultaneously more beautiful and less elite in order to appeal to communist audiences. The story of Kutiyattam's reinvention offers a meaningful contrast to studies of classical Indian arts that tend to foreground the deliberate "sanitization" of women's bodies-in-performance made to embody the new Indian nation. At the same time, the chapter advances Peterson and Soneji's (2008a, 2008b) efforts to broaden the historiography of South Indian classical performing arts beyond the "elite nationalist project" to focus on the region.

In chapter 6, "Claiming a Cosmopolis: Sanskritic Culture and Indian National Heritage," I trace the transformation of Kutiyattam into national heritage in the mid- to late twentieth century, emphasizing Guru Mani Madhava Chakyar's role in bringing the art to a wider national arena. I consider how, as traditional Sanskrit theater, Kutiyattam fits an idealized narrative of Indian national heritage as Sanskritic, upper caste, and Hindu that was foundational to a newly independent India. Through this nationalist narrative, the Indian state made political claims for the multireligious Sanskrit cosmopolis as Hindu. I detail how Kutiyattam's case exemplifies a wider process of Indian nation-building that was and is ultimately rooted in Orientalist constructions of an Indian national past that has both nationalized and Hinduized the diverse Sanskrit cosmopolis.

In chapter 7, "Kutiyattam as UNESCO Intangible Cultural Heritage: Politics, Aftermath, and Community Perspectives," I investigate the impact of UNESCO ICH inscription on the art both one and two decades later. Mapping out the results of the cosmopolitan designation that transformed Kutiyattam into a heritage of humanity, I consider the contested terrain of the art's UNESCO project implementation as well as the cultural politics behind its inscription. Presenting artist perspectives on how UNESCO inscription has affected their lives and art, I critically examine how the intangible cultural heritage enterprise in India has created new forms of cultural authority and agency as well as how it has both transformed and mirrored wider transformations in cultural practice across India.

In following Kutiyattam's rich cosmopolitan encounters over a thousand-year period, we get a sense of the many possibilities of cosmopolitan ways of being in the world through a non-Western perspective that bridges premodern and modern periods. Readers may be surprised and perhaps even delighted by the details of the encounters that appear here. With the art's cosmopolitan trajectory in mind, I revisit the question of decolonizing global heritage. Inspired by Mignolo's (2011) road map for decolonizing modernity—via decoupling modernity and tradition—*Deep Cosmopolitanism* explores how Kutiyattam provides a provocative model for doing so.

Figure 7. Kalamandalam Sajikumar lighting the *nilaviḷakkŭ* lamp that signals a performance about to begin. Photo by author.

Notes

1. I transliterate Malayalam and Sanskrit terms the first time they appear in the text; see Note on Transliteration.

2. See Bendix, Eggert, and Peselman 2013 for more on heritage regimes and UNESCO.

3. I use the term *non-Western/nonwhite* to reflect the colonial paradigm that privileged the Western/white subject as the norm.

4. Webb (2015, 11) defines deep cosmopolitanism more narrowly as the outlook of "great civilizations" (Greco-Roman, Muslim, Hindu, and Confucian China) on common ground and global citizenship.

5. Ricci (2011) extends Pollock's idea to an Arabic cosmopolis. For Kerala's role in the Arabic cosmopolis, see Prange 2018, and in the Hebrew cosmopolis, see Gamliel 2018.

6. Mignolo (2002) reiterated this by underscoring the need for a "critical cosmopolitanism" to reconceptualize cosmopolitanism from the perspective of coloniality and the "modern/colonial world."

7. See, for example, Appadurai 1996; Mardsen 2008; Notar 2008; Wardle 2000; Werbner 2008.

8. See Korom 1989 for an account of colonial folkloristics in Bengal.

9. Briggs and Naithani 2012; Naithani 2010; Otero and Martínez-Rivera 2021.

10. See Aikawa-Faure 2009; Blake 2001; Munjeri 2004.

11. See also Hemme, Bendix, and Tauschek 2007.

12. Bortolotto (2007) notes a 1963 critique of the UNESCO World Heritage program's definition of heritage as monuments from the Australian Institute for Aboriginal Studies.

13. For more details on this collaboration and timeline, see Blake 2001.

14. For the parallel development of the WIPO Committee as reaction against dominant Western discourses, see Wendland 2004. This culminated in the 2024 WIPO Treaty on Intellectual Property, Genetic Resources and Associated Traditional Knowledge.

15. See Kurin 2022 for a detailed examination of these efforts. The most notable not mentioned here are the 1989 Recommendation on the Safeguarding of Traditional Culture and Folklore and the 1993 Living Human Treasures program.

16. Kuutma (2016) notes that conceptual change did not accompany the terminological change.

17. From 1993 to 2003, Japan made an effort to export its "paradigm of heritage based on a non-linear view of history" to UNESCO (Bortolotto 2007, 24). Japan also facilitated the adoption of the 2003 Convention by accelerating its ratification in "developing countries" (Munjeri 2009).

18. See UNESCO 2001c.

19. Artists traditionally began training as young children in a *gurukulam* system living alongside their mentors.

20. See Shulman 2022a and Bar-On Cohen 2024 for in-depth accounts of performance.

21. Mudras are used for storytelling in many Indian art forms.

22. While Bhasa dates between 200 BCE and 200 CE, his authorship of Kutiyattam's Trivandrum plays is debated (Brückner 1999/2000). The Buddhist plays are *Nagananda* and *Bhagavadajjukeeyam*.

23. See Raja 1964 for earlier possible references to Kutiyattam.

24. See Chakyar 2015 for day-by-day accounts of temple performances.

25. While this is the general sequence, there are exceptions such as that described in the production manual of act 1 of *Ascharyachoodamani*, which calls for the following

order of performance: (1) Lakshmana's *purappad + nirvahanam,* (2) Lalitha's *purappad + nirvahanam,* (3) kutiyattam of Lakshmana and Lalitha, (4) Rama's *purappad + nirvahanam,* and (5) kutiyattam of Lakshmana and Rama (Jones 1984).

26. See also Richmond and Richmond 1985.

27. One example is the miming of bees, reminiscent of bees buzzing around Sita's honey lips and expanded into a lengthy narrative of Rama and Sita before returning to the original story. See Johan 2011a for more.

28. See Bar-On Cohen 2024 and Gamliel 2014 for more on the vidushaka.

29. For analysis of the history and performance of Nangiarkoothu, see Moser 2008. For Kutiyattam, see Gopalakrishnan 2011a; Johan 2014; Narayanan 2022; Raja 1964; Rajagopalan 2000; Rajendran 1989; Sowle 1982.

30. For more details, see Raja 1934; Śliwczyńska 2020. The *Puranas* are a genre of Sanskrit texts that synthesized earlier mythological narratives, legends, histories, and genealogies into a unified "history of everything" (Taylor 2022, 75–76).

31. For example, see Davis 2014; Kurien 2013, 9–14.

32. See Paulose 2003, 19.

33. Nangiars and Nambiars belong to the same subcaste. In Kerala, male and female members of the same subcaste are generally given different names. The female members of the Chakyar subcaste are Illodammas and are not involved in Kutiyattam.

34. I use a hyphenated caste/ethnic identity based on literature that associates ethnicity with caste in India, see Osella and Osella 2000a; Reddy 2005.

35. See also Daugherty 2011; Johan 2011b. I include professional and nonprofessional as categories of analytic distinction based on conversations with artists who described a tension between "trained" and "untrained" hereditary performers while discussing performance quality. Several were careful to explain that rather than representing a temporal break of before or after temple exit, performance caliber depended on whether "proper" training had been undertaken.

36. See also Brückner 1999/2000; Unni 2001.

37. For example, Paredes and Bauman 1972 and Cashman, Mould, and Shukla 2011.

1

GETTING INTO THE KUTIYATTAM BODY

Figure 8. Margi Usha performing Nangiarkoothu. Photo by author.

Two summers after first meeting Margi Usha, I find myself riding in an auto-rickshaw, barreling and weaving through heavy traffic toward Margi, the classical arts institution in Kerala's capital city of Trivandrum (Thiruvananthapuram) where she works and from where she takes her professional name.[1] Initially hesitant to accept the invitation to train with her, I come to realize that exploring the Kutiyattam body through my own is key to understanding the art. I train intensely with Usha-teacher, as I come to call her, for two months that summer leading up to my *arangettam* (stage debut) in Nangiarkoothu, the women's solo form of Kutiyattam.[2] My body becomes proof of my investment and artistic solidarity in terms valued by the Kutiyattam community. It creates a space where I belong as Margi Usha's student, embedding me in her wider web of relationships. Most importantly, this act of "kinesthetic empathy," of learning how to move with Kutiyattam artists as a way to feel with them, becomes an important way to gain a deeper understanding of their experiences (Sklar 1994). I do not anticipate that participating in this way would also place me in a teacher-student (*guru-śiṣya*) relationship fundamental to the making of every Kutiyattam—and, more widely, Indian—artist.

Usha-teacher postpones our first class for several days, as the original start date is not a good day, astrologically speaking, to begin a new endeavor. She instructs her husband to break a coconut for us at the nearby Ganesha temple, glinting smooth black in the bright sun. The clear coconut water's spray of liberation from its hard shell, smashed against the shrine wall alongside other projectile coconuts of hope, is a guarantee that our work together will be free of obstacles and blessed with success. Little do I know how blessed it will be, as I embark on a heartfelt journey of deep love, friendship, and respect.

In the vein of humanistic anthropology, this brief chapter describes my experience of getting into the Kutiyattam body, both physically through the rigorous molding of my body into the performance frame and emotionally through my growing relationship with my own guru. It is a response to a trend across several fields: dance scholarship that posits the body as sole access point for an alternate order of meaning termed *corporeal intelligence*; the "bodylore" turn in folkloristics; the anthropology of the performing arts as embodied practice; and the imperative of Wacquant's (2004, viii) "carnal sociology," challenging the researcher to place "his own organism, sensibility, and incarnate intelligence at the epicenter of the array of material and symbolic forces that he intends to dissect."[3] In recounting my experience training in Nangiarkoothu, I offer a window onto the embodied practice and performance of Kutiyattam necessary for understanding other arenas of the art—social, historical, political, and cosmopolitical—discussed in subsequent chapters.

Becoming A *Shishya*

"Raise your eyebrows, open your eyes wide, and follow my finger with your gaze," Usha-teacher instructs. Thus begins our first class of Nangiarkoothu. I sit cross-legged on the floor before her with folded arms, my wrinkled forehead a testament to the might of my brows. Eyes wide, I watch her finger slowly trace a line in front of me, back and forth, up and down, diagonal, then in a circle, clockwise, counterclockwise, and finally a figure eight, in both directions. It seems like the film reel of life has suddenly caught on the projector, with time slowing to a barely perceptible pace as my eyes follow her finger, my body and mind focused on nothing else apart from my breath. When she has me trace my own invisible lines, I focus my slowly moving gaze on every detail along my line of sight, experiencing my environment in an unfamiliar, hypervisual way. "Good. I need you to practice your eye exercises thirty minutes every morning and thirty minutes every evening," Usha-teacher instructs, carefully drawing the shapes and directions in my small notebook that will guide my home practice.

We then begin learning Kutiyattam's alphabet of twenty-four mudra hand gestures. Usha-teacher sits on the floor across from me so that I can mirror her, gesture by gesture. Sitting straight with elbows parallel to the ground, she begins a singsong chant naming the mudras, shaping her hands into the corresponding formations. "*Hasta patākō mudrākhya, katakō muṣtirityapi.*" I try to follow her, but some of the gestures feel like they are tying my hands in knots. I sometimes find myself using one hand to move the other into position rather than fluidly mirroring the gestures with both hands as I am supposed to be doing. Usha-teacher writes the words to the chant in Malayalam in my notebook and hands me a photocopied sheet with sketches of each gesture. I later learn how this basic vocabulary can be combined in innumerable ways to form words, numbers, suffixes, and grammatical cases through both single-hand and combined two-hand gestures.

Our last task for the day is to learn the nine basic *bhāvas* (emotional states), known more widely as *rasas*. The foundation of Kutiyattam's *rasābhinaya* acting technique whereby a performer enacts a series of emotions, they also form the basis of a wider South Asian performance aesthetic rooted in the two-thousand-year-old performing arts treatise, the *Natyashastra* (*Nāṭyaśāstra*). Actors use *bhavas* to convey a range of human emotions, with a special focus on expressing emotion through the eyes. Unlike Western method acting where a student imagines an emotional state inwardly and then expresses it outwardly, here the performer mechanically inscribes the emotion onto his or her body, thereby conveying that emotion to the audience. Whether or not mechanical

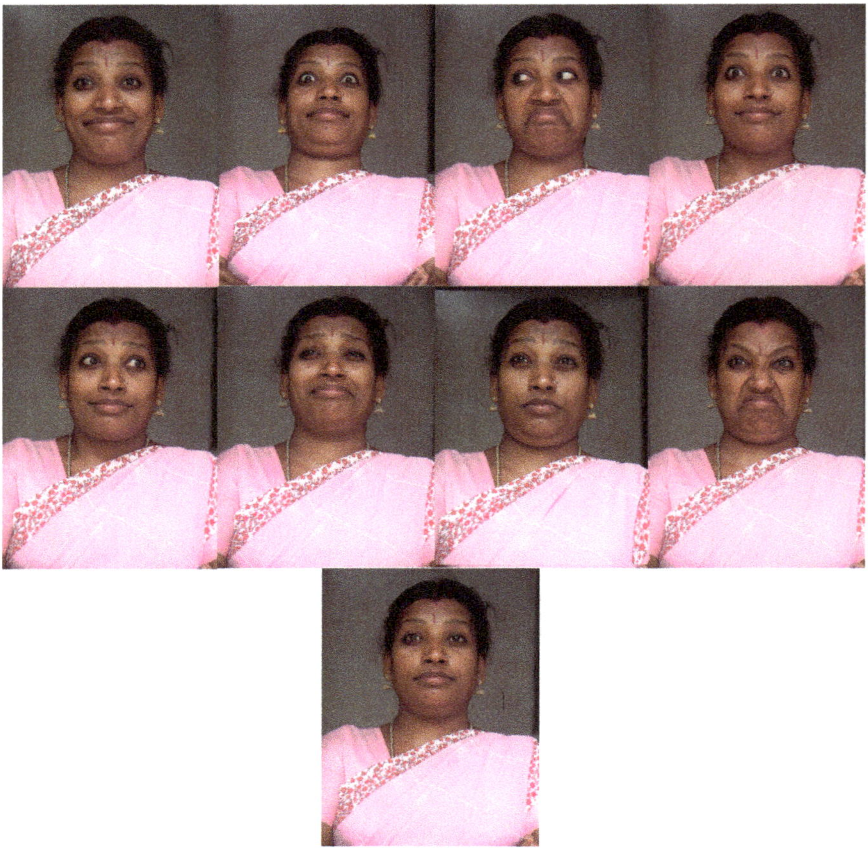

Figure 9. Margi Usha demonstrating the nine basic *bhavas* (*left to right*): *sringara*, *veera*, *hasyam*, *adbhutham*, *bhayanakam*, *karuna*, *raudram*, *veebhatsa*, and *shantham*. Photo by author.

acting creates an emotional response within the body of the actress herself is tangential, although Guru Ammannur Madhava Chakyar once said, "If in doing sringara you don't experience some joy inside, you will feel 'I did not do enough,' and the one who watches will feel that there is something wrong, that it is not true. In the training, the movement itself helps the actor to produce joy for sringara-bhava" (Pfaff 1997, 145).

Usha-teacher demonstrates the nine *bhavas* for me. *Sringara* (*śṛṅgara*): Love/ Happiness. Her face seems to burst with joy as she smiles widely, her eyebrows fluttering at an unbelievable speed, eyes sparkling. *Veera* (*vīra*): Valor. She angles her head back, her chin tucked into her neck for this *rasa* of kings, eyebrows raised and stationary, eyes widened. *Hasya* (*hāsya*): Humor. She gazes to the side, the corners of her mouth slightly downturned, and raises her eyebrows in an expression of wry humor, just on the brink of laughter. *Adbhutham* (*adbhutam*): Wonder/Amazement. Usha-teacher raises her eyebrows, widens her eyes, and smiles as she flutters air in and out of her lower cheeks. *Bhayanakam* (*bhayānakam*): Fear. She suddenly hunches her shoulders, bunches her eyebrows in worry, and darts her eyes quickly from side to side, searching for danger. *Karuna* (*karuṇa*): Sadness. Grief washes over her face as she raises her inner eyebrows and turns the corners of her mouth downward in quick succession, sniffling occasionally. *Raudram*: Anger. Usha-teacher's eyes seem to shoot arrows of rage as she twitches the muscles of her lower eyelids and upper cheeks fiercely, vigorously. I wonder despairingly how I will ever make this work on the palate of my own face. *Veebhatsa* (*vībhatsa*): Disgust. Outer eyebrows raised, the corners of her mouth downturned and nose crinkled, she contorts her face in an expression of extreme revulsion. My first reaction is to find this humorous—I know this one will be my favorite. And last, *Shantham* (*śāntam*): Tranquility. Looking straight ahead peacefully, her face is devoid of expression altogether.

Usha-teacher cycles through these intense emotions seamlessly, the only connecting thread the force of concentrated energy in her eyes. Taking my notebook again, she details each of the *bhavas* and tells me that I should use a mirror to practice the expressions. I labor in front of this mirror for hours, the movement of my lower eyelids for *Raudram* (Anger) the most difficult to grasp, just as I suspected. I move those muscles manually with my fingers, attempting to feel how they would move in isolation. I eventually succeed, developing the ability to move my lower eyelid muscles independently. "Practice, practice. Tension *vēṉda* [do not stress]," Teacher reassures me daily.

The Routine of Class

My summer is an intense combination of Nangiarkoothu and Malayalam training. My time in class with Usha-teacher is the highlight of each day. I find her constant sunny disposition refreshing and look forward to the daily hours we spend together, filled with gentle coaching and mutual, joking banter. In addition to molding my body and mind, my daily conversations with Usha-teacher have improved my Malayalam tremendously. I am finally getting used to prostrating before her before and after class, essential brackets that I kept forgetting. Each time, she patiently reminds me, "We can't end class until you *namaskār* (prostrate)."

Our lessons take place in the crumbling royal building where Margi has its main office and Kathakali center. The interior rehearsal space is cool and dark, with high brick walls capped by a long, snaking row of oil paintings depicting austere gurus of bygone days. Their stern gaze pervades the room as a constant reminder of the past in the present. We eventually shift our lessons to a small open-air stage located in an inner courtyard that glows in the golden light of the late afternoon sun. The stage, which has a black and white checkered floor, is surrounded by an expanse of soft sand and clotheslines hung with brightly colored costumes. Four thick columns support its red-tiled roof, protecting us from the hot sun and summer monsoon rains.

Usha-teacher chooses my performance piece, *Poothanamoksham* (*Pūtana-mōkṣam*), which depicts the demoness Poothana's spiritual liberation. For this, I must enact a summary of the story through mudras followed by a shortened, forty-five-minute version with full-body enactment. I begin by performing my initial salutations, vocalizing the drumbeats in synchronicity with my movements: "*Hrya keem da, koo koo koom.*" Surveying the imagined audience with my slow gaze, I sit down on a wooden stool, hands facing forward with elbows bent in a Saraswati posture, the right hand pointing upward and the left downward. I begin narrating a summary of the tale through my hands and facial expressions: "A long time ago, there was a demon-king Kamsa who, in an attempt to kill baby Krishna, instructed the demoness Poothana to kill all young children in the town of Ambady." The audience already knows the details of this popular story from the *Mahabharata* epic: a prophecy foretells that Kamsa's sister would bear a child that would eventually kill him. Murdering all of his sister's children at birth, Kamsa discovers that her eighth child was secretly given to a cowherding family in Ambady. Taking no chances, Kamsa orders all of the young children there killed. Poothana, a demoness who magically assumes the guise of a beautiful young woman, sets out with the intention of breastfeeding all of Ambady's young children, Lord Krishna among them, with poisoned nipples.

After finishing my summary, I stand up, move my stool aside, and prepare to jump, bend, and move my way around the stage enacting the tale. Most of the time, my body remains stationary, legs bent deeply in *aramaṇḍalam*—the basic stance of Kutiyattam—a feat of near superhuman strength that immediately raises my heart rate and sends sweat pouring down my face. Any attempt to wipe it away causes my black eyeliner, part of every middle-class Malayali woman's essential decorative quartet—eyeliner, earrings, necklace, and bindi—to streak down my face.

Usha-teacher and I cycle through the three basic stances of Kutiyattam, all of which demand a straight spine and thighs of steel: (1) the *aramandalam* posture, feet turned out one foot apart, the body in a deep bend; (2) the L-shaped posture, feet apart in an L-shape with legs bent; and (3) the sickle-shaped, bowlegged posture, feet together in a sickle shape, body weight shifted to the outside edges of the feet with the knees bent outward. To make things worse, as I tower above the brass oil lamp positioned onstage in front of me, Usha-teacher instructs me to bend even lower to achieve the art's small-bodied aesthetic. My body already feels like it cannot go any lower, with my legs bent and aching, yet she keeps telling me, "*Tāḻē, tāḻē*" (lower, lower). She also corrects the position of my feet and arms, almost always in a way that makes them more difficult to maintain, causing my muscles to shake with the effort. Half out of frustration and half out of playfulness, I occasionally exaggerate my movements and acting, crouching all the way to the ground instead of only halfway to make Usha-teacher laugh and concentrate less on correcting my movements and body position. This works every time, with the otherwise serious atmosphere devolving into laughter on both sides. The easygoing, joking relationship I have with Usha-teacher is full of laughter, and the usually strict lines of *guru-shishya* (teacher-student relationship) are blurred, as I am fairly close to her in age and a foreigner.

I mostly learn by mirroring Usha-teacher's movements during class and at home from short videos I take of each sequence. While I faithfully reproduce her mudras, I do not understand what each individual gesture signifies. Realizing this, I ask her to explain how the text correlates with my bodily narration. She writes out the entire tale from memory in her neat, curved letters. Each exact, highly Sanskritized, and often archaic word flows smoothly onto the paper. I marvel at the incredible memorization skills this art form requires. While she explains the meanings, the narrative world unfolds before me and it all suddenly makes sense. The mudras, after all, form their own language, and empty movements are as empty sounds, meaningless without knowing what they signify. I realize that I will have to memorize the highly literary Malayalam text word for word, forming an internal monologue that will mirror my nonverbal gestures. Kutiyattam is slowly becoming a total theater consuming my body and mind, words and images running through my mind then expressed through my body and, as I improve, expressed through my body before reaching my mind. As Browning (1995) writes, "I began to think with my body," as the text and its physical expressions become intertwined in my body itself.

Usha-teacher finally enacts the last scene of *Poothanamoksham*. The demoness, after hesitating upon seeing the ethereally beautiful baby Krishna, applies poison to her breasts and breastfeeds him. Instead of succumbing to the poison, Krishna sucks the life force out of Poothana's body. Being killed by a god, Poothana thereby attains *moksha* (*mokṣa*), or liberation from the cycle of rebirth. In

Figure 10. Laughter during practice with Margi Usha. Photo by author.

the humid heat of the late-afternoon sun, Usha-teacher directs me to perform the scene. I first pick up the heavenly child from his bed. "No, not like that, like you're cradling the head of a baby," she corrects me, gently scooping one cupped hand under the imaginary head of baby Krishna and the other under his body, gingerly taking the child into her arms. "*Da*, now you try," she encourages, and I take care to pick up the imaginary child carefully, as I would a real infant. After cooing to the child and asking through mudras if he is hungry, I begin to breastfeed baby Krishna, rocking him lovingly while gently patting his back.

The sky suddenly breaks around us on our open-air stage, ushering in the monsoon rains. Taking on an almost magical quality, the cool wind swirls and water sprays around us, seeming to dance to the soundtrack of the deafening downpour. I look around and take a deep breath, momentarily stepping out of the mythical world of divine children and murderous demonesses in which I am enfolded. Undeterred, Teacher scoots closer to me in her red plastic armchair and directs, "Continue." Diving back in, I begin to rock baby Krishna to death in my arms. Something is wrong. The poison is not working, so I smear more on my nipples and switch breasts.

Oww! I look down at the baby and frown, chiding him for biting, and continue breastfeeding. Suddenly, intense pain floods my body. My veins are being broken, sucked out of my body one by one. My eyes widen in horror as I realize it is the child. I desperately try to pull him off while staggering wildly around the stage, but to no avail. I finally collapse in exhaustion and await my death. Bracing myself in a sitting position on the ground, I alternate between contorting my face and body in agony and staring blankly with labored breathing. In one final breath, I look up to see Lord Krishna above me in his fully divine form, and fall over dead. The monsoon rain roars around me and then calms to a soft trickle.

An *Arangettam*

The day of my late-summer *arangettam* finally arrives. Before having my makeup applied, I tie the *cuvappŭtuṇi* (red thread) around my head. This signifies entry into a liminal world of performance, a "becoming" of the character so complete that not even the pollution of a death in the family can affect the one who wears it. As one actress tells me, smiling, "It's also pretty useful for holding back your hair." Usha-teacher begins my elaborate makeup, the sweet, earthy smell pleasantly enveloping my nostrils. Mixing yellow pigment and vermilion powder with water, she applies this to my face and neck. She rubs black pigment onto my eyes and eyebrows, dotting my eyebrows with rice paste. Red lipstick topped with pink pigment finishes the look.

Figure 11. Author's *arangettam* with (*left to right*) Kalamandalam Unnikrishnan Nambiar and Kalamandalam Ramanunni on mizhavu. Photo courtesy of Margi Usha.

At one point during my backstage preparations, my mother's elder sister Veena, who lives in Kerala, peeks in. Tiptoeing into the room smiling, my aunt is followed by a train of her jovial retired Western friends who live together in an ashram a few hours away. "I'm so excited!" my aunt beams, laughing as she touches my shoulder. She revels in her role as field trip leader, often pulling her friends out of their insular ashram life into the world of her niece, rooted in the performing arts scene of Kerala's capital city.

After they leave the greenroom, it is time to put the dreaded *chundapoo* (*cuṇṭapūvŭ*) seeds in my eyes. The young, soft seeds of the chunda flower are placed under artists' eyelids to inflame and redden the eyes, making the actor's *netrabhinaya* (acting through the eyes) more visible to the audience. As Usha-teacher places a seed in each of my eyes, I feel a sharp stinging as they quickly fill with water. "No problem, it will pass," she reassures me. Next begins my costuming. I feel my entire body constrained, bound tightly by skirts, vest, and headpiece. The costume conditions my body for the coming performance through constriction, forcing me into a heightened corporeal awareness. By straightening my spine and limiting the fluidity of my movement, the costume shapes my body into the rigorous form that Nangiarkoothu requires.

When ushered onstage, the sharp, metallic beats of the *mizhavu* drum overpower my other senses. I switch to autopilot, my mind floating away while my body deftly performs the sequences that have been drummed into it. My body feels cumbersome, hot, and heavy, and I am vaguely aware of a few audience members—my aunt smiling in front of me and Usha-teacher off to the side. After the last beat of the drum signals me to leave the stage, I stagger off exhausted. Usha-teacher smiles, obviously pleased, and ushers me over to reporters for press pictures.

Conclusion

Soon thereafter, Kutiyattam artists throughout Kerala see the news reports about my performance, if they have not already heard through word of mouth.[4] My initiation into the world of Kutiyattam has firmly legitimized my presence as a student of Margi Usha. Her status as a nonpolarizing figure within the community facilitates my introduction to artists from other institutions. Upon hearing that I am an American PhD student researching Kutiyattam, the first question artists usually ask is "Who is your teacher?" My reply immediately positions me within Kutiyattam's relational world.

Notes

1. The first word in a Kutiyattam artist's professional name is either the institution where they trained or their hereditary Kutiyattam family name.
2. For another personal account of Kutiyattam training, see Moser 2007. Training for my abbreviated *arangettam* was much shorter than the usual year.
3. For dance scholarship, see Browning 1995; for bodylore, see Sklar 1994, 2001; Young and Babcock 1994; and for anthropology of performing arts, see Royce 2004.
4. For example, see Mohandas 2008.

2

CONTEMPORARY KUTIYATTAM

Figure 12. (*Left to right*) Margi Raman Chakyar and Margi Usha in *Śūrpaṇakhāṅkam*. Photo by author.

As I descend from my auto-rickshaw and leave the cacophony of the main road behind—high-pitched honks of rickshaws and scooters mixed with deafening horn blasts of buses, the roar of masses of people in transit—I approach a cacophony of a different sort, loud but tranquil. Walking along a quiet side road toward the Mahadeva temple, I hear the sharp, hollow sounds made by Margi mizhavu students echo through the air—bare palms striking the hard, dried leather stretched taut over their small wooden practice drums—*digga takka digga takka digga takka*. I discern the fainter sound of a teacher's thick wooden peg tapping a steady beat—*tok tok tok tok*. A chorus of young voices suddenly challenges the percussive beats. Rising and falling abruptly in both pitch and volume, the singsong Sanskrit verses characteristic of Kutiyattam rise with the percussion to near-overwhelming proportions. Approaching Margi's wrought iron gates, hinged firmly onto the faded jungle of an adjacent cement wall, I enter the sandy courtyard.

Margi's Kutiyattam center is in a small cement building on a discreet piece of temple-adjacent land owned by the Travancore Devasom temple board, which governs temples in an area corresponding to the former Kingdom of Travancore. To the center's right sits an unused, leaf-filled bathing tank. Palm trees laden with coconuts form a canopy over the verdant courtyard. A stray coconut occasionally falls, hitting the center's tin roof with an explosive crack before rumbling thunderously to the sand below. The Kutiyattam center is a single, low-roofed structure with three small rooms attached to an open-air performance space that tends to flood during heavy monsoon rains. Two rooms, slightly elevated by three steps, adjoin this performance space. One belongs to Unni-ashan, Margi's senior mizhavu guru, while the other is a general room where the artists lounge, Sanskrit classes are held, and students eat their lunches and socialize. Behind these rooms is a long, narrow room where the percussion students practice that follows the length of the building.

I survey the familiar early-morning scene. Directly in front of me sits a low red brick wall that separates the space from the surrounding lush courtyard. The *vesham* (*veṣam*, meaning "acting," literally "costume") students—girls and boys ranging in age from eight to seventeen—chant their Sanskrit *shlokas* (*ślokas*, verses) here while percussion students drum from the back room. I am struck by the dissonance of the different rhythms occupying the same aural space and how this does not seem to affect either group's concentration. The actors and actresses teaching the students lounge before me in high-backed, brown plastic armchairs. Some prop their feet up on wooden stools, half-attentively watching the young students while reading newspapers, checking their phones, or chatting among themselves. The students are positioned in the difficult *aramandalam* stance, outturned knees bent deeply, thin rivulets of sweat running down faces tense with concentration. Chanting in unison, their voices rise and fall with each rhythm and tone of the various *svaras*, or musical moods, of each Sanskrit verse. With bent elbows and forearms parallel to the ground, they simultaneously rotate their wrists, hands held in tight fists. Ensuring flexibility of the wrists and forearms, this exercise facilitates the mudra hand gestures and stamina required of Kutiyattam.

Sajeev-ashan paces back and forth in front of the students, sternly directing them with a furrowed brow. He hears a mistake. "Stop, stop!" he shouts, directing, "Vishnu, chant the verse." The boy chants hesitantly, maintaining his bent position and rotating fists. "Enough!" Sajeev-ashan instructs with a wave of his hand, and the group chants once more in unison. I slip off my shoes and enter the space, sitting down on a straw mat at Usha-teacher's feet to observe the class. As several students' legs begin to tremble with the sustained effort of holding the strenuous position, I feel a bit guilty to be sitting so comfortably on my mat.

~

Most in-depth studies of Kutiyattam focus on its hereditary performance community and context.[1] Others concentrate on its contemporary performance by hereditary and nonhereditary artists, in hereditary and nonhereditary contexts, or both.[2] Most recent studies of Kutiyattam shift focus from context to performance.[3] I contribute an in-depth study of the processes whereby Kutiyattam artists actively negotiate the art's contemporary diversity, a diversity that I argue is key to understanding contemporary Kutiyattam and the ways artists move in the world today.

In this chapter, I present my experiences and observations at Margi's Kutiyattam institution as a microcosm of the larger contemporary world of a diverse Kutiyattam. While I spent time at every Kutiyattam institution, including six months at Kerala Kalamandalam, I spent most of my time at Margi or traveling with Margi's artists to performances around the state. Margi is uniquely positioned to represent the larger Kutiyattam community due to the diversity of its actors' training backgrounds and resultant acting styles.[4] This diversity stems from the fact that Margi has principally been an institution of higher rather than primary study. In contrast, other senior institutions are staffed mainly by actors and actresses trained in-house. Margi artists therefore have a range of perspectives and styles reflective of the wider Kutiyattam community and comprise both hereditary and nonhereditary artists trained in a variety of institutional and hereditary contexts. Here, I consider several issues relevant to a diverse, contemporary Kutiyattam—the fluid boundaries between the worlds of performance and everyday life, the contested terrain of caste versus artistic titles, and the discourse of style—by exploring how they play out in the lives of Margi artists.

Margi

Margi was founded in 1970 as a society for the promotion of classical arts in Kerala's capital city of Trivandrum. Its founder, D. Appukuttan Nair, was an engineer known for constructing *koothambalam* temple theaters at the renowned performing arts institutions Kerala Kalamandalam and Kalakshetra. Margi established a center for the higher study and performance of Kathakali dance drama in 1974, recognizing the need for a center in Trivandrum that could provide performance opportunities to recent Kalamandalam Kathakali graduates. A few years later, this expanded to include the public promotion of Kutiyattam. In 1981, Margi established a *gurukulam*-based center for Kutiyattam higher training with funding from the Kerala state government.[5] Under the direction of Padmasree Guru Moozhikkulam Kochukuttan Chakyar, Margi's first Kutiyattam students were his two sons Sajeev and Madhu, and his grand-nephew Raman. Guru Kochukuttan's maternal uncle, Padmabhushan Guru Ammannur Madhava Chakyar, served as Margi's senior visiting guru from 1981 to 1989. By 1991, Margi had a full Kutiyattam troupe with four actors, two actresses, and five percussion artists: three mizhavu, one *thimila* (*timila*), and one *edakka* (*iṭaykka*).

Margi prioritized the revival of Kutiyattam plays that were no longer being performed, bolstered by Ford Foundation support from 1989 to 1992 (Iyer 1989). The institution commissioned Guru Ammannur to write stage manuals (*attaprakarams*) for three lost acts of Shakthibhadra's ninth-century play, *Ascharyachoodamani* (Wondrous Crest-Jewel), which Guru Kochukuttan staged with the Margi troupe.[6] This significantly opened up more repertoire to non-hereditary artists, who are generally not given access to traditional stage manuals.[7] Margi also focused on reviving Nangiarkoothu, Kutiyattam's female solo performance, in collaboration with actresses Margi Sathi and Margi Usha. Starting in 1991, the school began offering free weekly performances of *Ascharyachoodamani* (*Aścaryacūḍamaṇi*) and the newly revived Nangiarkoothu for the public as part of a national Sangeet Natak Akademi (SNA) funding scheme.[8] Margi has also emphasized higher training in unedited performances, in contrast to the highly edited performances of Kalamandalam. For example, Margi artists have trained in the extended performance of *Aṅgulīyāṅkam*, otherwise only performed as a temple *adiyanthiram* (ritualistic duty).[9] It also enlisted Padmasree Guru P. K. Narayanan Nambiar to train its artists in the full performance of *Mantrāṅkam*, a piece virtually unknown outside of the temple.[10] In 2000, Margi submitted a successful application for Kutiyattam to UNESCO's Intangible Cultural Heritage (ICH) program and subsequently became a nodal agency for the art's UNESCO project, as later chapters discuss.

Margi's Kutiyattam troupe consists of ten performing artists—three actresses (all nonhereditary), three actors (two hereditary, one nonhereditary), and four drummers (one hereditary, three nonhereditary).[11] In this chapter, I present a brief character sketch of Margi's artists to give the reader a sense of the actresses, actors, and drummers performing in the field of contemporary Kutiyattam. As is standard in Kerala, all of the suffixed titles reflect the speaker's position in terms of age and status vis-à-vis the individuals referred to. *Teacher* is a term of respect for female gurus; *ashan* (*āśān*) is a term of respect for male gurus; *chechi* (*cēchi*) and *chetan* (*cēṭṭan*), meaning "elder sister" and "elder brother," respectively, are terms of respect for individuals generally within a decade or two older than oneself; and no title is used for younger individuals.

Actresses—Streevesham (Strīveṣam)

Usha-teacher (Margi Usha), who we encountered in chapter 1 as my teacher, is a nonhereditary actress in her early forties. She exudes warmth and laughs easily with most people she meets—she has a talent for making others feel at ease in her presence. As a young girl, she was initially attracted to Kutiyattam by the beauty of its female costume. Throughout her life, Usha-teacher has broken several societal expectations for women in Kerala, including moving alone as a young, unmarried woman to the capital city to join Margi after finishing her Kalamandalam studies. She devoted her life to Kutiyattam before her late "love marriage" (nonarranged) at the age of thirty-eight across religious lines to a Christian man, Joby-chetan (Margi Joby), who now serves as the institution's greenroom assistant and procurer extraordinaire. She fondly recalls Margi's early days under the tutelage of Guru Kochukuttan, whom she greatly admires for treating everyone equally regardless of caste background. In the world of Kutiyattam where gossip abounds, I never heard Usha-teacher say a negative word about anyone. Enrolled in the new Kutiyattam BA degree distance learning program at Kalamandalam, she always has a book in her hand, studying. Usha-teacher spends long hours at Margi's Kutiyattam center, waiting for Joby-chetan to finish his administrative work for Margi before heading home. After the other artists leave for the day, I often stay talking and laughing with her for hours, sometimes joined by a few jokesters—her husband and Unni-ashan.

Sathi-teacher (Margi Sathi) is a nonhereditary actress in her midforties. With an elegant flair and likability that appeals to wider audiences, she has made a name for herself as one of the most well-known Kutiyattam and Nangiarkoothu actresses in Kerala. She trained at Kalamandalam under Guru Painkulam Rama Chakyar, whom she joined on Kutiyattam's first international tour to Paris in 1980. She was the first actress to join Margi and was instrumental in popularizing Nangiarkoothu through extensive practice and weekly performances, alongside Usha-teacher, based on P. K. Narayanan Nambiar's (1984) acting manual, *Srikrishnacharitham Nangiarammakoothu* (*The Story of Lord Krishna in Nangiarkoothu*). Sathi-teacher left Margi a few years ago to take a teaching position at Kalamandalam after her husband was tragically killed in an accident on the set of her first film, leaving her to raise her two children alone.[12] Despite leaving, she continues to serve Margi as a visiting professor, traveling to Trivandrum every weekend. Making regular television appearances,

Figure 13. Margi Usha. Photo by author.

she strives to make her performances as intelligible as possible for the wider, noninitiated public. Her roles in several Malayalam films have further boosted her popularity across the state. Sathi-teacher has a busy performance schedule both in Kerala and abroad, and among the artists at Margi, she holds the most influence with the management.

Sindhu-chechi (Kalamandalam Sindhu) is a nonhereditary actress in her early thirties and Margi's youngest acting teacher. Easygoing, she speaks her mind easily and loves to laugh. Sindhu-chechi is infatuated with Kutiyattam and developing ways to improve her performance. I have seen her on the edge of her seat, enthralled, watching actresses onstage she admires. Mentioning this to her, she laughs and says she simply imagines how she would perform the scene herself. After finishing her Kalamandalam studies, Sindhu-chechi had difficulty finding employment. Like many Kutiyattam actresses before her, she learned Mohiniyattam (all-female classical dance) in her spare time at Kalamandalam as a backup employment option. While teaching Mohiniyattam after graduation, Sindhu-chechi applied several times for an annual scholarship from India's national Ministry of Culture for higher study in Kutiyattam. Nearing the age limit, she received the scholarship on her fourth try. This supported two years of study with Usha Nangiar, a renowned hereditary

Figure 14. (*Left to right*) Kalamandalam Sindhu with son and Margi Sathi with daughter. Photo by author.

actress. Sindhu-chechi struggled further after marrying a man who forbade her from performing the art she loves, but she eventually persuaded him with the prospect of a second income when a position at Margi became available.

Actors—Purushavesham (Pūruṣaveṣam)

Sajeev-ashan (Margi Sajeev Narayana Chakyar) is a hereditary Kutiyattam artist born matrilineally into the Pothiyil Chakyar family. A comic in daily life, he has a wry sense of humor that shines onstage, especially during his humorous portrayals of animals and witty wordplay in Chakyarkoothu, Kutiyattam's male solo verbal performance. As a hereditary performer, Sajeev-ashan performs both on public stages and on hereditary temple stages. In his midforties, he is one of the senior actors and teachers at Margi, a stern figure who is all bark and no bite. Contrary to tradition, Sajeev-ashan was taught by his father and paternal great-uncle rather than his maternal uncle. Following Kutiyattam's conventional training methods, early Margi students—he, his brother, and his cousin—were not allowed to attend school or any type of outside training in order to devote themselves full time to studying the art.

The students (*shishyas*) lived with their guru (*ashan*) and followed a strict—and as he remembers, tedious—training routine. Arising in the morning to practice eye and body exercises from 4:00 a.m. to 6:00 a.m., they then bathed and ate breakfast, practiced again from 9:00 a.m. until noon, ate lunch, had class from 2:00 p.m. to 4:00 p.m., took another break, and then had class from 7:00 p.m. to 9:00 p.m., six days per week. Sajeev-ashan recounted his frustration with the repetition of learning and perfecting only one performance piece for years at a time. "Sometimes I got angry," he told me, "but now I understand why *Ashan* did that, because an actor must have a strong base. We are doing the same with the kids at Margi." In his youth, Sajeev-ashan's true passion was drumming—his father humored him and let him and his brother study both mizhavu and edakka on the side. Sajeev-ashan used to regularly play mizhavu accompaniment at performances and once even played edakka on a London tour with Guru Ammannur. While telling me that he did not like Kutiyattam acting at first, he grew to like it over time. Yet, his love for drumming persists, and I often glimpse him drumming percussive beats on his lap in perfect synch with the drummers during practice or performance.

Ravi-ashan (Kalamandalam Ravindran) is a nonhereditary performer in his midforties who began his six-year training at Kalamandalam at age fifteen. Good-natured, Ravi-ashan took an eleven-year break from Kutiyattam before joining Margi. Upon completing his Kalamandalam training, he joined the Ammannur Chachu Chakyar Smaraka Gurukulam for a few years. Unsatisfied there, he quit to join a modern theater troupe that performed European dramas in translation. Modern theater troupes in Kerala began integrating traditional performing arts techniques into their training and repertoire, and Ravi-ashan became a Kutiyattam teacher and resident expert, leading his troupe members in an hour of Kutiyattam training and acting exercises every morning. Alongside this, other members led the troupe in *kalaripayattu* exercises, Kerala's martial art form, as well as other Kerala arts. When Ravi-ashan's group lost their Ford Foundation funding in the late 1990s, he needed to find a job to support his family, and Sathi-teacher encouraged him to apply for an opening at Margi.

Raman-ashan (Margi Raman Chakyar) is Sajeev-ashan's cousin and a hereditary Kutiyattam artist born matrilineally into the Ammannur family. He trained with Guru Ammannur for six years before coming to Margi. In his midforties, he is soft-spoken and quiet, a good listener with a positive, unassuming attitude. Like Sajeev-ashan, he wears the sacred thread that Chakyars, as half-Brahmins, are entitled to wear. Raman-ashan's nine-year-old son Anandu belongs to Margi's newest batch of students who study Kutiyattam on weekends and school holidays. Since his mother has a different caste background, Anandu knows he is not allowed to perform on hereditary temple

Figure 15. (*Left to right*) Margi Sajeev Narayana Chakyar in Chakyarkoothu and Kalamandalam Ravindran in Kutiyattam. Photo by author.

stages, defiantly commenting, "I'm glad I'm not a Chakyar." Raman-ashan enters Margi's courtyard every morning carrying Anandu's child-sized bright orange umbrella, handy protection against both the sun and rain during his short walk from home. Worried about future employment and marriage prospects with Margi's low salaries, Raman-ashan left Kutiyattam for three years after his studies to work as a security guard. When Margi increased artists' remuneration in 1989 through a Ford Foundation grant, Raman-ashan rejoined Margi and has been there ever since.

Percussion—Mizhavu

Unni-ashan (Kalamandalam Unnikrishnan Nambiar) is a senior mizhavu player in his early fifties who often emerges from his daily afternoon nap with a twinkle in his eye and a joke on his lips. He and I have a joking relationship. He teases me good-naturedly, posing a question he usually answers himself followed by a soft explosion of high-pitched chuckling that rises and falls on the waves of his mirth. He playfully mimics my Malayalam accent: "Hee hee hee, *ennikkŭ āṟiyilla* [I don't know]," palms upturned, the last two of his nimble fingers pointing up

Figure 16. Margi Raman Chakyar with his children. Photo by author.

toward the sky. This is always accompanied, of course, by Kerala's distinctive head waggle. As a Nambiar, Unni-ashan was born into playing the mizhavu. He was trained at home before and after school by his maternal uncle, and when his grades began to falter, his uncle sent him to Kalamandalam to study the mizhavu full time. There he became Guru P. K. Narayanan Nambiar's first student, and he participated in Kutiyattam's first international tour to Paris with the Kalamandalam troupe in 1980. After completing his studies at Kalamandalam, Unni-ashan joined the Ammannur gurukulam. There he played mizhavu and performed other duties traditionally assigned to Nambiars like mending and preparing costumes, often late into the night with Guru Ammannur. After many years there, he joined Margi's newly formed Kutiyattam troupe in 1982. Because his home in Thrissur is a seven-hour train ride away, Unni-ashan lives full time at Margi, often supplementing his income with privately sponsored performances of the witty wordplay of Pathakam (a solo narrative form performed traditionally by Nambiars) and Chakyarkoothu.

Mohanan-ashan (Kalamandalam Mohanan) is the only thimila player, a drum traditionally played as part of a five-piece temple percussion ensemble called *panchavadyam*, in all of Kutiyattam. Stately and reserved with a warm smile, Mohanan-ashan trained at Kalamandalam for seven years before coming to Margi in 1990. He is a hereditary thimila percussionist but not a

Figure 17. (*Left to right*) Kalamandalam Unnikrishnan Nambiar and Kalamandalam Mohanan. Photo by author.

hereditary Kutiyattam performer, as the thimila is not traditionally recognized as part of Kutiyattam performance. Some say that the thimila used to be part of Kutiyattam temple performance in Thrissur's famous Vadakkumnathan temple, which inspired Margi's founder to recruit him. The thimila plays a supporting role to the mizhavu percussionists, similar to the role of the edakka. Like Unni-ashan, Mohanan-ashan lives near Margi, while his wife and daughter live in Thrissur.

Ramanunni-chetan (Kalamandalam Ramanunni) is a nonhereditary mizhavu player in his late thirties. He is quiet and reserved, often observing conversations rather than participating in or initiating them. A year after completing his training at Kalamandalam, he began working at Margi. Like most of the other drummers, he lives apart from his wife and children—who are in the neighboring state of Tamil Nadu—and seldom sees them. Ramanunni-chetan lives in a nearby rented house with all of the Margi drummers except for Unni-ashan. I often see him walking down the lane with Saji on his way to Margi, both wearing the typical clothing for young men in Kerala: patterned, short-sleeved collared shirts

Figure 18. (*Left to right*) Kalamandalam Sajikumar and Kalamandalam Ramanunni on mizhavu. Photo by author.

paired with a colored *mundu*, a floor-length fabric wrap worn around the waist, alternately tied up and let down in displays of Malayali masculinity.

At twenty, Saji (Kalamandalam Sajikumar) is the youngest member of the troupe. A nonhereditary drummer, he trained at Kalamandalam and started his job at Margi only three months after finishing his studies there. He immediately benefited from the new salary scheme set up by the Kutiyattam Kendra, established after UNESCO's recognition. This scheme raised Margi salaries by 300 percent in 2007, although they are still low by Kerala standards. Saji assumes the cool persona of an older teenage Malayali boy, always ready with a sly smile and joking demeanor. He is interested in new technology and gadgets and proudly shows me his new phone from China. It holds an impressive two SIM cards, allowing him to have two separate numbers on the same phone. Saji is the only unmarried and local member of Margi's Kutiyattam troupe; everyone else is from the Thrissur region in central Kerala.[13]

Discussion

Margi is a microcosm of the larger world of contemporary, professional Kutiyattam today. The diversity of Margi's Kutiyattam artists encompasses the breadth of professional Kutiyattam artists—hereditary and nonhereditary performers trained at a variety of institutions with a diversity of acting styles. Margi also represents the institutional structure in which contemporary Kutiyattam identity is located. While Kutiyattam's artistic identity was formerly rooted exclusively in the family, today it is primarily associated with the institution where artists train, evidenced by professional naming practices. Artists' professional names generally begin with the institution where they trained, often even taking the place of a hereditary family name.[14] I observed an incident that highlights the complexity of artistic names and the emotions invested therein. Roughly one year after joining Margi, Sindhu-chechi was introduced as Margi Sindhu at a program. On the long ride home from the performance, she let everyone know how much this upset her—she had trained at Kalamandalam and was not going to ignore the role her teachers had played in her artistic formation by erasing Kalamandalam from her name. As she stressed to those of us on the bus, she would always be Kalamandalam Sindhu no matter how many years she worked at Margi. It was everyday backstage moments like these that best illuminated for me artists' lives and values. I explore several more such moments in the coming sections.

Intertwined Worlds: The Stage and Everyday Life

Figure 19. (*Left to right*) Margi Amritha and Kalamandalam Sindhu rehearsing before a performance. Photo by author.

It is a warm, humid morning, the air heavy and thick around me. When I arrive at Margi, Usha-teacher is not yet there. I am sporting a new pair of earrings—medium-sized round golden disks. The students immediately notice, giggling that I have *thalam* (small cymbals played to accompany Kutiyattam) hanging from my ears. I bring out a small straw mat from the side room and sit down to observe the students begin their morning eye exercises. When Usha-teacher finally arrives, her face brightens upon seeing me—she immediately walks over, cups my chin in her right hand, and gazes a warm greeting down to me. Sindhu-chechi laughs openly at the gesture, "Ayyo! What *vālsalyam,* I can't stand it!" Teacher laughs and I smile, recognizing that Sindhu-chechi had characterized Teacher's emotional sentiment toward me in that moment as *valsalyam,* a specific flavor of the *Sringara* rasa that denotes the love of a mother for her child.

Over lunch, I go to Sindhu-chechi's house with Coralie, a French student studying Nangiarkoothu at Kalamandalam. The three of us sit on straw mats, drinking chai and discussing the individual acting styles of different actresses while Sindhu-chechi breastfeeds her young son. He pulls at the scarf covering his head, causing Sindhu-chechi to laugh and let loose a quick "Ayyo!" before she covers him back up and cradles him. The conversation stops as she gazes down at him for a moment. Looking back up at us, she smiles and, knowing that both Coralie and I have performed the piece, mischievously says, "*Poothanamoksham.*" We all laugh, and Sindhu-chechi muses, "I always think of Poothana when I nurse him, I can't help it."

Returning from lunch, I slip off my shoes in the courtyard sand and enter Margi's performance space. The mizhavu students have already resumed their practice in the back room, the sharp sounds echoing throughout the courtyard. As I enter, I see Unni-ashan emerge from his room. He beams a smile and signs in mudras across the loud expanse of empty space. "Have you eaten?" his hands ask. "Yes, yes," I waggle my head from side to side in affirmation, smiling back at him. This was the first time an artist included me in the mudra communication that pervades Kutiyattam artists' on- and offstage lives, and it felt like a milestone, marking my true acceptance into the world of Kutiyattam.

~

In moments like these, I was struck by the fluidity between the worlds of performance and everyday life for Kutiyattam artists. Stories performed onstage like *Poothanamoksham,* the onstage emotional vocabulary of bhava/rasa, and communicative techniques like mudra hand gestures are all resources artists draw on while blending their on- and offstage worlds. Folklorist Katharine Young (1987) introduces the terms *taleworld* and *storyrealm* to analyze the phenomenology behind oral storytelling performance, adding to existing discussions of text and context, or entextualization and contextualization.[15] Young (1987) defines the taleworld as a "realm of events . . . inhabited by characters acting in their own space and time," which in Kutiyattam is the realm of divine events from the great epics, the *Ramayana* and *Mahabharata* (Young 1987, viii). Young refers to the world of the storyteller as the storyrealm, defining it as "an enclave in the realm of conversation, itself an aspect of the realm of the ordinary" (Young 1987).

Kutiyattam's storytelling events, which involve costumed performers onstage, do not quite fit into this framework. They are not "breakthrough(s) into performance" in the ordinary realm of everyday conversation (Hymes [1975] 1981). Strictly marked off from everyday life by the formalities of the stage, Kutiyattam's storytelling events are largely narrated nonverbally through facial expressions, bodily movements, and mudra hand gestures. Even so, Young's terms are useful for examining how artists conjure the text and context of the stage in everyday life without actually breaking into performance. The taleworld that Kutiyattam creates onstage is not simply a process of entextualization, or creating a text that can be extracted from discourse. The worlds the artists conjure are both well-known and lesser-known tales of gods and goddesses at war, in love, or at play, tales of Poothana, Ravana, Rama, Sita, Hanuman, Arjuna, and Subhadra. Many of these tales fill the imaginations of the Hindu Malayali since childhood, who sees these epic stories embodied on temple and festival stages in a variety of forms and hears them read aloud by grandmothers during *Karkidakam*, or Ramayana month, to the accompaniment of the monsoon rains every year.

Poothanamoksham, the piece described in chapter 1 that I performed for my *arangettam* (stage debut), is, through its Nangiarkoothu solo, one of the most commonly recognized stories in Kutiyattam. Would Sindhu-chechi have made the connection between the tale and nursing her son if she hadn't performed it herself? Perhaps. Nevertheless, her enactment of the story onstage—miming Poothana's poisoned breastfeeding, rocking babies, cooing to them, patting their backs softly, and placing them carefully back into their cradle to die—brings the taleworld into her body where it sits, ready to be activated again in performance. As a mother, these familiar actions—movements performed now with a real child in her arms—awaken the story in her body each time she performs them, resulting in a strange juxtaposition of a demoness's cruelty and a mother's love. In revealing her experience to Coralie and me, knowing that we, too, shared the experience of embodying Poothana onstage, Sindhu-chechi included us in Kutiyattam's symbolic world. In the context of breastfeeding, her single remark "*Poothanamoksham*" conjured the taleworld among us in one brief moment of shared experience.

Artists likewise conjure the storyrealm in everyday life by reframing everyday objects and actions through the conventions of stage performance as well as using the nonverbal language of the stage to communicate with each other. By recognizing my earrings as small *thalam* and reframing Usha-teacher's affectionate gesture as *valsalya,* the students and Sindhu-chechi both briefly conjured the storyrealm in everyday life. Similarly, by speaking to me through mudras from across the room, a common practice among artists, Unni-ashan used a narrative technique of the storyrealm to establish a community of shared reference outside of the performance context. For Kutiyattam artists, the text and context of the stage—the taleworld and the storyrealm—are not self-contained but are continually and fluidly referenced within the context of their everyday, lived experiences. Rather than existing in separate, concrete units, artists' lives on- and offstage occupy a continuum of blended spheres of experience. As Kutiyattam researcher John Stevens Sowle (1982, 224) has noted, "In a life so totally involved in the theatre, every event that occurs to the actor is interpreted in terms of the characters he has come to know intimately. The newspaper is read for the material it presents for use in Kuttu, love and marriage are seen in the light of the ideal presented by the characters enacted . . . like other things in Kutiyattam this merger of life and art is complete and automatic because of total involvement." While mid-twentieth-century Kerala's emerging public sphere pulled apart Kutiyattam's previously intertwined realms of art, family, and occupation, the boundaries between life and art in a contemporary, democratized Kutiyattam have remained fluid, and the art has persisted in demanding total involvement from its artists.

The Art of the Chakyars—Caste versus Artistic Titles

This morning, Sindhu-chechi teaches the students while all of Margi's other actors and most drummers are on a sixty-hour train ride to Varanasi for a performance. Sindhu-chechi is a conscientious teacher who takes special care with her students. After a physical warm-up, she asks one of the boys to recite his text for today's scene. This text becomes an internal script the actor silently mimes to the audience through mudras and facial expressions. Only when he masters the art will he be able to supersede this internal text through *manōdharma,* the art of improvisation. The boy has trouble with the correct pronunciation of the Sanskritized Malayalam words, especially with aspirated letters like *dha,* which he is made to repeat several times while the other students look on disinterestedly.

Sindhu-chechi quickly shifts gears, taking the opportunity to give the students a small lesson in Kutiyattam. Gathering the six girls and boys in front of her, she asks them, "How long is a movie?" Several enthusiastic voices reply, "Two and a half hours!" Sindhu-chechi continues, "You know what makes Kutiyattam so special? It is because a story that can be told in one hour, in Kutiyattam only one part of that, one act, can last for even twelve days. The Chakyars were the only ones who used to perform Kutiyattam in the temples, and then Painkulam Rama Chakyar-ashan came along and opened it up to everyone. He started a Kutiyattam department at Kalamandalam in 1965. Other Chakyars became very angry at him, but this didn't stop him. So earlier only some people got to perform Kutiyattam, but now . . ." she waves her hand at the acting students sitting in front of her and then at the mizhavu students sitting farther off to her left. "Now, you are all Nambiars," she proclaims to the mizhavu students, "and you are Chakyars," looking at the boys in front of her. "And we are all Nangiars," she tells the girls.

~

Despite the mid-twentieth-century democratization of Kutiyattam performers, or perhaps because of it, the issue of caste is fraught and rarely discussed openly. Even though the Kutiyattam stage opened to nonhereditary performers nearly sixty years ago, in Kerala's popular imagination, Kutiyattam is still widely conceived of as the art of the Chakyar. Members of the public generally assume that artists are Chakyars, Nambiars, or Nangiars. Journalists sometimes even add these caste titles to artists' names without checking. My teacher, Margi Usha, is often confused in media reports with Usha Nangiar, a professional hereditary actress in central Kerala.

Nonhereditary performers generally lack access to Kutiyattam's hereditary koothambalam temple theater performance spaces. When I asked about this, most nonhereditary artists shrugged it off with comments like "Let the Chakyars have the koothambalams, there are plenty of other places for us to perform." As Usha-teacher explained,

> I don't perform in traditional festivals. I'm not allowed, because I'm not part of the family. And I don't wish to, because what I really wanted was the chance to study Kutiyattam. Getting this chance made me really happy, and I gave thanks to God for the opportunity. The most important thing is to have dedication to God, so I don't wish to perform in the koothambalam, because my caste occupation is *kalaripayattu* (martial art). Our family tradition was kalaripayattu, but my family doesn't practice it. We lost our family tradition, and when we do someone else's family tradition, we need to respect it. I don't wish to go and say, "I want, I want," because

> we have plenty of other stages. If we are dedicated to God when we perform, this is the same as in the koothambalams.

Sindhu-chechi's symbolic use of Kutiyattam caste names, however, tells a deeper story. She used the names as terms of inclusion to make her students feel invested and part of the longer history of Kutiyattam. While she would never call herself Sindhu Nangiar, she imagines herself and her female students as contemporary Nangiars in the sense of contemporary Kutiyattam actresses, fully invested with the ability and right to perform on the Kutiyattam stage. Gopal Venu—Kutiyattam actor, director, and longtime administrator at Ammannur Chachu Chakyar Smaraka Gurukulam and Natana Kairali—is vocal in his opinion that Kutiyattam's caste titles have always been artistic titles and should thus continue to be used this way. Venuji, as Venu is more widely known, argues that it was never possible to be born a Nangiar, Nambiar, or Chakyar, as the titles are traditionally only awarded to caste members after the successful completion of their arangettam. If they never debut onstage, they never earn the name. In light of this, he feels that all Kutiyattam artists who have performed a successful arangettam have the right to call themselves Nangiars, Nambiars, or Chakyars. When he tried to apply this reasoning to his daughter's professional name by adding "Nangiar" to it, however, he sparked a small uproar, evidencing the ongoing conservatism of Kutiyattam's hereditary community and wider Kerala society.

Venuji likewise values the use of Kutiyattam caste names by artists today, reflecting, "Nowadays, nobody uses their caste names, but for professional performers, names matter a lot." He continued to tell me a story of his influence on the professional names of two artists at the Ammannur gurukulam, Usha Nangiar and Sooraj Nambiar. Both had wanted to follow Kerala's contemporary naming practices that erase caste names altogether. Venuji insisted that the former retain "Nangiar" in her professional name. Though she was apparently unhappy about it at the time, he reported that she is now glad she kept the name. Sooraj Nambiar, on the other hand, is a nonhereditary artist who hails from a non-Kutiyattam Nambiar community. Venuji laughingly explained, "He wanted to be known as T. R. Sooraj, but it didn't look nice. So I have written Sooraj Nambiar and told him, this may help you in the future, and you *are* a Nambiar."

The emotional value that inclusion in Kutiyattam's hereditary world can hold for nonhereditary artists is poignantly shown by how Sathi-teacher once responded to a question I posed. I asked her if she had experienced any difficulties as a nonhereditary artist. She replied by telling me a few anecdotes.

> A Nangiaramma from Kunjan Nambiar's family was once at a function I attended.[16] She asked me, "You're a Nangiar, aren't you?" So I said, "No, I'm not." Then she said, "You're Sathi, right?" "Yes." She asked, "Then why are you saying you're not a Nangiar?" "Because I am not a Nangiar, I am a Namboodiri [Kerala Brahmin]," I said. "You're the Sathi that performs Nangiarkoothu, right? What do I mean when I say Nangiar? One doesn't become a Nangiar through birth but through action," she told me. So even if I was born a Namboodiri, I am a Nangiar because I do the work of a Nangiar. That is what a Nangiar from Kunjan Nambiar's family said to me. It made me really happy.
>
> Similarly, in Kottayam Kaviyur temple, Nangiarkoothu was performed for many years but stopped twenty or thirty years ago. They weren't able to do it anymore. This made one of the old Nangiarammas there very upset. After a problem arose and they looked into the astrology behind it, they determined that it was God's wish that they start Nangiarkoothu in the temple again. After hearing this, the Nangiaramma there was very upset, because she was unable to perform due to her advanced age. They didn't have anyone there who could perform Nangiarkoothu. Then they saw one of my programs on Doordarshan television. They called Margi and said they wanted me to perform Nangiarkoothu at their temple. At the temple, the Nangiaramma even gave me a *settŭmuṇḍŭ*.[17] This was the greatest thing in my life, that a Nangiar requested my Nangiarkoothu, invited me to perform at her temple and gave me a *settumundu*. Instead of experiencing any difficulties for being a non-hereditary actress, these two experiences were like an award.[18]

While Sathi-teacher's positive experiences were undoubtedly influenced by her high-caste Brahminic background—higher than Nangiars—it is obvious how much these gestures meant to her. For the filming of the UNESCO ICH application's documentary, she performed alongside other nonhereditary artists in Kidangur koothambalam in south Kerala.[19] Despite many of these artists telling me that they did not wish to perform in koothambalams and that there are plenty of other stages on which to perform, they nevertheless revealed how lucky they felt to have had the opportunity to perform there. Thus, while claiming to eschew the sphere of hereditary performance, many nonhereditary performers nevertheless highly value inclusion on Kutiyattam's hereditary stages.

Discussion

Just as Margi is a microcosm of the wider Kutiyattam community, Kutiyattam offers a window onto caste in Kerala—an issue not often discussed but present just below the surface. While many nonhereditary artists say they don't care about their exclusion from Kutiyattam's hereditary performance sphere, stories like those of Sathi-teacher show that they give a great deal of emotional significance to this inclusion. As Lukose (2009) has noted, an important thread of the narrative of Kerala's modernity, intimately impacted by the rise of Communism in the state, has been vigorous, caste-based social reform that attempted to create an egalitarian, secular public space in which caste became "unspeakable." In the world of Kutiyattam, this unspeakability is counteracted by caste as manifested through who is and who is not allowed to perform Kutiyattam on hereditary temple stages. Caste is thus spoken through the performer's body, much like the rest of Kutiyattam narrative. Lukose (2009) asserts that the unspeakability of caste in Kerala was further cemented through naming norms. With the goal of shedding all caste markers, the predominant naming practice in Kerala uses a person's first name preceded by their last initial—my name would thus be L. Leah.[20] As we saw, Usha Nangiar and Sooraj Nambiar wanted to use these naming norms for their professional names as young artists, but Venuji convinced them to keep their caste markers. Venuji's observation that caste names still matter for professional performers is something I have noticed on a wider scale in Kerala. Professional performers of classical arts often have a caste name in their artistic title, but only if they are upper caste. In Kerala, this means Nair; the various *ambalavasis* (temple service castes) such as Chakyars, Nambiars, and Nangiars; and Namboodiri Brahmins.

As expressed in the bodies and names of Kutiyattam performers, caste still represents a significant amount of social and cultural capital. Because of this, its boundaries are strictly policed. When Venuji tried to use the Nangiar name as an artistic title in a contemporary, nonhereditary context, he was quickly shut down. Similarly, although Sindhu-chechi used caste names as metaphors for the symbolic inclusion of her nonhereditary students, this was done privately. Although she was comfortable claiming the title in her affirmation to Margi students—"And we are all Nangiars"—she never would have ventured to do so on a wider, public scale. This strict policing of boundaries is also why Venuji reveled in the fact that a performer at his institution, though not a Chakyar-Nambiar, still claims the name in his artistic title—because he *is* a Nambiar—thus successfully subverting these boundaries.

The Discourse of Style

At Margi this morning, the students have split off into separate groups after training together for their morning warm-up, the girls on the left with Usha-teacher and Sindhu-chechi and the boys on the right with Ravi-ashan. Both groups are learning the *nityakriya* piece that will form the first part of their *arangettam* initiation into Kutiyattam. The *nityakriya* is one of the few extended sequences in Kutiyattam that focuses predominantly on dance and bodily movement rather than on acting and the expression of bhava sentiments. The students are vocalizing the steps and movements in proscribed, rhythmic syllables—*da da da kitti koo koo koom*. In Western musical notation, the eight-beat cycle of syllables would be one, two, three-and-four, -and, -and, -and, (rest).[21] The vocalizations correspond with the percussive accompaniment, eliminating the need for live accompaniment during rehearsal or, as is common among Western dance practices, recorded music. I have never seen a Kutiyattam performance or practice accompanied by recorded percussion. The interplay between the drummer and actor or actress is too dynamic to capture and reproduce mechanically.

After practice, I ask Ravi-ashan why he teaches the boys alone. He explains:

> Margi decided that I should teach the boys *nityakriya* because Sajeev-ashan and Raman-ashan learned it differently, they have a different style (*śaili*). This is problematic for the children. They should pick the style they like, which mudras, and they should perform that way all of the time.... There are several differences, in mudras especially—the twenty-four mudras are the same, but the way they show them is different. You can't say that one is right and the other is wrong.... When I was at Kalamandalam, they said their way was correct, but when I went to Ammannur gurukulam, they said their way was correct. While I'm learning I can make small changes, but when I get onstage my old style will automatically come out.

Contemporary Kutiyattam is performed by artists trained at different institutions in different acting "styles." The notion of style (*shyli*) is debated in the Kutiyattam community. For the most part, artists agree that the art is "basically one style"; its stylistic differences are not as significant as the major differences in, for example, Kathakali performance styles. Despite this claim, I heard numerous artists refer to the Kalamandalam and the Ammannur styles of performance and state that each Chakyar family used to have their own style. As an orally and mimetically transmitted art form, Kutiyattam evidences the "multiple existence and variation" of the classic definition of folklore that considers the existence of different versions a primary characteristic of expressive culture (Dundes 1999). The historical multiplicity and variation of performance styles among the former eighteen Chakyar families, which Narayanan (2005, 37) calls "microtraditions of acting," shows how Kutiyattam's repertoire of embodied knowledge has been passed from the body of the teacher to the body of the student watching, listening, and imitating, from generation to generation. The recognized variation among family styles is exemplified in a well-known saying that describes the strengths of different Chakyar families: "Kuttancherry *hasya* (humor), Ammannur *vesham* (acting), Pothiyil *vachika* (wordplay)." Artists describe such differences as spanning all aspects of performance, including the way the body is held, the mudras used, the dance sequences, the musical variation among songs, and the *svaras* (musical scales) in which the Sanskrit verses are chanted.[22] Sowle (1982) notated the differences in pitch among the three great Kutiyattam masters of the twentieth century—Ammannur Madhava Chakyar, Mani Madhava Chakyar, and Painkulam Rama Chakyar—performing the Indalam *svara* in 1974 (see fig. 20). He notated the pitch as well as the variation in ornamentation among the three gurus chanting the Shailaya shloka from the act of *Shurpanakhankam*, as we see below.

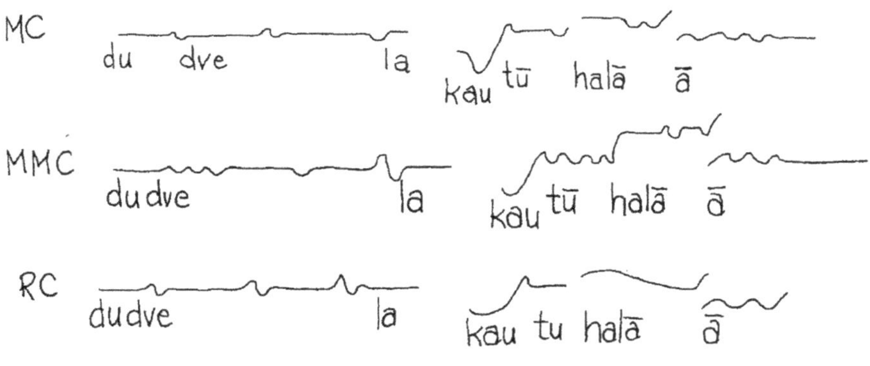

Figure 20. Ammannur Madhava Chakyar (MC), Mani Madhava Chakyar (MMC), and Painkulam Rama Chakyar (RC) chanting the Indalam *svara* (Sowle 1982, 151). Image courtesy of John Sowle. (For audio, see the three audio clips under the Audio Files section of http://kaliyuga.com/JohnDissertationPg.htm.)

There were historically eighteen Chakyar families in Kerala, but many either merged or ceased to produce a female heir to continue the line. Only six remain today: Pothiyil, Koyppa (Painkulam), Kuttancherry, Ammannur, Mani, and Kidangur (Chakyar 2015). Out of these families, only Painkulam and Ammannur have successfully trained a younger generation of artists who perform their style through the present day. The Painkulam style is considered equivalent to the Kalamandalam style developed by Guru Painkulam Rama Chakyar at Kerala Kalamandalam state arts institution in the 1960s, which I discuss in more detail in chapter 5. Through a process of conscious reinvention, this style emphasizes *lokadharmī* (realistic acting) to make Kutiyattam more intelligible to wider audiences. Guru Ammannur Madhava Chakyar, the most conservative among the three gurus listed above, imparted the Ammannur style to a new generation of students. This style is generally considered the "traditional style" that emphasizes the more complicated *nāṭyadharmī* (stylistic acting). Guru Ammannur is renowned for his rejection of audience intelligibility as a concern during performance. Interestingly, Guru Painkulam and Guru Ammannur trained together under the same guru—the former's brother-in-law and the latter's maternal uncle—Ammannur Chachu Chakyar.[23] Both the Kidangur and Mani families have no young professional Chakyars in the current generation of artists, although the Mani gurukulam has continued the Mani family style to some degree, passing it to the non-Chakyar children and grandchildren of Guru Mani Madhava Chakyar. Several of the Pothiyil family's younger artists trained in the Ammannur style, and the only practicing artist from the Kuttancherry family trained at Kalamandalam. All professional artists today, both hereditary and nonhereditary, practice either the Ammannur or Kalamandalam styles. The two styles differ in terms of mudras, in both position and form, and several other details such as the positioning of the stool onstage, the rendering of the shlokas, and the singing of songs. Sathi-teacher compared the current differences in Kutiyattam to the differences in how Malayalam is spoken in Kerala's various districts, saying, "Like the differences in language, there are small differences in Kutiyattam."

I never heard artists mention varying styles between Nambiar and Nangiar families. While hereditary Nangiars were usually taught by their mothers, grandmothers, or Chakyars, the current generation of professional actresses trained at either Ammannur gurukulam or Kalamandalam, thereby preserving the same style binary. Regarding Nambiars and the realm of mizhavu percussion, every contemporary professional mizhavu player trained either at Kalamandalam under Guru P. K. Narayanan Nambiar or under his student Kalamandalam Easwaranunni. Thus, while there had previously been differences in percussion styles among Nambiar families, the Kochampilli Nambiar-cum-Kalamandalam style of Guru P. K. Narayanan Nambiar is the only one played professionally today.

Margi is unique because it has predominantly been an institution of higher study. Margi's Kutiyattam troupe thus has a mix of artists from both the Ammannur and Kalamandalam styles. As noted earlier, Sajeev-ashan and Raman-ashan trained in the Ammannur style, while everyone else at Margi trained in the Kalamandalam style. All three actresses at Margi, despite basic training at Kalamandalam, underwent advanced training in the Ammannur style—Usha-teacher and Sathi-teacher at Margi, and Sindhu-chechi with Usha Nangiar. All described how their Kalamandalam training formed a strong base for their art by concentrating on the strength and aesthetics of the body, whereas their higher study enabled them to focus on acting techniques and the power of emotional expression seminal to their artistic development. The actresses thus embody both styles, picking and choosing a mix of whichever style they prefer at any time. I first noticed this variation when training with Usha-teacher. When she first demonstrated the mudra representing Lord Krishna, she gave me a choice between two ways of performing it—the stylized *natyadharmi* version—the same as the mudra for Lord Vishnu except with a slightly more enthusiastic facial expression—or the more realistic *lokadharmi* version, iconic of Krishna, hands positioned as though holding a flute. Usha-teacher told me to pick the one I preferred and gave me similar style choices throughout my training. I later learned that these were choices between the Ammannur and Kalamandalam styles, both of which she incorporated into her own performance.

As a result of Kutiyattam's UNESCO inscription, Margi became an institution of basic training and today teaches children acting and drumming. Similar to Ravi-ashan teaching the *nityakriya* in the Kalamandalam style, Margi students learn different pieces in different styles from different teachers. In the process, they navigate the terrain of shifting performance styles by gaining competence in both. When I asked one of Margi's senior students about this, she clarified that she performs the style of the teacher currently instructing her. Ravi-ashan emphasizes that the students should pick one style and stick with it. Sajeev-ashan feels similarly, saying, "Margi students should choose whichever way they like performing the best and stick to that, no matter who is teaching them at the moment. Constantly switching back and forth causes confusion for students, and is ultimately detrimental to their Kutiyattam education. At other institutions the students all do the same mudras, making it easier. Of course there will be differences between individuals, but on the whole they are doing the same mudras."

Style and the Individual

Sajeev-ashan ruminated on the importance of the individual in performance in relation to style. Despite being trained by Guru Ammannur, he revealed that he and Raman-ashan learned some mudras differently than the guru's later students. After pausing for a moment, he remarked, "Ammannur-ashan developed and improved his performance style throughout his lifetime. He had no children and therefore no distractions. He had a lot of time to think about and meditate on how to improve Kutiyattam, and devoted his life to the art. So when he taught us the mudra for palace, he taught us like this." Sajeev-ashan demonstrated for me: both hands in *Patāka* mudra, the right wrist crossed the left from behind—once to the left of his head, again at his chest, moving his right hand in front, and finally up again to the right of his head, his right hand crossing from behind again. He continued, "But after a few years of meditating upon it, Ammannur-ashan decided to change it to this." He demonstrated again using the same mudra, once to the left of his head, then moving higher to the center above his head, and then down again to the right of his head. "Why? Because it looks more like the roof of a palace! So that is how he taught his younger batch." Sajeev-ashan's eyes gleamed in admiration, and he leaned forward: "And Ammannur-ashan's special contribution was that while singing shlokas (verses), there should be *bhava* (emotion). *Bhava* should be evident in the singing, and that is how he taught them. Other institutions don't really do that."

The importance of individual style in Kutiyattam was clear throughout my fieldwork. A poignant example is a performance by Sathi-teacher of *Poothana-moksham* during a Kutiyattam Kendra festival in Trivandrum. I had previously seen several actress's renditions of the piece and was familiar with it from my own performance. A pivotal scene sees the demoness Poothana attempting to kill baby Krishna by breastfeeding every young child in town with poisoned nipples. The scene is often enacted tenderly, with the demoness delighting in each child and nursing it gently to death, followed by the mournful cries of the mother upon discovering her child. Sathi-teacher, in contrast, enacted the scene with all the violence she imagined a demoness would inflict, breaking children's necks and ripping their heads off in the process. The palpable violence onstage made me wince, as it did the actress Usha Nangiar sitting in front of me. While visiting Ammannur gurukulam the following week, a drummer there asked what I had thought of Sathi-teacher's performance. I answered honestly, sharing that I found it a creative interpretation but that I preferred a gentler depiction of the scene. He quickly countered, "Well I really liked it, because that is how a demoness is supposed to act. It is different than all of the others. I find those a bit boring."

"Old" versus "New" Kutiyattam?

One last manifestation of the style debate concerns the types of Kutiyattam artists performing today: (1) hereditary nonprofessional artists who perform exclusively within temples to fulfill their familial/caste duties, (2) hereditary professional artists who perform on both public and hereditary temple stages, and (3) nonhereditary professional artists who perform exclusively on public stages. Painkulam Narayana Chakyar, a professional hereditary artist who trained at Kalamandalam under his great-uncle Guru Painkulam, took issue with what some call Kutiyattam's "traditional" or "old style." Referring to the less rigorous temple performance of hereditary nonprofessional artists that some regard as the art's "old style," he emphasized, "This is not a style issue, it is a training issue." He explained that hereditary nonprofessional artists perform to fulfill their familial duty regardless of their training. "I will show you—King," he offered, bringing his hands regally in *Patāka* mudra to either side of his face, elbows parallel to the ground. "People who haven't trained, sometimes they do this," he said, demonstrating with elbows down, hands not forming a proper mudra, "with no clarity or beauty. But it is not another school, they just haven't trained. There is no such thing as old and new Kutiyattam. We got training and they didn't." As discussed in chapter 4, legends abound of past feats of Kutiyattam performance, indicating that hereditary temple performance has not always been equated with poor quality. As Sathi-teacher reflected,

> I think that Kutiyattam had very good acting and percussion techniques earlier, but after it came to be performed only as an adiyanthiram [ritualistic duty] in the temple, there started being problems with performance, people were less interested, and so performing like that became enough. . . . That's what I think, because people say there were performances like the floating Nangiar and the flying Chakyar. The floating Nangiar was a scene in which acting skills were very important, and Nangiarammas performed it. Like that the hanging scene which Nangiarammas performed was very difficult to do. Similarly there were Chakyars who performed Garudan [the eagle] flying, which was very famous in earlier days. The number of people able to do such performances has since decreased, but now it is increasing again.

Known as adiyanthirakoothu (*aṭiyantirakūttu*), hereditary temple performances are scheduled at the same astrologically determined time every year for a specific number of days, usually as part of a temple festival. The responsibility of specific Chakyar and Nambiar families at particular temples, these performances notably have an unlimited number of performance hours, in stark contrast to public performances. Some credit hereditary performance contexts with inspiring an unexplainable positive increase of energy within the actor as compared to public stages, as Sajeev-ashan describes below. Artists alternatively define the term *adiyanthirakoothu* as meaning "for God," that which is performed in temples, "ritual," and that which is performed "in a devotional manner." It is believed that if an adiyanthirakoothu is not performed, some misfortune will befall the responsible family. Consequences vary from temple to temple, ranging from sickness to barrenness to poverty. Hereditary performances thus must be performed at the specified time even with no audience present, or the family responsible could face dire consequences.[24] There is consequently a strong sense of duty pervading these performances.

The hereditary performance context has several restrictions, like purificatory bathing before a performance. Hereditary artist Dr. C. K. Jayanthi recounted her childhood memory of having to watch each step after her bath for fear of stepping on a rogue thread or other nontemple material and being sent back to bathe repeatedly. She similarly stressed that this context requires a perfect rendition of a complete performance piece, explaining, "In the temple you need *everything*, you can't omit anything, (and) you can't make any mistakes. . . . If you make a mistake, you have to start from the beginning again." Adiyanthirakoothu takes its root from the word *adiyanthiram*, which in Malayalam refers to all hereditary services rendered for the temple, with duties accorded to different *jātis*, or caste groups. The word has colloquially come to mean something that is generally of low quality and done quickly because one must, not because one chooses to. Changing connotations of the word *adiyanthiram* thereby reflect the devaluation of hereditary temple services within wider Kerala society.

Unlike the unlimited performance time of adiyanthirakoothu, the democratized public sphere of Kutiyattam performance is subject to strict time limits, something that artists often lament. Open to artists of any caste, public performances can range from weekly shows at venues such as tourism festivals, universities and schools around the state, and temple festivals on stages inside and outside of the temple compound. If there is no audience for this type of performance, I was told that artists "wouldn't want to come to the stage" and the performance could be canceled. While the strict purity and pollution rules of the temple should ideally be followed anywhere, the public context does not require them. In contrast to the expensive stage decorations needed for temple performance, the only requirement for public Kutiyattam is the presence of the lamp onstage; anything else—flowers, grain, banana trees, and so on—is optional. The goal of public performances is to make Kutiyattam broadly intelligible to audiences, with story summaries usually narrated or distributed beforehand.

As a hereditary artist, Sajeev-ashan performs on both public stages and hereditary temple stages. On the latter, he performs with the idea that he is performing for God and for the community as a whole. Sajeev-ashan referred to this performance context as the "old way" (*paḻaya rīti*). His family once performed Kutiyattam as a hereditary occupation in exchange for land and sustenance, but today, temple remuneration rarely covers his travel, and he often has no audience. Despite this, Sajeev-ashan revealed, "I prefer these performances because I can improvise and perform as long as I want, and no one can kick me off the stage." He further clarified:

> Performing inside the koothambalam and outside of the temple is very different. When I perform inside the koothambalam, I feel a special energy or power in my body and mind, so that the words automatically come without having to think about it. I don't know what it is. Last year I performed Chakyarkoothu in the Guruvayur koothambalam in the afternoon. Later that evening, I performed the same story, same portion, same shloka, for a tourism program in Thrissur. I didn't feel the way I did in Guruvayur, it was very different. Ramanunni was at both, he can tell you. He watched the Guruvayur performance and played for the Thrissur performance, and he told me afterwards, "*Chetan*, those two performances were so different, I can't believe how different they were." Like that we get an automatic power in the temple.

Discussion

The discourse on style, such as that on caste and artistic naming practices, reflects larger transitions within Kerala society. Kerala's wider devaluing of *adiyanthiram* hereditary temple duties comes into play in discussions of "old" versus "new" styles and the rejection of this binary altogether. Instead of a question of style, many artists attribute the generally lower rigor of hereditary nonprofessional performance to a difference between "untrained" and "properly trained" bodies, with the latter equated with the institutionally trained body. Yet we see institutionally trained, hereditary artists like Sajeev-ashan perform adiyanthirakoothu the same way they do public performances except with greater temporal and artistic freedom. As we have seen here, artists experience a palpable difference between the two contexts. While Sajeev-ashan could not put his finger on why that was so, his wife chimed in: "Because it is for God." He quickly followed up with, "Yeah, for whatever reason, I feel differently," pointing out that others feel a special energy on hereditary stages as well.

Kutiyattam's decreasing stylistic diversity over time is also related to a changing Kerala. Extreme socioeconomic changes in the twentieth century, discussed at length in chapter 5, caused many hereditary family members to abandon Kutiyattam, which reduced the art's stylistic diversity. What were once numerous family styles were thus whittled down to the current two, the

Ammannur style and the reinvented Kalamandalam style. Artists paradoxically see the ability to seamlessly transition between the two—as we saw students at Margi doing—not as an advantage but as a disadvantage that causes confusion and a potential lack of fluency in either style.

My foray into conceptions of style elucidates the relationship of the individual to tradition in Kutiyattam. The individual artist is not effaced but celebrated and expected to innovate. When a senior guru innovates, the innovation has a potential long-term impact on the wider style, as we saw with Guru Ammannur. The overall number of Kutiyattam styles has decreased, but artists' ongoing innovation maintains the art's diversity in performance. According to folklorist Henry Glassie (1994, 252), "Tradition lives only in individual minds as part of the adaptive process of daily life, so it exists in a steady state of change." Contemporary Kutiyattam performance adapts to the process of daily life insofar as daily life impacts the way its artists interpret the world and translate their interpretation into artistic innovation.

Conclusion

This chapter has more broadly explored how the diversity of contemporary Kutiyattam mirrors the diversity of contemporary Kerala in myriad ways. We have witnessed an art form grappling with issues of caste; the continuum between work/art and life; varying arenas of performance; and conceptions of style, institutionalization, and innovation. I have argued that examining the art's diversity is key to understanding present-day Kutiyattam, which embodies Kerala's larger social and political changes over time. In chapter 3, we jump from the present day back to the creation of Kutiyattam a millennium ago as part of the larger world of the Sanskrit cosmopolis, thereby mirroring the art's circular storytelling.

Notes

1. See Johan 2014; Jones 1967; Moser 2008; Narayanan 2022; Paulose 2006; and Śliwczyńska 2009. Examining Kutiyattam's training and performance at 1970s Kerala Kalamandalam, Sowle 1982 is a notable exception to this trend, as are Gopalakrishnan 2011a and Madhavan 2010. Bar-On Cohen 2024 and Shulman 2022a consider Nepathya's nontemple koothambalam performances that parallel hereditary performance contexts in many ways.

2. For the former, see Casassas 2012; Daugherty 2011; the middle, see Johan 2011b; and the latter, see Daugherty 2019; Ducomb 2007; Gopalakrishnan 2011a; Moser 2013a; Venu 2002.

3. See Madhavan 2010; Oberlin and Shulman 2019; Salini 2021; and Shulman 2022a. Bar-On Cohen 2024 and Narayanan 2022 focus on both. Mucciarelli and Sathaye 2024 innovatively employ Kutiyattam performance to aid the translation of Sanskrit plays.

4. Margi artists trained at Kerala Kalamandalam, the Ammannur gurukulam, and/or in hereditary Kutiyattam families. By contrast, most mizhavu players, except those at Mani gurukulam, trained at Kalamandalam.

5. A gurukulam is an educational system whereby students live with or near their teacher/guru, helping with daily chores alongside their training.

6. In a 2023 personal communication, Diane Daugherty clarified that these acts are *Parṇaśālāṅkam*, *Māyāsītāṅkam*, and *Agnipraveshāṅkam*. Margi likewise commissioned Guru Ammannur to write an attaprakaram for the second act of Kulashekhara's *Subhadradhananjayam* (Wedding of Subhadra and Dhananjaya), staged in 2001 with funding procured by Diane Daugherty from the American Institute of Indian Studies.

7. To performers at Margi, and with the manuals' publication (Venugopalan 2009), nonhereditary performers more broadly.

8. Shaktibhadra's *Ascharyachoodamani* (*The Wondrous Crest-Jewel*) is the first Sanskrit drama from South India (Kerala), see Jones 1984.

9. *Anguliyankam* (*The Act of the Ring*), also known as *Anguliyankamkoothu*, is the sixth act of *Ascharyachoodamani*.

10. *Anguliyankam* and *Mantrankam* each require forty-one days in the temple, but Margi extended them even further.

11. During my primary research period, 2008–2010. As of 2024, Margi has one hereditary actor (Margi Sajeev Narayana Chakyar), two nonhereditary actresses (Margi Usha, Margi Vishishta), two nonhereditary mizhavu players (Kalamandalam Sajikumar, Margi Mahesh), and one edakka player (Margi Akhil).

12. The 2006 film *Nottam* (dir. Sasi Paravoor).

13. Saji is now married and a father.

14. For example, Kalamandalam Rama Chakyar. Artists trained at Ammannur gurukulam are the exception.

15. For example, Bauman and Briggs 1990.

16. Kunjun Nambiar was a celebrated eighteenth-century poet and Kutiyattam drummer who defied tradition to start a new art form called Otan Thullal. See Gilchriest Hatch 1933, 263; Reddington 2021.

17. A settumundu is the Kerala equivalent of a sari but with two pieces—one around the waist and one around the upper body. Hereditary Kutiyattam temple performance protocol entails presenting an actress with a settumundu and actors and drummers with a mundu (lower wrap only).

18. These experiences cannot be generalized to actresses with a lower-caste background.

19. Strict rules of heredity for artists performing in koothambalams, while still unbendable in temples belonging to central Kerala's Cochin Devasom Board, have long been somewhat flexible in temples under the control of south Kerala's Travancore Devasom Board. Venuji also helped organize a 1996 SNA-funded project called Koodiyattam to People, whereby young hereditary and nonhereditary artists performed Kutiyattam, led by Guru Ammannur, on two south Kerala koothambalam stages unused in over a century, Harippad and Tirunakara (Ramanath 1996).

20. This naming practice emerged from the teachings of Narayana Guru, an important late-nineteenth/early-twentieth-century low-caste social reformer in Kerala who preached "One Caste, One Religion, One God" (Lukose 2009).

21. Based on 4/4 time.

22. For example, see Chakyar 2015, 68; K. P. S. Menon 1994, 130.

23. For Guru Painkulam, this constituted higher training—his basic training was under his uncle Kidangur Raman Chakyar (Sowle 1982).

24. Kalamandalam Narayanan (Vijayan) Nambiar specified that these consequences do not apply if temples stop performances.

3

THE SANSKRIT COSMOPOLIS AND EMBODIED COSMOPOLITANISM

Figure 21. Ammannur Kuttan Chakyar as Bali with (*left to right*) Kalamandalam Narayanan Nambiar and Kalamandalam Shivadas. Photo by author.

As I enter Margi today for my lesson, I find Usha-teacher perched atop a low wooden stool, a sliver of soft light falling on her face as her pink polyester sari floats around her like fresh cotton candy. She has a book in her lap, a common scene I encounter when I tiptoe into her moments of solitude. As class begins, Teacher tells me that I should always sit and pray before starting practice to ensure both strength of memory and success. She has mentioned this to me previously, in what I thought was a humorous jab at my memory or a commentary on my apparent lack of practice that day. Today, however, she explains solemnly that she does this before each practice, and it is important for me to do so as well. Usha-teacher begins chanting a Sanskrit invocation to Saraswathi, the goddess of learning; Ganesha, the elephant god and remover of obstacles;

and all of the respected gurus who have come before. The verse has a repetitive, lilting quality that, although I do not understand the Sanskrit words, I find beautiful and calming.

Usha-teacher writes the verse in my notebook, the words in the Devanagari script crisply angular. Just underneath, she pens the Sanskrit verse in the Malayalam script, her rounded letters curving and looping across the page. Usha-teacher goes over the verse several times with me, making me repeat it after her, and it becomes something I often return to in the years that follow.[1]

SANSKRIT
ॐ गं गणपतये नमः
ॐ श्री गुरुभ्यो नमः
सरस्वति नमस्तुभ्यं वरदे कामरूपिणि ।
विद्यारम्भं करिष्यामि सिद्धिर्भवतु मे सदा ॥

MALAYALAM
ഓം ഗം ഗണപതയേ നമഃ
ഓം ശ്രീ ഗുരുഭ്യോ നമഃ
സരസ്വതി നമസ് തുഭ്യം വരദേ കാമരൂപിണി
വിദ്യാരംഭം കരിഷ്യാമി സിദ്ധിർ ഭവതു മേ സദാ

TRANSLITERATION
Ōm Gam Gaṇapatayē Namaha,
Ōm Srī Gurupyō Namaha,
Saraswati Namastupyam Varatē Kāmarūpiṇi
Vidyārambham Kariṣyāmi Siddir Bhavatumē Sadā

MEANING
Salutations to Lord Ganesha,
Salutations to all gurus,
Salutations to Goddess Saraswathi, giver of boons, fulfiller of desires.
Bless me with success in beginning my studies,
Bless me with accomplishments.

I come to marvel at Usha-teacher's ability to seamlessly transition between Sanskrit and Malayalam. Most of my lessons concentrate on acting through the body (*āṅgikābhinaya*) and emotion-laden facial expressions (*sāttvikābhinaya*). Even though I do not have to chant it for my Nangiarkoothu *arangettam*, I also learn the Sanskrit verse that features in my performance—memorizing it, learning its meaning in Malayalam, and acting it out through mudra hand gestures.

While teaching me the verse describing the death of the demoness Poothana, Usha-teacher first writes the Sanskrit neatly in the Devanagari script, followed by the Malayalam translation in the Malayalam script, and then she teaches me the corresponding mudras and facial expressions in the embodied language of the Kutiyattam stage.

Multilingual navigation like this is an important part of Kutiyattam performance in its many variations. Sanskrit drama more broadly was multilingual at its inception approximately two thousand years ago, with the hero speaking Sanskrit and all others—the companion to the hero as well as female and other lower-status characters—speaking Prakrit or local dialects alongside mudra hand gestures. As Sanskrit drama was adapted for the Kerala stage, the number of languages used in performance came to include, in various contexts, Sanskrit, Prakrit, Malayalam, Manipravalam, Tamil, and mudras.

In this chapter, I explore Kutiyattam's cosmopolitan origins as a form of Sanskrit drama adapted to the Kerala stage, where plays penned by ancient playwrights from across the Indian subcontinent were and still are performed. In so doing, I situate the art's ninth- or tenth-century CE beginnings within the wider Sanskrit cosmopolis, the circulation of Sanskrit poetry across South and Southeast Asia in the first millennium CE (Pollock 2006). Connecting this to present-day performance, I make a case for Kutiyattam's embodied cosmopolitanism by exploring how artists today experience performing in multiple languages while considering the changing relationships between language and power over time.

The Sanskrit Cosmopolis, Sanskrit Drama, and Kutiyattam

Pollock's (2006) model of the Sanskrit cosmopolis encompasses a premodern cosmopolitan world that spanned South and Southeast Asia for a millennium. In this section, I explore the Sanskrit cosmopolis and the subsequent vernacular turn that marked its end. Considering Sanskrit drama a phenomenon within the larger Sanskrit cosmopolis, I ask what its performance looked like as outlined by the iconic *Natyashastra* (*Science of Drama*) treatise. I then ultimately locate Kutiyattam's origins squarely within this wider cosmopolitan world. As we will see throughout the rest of the book, Kutiyattam's cosmopolitan origins were only the first of several cosmopolitan engagements the art form would have over the next thousand years, culminating in its inscription as a United Nations Educational, Scientific and Cultural Organization (UNESCO) Intangible Cultural Heritage of Humanity.

What Is the Sanskrit Cosmopolis?

Pollock (1996) describes the Sanskrit cosmopolis as an alternative cosmopolitanism spanning ancient South and Southeast Asia from approximately 300 to 1300 CE, premised on voluntary membership in a wider Sanskrit literary world. Sanskrit, long a sacred language confined to the realms of Hindu religious practice, became a mode of literary and political expression around the start of the Common Era. Sanskrit literary culture soon spread throughout South and Southeast Asia, from today's Malaysia to Afghanistan and Sri Lanka to Nepal, constructing what Pollock (2006) characterizes as a "voluntaristic cosmopolitanism" created through voluntary affiliation with a wider Sanskrit literary world. This centered around Sanskrit literary forms such as *kāvya* (poetry), circulating as a form of cosmopolitan literary communication that was "unbounded, unobstructed, [and] unlocated" (Pollock 2000, 599). As Pollock (2000, 599) provocatively asserts, "There was nothing unusual about finding a Chinese traveler studying Sanskrit grammar in Sumatra in the seventh century, an intellectual from Sri Lanka writing Sanskrit literary theory in the northern Deccan in the tenth, or Khmer princes composing Sanskrit political poetry for the magnificent pillars of Mebon and Pre Rup in Angkor in the twelfth."

Though meant to create a sense of belonging across time and space through its widespread readability, Pollock (2006) notes that Sanskrit, unlike its cosmopolitan contemporary Latin, never theorized its own universality. Sanskrit never created specific descriptors for either its political or cultural spheres of influence, in contrast to Latin's political category *imperium romanum* (Roman Empire) and literary and cultural category *latinitas* (2006, 571). While the Latin cosmopolis was created through Roman conquest that destroyed all other languages in its wake, the Sanskrit cosmopolis emerged through voluntary movement unassociated with conquest or political coercion. The latter never considered other languages a threat, nor did it proselytize any particular religion, with Jains, Shaivites, Vaishnavas, and Buddhists all producing similar poetry and political practices concurrently. The Sanskrit cosmopolis thus allowed for cultural and political diversity with no specific coercive agenda regarding its own universalism.

Pollock (2006) also highlights the Sanskrit cosmopolis's relationship with place, emphasizing that place was irrelevant in a cultural-political formation with no recognizable core or peripheries. In a world of all centers and no peripheries, there was no center to dominate or emulate. Kashmiri poet Bilhana, who traveled extensively throughout the Indian subcontinent in search of patronage, described this world from an insider's perspective in the eleventh century CE: "There is no village or country, no capital city or forest region, no pleasure garden or school where learned and ignorant, young and old, male and female alike do not read my poems and shake with pleasure" (2006, 23).

Around 1000 CE, vernacular languages rose over the next several centuries to challenge Sanskrit's dominance as the language of poetry and politics, eventually fracturing the Sanskrit cosmopolis and heralding Sanskrit's decline by 1300 CE. Pollock (2006) calls this the beginning of the "vernacular epoch" that witnessed the creation of new reading communities and new conceptions of vernacular political space. These vernaculars became languages of Place (*desī*), not of a region of birth, as the Latin *natio* implies. They were never tied to notions of biology or ethnicity as languages in Europe were. According to Pollock (2006, 573–574),

> No discourses exist in southern Asia on the origins of languages or peoples, like the myths of languages and peoples, transmogrifying into chronicles and histories of kingdoms and peoples, that can fairly be called an obsession in medieval Europe. . . . No writer in southern Asia ever linked political power with linguistic particularism. . . . No language in southern Asia ever became the target of direct royal regulation; sanctions were never imposed requiring the use of one and prohibiting the use of another. At the time when episodes of vernacular extermination were occurring in Europe, kings in Karnataka were issuing royal records in Kannada for the core of their culture-power *desa*, in Telugu for the eastern sector, and in Marathi for the western, and in their courts these kings were entertained with songs in these languages as well as Avadhi, Bihari, Bangla, Oriya, and Madhyadeshiya—producing, in fact, a virtual cosmopolitanism of the vernaculars.

Pollock's model of the Sanskrit cosmopolis is part of his larger examination of two critical transformations in culture and power in premodern India—the first transforming Sanskrit from a religious into a cosmopolitan literary language around the beginning of the first millennium and the second transforming vernacular languages into literary languages around the beginning of the second millennium. Pollock (2000) more comfortably associates the cosmopolitan and vernacular with the equivalent terms in Indian languages—cultural practices of the great "Way" (*mārga*) and those of "Place" (*desī*)—that harbor fewer assumptions than the English terms.[2] In considering these alternate formations, Pollock ultimately argues that ways of being vernacular or cosmopolitan in the world today—often assumed "natural" or "unnatural"—have been constructed over time. In so doing, he points out that the contemporary tendency to naturalize the diversity of vernacular languages and culture is itself historically constructed.

> Few things seem as natural as the multiplicity of vernacular languages used for making sense of life through texts . . . and few things seem as unnatural as their gradual disappearance in the present, especially from the pressures exerted by globalizing English. Literary-language loss is in fact often viewed as part of a more general reduction of diversity in a cultural ecosystem, a loss considered as dangerous as the reduction of biological diversity, to which . . . it is often compared. Today's homogenization of culture, of which language loss is one aspect, seems without precedent in human history, at least for the scope, speed, and manner in which such change is taking place. (2006, 567)

Pollock (2006, 567) makes two arguments concerning the historical construction of the categories of the cosmopolitan and vernacular. First, that vernacular cultural orders that now appear threatened were fashioned over time and are not "primeval" ways of being in the world. And second, that what he calls "the new vernacular cultures" substituted a multiplicity of "much older practices that affiliated their users to a global space rather than to a local place" (2006, 567). Pollock (2006, 567) concludes by observing that "it is only now, when the millennium-long vernacular epoch is coming to an end, that this past can be seen as a whole—the grand transformations from the old cosmopolitan to the new vernacular order, and from the vernacular to the new and far more disquieting global order of the present day—and so can be drawn upon for understanding that long history of culture and power."[3]

One problematic aspect of Pollock's argument is his seemingly uncritical acceptance of the stance, propounded by UNESCO and many others, that views culture around the world as imminently homogenizing.[4] Nevertheless, he significantly contributes a wider historical perspective that puts current vernacular-cosmopolitan transformations into a larger dynamic context and questions their conceptual basis. In examining the cosmopolitan and vernacular formations shaped by Sanskrit throughout premodern South and Southeast Asia, Pollock critically offers alternatives to contemporary culture-power formations and thereby rejects the widely accepted, narrow European analytical and temporal frameworks that consider cosmopolitanism a cultural-political form of universal reason. In the next section, I examine how Kutiyattam has been embedded in both cosmopolitan and vernacular transformations.

Sanskrit Drama and the Sanskrit Cosmopolis

The production of Sanskrit drama was part of the circulation of Sanskrit poetry that constituted the Sanskrit cosmopolis. According to the classical dramatic treatise the *Natyashastra* (c. 200 BCE–200 CE), the text of a drama is considered *kavya* (poetry) while its performance onstage is *nāṭya* (drama).[5] Premodern critical literature refers to Sanskrit drama as *drishyakavya* (*dṛśyakāvya*), or visual poetry (Stoler Miller 1984). Keith (1924, 276) describes it as "the highest product of Indian poetry," and art critic Vamana praises Sanskrit drama as the "greatest form of literature" in the eighth or ninth century CE (Raghavan 1993a, 21).

The *Natyashastra* is the foundational theoretical and practical text of Sanskrit theater and performing arts, "adhered to by theoreticians and practicing artists for a period of approximately 2000 years . . . throughout the [Indian] subcontinent" (Vatsyayan 2001, 26). There is no definitive critical edition of the text; many incomplete manuscripts have been discovered from Nepal to Kerala, resulting in numerous editions that vary in terms of content and number of chapters and verses (Pollock 2016).[6] This variation fulfills the basic criteria of folklore, and it is generally accepted that the *Natyashastra* was previously in oral circulation.[7] Sanskritist and Kutiyattam scholar Bruce Sullivan (email communication, 2022) explained an alternate source of variation, telling me, "Written texts recopied every generation can develop a lot of variation due to errors of omission, annotations being added in, a patron's wisdom being added since he's paying for the copying, etcetera." Consistent across all versions, however, is the claim by the attributed author, the sage Bharata, that the text is the fifth Veda, or Hindu scripture, delivering the gift of dramatic arts from the gods to humanity. The approximately six-thousand-verse text exhaustively outlines such details as specific stage measurements, character types with corresponding makeup and language use, details of preliminaries performed at the beginning of each play, and how emotions should be expressed onstage and received by audiences. It describes a total theater combining drama, music, and dance, and the term *natya*, often translated to English as "drama" or "theater," actually refers to dramatic art that unifies these three elements (Raghavan 1993a).

What did Sanskrit drama actually look like in performance?[8] What we know comes from the *Natyashastra* as well as tenth-century Kashmiri philosopher Abhinavagupta's commentary on it, the *Abhinavabhāratī*, whose manuscript was discovered in Kerala in the early twentieth century (Vatsyayan 2001). Theater scholar James Brandon (1993, xviii) provides an apt summary of the "amazingly sophisticated and elaborate" system of performance.

> The lines of a play are not merely "spoken" on stage. The dramatic text, which is written in alternating passages of prose and of verse in various meters, is chanted and sung (and perhaps in part spoken) and is enacted visually through formal schemes of dance movement, symbolic hand gestures, and codified facial expressions. With the support of costume and makeup patterns, actors and actresses represent specific types of characters in carefully determined situations which are appropriate to convey certain chosen emotional states. The whole is accompanied by instrumental music and interpolated songs (which do not necessarily appear in the author's play text). The proper procedures for constructing a theater, for carrying out preperformance ritual offerings, for warming up the audience with preliminary songs and dances, and for placing the different social groups within the auditorium are known and prescribed. The aim of performance is to induce in the spectator a feeling of aesthetic delight (*rasa*), and each element of the production is judiciously chosen and arranged so that this highest aesthetic affect may be achieved through the performance.

According to Bharata, theater is "no more and no less than the nature of the world with its happiness and despair represented through acting" (Byrski 1993, 143).[9] As such, the Sanskrit theater was considered a microcosm of the universe, including all caste groups and genders, with even the gods conceptualized as being present for performances (Sullivan 1997). The *Natyashastra*'s origin story evidences a democratizing aim of making the art accessible to all castes (i.e., humanity) as the fifth Veda, in contrast to previous Vedas restricted only to Brahmins (Byrski 2015, 65).[10] Within the theater, the troupe's director (*sūtradhāra*, literally "thread-holder") was a prominent figure, presiding over each play's preliminaries (*pūrvaraṅga*). These included religious propitiations; a series of musical items and dances; a benediction (*nāndī*) invoking a divine blessing for Brahmins, the king, and the playwright; and the prologue (*prastāvanā*), whereby the director introduced the play (Enros 1979). Plays, often based on the *Ramayana* and *Mahabharata* epics already familiar to audiences, generally emphasized character development over plot.[11] As Raghavan (1993a, 29) explains, "The Sanskrit dramatist is always interested in the effect of events on his characters, rather than in the actual incidents themselves."

The *Natyashastra* outlines four essential elements of acting (*abhinaya*). These are *āṅgika*: body movements like mudras, dance, and various gaits for different characters; *vachika* (*vācika*): verbal expression; *āhārya*: costuming, makeup, ornaments, and stage decoration or props; and *sāttvika*: emotional expression through the eyes, face, and involuntary emotional responses of the body.[12] Narrative pantomime was a core element of Sanskrit theater, as bodily acting was valued on par with verbal acting. Stylized costuming and makeup were also important, with the type of dress and colors painted on the face and limbs varying according to region, status, caste, and age. As opposed to realistic acting (*lokadharmi*), which Bharata considered inferior, Sanskrit theater was dominated by stylized acting (*natyadharmi*), giving it the "utmost scope to imagination and fancy" (Ghosh 1951, 58).

The theory of rasa (aesthetic flavor), which conceptualizes how emotional expression impacts audiences, is perhaps the most well-known aspect of the Sanskrit theater today.[13] As Bharata famously declared, "Nothing proceeds on the stage without reference to rasa" (Raghavan 1993a, 21). Rasa theory has had a lasting impact on Indian performing arts through the present day, part of the *Natyashastra*'s ongoing impact as an "active, oral, and corporeal [tradition] . . . present in performers, their teachers, and their performances, . . . an embodied set of ideas and practices . . . more danced than read" (Schechner 2001, 28). The *Natyashastra*'s description of rasa is renowned for its metaphor of taste.

> Just as when various condiments and sauces and herbs and other materials are mixed, a taste is experienced, or when the mixing of materials like molasses with other materials produces six kinds of taste, so also along with the different *bhavas* [emotions] the *sthayi bhava* [permanent emotions experienced "inside"] becomes a rasa. But what is this thing called rasa? Here is the reply. Because it is enjoyably tasted, it is called rasa. How does the enjoyment come? Persons who eat prepared food mixed with different condiments and sauces, if they are sensitive, enjoy the different tastes and then feel pleasure; likewise, sensitive spectators, after enjoying the various emotions expressed by the actors through words, gestures, and feelings feel pleasure. This feeling by the spectators is here explained as the rasas of natya. (Bharata-Muni 1996, chap. 6, v. 31)

The text outlines eight rasas: *shringara* (desire, love), *hasya* (humor, laughter), *karuna* (pity, grief), *raudra* (anger), *vira* (energy, vigor), *bhayanaka* (fear, shame), *bibhatsa* (disgust), and *adbhuta* (surprise, wonder). Abhinavagupta famously added a ninth rasa, *shantha* (bliss/tranquility), which has been widely accepted.

Performance studies scholar Richard Schechner (2001) contrasts rasa-based acting with the Stanislavsky method dominant in Western acting. Whereas the rasic system considers "artistically performed emotions" objective and impersonal, inscribed onto the actor's body through facial expressions and eye and body movements, the Stanislavsky method conceptualizes emotions as a personal, individual experience, accessible only by recalling an "emotional memory." As Schechner (2001, 32) observes, "In the rasic system, the emotions *in the arts, not in ordinary life* are knowable, manageable, and transmittable in roughly the same way that the flavors and presentation of a meal are manageable by following recipes and the conventions of presenting the meal." On the reception end, the rasic system conceptualizes the spectator as being of "one heart" (*sahṛdaya*) with the playwright and his characters, feeling deeply the emotions the actor or actress presents onstage (Raghavan 1993a).

Plays were performed in their entirety in Sanskrit theater, although opinions differ on whether they were performed in temples or palace theaters in a single night (e.g., Sullivan 1995) or over the course of several days, with one act performed per day (e.g., Raghavan 1993a). Actors and actresses performed together onstage, and troupes were known to be composed exclusively of actresses who performed both male and female roles (Raghavan 1993a). The theater was undergirded by a "total optimism" in which conflicts were always resolved and desires fulfilled by the end of the play (Byrski 1993, 145). With the hero and heroine's desired results in heroism or love always achieved in the end, the "idealist" Sanskrit drama was never a true tragedy (Keith 1924, 278). The stage itself had no scenery and very few props. The theater used curtains sparingly as well: a few covered the two doors on the back wall leading to the greenroom, and an eight-by-four-foot rectangular curtain called *yavanika* was held by stage assistants during the entries and exits of characters (Richmond 1993). The *Natyashastra* considered music the "bedrock of drama," with drummers and musicians placed prominently upstage center between the two greenroom doors (Bharata-Muni 1951, chap. 33, v. 301). Bharata writes: "As without color, a drawing is not beautiful, so is drama not attractive without music" (Raghavan 1993a, 39).[14] As Raghavan (1993a, 39) notes, there is even a saying in Sanskrit that anything strange is like "a drama without a drum."

Finally, the *Natyashastra* outlines the polyglot nature of Sanskrit theater, describing multiple languages used onstage: Sanskrit, Prakrit—often glossed as the vernacular form of Sanskrit yet a strictly literary language—and Deshabhasha, or regional languages.[15] Sanskrit was to be spoken by heroes, sages, Buddhists, or anyone who studied the Vedas; Prakrit by "children, persons possessed of spirits of lower order, women in feminine character, persons of low birth, lunatics and phallus-worshippers" and others, including the *vidushaka*, or jester; and varying Deshabhasha were spoken according to character type—Magadhi by those in the king's harem; Shauraseni by the heroine and her maids; Prachya by the jester; Ardhamaghadhi by royal servants, military men, and merchants; Avanti by rogues; Dakshinatya by soldiers and police; and Bahliki by the Khasas from the North (Bharata-Muni 1951, chap. 18, vs. 34–36, 47–51). The hero's companion, the vidushaka, played the key role of commenting on and translating Sanskrit dialogues into Prakrit to make them easier for audiences to understand. Culp (2021) observes that characters would sometimes even transcend these rules to code switch according to context during a single conversation—using Sanskrit for politics and Prakrit for romance. Ollett (2017) points out that while the *Natyashastra* outlines these three literary language categories, later premodern writers considered Prakrit and Deshabhasha synonymous, a model that continues to dominate scholarship today, with scholars collectively referring to a wide range of languages related to Sanskrit with the plural *Prakrits*.

Keith (1924, 282) describes the quality of language used in Sanskrit drama: "We are treated to an artificial court speech, which assorts with stereotyped emotions, refined, elegant, sentimental, rich in the compliments of court gallantry, . . . marked with a distinct strain of philosophical commonplace, and fond of suggested meanings and double entendres, hinting at the events yet to come." As Gopalakrishnan (1988) notes, different layers of meaning are a characteristic feature of Sanskrit verse as seen in dramas, including specific types known as multiple meaning (*śleṣa*), implied meaning (*vyaṅgyārta*), "crooked" expression (*vakṛōkti*), and obscure meaning (*gūḍhārtha*). The next section discusses an example of suggestive language use in Kutiyattam.

Sanskrit drama in performance reached its peak with the poet Kalidasa in the fifth century CE and by the eighth century had begun to decline, although poets penned new plays as literary works through the nineteenth century (Swann 1993). Despite the *Natyashastra*'s democratizing goals for Sanskrit theater, in terms of status, the art was "essentially aristocratic," with caste and class distinctions reflected through language (Keith 1924, 276). Raghavan (1993a) observes that, according to Vatsyayana's *Kama Sutra*, drama is among the sixty-four arts that men and women "of taste" should master and is considered an opportunity for making and developing love. Spanning the Indian subcontinent from Kerala to Kashmir and even to Turfan in central Asia, where first- or second-century CE play fragments about the life of Buddha have been found, this aristocratic art had an immense geographical scope that united playwrights, actors, and audiences of diverse backgrounds under the cosmopolitan banner of Sanskrit theater (Raghavan 1993a).

Situating Kutiyattam in the Sanskrit Cosmopolis

As the production of Sanskrit drama in a Malayalam-speaking region, Kutiyattam began squarely situated within the circulation of Sanskrit poetry that made up the Sanskrit cosmopolis. Kutiyattam emerged on the cusp of vernacularization, "roughly coinciding with the breakdown of the unity provided by Sanskrit and the growth of regional languages and literature" (Vatsyayan 1980, 15). King Kulashekhara is credited by oral tradition and historical records with the reshaping of Sanskrit dramatic performance for the Kerala stage that marked the birth of Kutiyattam (Raja [1958] 1980).[16] In composing the plays still part of Kutiyattam's contemporary repertoire, *Subhadrādhanañjayam* (*The Wedding of Arjuna and Subhadra*) and *Tapatî-saṃvaraṇam* (*The Sun God's Daughter and King Samvarana*), the ninth- or tenth-century CE king of Kerala consciously affiliated with the larger world of Sanskrit drama and theater while making intentional deviations from it, as we see below.[17] Kutiyattam's membership within this cosmopolitan world is further solidified by its performance of works by classical playwrights such as Bhasa, Shaktibhadra, Bodhayana, and Harsha, who composed Sanskrit dramas from the fourth to eleventh centuries from different regions of the subcontinent.[18] And while most of the plays in Kutiyattam's repertoire are heroic *nāṭaka* plays, which are based on material from the Hindu epics the *Mahabharata* and *Ramayana*, a few are Sanskrit farces that feature Buddhist characters—Bodhayana's *Bhagavadajjukam* (*The Ascetic and the Courtesan*) and Mahendravarman's *Mattavilasa-prahasana* (*The Delight of the Drunkards*)—and one is a Buddhist play, Harsha's *Nāgānanda* (*Joy of the Serpents*).[19] Kutiyattam's production of a wider body of Sanskrit drama proves that it was, at least at its inception, consciously part of this voluntary, larger-than-local poetic world.

As part of the larger phenomenon of Sanskrit dramatic production, Kutiyattam shares a striking number of similarities with the *Natyashastra* in performance, particularly in its temple context. On a broader scale, Indian regional theaters like Kutiyattam are thought to share several features in common with the *Natyashastra*, namely, the *purvaranga* preliminaries—a series of rites conducted onstage before the play commenced—rasa-oriented aesthetics, a nonlinear conception of time and space, and the philosophy and practice of *abhinaya* (acting), especially the use of gestures (Tripathi 2013, 12).[20] What distinguishes Kutiyattam from other regional theaters, however, is its degree of adherence to the *Natyashastra*. This entails everything from detailed preliminaries to the use of Sanskrit and Prakrit languages, the *yavanika* (curtain), particular gaits and makeup for certain characters, fourfold acting described earlier—*angikabhinaya, vachikabhinaya, aharyabhinaya,* and *sattvikabhinaya*—theaters constructed especially for the purpose, and an emphasis on stylized acting, among other similarities.[21] In fact, much of Brandon's (1993) description of Sanskrit drama above rings true for Kutiyattam, while Farley Richmond (1990, 22) calls Kutiyattam "the closest living relative of the ancient Sanskrit theatrical tradition." As chapter 6 details, Kutiyattam has been widely viewed by scholars and Indian government officials alike as a direct link to ancient Sanskrit theater and has often been claimed as part of India's "national" past. Despite these myriad similarities, Kutiyattam also significantly diverges from the *Natyashastra,* as I explain below.

At the time of Kutiyattam's emergence, Sanskrit plays were already known and flourishing in Kerala (Unni 2013). King Kulashekhara sought to reform the Sanskrit stage by incorporating the aesthetic theory of *dhvani,* conceived by ninth-century CE Kashmiri philosopher Anandavardhana, which emphasizes the suggested or inner meaning of poetry (Paulose 2013). Adapting this idea to theater, Kulashekhara tells audiences that he "wrote two dramas pregnant with inner meaning," *Subhadradhananjayam* and *Tapati-samvaranam* (Paulose 2013, 41). Let's look at one example of dhvani from *Tapati-samvaranam.* The vidushaka asks the hero, "The gloom of your lotus face indicates the grief concealed by your heart. Why is it so?" To this, the hero King Samvarana replies: "Friend, you have guessed it right. During the previous night I was worshipping the sun in my dream, when—There appeared from the sky the orb of the sun before me, drying up the dew drops, and observed by the lotuses of the lake, opening their petals, and releasing the bees entrapped" (Unni and Sullivan 1995, 156). In a footnote to the verse, Unni and Sullivan explain, "Double meanings in the verse equate the lotuses to maidens, lotus petals to their opening eyelids, and the releasing of bees to the movements of their black pupils, an often-repeated trope in Sanskrit poetry" (1995, 211).[22] It is the Kutiyattam actor's role to convey these hidden meanings to the audience through nonverbal, bodily narration (*angikabhinaya*). Some verses may have up to three or four different meanings.

Kulashekhara's goal in introducing dhvani to the theater was to liberate the actor from the constraints of the dramatic text and its conventions. Widely thought to be assisted by his Brahmin minister Tolan, Kulashekhara introduced a number of performative innovations that facilitated suggestive acting and improvisation (*manodharma*), still a characteristic feature of Kutiyattam today.[23] The *Vyaṅgyavyākhyā,* the Sanskrit commentaries for Kulashekhara's two plays, together serve as performance manuals that explain both the overt meanings of the texts and the dhvani subtexts the actor should elaborate when performing.[24] The *Vyangyavyakhya* is written from the perspective of a scholar whom Kulashekhara invited to comment on his plays. In the text, the anonymous author describes how, in the "autumnal season with its breeze cool and heat so gentle, water as clear as crystal," the king of Kerala summoned him to the capital at Mahodayapuram, furnishing his travel "through the river Churnika in a canoe provided with cot, bed, and other comforts" (Paulose 2013, 71–73). Upon arriving, he describes how the king received him with "sweet words" and provides a rich, embellished description of ninth- or tenth-century King Kulashekhara.

> There I met the king seated on a throne. His natural lustre seemed to have increased owing to the radiance of the rich stones adorning his crown. An elevated forehead, a prominent nose, lofty shoulders, long eyes and lengthy shanks contributed much to adorn his person. Surely, the red painted forearms and feet betrayed the signs of a king since they possessed auspicious marks of a wheel, conch-shell, etc. His face-lotus glittered in the brilliance of the rich stones of his earrings. His neck surpassed the conch-shell in sound and shape. His breast was anointed with saffron, camphor and sandal pastes. The blue silken garment worn by him attracted the attention of onlookers. . . . He was loved and admired by one and all. (Unni 1995, 3)

Kulashekhara requested the scholar judge his plays and evaluate their merit. If judged well, the king would perform each character to demonstrate and then have the plays staged by professional actors. As the scholar writes, "The King, determined as he was, put on the costumes and ornaments of different characters and showed the mode of their acting" (Paulose 2013, 300). He took note of the sentiment, mode of enactment, and entrance of characters in each drama, which became the text of *Vyangyavyakhya*.

Which deviations from the *Natyashastra* are attributed to Kulashekhara's efforts to give the actor unlimited imaginative scope?[25] The king's innovations generally thought to herald the birth of Kutiyattam are (1) the reduction of performance to only one act of a play at a time; (2) the associated introduction of *nirvahanam*, or solo retrospective narration, at the beginning of each playact that summarizes all previous acts as well as the life history of particular characters; (3) further movement away from *lokadharmi* (realistic acting) toward *natyadharmi* (stylized acting) through theatrical elaboration that included a fourfold interpretation of each Sanskrit verse (oral recitation, grammatical rendering through mudras, exploration of the verse's inner meaning through mudras, and the interpretation of all possible implied meanings through mudras); (4) the introduction of the *pakarnnattam* (*pakarnāṭṭam*) technique, whereby the solo actor or actress switches back and forth seamlessly between various roles as an omniscient storyteller;[26] (5) the confining of Sanskrit stage production within the temple and the Nambiar/Nangiar/Chakyar hereditary performance communities;[27] (6) the addition of humorous material to a performance by adding material outside of the dramatic text such as the parody of the four *Purusharthas* (*Puruṣārthas*; The Aims of Human Life); and (7) the introduction of local language used by the vidushaka, jester figure and companion to the hero, to explain the Sanskrit and Prakrit passages to the audience (Gopalakrishnan 2011a; Raja 1964).[28] The ability of the Kutiyattam vidushaka to speak Malayalam and diverge from the dramatic text by drawing parallels between the action of the play and contemporary issues as a mode of critique is credited by many with the art's survival, keeping the art ever relevant to the changing times.

While these innovations have led Kutiyattam to be called a "theater of the imagination" (Paniker 1994), it is important to note that degrees of improvisatory license vary within Kutiyattam performances themselves, often along gendered lines (Lowthorp 2016). Artistic freedom peaks during a solo performance. In a full performance context, this means multiple days of solo nirvahanam retrospective acting where the usually male actor is an all-knowing narrator using pakarnnattam to embody heroes, heroines, demons, goddesses, or animals. In the multicharacter kutiyattam proper at the end of a performance cycle, however, actors and actresses are constrained by their roles.[29] I have explored the issue of imaginative freedom among actresses, whose artistic license peaks in Nangiarkoothu, technically considered an extended nirvahanam performance (Lowthorp 2016).[30] Significantly, actresses are not often given a nirvahanam solo opportunity in Kutiyattam.[31] When I asked actresses if they prefer performing Kutiyattam or Nangiarkoothu, the vast majority chose Nangiarkoothu, citing the freedom it gives them in performance. As Margi Sathi told me, "In Kutiyattam there are several characters onstage and you play only one of them, so from start to finish you must stay in the mind of only that character. . . . In Nangiarkoothu, we have the freedom to become anything." Usha-teacher (Margi Usha) elaborated, "Because Nangiarkoothu is a solo performance, we can decide to do as much improvisation as we like . . . Nangiarkoothu uses *pakarnnattam*. Even though it doesn't have the character Arjuna, we can still become Arjuna onstage. Nangiarkoothu therefore has the greatest potential for acting, it gives us the freedom to act to our highest ability."[32] Solo acting filled with retrospection and elaboration is thus where we can see the fulfillment of Kulashekhara's dream of imaginative liberation.

Figure 22. Actresses in Nangiarkoothu: *left*, Kapila Venu with Kalamandalam Rajeev on mizhavu versus Kutiyattam; *right*, Kalamandalam Sindhu alongside Margi Raman Chakyar. Photos by author.

Not everyone was excited about the vernacularization of Sanskrit theater these changes signified. The anonymous author of the fifteenth-century CE Sanskrit commentary the *Naṭāṅkuśa* (literally, a "restraining hook" for actors) is one example.[33] Written from the perspective of a learned spectator of the temple theater, the sometimes humorous manuscript vehemently critiques Kutiyattam's deviations from the *Natyashastra*. These include the use of *kriya* (ritualistic dances) outside of the preliminaries, the extension of the dramatic text through the addition of nirvahanam, the technique of pakarnnattam, and the vidushaka's use of Malayalam. Claiming that *kriya* interrupts the "ultimate aim of performance"—the spectator's realization of rasa—the author offers a humorous metaphor: "This 'Kriya,' useless in all respects, is like the teat nipple that hangs down from the neck of a she-goat" (Paulose 2013, 160). On nirvahanam, the author asserts that "the attempt of the actor to elaborate [the script] is not proper. . . . By adopting this method of extension one can connect anything to everything. The mud in the hands of the potter can be described as embedded with the knowledge of the absolute. . . . By elaborating incidents unconnected to the theme, the actor actually throws the axe at the root of the tender creeper the plot" (2013, 162, 180).

The *Natankusa* author focuses much of his critique on the performance of *Anguliyankamkoothu* (*The Act of the Ring*), the sixth act of Shaktibhadra's play *Ascharyachoodamani*. Here, the actor, in the guise of Hanuman the monkey god, narrates the entire *Ramayana*. He takes particular issue with the pakarnnattam technique, whereby the actor as narrator assumes multiple roles, telling his readers, "There is a tendency among the actors to imitate a character, in the dress and makeup of another whose character he has originally assumed. The propriety of this has to be questioned" (Paulose 2013, 164). He continues, sarcastically, "Wonderful indeed is the imitation of the effeminate elegant movements of Sita in the robe of a monkey, with a tail hanging behind!" (2013, 164). The author describes a technique that male actors still use today to transform into female characters: "When the actor in the role of Hanuman begins to imitate Sita, ties up in front the tip of the garment, what is it for? . . . What will you do to imitate a bee? You cannot accomplish the impersonation of Sita by this action alone" (2013, 166).

The incensed author finally takes issue with the Kutiyattam vidushaka speaking Malayalam instead of Prakrit as per the *Natyashastra*. He stresses that the conventions of the stage need not match everyday life, emphasizing, "The women of Kerala usually keep their breasts exposed. But they are presented on the stage with their bosom covered" (Paulose 2013, 178). He seems to find the vidushaka's Malayalam particularly egregious, alleging, "The actor is ridiculing the sensibility of the learned audience. The meaning of what he says ends in this: 'O learned spectator, you do not seem to have understood what we have presented so far on the stage. Hence I will enlighten you by narrating it in the popular tongue'" (2013, 181). While scholars previously considered the *Natankusa* as the localized critique of a Brahmin scholar with an axe to grind with local performers, Paulose (2003) considers the critique a case of performer-spectator interaction. In light of Pollock's (2006) vernacular epoch described previously, I instead reframe the *Natankusa*'s critique as resistance to larger processes of vernacular transformation occurring throughout the subcontinent at the time.

Embodied Cosmopolitanism: Language and Performance in Kutiyattam

Let us now consider Kutiyattam's embodied cosmopolitanism, by which I mean aspects of the artist's body-in-performance that index larger-than-local worlds.

Kutiyattam's embodied relationship to the wider phenomenon of Sanskrit theater described above is certainly a form of embodied cosmopolitanism. What I explore here, however, is Kutiyattam's incredible multilingualism onstage. A conversation with Sooraj Nambiar, a young nonhereditary actor at the Ammannur gurukulam in Irinjalakuda, sparked my deeper interest in this arena.[34] When I asked if he considered Kutiyattam a Keralan, Indian, or world theater, he first reflected on the relationship between Sanskrit and Malayalam in performance, telling me,

> Kutiyattam is called a Sanskrit theater, it uses Sanskrit plays. These are Indian plays, not Keralan plays, but this survived because only the text is in Sanskrit. The whole *attaprakaram* (acting manual) is in Malayalam, the mother tongue. You cannot do theater in a foreign language. Okay you can, but only after first doing it in your mother tongue and then translating it. Body language and your thinking and your expressions and everything are all close to your mother tongue, so there is no problem that this is Sanskrit theater, because only the text is in Sanskrit. All other things are in the mother tongue, the language of your dreams.

"Do you ever dream in Sanskrit?" I asked.

"Never," he replied.

Sooraj's poetic descriptions of the impossibility of theater in a foreign language and one's mother tongue as a "language of . . . dreams" stuck with me, prompting me to inquire further into language and performance in Kutiyattam during subsequent visits to Kerala. The polyglot art vacillates at various times between Sanskrit, Prakrit, Manipravalam, Tamil, the language of mudra hand gestures, and Malayalam. In this section, I explore Kutiyattam's multilingualism and how artists today experience performing in multiple languages onstage.

Language Use Onstage

I begin with a reminder of the different stages of a full Kutiyattam performance: (1) solo *purappadu* character entry, (2) solo nirvahanam character retrospection, (3) repetition of sequences 1 and 2 for additional characters, and (4) kutiyattam proper with multiple characters onstage. In terms of languages, Sanskrit, Malayalam, and mudras dominate Kutiyattam performance. When considering all of Kutiyattam's languages and the worlds they evoke, Sanskrit and Prakrit index cosmopolitan worlds; Manipravalam, Tamil, and mudras signify local/larger-than-local hybrids; and Malayalam represents the region.

Let us first consider the cosmopolitan languages Sanskrit and Prakrit, whose explanation and use in wider Sanskrit drama were detailed earlier this chapter.[35] In the multicharacter kutiyattam proper, the male hero employs Sanskrit alongside the multilingual vidushaka jester figure, who translates the hero's lines for the audience. In Kutiyattam's nirvahanam segments and other solo performances like Mattavilasamkoothu, Anguliyankamkoothu, and Nangiarkoothu, the actor does not recite his or her own lines but instead acts them out through pantomime and mudras.[36] In these instances, an actress-cum-musician seated stage right recites the actor's Sanskrit lines while playing *kuzhithalam* cymbals.

Prakrit only appears in kutiyattam proper, where women and other lower male characters, including the vidushaka, chant their lines in Prakrit. As Sindhu-chechi (Kalamandalam Sindhu) told me, the type of Prakrit or Prakrits in each play can vary according to both the time and place of the playwright as well as the status of the characters speaking it. Sajeev-ashan (Margi Sajeev Narayana Chakyar) similarly told me that the vidushaka's Prakrit is generally different from that of female characters. Particularly, the Prakrit used by the demoness Shurpanakha in Shaktibhadra's *Ascharyachoodamani* is different from that used by the same character in the guise of an attractive woman, Lalita, whom he described as "a little more beautiful." Interestingly, this Sanskrit and Prakrit language use roughly follows that outlined in the *Natyashastra*, although the use of other languages, as I discuss below, diverges significantly.

The languages I classify as local/cosmopolitan hybrids in Kutiyattam are Manipravalam, Tamil, and mudra hand gestures. In the Kerala context, Manipravalam is a hybrid literary language that mixes Sanskrit and a Tamil dialect considered an early form of Malayalam (Freeman 1998). It only appears in Kutiyattam when used by the vidushaka, who chants his lines first in Prakrit, then Sanskrit, and then Malayalam, when he expands all of the various meanings of the hero's verse. It is only after this expansion that he performs an abbreviated summary of the hero's lines in Manipravalam. According to Sajeev-ashan, Manipravalam is used "to make fun of the hero (through a) parody of the hero's verse." According to Goren Arzony (2019, 307), Manipravalam is more specifically "a lingual genre in which most of the early literary non-Sanskrit texts in Kerala were composed."[37] It was closely connected to the stage and may even have been developed by Chakyar actors.[38] As the vidushaka only appears in a limited number of performances as compared to the wider Kutiyattam repertoire, Manipravalam is a minority language onstage.

An even greater minority language onstage today is Tamil, also known as Nambiar Tamil, which Betty Jones (1984, 172) defines as "the recitation by the

Nambyar in Old Malayalam which explains or elaborates upon the act of the drama which is being presented."[39] Unni-ashan (Kalamandalam Unnikrishnan Nambiar) noted that it is only used today in Anguliyankamkoothu, although he has heard it was also previously used in Mattavilasamkoothu. He described the language as basically Malayalam, with some of the words having "the taste of Tamil." Unni-ashan gave the example of the past tense of the verb *to do*, which in Malayalam is *cheythu*. When speaking Tamil, he would instead say *cheythan*. "Like that," he told me, "some words have the taste or the music of Tamil. Even if it's not directly Tamil, it's similar to it." While today we know Tamil as the language of the neighboring state of Tamil Nadu, Tamil here refers to an early form of Malayalam that developed from Early Middle Tamil (Shanmugam 2018). As late as the fourteenth century CE, Malayalam was regularly referred to as Tamil, alongside *bhāṣa* (language) and *kēraḷa-bhāṣa* (Kerala language), only becoming known as Malayalam in the nineteenth century (Gamliel 2020, 1). Despite being Old Malayalam, I consider Tamil in this context hybrid in the sense that it simultaneously indexes a local and larger-than-local imagining.

The mudra hand gesture language, by contrast, is a dominant language onstage. When I asked artists which languages one must know for Kutiyattam performance, most did not include mudras. Usha-teacher, however, emphasized, "Just like other languages have alphabets, mudras are the alphabet of Kutiyattam. With these letters, we make sentences. With these sentences, we make paragraphs. And with ten paragraphs, we enact a story." Indeed, one thing that makes Kutiyattam mudras so special is that they are equipped to express full sentences, replete with grammatical markers such as dative, possessive, locative, and plural.[40] As we saw in the last chapter, artists also use mudras as an insider language of offstage communication. On the Kutiyattam stage, the majority of dialogue and storytelling happens through mudras, with spoken dialogue generally scarce outside of the vidushaka's performance. The mudra language is hybrid in the sense that, while the use of mudras was specified in the *Natyashastra* and they are still widely used today in arts across the Indian subcontinent, Kutiyattam's mudras are a local variation of this wider cosmopolitan phenomenon, inspired by a Kerala treatise known as the *Hastalakshanadeepika*.[41]

Likewise, the regional language Malayalam is dominant, although sometimes invisible, on the Kutiyattam stage. While most evident in the vidushaka's banter, its prominence as the language of artists' interior dialogue guiding their mudra storytelling is less obvious to audiences. This becomes evident in grammatical differences between the enactment of Sanskrit verses, where mudras follow Sanskrit grammar, and mudras throughout the rest of performance,

Figure 23. Painkulam Narayana Chakyar as the demoness Shurpanakha. Photo by author.

which follow Malayalam grammar. Malayalam is also an important behind-the-scenes language, with most Kutiyattam *attaprakaram* acting manuals and *kramadeepika* production manuals written in Malayalam. It should be noted that this is not everyday Malayalam but an extremely refined, highly Sanskritized register of the language. Sindhu-chechi told me that it is a different kind of Malayalam, one she had to study to master. Other registers of Malayalam also occasionally appear in performance, like in the demoness Shurpanakha's Malayalam dialogue in *Ascharyachoodamani*, where she speaks a lower-caste dialect that, for example, uses *cundari* instead of *sundari* as the word for *beautiful*.[42]

In the closely allied forms that belong to the wider Kutiyattam complex—Nangiarkoothu, Chakyarkoothu, and Pathakam—language use varies. In

Nangiarkoothu, an expanded nirvahanam form, the actress as storyteller does not employ Prakrit as do female roles in Kutiyattam, despite wearing the same costume. As in other solo performances, the Nangiarkoothu actress enacts the tale through pantomime and mudra gestures while the actress-cum-musician accompanying her on cymbals chants the verses in Sanskrit.[43] Similarly, while Chakyarkoothu (a.k.a. Prabandhakoothu) uses the same costume as the Kutiyattam vidushaka, the actor's languages differ, using only Sanskrit and Malayalam without Prakrit or Manipravalam. Finally, Pathakam, the traditional verbal solo performance of Nambiars—similar to Chakyarkoothu but without the privilege of social critique—employs strictly Sanskrit and Malayalam alongside as its own unique costume.

Conceptualizing Sanskrit

Sooraj Nambiar's emphasis that one cannot do theater in a foreign language stuck with me over the years, and I decided to explore the topic on a later research trip. As our conversation had centered around Kutiyattam, I interpreted Sooraj's statement to mean that he considers Sanskrit a foreign language, although he never explicitly said so. After asking him again, however, I realized that I was approaching the topic from an English-centric perspective that considers any language other than one's mother tongue a foreign language. In Malayalam, there are two words to describe a nonmother tongue: *videshabhasha* (*vidēśabhāṣa*; foreign language) and *anyabhasha* (*anyabhāṣa*; other language). While Sooraj used the English term *foreign language* in our initial conversation in English, he thoroughly rejected my attempt to characterize Sanskrit as a *videshabhasha* in a follow-up conversation in Malayalam. "Oh no, Sanskrit is not a foreign language. It is a language of India itself," he corrected me. When I shifted, asking if he considers Sanskrit an anyabhasha, he similarly rejected this, telling me that Sanskrit is part of Malayalam, so it cannot be considered an "other" language. I subsequently posed the same question to several other artists. Despite varying justifications, all artists strikingly agreed that while Sanskrit was not their mother tongue, neither was it an "other" language. In this section, I explore the ways Kutiyattam artists conceptualize Sanskrit, the most prominent of the nonmother tongue languages on the Kutiyattam stage, through their answers to my question "Is Sanskrit an anyabhasha (other language)?"

Amminikutty Nangiaramma, the youngest daughter of Padmasree Guru Mani Madhava Chakyar, first clarified what the term means, reflecting on it in relation to artist and audience interaction. She queried, "What's an *anyabhasha*? It's a language that we don't know. The vidushaka is there to help audiences understand the Sanskrit acting, right? That's why we don't feel it's an *anyabhasha*." While everyone I spoke to unequivocally agreed that Sanskrit is not an anyabhasha, a few contrasted their relationship with the language before they began to study Kutiyattam. Both Kalamandalam Shylaja and Sindhu-chechi admitted that before they began their Sanskrit studies in Kutiyattam, Sanskrit felt like an anyabhasha. As Kalamandalam Shylaja told me, "Sanskrit definitely felt like an anyabhasha then, because we didn't learn Sanskrit in school [before coming to Kalamandalam], some students take it and some take Malayalam. For those that take it, it's easy. But for those who didn't, it's very challenging." Sindhu-chechi similarly shared, "When I arrived as a student, I didn't know Sanskrit. When I began to study, it was totally an *anyabhasha*. Now it's not." Usha-teacher offered a different perspective of her experience before her Sanskrit studies, reflecting, "I hadn't learned it yet, but I didn't feel that Sanskrit was an *anyabhasha*, because there is a lot of Sanskrit in our prayers. We pray every morning when we get up, and I learned the meaning of these *shlokas* [verses] in order to understand them." She continued, laughing, "I also knew sooo many *shlokas* whose meaning I didn't know. Most people chant *shlokas* without knowing their meaning."

Sindhu-chechi followed up by clarifying how she integrated Sanskrit into her life through stage practice, telling me, "After studying and studying, just like the language I use in my everyday life, Sanskrit became the language of my life onstage. Because of that, I no longer feel it's an *anyabhasha*. These two lives—my artistic life and everyday life—are very close to each other, they are not detached, and their languages (Malayalam and Sanskrit) are very close also." Sooraj similarly reflected, "When you are performing in Sanskrit, it's not your mother tongue. But we have another journey with the language because we have a practice where we make it ours. If you recite a play one thousand times or more, you make it yours, so in a way it becomes your language." Dr. Aparna Nangiar, a young hereditary Kutiyattam actress and Sanskrit professor, revealed how through her Kutiyattam practice, Sanskrit became like a mother tongue: "From our childhood we are studying Sanskrit, all the basics of Sanskrit, so personally I don't have those feelings, that Sanskrit is not my mother tongue." She continued, smiling, "Sanskrit is everything for me, my favorite language—it is my studies, my profession, my passion, everything."

One common justification artists gave for rejecting Sanskrit as an anyabhasha was that it is a language of India. Some called it the mother tongue of India, while others characterized it as the root of all Indian languages. Sajeev-ashan associated this idea with the pan-Indian performance of Sanskrit drama. As he explained, "Sanskrit is Bharatha's [India's] language. There were Sanskrit dramas all over India earlier." When I asked about his idea of Bharatha, Sajeev-ashan indicated an older conception larger than India's current national borders, emphasizing, "It was all one before they divided it, right? When I say Bharatha, I mean before all of these national divisions happened." Dr. C. K. Jayanthi, a hereditary artist and Sanskrit professor, underscored, "Every Indian language has a connection to Sanskrit that speakers are mostly unaware of. In Sanskrit aesthetics the ultimate theory is rasa. Most Malayalis don't know that *rasa* is the ultimate theory of Bharata's theater. They don't know Bharata, they don't know Sanskrit. But when asked how a performance was they'll say, 'It was really *rasam* [enjoyable].' Another example is food. How was the food? It was very *rasam*. Malayalis and Tamils even have a dish named rasam. Rasa is enjoyment. Rasa is aesthetic experience. Everywhere in India they'll quickly recognize this word, every language has it." Several artists brought to my attention a related characterization of Sanskrit as the language of the (Hindu) gods. Kalamandalam Shylaja asserted, "Sanskrit is our language itself, the language of the gods, the language of the Vedas." She then followed up, humorously, "They say that when we speak Sanskrit, the gods listen." With an exaggerated expression, she cast her eyes to the heavens and jokingly queried, "My Lord, are you listening?"

The consensus of most artists was that Sanskrit is not an anyabhasha because Sanskrit is part of Malayalam. Many referred to Malayalam's origins as the merging of Tamil and Sanskrit, with Ammannur Kuttan Chakyar musing, "There would be no Malayalam if not for Sanskrit. Most of its words are Sanskrit words. When you join Sanskrit and Tamil, you get Malayalam." Despite the fact that the languages belong to different language families, Malayalam to the Dravidian and Sanskrit to the Indo-European, Malayalam is a highly Sanskritized language whose alphabet encompasses the full range of Sanskrit phonemes. Higher, formalized registers of Malayalam are particularly Sanskrit-heavy, although everyday language has its fair share of Sanskrit words as well. As Kalamandalam Shylaja explained, "Many words we use in Malayalam are Sanskrit words, without even being aware of it. When people speak, they think it's Malayalam, but it's all Sanskrit. For example, *mukhaṃ* [face] is a common word in Malayalam, but *mukham* is a Sanskrit word! The Malayalam word is *mōnta*, you can use the words interchangeably. *Monta* is from a lower level of the language, and *mukham* from a higher level." Dr. Jayanthi similarly elaborated, "Sanskrit doesn't need to be a mother tongue. My language, Malayalam, is full of Sanskrit. In a *shloka* [Sanskrit verse], 75 percent of the words we already know, because they're Malayalam words. They're Sanskrit words, but have a Malayalam meaning, so we would never say or write that Sanskrit feels like a different language." She mentioned that for much of history, most Sanskrit works in Kerala were written in the Malayalam script, as we saw with Usha-teacher's Saraswathi prayer at the beginning of this chapter. This practice further blurred the lines between the two languages, with Devanagari script becoming common only after the spread of printing in the nineteenth century.

This blurring of Sanskrit and Malayalam is also evident in Kutiyattam stage manuals (attaprakaram). Written in the Malayalam language, Sanskrit verses likewise appear in the manuals in Malayalam script. Several artists commented that the Malayalam in these stage manuals is distinct. As Kalamandalam Shylaja told me, "*Attaprakarams* have a different language style. So when we write new *attaprakarams*, we have to follow that." Sindhu-chechi elaborated, "We don't use everyday Malayalam in the *attaprakaram* language. This Malayalam is a translation of the Sanskrit; it follows Sanskrit rules. That is why case endings are so important, otherwise we don't give them much importance in everyday Malayalam." Dr. Jayanthi clarified that while Malayalam has case endings like Sanskrit, many of them are dropped in contemporary usage.[44] However, these case endings remain strictly required in Sanskrit, a principle carried over to the Malayalam used in attaprakarams.

Embodied Integration

Intimately related to Kutiyattam artists' conceptions of Sanskrit, this section explores embodied cosmopolitanism through the lens of how artists experience performing in multiple languages onstage. By doing so, I consider artist responses to the questions: "How do you negotiate between languages in performance?" and "Do you ever feel a moment of switching languages onstage?" I asked these questions immediately after inquiring if artists consider Sanskrit an anyabhasha, so although I intended this question to encompass all languages in Kutiyattam performance, the majority of answers focused on artists' experiences of performing in Sanskrit.

Several responses focused on the embodiment of the practice over time. When students begin learning, they translate the Sanskrit into Malayalam, perceiving a strict distinction between the two languages, as Sindhu-chechi described of her learning experience. Once becoming a fully trained actor or actress, however, she told me, "We feel that Sanskrit and Malayalam are the same, there is no difference. In our mind, they're part of our everyday life." Sooraj clarified a practical distinction in performance, explaining that "when you are reciting and doing a mudra, it follows Sanskrit grammar. Otherwise, with mudras and no recitation, it follows Malayalam grammar." Despite this, he clarified that there is no conscious switching involved, explaining, "It's because of the practice." G. Venu also emphasized, "It's so deep that you don't feel a switch."

Similarly, several artists spoke in terms of images conjured in their minds in lieu of words, which further deemphasized transitions between languages. As Usha-teacher expressed, "Whichever language you're speaking, the content is the same, you don't need the words. We have the meaning inside, in our thoughts." Dr. Aparna Nangiar affirmed that she feels no such switching in performance, underscoring, "It's because we are thinking of the real meaning of the Sanskrit *shlokas* while reciting. If I'm reciting *himakara, himakara* means moon, so in my mind I see the image of a moon." Dr. Ammannur Rajaneesh Chakyar similarly explained, "While reciting we will see the image from that Sanskrit *shloka,* the content, and then we will explain the image by adding questions in Malayalam. How was that, how did that happen? Then we will elaborate the image. That is the process." Always tied to practice, senior artist Painkulam Narayana Chakyar, great-grandnephew of Painkulam Rama Chakyar and one of the early Kutiyattam students at Kerala Kalamandalam, also emphasized, "There's no feeling of switching languages. It's a fluid process, the languages come together if you've really studied Sanskrit. If not, if you don't know the meaning, it doesn't come. In practice if I chant *shlokas* while acting, students who don't know Sanskrit have to learn the mudras by heart, but when we do it, we know what we're acting. I don't think of the Malayalam word at all, actually, I think of the Sanskrit word and the Sanskrit meanings come automatically."

A few offered insights into how earlier artists related to Kutiyattam's languages, which differs from today. As Dr. Sreekanth V., great-grandson of Mani Madhava Chakyar, explained, "In olden times, they didn't feel any inherent difference between Sanskrit and Malayalam. For example, Manipravalam *shlokas.* These are half Malayalam and half Sanskrit, so the switchover to complete Sanskrit or complete Malayalam wasn't much. And what is Malayalam? It's 90 percent Sanskrit words, so the inherent difference others feel, they didn't feel." Dr. Jayanthi clarified further: "Those studying Kutiyattam traditionally, they weren't told that they were learning Sanskrit, they didn't know. Since *shlokas* are written in the Malayalam script, they were reading them without knowing it's Sanskrit, they thought that they were reading and learning Malayalam. It was the scholars who came and told them that this is Sanskrit, this is Prakrit, and these are Bhasa's plays. They didn't need to know this when they were studying traditionally."

Dr. Jayanthi offered further valuable insight into language comprehension in hereditary practice, telling me, "Only if you show the mudras do you know the meaning of the *shlokas.*" As a Nangiar with extensive experience chanting shlokas from the side of a Kutiyattam stage in hereditary contexts, she admitted that she grew up learning all of the shlokas by heart without knowing their meaning, even the five hundred verses of *Anguliyankam*. She related this to past practice, describing the experience of her grandmother: "My grandmother didn't know how to read or write, but she could chant all the *Anguliyankam shlokas* and show you where they were in the palm leaf manuscript." She laughed, continuing, "She didn't know Sanskrit or how to read or write in Malayalam, but she knew all the *shlokas*. That is oral tradition. Some grandmothers were like that, some chanted with knowledge of the language, and some chanted without. There were many like that." Dr. Jayanthi mused that one likely reason for the grave consequences associated with mistakes during recitation in hereditary contexts—ranging from curses of illness to childlessness—was to prevent the introduction of mistakes to the oral texts over time.

Oral tradition being what it is, however, errors alongside other changes were inevitable. Indira, a Sanskrit teacher and hereditary performer, related a similar experience from childhood of shloka memorization and recitation without Sanskrit knowledge. Learning Sanskrit at college, she told me, was the first time she realized that some of the shlokas her family chanted contained errors, which she corrected for future performances. The experience of learning extensive Sanskrit verses for recitation onstage is a specifically gendered hereditary experience for Nangiar performers, who recited verses for all solo acting performances such as nirvahanam, Anguliyankamkoothu, Mattavilasamkoothu, and Nangiarkoothu. Over the course of several centuries, Nangiars were for unknown reasons increasingly erased from acting roles on Kutiyattam stages through a number of strategies, becoming, as Johan (2011a) terms, "voice only" recited from the side of the stage.[45] As the *Natyashastra* mandated the participation of women in theater, Madhavan (2010) sees this elimination as part of a larger historical trend of erasing women from the stage throughout the Indian subcontinent.

For women on the Kutiyattam stage, recitation and acting thus became largely divorced from one another over time, with recitation focused on faithfully reproducing large numbers of meticulously memorized Sanskrit verses onstage. This is not to say that there were no actresses on the Kutiyattam stage. The legends of extraordinary actresses discussed in chapter 4 indicate their sustained presence over time. This was nevertheless in a context of wider erasure that did not change until the late twentieth-century revival of women's roles that I describe in chapter 5; this erasure even largely continues on hereditary temple stages today (Johan 2014). As Dr. Jayanthi described, "When we learn orally, we don't reflect upon the meaning. When you memorize the *shlokas* for chanting, there is no need to make the connection to meaning." The realm of meaning thus became the purview of the primarily male actors acting through mudras onstage, as well as those with the privilege of Sanskrit learning, to which not all had access.

Sanskrit knowledge, for its part, facilitated the conscious modification of oral tradition. In a time when most women were denied Sanskrit learning, Guru Mani Madhava Chakyar insisted that all of his daughters study Sanskrit, beginning in the 1920s with his eldest daughter Thankamma Nangiaramma, who even qualified as a Sanskrit teacher. Dr. Jayanthi told a tale of one of the guru's younger daughters, her aunt Vasumathy Nangiaramma, who used her Sanskrit knowledge to make a creative change to the text. She was chanting a shloka that referred to the god of love, Kamadeva, by the name Chakyars use for him—Meenaketu, which conjures images of the god's fish emblem. Her aunt substituted this name for that commonly used by Nangiars—Pushpadhanwa, which refers to Kamadeva shooting flower-tipped arrows of love. "The images vary, but both are correct," Dr. Jayanthi explained. She similarly recalled an instance where she modified a shloka in performance. Smiling, she recounted:

> The only one who noticed was Father [P. K. Narayanan Nambiar].[46] He learned all of the dramas by heart, as well as the *shastras* (*śāstras*) and Ayurvedic texts. Long ago in the gurukula system, starting with 3 years old until 12, children had to memorize all shastras by heart, and then afterward connect them to theory. Learning everything by heart increases your memory capacity. If someone comes to me with a question, I consult the book then forget. Father doesn't forget, he learned everything by heart. Learning by heart is the first step, then analyzing is the second, and the third step is creation.

Conclusion

In this chapter, we have witnessed Kutiyattam's cosmopolitan origins as part of the wider circulation of Sanskrit drama across the Sanskrit cosmopolis of premodern South and Southeast Asia. We have likewise explored what I term the art's embodied cosmopolitanism via its fascinating multilingualism today. Without explicitly saying so, this chapter has also charted the changing relationship between language and power over time, specifically of Sanskrit in the wider world and the world of Kutiyattam. Once the exclusive domain of Brahminic religious practice, Sanskrit transformed into a more widely accessible, albeit still elite, literary language whose circulation defined an emergent

Sanskrit cosmopolis. Situating Kutiyattam within this cosmopolitan world, we saw the art originate with a ninth- or tenth-century CE Kerala king who sought to consciously affiliate with a wider Sanskrit dramatic world and the powerful imaginary that came with it. Yet the art emerged on the cusp of wider vernacularization across the subcontinent, evidenced by King Kulashekhara's vernacular modifications to the Sanskrit theater in Kerala. The local-yet-cosmopolitan birth of Kutiyattam thus signified an acknowledgment of the power and value of both Sanskrit, the cosmopolitan language, and Malayalam, the vernacular.

Despite the rise of the vernacular, Sanskrit retained its position of power among Kerala's caste elite over time, with the perseverance of Kutiyattam as part of upper-caste temple culture evidence of this. We witnessed the particularly striking example of the fifteenth-century *Natankusa* author demanding that Kutiyattam adhere more strictly to the *Natyashastra* by purging itself of its vernacular innovations. Sanskrit's dominance in Kerala's elite arts and literature persisted, wavering only in the mid-twentieth century with the rise to power of the Communist Party, further described in chapter 5. As we will see in chapter 6, the situation on the national stage was exactly the opposite, with Sanskrit gaining greater power and influence in the context of both colonialism and Indian nationalism.

Within the world of Kutiyattam, the power of Sanskrit persisted, not only as the key to knowledge and meaning onstage but also as an avenue of innovation. Centuries of oral and mimetic tradition connected Sanskrit dramatic verses with their meaning through mudra hand gestures. As actresses were erased from the Kutiyattam stage over time, they were deprived of the connection to textual meaning that mudra enactment provided them. As many Nangiars were not given access to Sanskrit learning, their relationship with the language became restricted to the memorization of words for the sole purpose of recitation. They likely understood several words since Malayalam and Sanskrit share many words in common, but they would not have grasped the verses' full meaning. As Dr. Jayanthi outlined, "Learning by heart is the first step, then analyzing is the second, and the third step is creation." With no access to either acting or Sanskrit knowledge, many Nangiars were deprived of the opportunity to analyze and thereby to innovate. Through their dominance onstage, therefore, Chakyar male actors hegemonized both meaning and innovation on the Kutiyattam stage for centuries. Today, Kutiyattam is firmly embedded in the public sphere and institutional training, with all students regardless of gender or caste being required to learn Sanskrit. Actresses are likewise a prominent force onstage today. As we shall see in chapter 5, the reintroduction of women's roles onstage at Kerala Kalamandalam alongside institutionalized training that includes mandatory Sanskrit lessons has led women in Kutiyattam today to dominate the domain of innovation.[47] As drummer Kalamandalam Sajith recently told me, "Nowadays, actually the ladies are doing most of the work in everything, most of the programs and new stories."

Notes

1. This is a shortened version of an invocation Usha-teacher teaches her students that combines the prayer used while donning the Kutiyattam costume; the verse is used when beginning new studies.

2. For more on *marga* and *desi*, see Ramanujan 1989.

3. For more on the vernacular concept in South Asia, see Harder, Zaidi, and Tschacher 2023.

4. Anthropological literature counters this claim, emphasizing that cultures worldwide actively mediate, negotiate, and indigenize the "homogenizing" forces of globalization (Inda and Rosaldo 2002).

5. See Vatsyayan 2001 for more on the *Natyashastra*, including debates surrounding its authorship (6–7) and age (24).

6. For more on the absence of a critical edition, see Sullivan 2007; Vatsyayan 2001. Kerala collections hold 30 percent of all manuscripts, many in Malayalam script (Vatsyayan 2001).

7. Clifford Jones once told me that the Madras *Natyashastra* manuscript was accidentally dropped midcentury, losing the original palm leaf order. For an example of variation, see footnote 73.

8. See Raghavan 1993a and Madhavan 2010 for detailed summaries of Sanskrit drama in performance.

9. Byrski (2015, 63) translates *abhinaya* not as acting but as "a lead," derivative of the verb meaning "to lead towards." He depicts the director as a leader who through rasa "leads spectators from mundane emotional entanglement into the virtual sphere (*sadharana*) of tasting pure emotions untainted by everyday mundane concerns" (2015, 70).

10. As Byrski (2015, 65) translates, the god Indra told Brahma that "since the members of shudra castes cannot listen to the recitation of the Vedas, he may create the fifth Veda, which will be accessible to all varnas [i.e., to all humanity]." See also Vatsyayan 2001, 21.

11. As Gopalakrishnan (1993, 92) notes, poets dramatized ancient legends and epics, adapting them to their own "imaginative interpretation."

12. For a deeper analysis of these categories, see Raghavan 1993a.

13. See Pollock 2016 for a survey of the concept of rasa from the time of the *Natyashastra* through 1700.

14. This offers a good example of the multiple existence and variation of the *Natyashastra*. Raghavan cites his translation from the 1934 Gaekwad Oriental

Series Sanskrit edition as chapter 32, verse 425. In the Ghosh English edition, the equivalent verse is chapter 32, verse 86 with the variant "Just as a well-built dwelling house does not become beautiful without any colour, so without any song the drama does not attain [the capacity of giving] joy."

15. See Ollett 2017, 123–128 for deeper discussion.

16. While Raja and others make this claim, Moser (2008) concludes that innovations attributed to Kulashekhara are based solely on oral tradition. Moser (2011) suggests eleventh- or twelfth-century Kutiyattam origins independent of Kulashekhara. Paulose (2013) claims that Kutiyattam emerged centuries after Kulashekhara's modifications to Sanskrit theater.

17. Dating King Kulashekhara is problematic (see Devadevan 2019, 277–284; Paulose 2013, 52–53; Unni and Sullivan 2001, 49–52). I find Devadevan's (2019) ninth-century CE argument the most compelling, wherein he cites a tenth-century record of a *Tapati-samvaranam* performance. I maintain Kutiyattam's origins with Kulashekhara, the consensus among artists and many scholars, declining Devadevan's outlier sixteenth-century claim.

18. Shulman (2022a, 17) claims that only two Kutiyattam plays originate outside of Kerala.

19. See Paulose 2000 for more on *Bhagavadajukkam*, Unni 1998 on *Mattavilasa*, and Unni 1990 on *Nagananda*.

20. See Nair 1994c for how Kutiyattam's preliminaries compare to the *Natyashastra*.

21. See also Gopalakrishnan 1988; Madhavan 2010, 2015.

22. See Nair 1994b, 55–56 for details on this verse enactment.

23. Paulose (2013, 492–493) asserts a lack of historical evidence to support Tolan's existence.

24. The original name for the text was *Dhanañjayasaṁvaraṅadhvani*. See Paulose 2013 and Devadevan 2019 for deeper discussion.

25. A well-known deviation not attributed to Kulashekhara is the enactment of dying onstage, see Sullivan 2007. The performance of *sringara* (love/happiness) rasa in Kutiyattam is also more nuanced than in the *Natyashastra*, with variations according to different types of love—the love of a mother for her child, a woman toward a man, a man toward a woman, and devotion to God (see Madhavan 2010, 109–110).

26. See Madhavan 2010; Moser 2013b; Venu 2009 for more on *pakarnnattam*.

27. This is not the scholarly consensus. Some date the art's temple entry to the thirteenth or fourteenth century; see Narayanan 2006.

28. Paulose (2003) argues that innovations 6 and 7 listed above were made after Kulashekhara.

29. Daugherty (2011) observes, however, that even in multicharacter kutiyattam, the focus remains on the individual performer, with other characters often exiting the stage and only reentering right before their next line.

30. As Moser (2008) demonstrates, Nangiarkoothu is the nirvahanam of Kalpalathika, the heroine's maid in Kulashekharavarman's *Subhadradhananjayam*.

31. See Daugherty 2011 on the revival of *purappad* and nirvahanams of female characters.

32. Actor Margi Madhu similarly details *dhvani* in the vidushaka's verbal performance, noting, "There is also the matter of encoded language, where he says something and shows the gestures of other, hidden meanings." Devadevan (2019, 274) observes that these changes transformed the actor into an instructor explaining the meaning of verses, writing that the *Vyangyavyakhya* "hijacks the performance of Sanskrit drama from the realm of emotions . . . and lands it in a reflective universe that is obscure, intimidating, and intellectually demanding."

33. See Paulose 1993, 2003.

34. Ammannur Chachu Chakyar Smaraka Gurukulam.

35. Ollett (2017, 128) terms Sanskrit and Prakrit "transregional" languages.

36. Mattavilasamkoothu performs Mahendravarman's Sanskrit farce, *Mattavilasaprahasana* (*The Delight of the Drunkards*).

37. While Kutiyattam artists today categorize Manipravalam as a language, Goren Arzony (2019) points to early evidence that it was conceptualized differently, as a context-dependent "performative science."

38. See Goren Arzony 2019 and Veluthat 2013.

39. As Appukuttan Nair (1994a, 32) notes, Mani Madhava Chakyar suggested that Nambiar Tamil should be translated into Malayalam as a "scene-by-scene account," a technique sometimes used more broadly to explain onstage actions to the audience today.

40. Madhavan (2010, 99) notes that the seven different hand positions of the *pataka* mudra denote all seven clitics (word prefixes and suffixes) of Malayalam grammar—nominative, accusative, ablative, dative, instrumental, possessive, and locative.

41. Mohiniyattam and Kathakali mudras also draw on this text. See Venu 2013 for detailed documentation of Kutiyattam mudras.

42. Rajagopalan (1997, 42) refers to this as slang of "lower born people," while Salini (2021, 456) identifies it as "a crude unrefined mixture of Tamil and Malayalam," indicating that Shurpanakha belongs to the lowest social strata.

43. In contrast, in several of G. Venu's Nangiarkoothu choreographies like *Narasiṃhāvatāram* (*The Man-Lion Avatar*), the actress recites her own lines onstage.

44. The example she gave was "I ate an idli." The technically correct "*Ñān iḍḍaliye tinnu*" today gets the case ending dropped, becoming "*Ñān iḍḍali tinnu*."

45. For more on this erasure, see Lowthorp 2016; Paulose 2006.

46. Nambiar drummers were also renowned for their Sanskrit knowledge, showcased in their Pathakam performances, with many being Sanskrit teachers themselves.

47. Significant exceptions to this trend are Padmasree P. K. Narayanan Nambiar, G. Venu, Margi Madhu, and Dr. Ammannur Rajaneesh Chakyar.

4

KINGS, SULTANS, AND COLONIALISTS

Legendary Circulation and Encounters with the Other

Figure 24. Guru P. K. Narayanan Nambiar as *vidushaka* in *Mantrankam* with (*left to right*) Unnikrishnan Nambiar, Hareesh Nambiar, and Vinod Sathanam. Photo by author.

In my nearly two years in Kerala, Trivandrum has been my home base. The small capital city, which sometimes seems more like a large village, is where I spend most of my time when I am not traveling around Kerala or India for research. Many of my days are spent at Margi. After classes or rehearsals, I often spend the afternoons with Usha-teacher in a small side room whose windows let in sounds of temple bells, birdsong from nearby palm trees, and rays of the late-afternoon sun that bathe the room in a soft, golden glow. The room's walls are a light shade of violet, reminding me of the sarong-type wraps called *mundus* that many older men wear, which start out white but develop a slight violet hue over time from a commonly used washing product. The walls are decorated with photos of Margi's Kutiyattam artists alongside colorful pictures of various deities—Saraswathi, the goddess of learning; Ganesha, the remover of obstacles and guarantor of success; and Shiva of the blue skin and dreadlocked hair, the god of destruction who, alongside Vishnu with his many incarnations like Rama the righteous god-king, is one of the two main deities of temples in which Kutiyattam is traditionally performed.

Evidence of the room's daily use lies scattered along its periphery—plastic bags filled with items for performance, piles of books and newspapers, mizhavu copper drums, leather drum heads, small wooden practice drums, phone chargers hanging out of electrical sockets, stacked plastic armchairs, rolled-up straw mats, and a large wooden cot along one wall used for afternoon naps. Although the room serves as a common area for Margi's Kutiyattam center, Usha-teacher usually has it to herself after the artists leave for the day. She often stays until nine or ten at night, studying and teaching private classes while waiting for her husband to finish work and drive her the twenty kilometers home on their scooter. The adjacent room belongs to Unni-ashan, who lives there full time, as his home is an eight-hour train ride away in Thrissur. With his ever-ready chuckle, he often joins us for lunch and afternoon chai and is always a small shout away.

Now that my *arangettam* (stage debut) is over and I have switched to full-time research, Usha-teacher's role as my performance guru has shifted to that of research adviser and friend. Her thoughtful suggestions and guidance during our frequent conversations have been invaluable, and I am grateful for her generous insight. Today we discuss my research interview questions, which my Malayalam teacher helped translate from English. I planned to ask artists to share legends they knew about Kutiyattam performers from the past, which, from my folkloristics training, I define as historical narratives believed to be true. I did not know how to translate the word *legend* into Malayalam, so I explained to my language teacher that I wanted to ask artists to relate old stories about the art. After hearing my explanation, she suggested using the term *pazham katha* (*paḷaṃ katha*), meaning "old story." I used this word during an interview with Sajeev-ashan, asking him to tell me any *pazham kathakal* (plural) he knew about Kutiyattam performers of yore. He furrowed his brow, saying, "But *pazham kathakal* are not true. What one hears about in a *pazham katha* did not actually happen. You mean *aithihyangal* (legends: plural), which are true." Rather than simply an "old story," therefore, the *pazham katha* genre refers to fictional tales of yore.

I mention this to Usha-teacher, and she nods and explains the difference: "We tell *pazham kathakal* to children to teach them a lesson. *Aithihyangal* are about individuals from the past."[1] She pauses and then reflects: "It's like when I tell my students about how you came to study and perform. We know that this happened. Once it gets to a point where we can't be completely sure that it happened, then it becomes an *aithihyam* (*aitihyam*, legend: singular)."

~

This chapter explores legendary tales (*aithihyangal*) of Kutiyattam performers of yore, continuing the narrative of Kutiyattam's historical cosmopolitanism. As the young hereditary actor Dr. Ammannur Rajaneesh Chakyar told me, the word *aithihyam* literally means "that which exists here": *iha* ("here") + *sthiyathi* ("existing here"). Implying something that has been experienced visually, he revealed the term more correctly translates to "that which has been seen" or witnessed. Generally believed to be true, the aithihyam occurs beyond the reach of living memory yet is firmly rooted in historical time, closely resembling the genre that folklorists call legend and generally translated in Kerala as such. As Usha-teacher explained, these narratives are about individuals from the past, which most closely correlate with the subgenre folklorists refer to as the "personal legend." According to Ray Cashman (2008, 108), the personal legend is a "type of historical legend that focuses on the actions and traits of an actual person or persons from a previous historical period." Closely related to the anecdote, which memorializes individuals within living memory, the personal legend memorializes individuals who lived during lifetimes before that of the teller. The genre tends to focus on content over poetics, and generally emerges in conversational moments "when the past becomes relevant to people's thoughts about the present" (2008, 109).[2] Although there are slippages between the categories of aithihyam and personal legend, I use the terms interchangeably because they seem to have the same basic elements.

For Kutiyattam artists, these types of legends have a personal element as tales of their ancestors. For nonhereditary performers, these tales involve characters with a shared artistic inheritance, and for hereditary performers, a shared artistic and familial inheritance. The tales offer both groups continuity with the past and a claim to group membership in the present. Each telling and retelling brings the past alive in the present moment of narration, allowing contemporary tellers and listeners the imaginative space to observe, reflect on, and identify with those who have gone before. In narrating these personal legends, artists actively "imagine and enact community, forging individual and collective identities" (Cashman 2008, 148).

Here I consider three personal legends of Kutiyattam artists involving kings, sultans, and colonialists that reveal the art's sixteenth- to nineteenth-century encounters with cultural Others, as well as the circulation of artists across borders in the centuries before Kerala statehood.[3] For each legend, I include the ethnographic context of its narration, an interpretation by its teller, my own analysis, and the wider historical context. Coined by my mentor Alan Dundes (1966) as "oral literary criticism," the interpretation of folklore by those who circulate it is one of the most important elements of contemporary folklore fieldwork. According to this model, it is essential to ask tellers and listeners the meaning of their narratives in order to understand how they function as part of social life.[4] With this approach, the folklorist remains free to make their own interpretations but must do so with an explicit recognition of the narrative or practice's emic, or insider, meaning.[5] My exploration into the meanings these personal legends hold for the artists who tell them offers insight into the myriad ways Kutiyattam community members imagine and make meaning out of the past today, as well as how narrative connections with the past reveal present claims to community membership.

In situating each legend historically, I approach these narratives as a lens onto the cosmopolitan history and historical consciousness of Kerala, as well as a source of insight into how Kutiyattam artists place themselves within that history. As Cashman (2008, 117) reveals, legends generally claim historical truth value regardless of whether tellers or audiences actually believe them. In so doing, they participate in a form of historical discourse that evaluates the status quo by comparing the past and present. The historical claims of legends, however, tend to be dismissed by scholars of both folklore and history. Here, I take the historical elements of Kutiyattam personal legends seriously, drawing on recent South Asian historiography that considers written folk narratives to be an important form of inquiry into Indian regional history.[6] Since early colonial times, Western historiography has notoriously claimed that India has no sense of historical consciousness or native history. Historian Kesavan Veluthat (2009, 130) describes this as "not just a matter of Eurocentrism, [but] . . . part of the baggage of colonialism." He situates the move toward seeking expressions of historical consciousness that fall outside of Eurocentric conceptions of history within a postcolonial historiography that challenges the Western tradition as "*the* standard" (2009, 130).

This approach rejects a universalized, Eurocentric concept of history, arguing instead that history is always time and place specific. According to Rao, Shulman, and Subrahmanyam (2001, 5), "Each community writes history in the mode that is dominant in its own literary practice." These authors demonstrate how history in South India was written in several different genres, including folk-epic and courtly poetry, that were not recognized as history according to Eurocentric frames of judgment. The *Kēraḷōlpatti* is a set of Brahminical texts that chronicle Kerala's earliest history through a mixture of myth and legend.

In approaching the *Kēraḻōlpatti* as history, Veluthat (2009, 141) argues that "Kerala too had a sense of history, which it expressed in forms that were found most suitable for its needs." While South Asian historians have generally examined written folk narratives within this framework, I apply the framework to folk narratives that are still orally circulated. The personal legends I discuss in this chapter evidence a history from below, in the sense that they provide a nonruling perspective of Kerala history. Unlike the *Keralolpatti*, which functioned to justify the power and position of both Brahmins and ruling dynasties, these legends reveal a perspective from just below—that of an elite group of artists with close ties to these ruling groups but not rulers themselves.

Legend 1: Performing in the Time of Tipu Sultan

Figure 25. Guru P. K. Narayanan Nambiar and granddaughter Sweda as spectators. Photo by author.

I always feel a sense of joyful anticipation when I am on my way to visit drumming guru Padmasree P. K. Narayanan Nambiar and his family. Born in 1927, Nambiar-ashan is Kutiyattam's senior-most drummer and is responsible for the innovations at Kerala Kalamandalam, as detailed in the next chapter, that made Kutiyattam drumming what it is today.[7] He inherited his mizhavu drumming occupation matrilineally from the family of his mother, a Nangiar actress, but he is also the son of one of the most celebrated Kutiyattam actors of the twentieth century, Padmasree Mani Madhava Chakyar. From a young age, Nambiar-ashan regularly traveled with his father and other family members for up to nine months a year, performing at temples near and far, sometimes in the audience of kings. Taking a train where they could, most of their travel was on foot. They often walked for days at a time and, due to the rigid caste restrictions in those days, were unable to eat anything along the way until they had arrived at their destination and bathed, usually after nightfall. They passed time during their journey reciting Sanskrit verses, discussing performances, or listening to their father tell stories. Nambiar-ashan's mother used to travel with them, but when she started having more children, his older sister Thankamma accompanied them instead. After she married and had children, his next-oldest sister stepped in. By the time Nambiar-ashan performed with his father in 1962 in the first-ever performance of Kutiyattam outside of Kerala, his youngest sister Amminikutty was playing the female roles onstage when needed.[8] Known affectionately by the family as Mema—meaning "father's younger sister"—she lived a few doors down in the family's *tharawad*, or matrilineal home. With her sunny disposition and ever-ready smile, I grew particularly fond of Mema and made a point to visit her whenever I visited Nambiar-ashan.

Today I hop off the bus and turn onto a narrow dirt road, dotted on either side by houses partially obscured by verdant foliage, some of which belong to Nambiar-ashan's relatives. I have never followed the short road to its end, but I know that it leads to the temple where Nambiar-ashan's children had their *arangettams* and where Mema reads the *Ramayana* for temple audiences every year during the Malayalam month of Karkidakam, marking the end of the monsoon season when Hindu families around the state read the beloved epic daily. After a short walk, I find myself in front of the steps to Nambiar-ashan's house, which sits atop a small hill. It is a large structure in a midcentury style that melds modern construction materials with elements of traditional Kerala architecture. The upper floor has one wall of evenly spaced, overlapping vertical and horizontal wooden slats that curve generously outward in an S shape, welcoming the wind indoors during the hot months of winter and spring and the cool months of the monsoon summer.

Usha-teacher first brought me here to visit Nambiar-ashan, one of her gurus. She became friends with his daughter Vasanthi when they studied Kutiyattam together as young girls at Kalamandalam, where Nambiar-ashan taught for decades. Upon our first visit, Usha-teacher and I were warmly welcomed. We visited and ate dinner with the family, at the time consisting of Nambiar-ashan, his wife Sarada Nangiaramma, and their children Hareesh, Dr. Jayanthi, Unnikrishnan, Unnikrishnan's wife and daughter, and Vasanthi and her two children (her husband was working in the Middle East at the time). Usha-teacher and I spent the night in Vasanthi-chechi's room, awakened the next day in the chill early morning by the sounds of mizhavu percussion students practicing before breakfast. I stayed with Nambiar-ashan's family on later visits and was welcomed into their home just as they had welcomed the first foreigner to study Kutiyattam there fifty years earlier.[9]

This morning, I am here to interview Nambiar-ashan and, despite the many hours I spend interviewing him throughout my time in Kerala, I am hardly able to scratch the surface of his vast knowledge of Kutiyattam. I present him with a small offering (*dakṣiṇa*), a bag with fruit and his favorite biscuits, and prostrate before him in a namaskar, touching my forehead to the ground in front of his feet until I feel his soft touch on the crown of my head signaling me to rise. The blessing finished, he greets me with a slow smile accompanied by a characteristic twinkle in his eye. Others with his seniority might seem intimidating, but Nambiar-ashan is open and welcoming, known for generously sharing his knowledge with anyone who comes in search of it. I ask him to tell me *aithihyangal* of Chakyars, Nambiars, and Nangiars of yore, and he begins to regale me with tales of his ancestors. Among these, he talks of performing in the time of Tipu Sultan, a Muslim ruler from the neighboring Kingdom of Mysore who invaded Kerala in the late eighteenth century. Looking at me solemnly, he narrates:

> Tipu Sultan attacked this area. Many of the temples here were destroyed. He had a fort nearby in Palakkad where he lived. This was long ago, before the time of British rule.
>
> In those days, out of fear of Tipu Sultan, people were afraid to make any sound in the temple. Even then, Koothu didn't stop—three people went to perform together, hiding during the day and playing the mizhavu quietly at night. My *ammāvan* [maternal uncle] used to tell me they kept the lamplight dim, donned their costume, and performed Mantrankam-koothu for 41 days without interruption. They drummed quietly in case someone might hear and come to lock the temple. They drummed quietly,

chanted the shlokas softly, and lit only a small wick in the lamp. In this way, they stayed in the forest and performed Koothu at night when no one was around.

My *ammavan* used to tell me that just like they didn't let the art stop then, I too needed to ensure it continued without interruption.

Meaning and Analysis

At the end of his narrative, Nambiar-ashan emphasizes the meaning of this personal legend.[10] His maternal uncle, an important figure in Kutiyattam's matrilineal family system, shared this story as a lesson to show that their family had risked everything to continue performing and to teach him that he must also be prepared to do so. His ancestors had risked their lives to perform, yet took precautions according to the circumstances—performing in the dead of night instead of during the day, dimming the lamp, softly playing percussion, and nearly whispering their chanted lines. Nambiar-ashan's childhood training with his uncle in the 1930s—which took place across the road from Mema's current home—happened during a period marked by intense social, economic, and political upheavals in Kerala. It was a time, much like the time of Tipu Sultan, when the future of the art seemed uncertain. Through this tale, Nambiar-ashan's uncle emphasized that if their family was willing to risk their lives to perform in the time of Tipu Sultan, Nambiar-ashan must do everything in his power to continue performing as well.

I discussed the legend with Nambiar-ashan's daughter, the Sanskrit professor Dr. C. K. Jayanthi, who told me that they must have put water on the head of the drum, as was common in Tipu Sultan's time. She explained that this was done regularly to dampen the sound: "If the leather drum head is dry it has a very loud sound, but if the leather is wet, the sound lessens." When I asked for her interpretation of the legend, she responded, "Its meaning is that society will change economically and politically, but art never changes." I inquired if this meant that art resists economic and political change, and she paused, explaining that to an artist the legend means that "I must do my duty in all circumstances, even if there's no one to watch." With this interpretation, just like her great-uncle, she connects the meaning of this eighteenth-century legend to her present, a time when artists often perform to empty temple halls.

These interpretations reveal a strong sense of duty among hereditary artists to perform Kutiyattam, whether it means risking one's life as described in the legend or risking one's pride performing to an empty hall.[11] Change, in the sense used by Dr. Jayanthi, pertains to the context but not the content of performance. She does not mean that art never changes its form—she had expressed on other occasions that she considers change over time to be a fundamental characteristic of art. Rather, she means that art must not stop even in the face of great obstacles—the show must go on no matter the risk. This strong sense of duty to perform still pervades hereditary Kutiyattam families today and is bolstered by tales of great personal sacrifices made by ancestors to ensure these duties were fulfilled.

On another occasion, Dr. Jayanthi solemnly narrated the story of her great-grandmother, an actress who continued to perform the dangerous hanging scene of the play *Nāgānanda*, knowing it would cause her physical harm.[12] Despite being pregnant, she continued performing the scene, which required falling violently from a great height to the ground with a rope twisted around her neck. As a result, she miscarried seven times. "Such was her devotion to her art to perform her duty for the community," Dr. Jayanthi told me, quietly but firmly, with an intensity burning in her eyes. These personal legends are emotionally significant and reveal a deep emotional investment in the art as a fundamental part of Kutiyattam family identity, whose members are invested in ensuring its continuation at all costs.

Dr. Jayanthi has a special way of explaining concepts through rich metaphor and evoking vibrant, and at times poetic, imagery that clearly communicates her ideas. The language she used to describe this sense of duty to perform Kutiyattam was simple and straightforward. Comparing it with the duty of farmers to farm, she explained, "If they don't do their duty to farm, everyone in society will suffer as all will be at the mercy of the higher prices of imported food. Like that a lot of traditions suffered and disappeared." This comparison, along with the example of her great-grandmother, introduces a social element to the familial or caste duty that she describes. It is a sense of duty to perform roles that affect not only the individuals or families concerned but society as well. This imagery emphasizes Kutiyattam's social role of contributing to the annual temple cycle and thereby ensuring the temple deity's blessing for the community at large. Dr. Jayanthi also told me about specific aspects of the art's social role, namely, that performances used to involve members of the larger community, even those not allowed onto the high-caste temple premises. At a time when one's occupation strictly aligned with caste, performances required not only actors, actresses, and drummers but also garland makers to make garlands for costumes, lower-caste washermen to bring fresh linens, and so on. Whereas many members of the wider community were previously involved in a temple performance, she stressed, it is mainly Kutiyattam community members who participate today, indicating how disconnected the art has become from its earlier social context, even in temple performances.

The sense of duty to perform Kutiyattam persists strongly in Nambiar-ashan's family today, with many family members still involved with the art. Nambiar-ashan's four children, three grandchildren, and two grandnephews, among others, have all studied and regularly perform at the gurukulam Nambiar-ashan founded in his father's memory. Among the extended family, most have performed their *arangettam*. Even those who do not actively perform still seem to value the art, its associated Sanskrit knowledge, and the legacy of their illustrious ancestor Guru Mani Madhava Chakyar. Local extended family members regularly attend performances, festivals, and talks organized by the gurukulam. According to conversations with a range of hereditary artists, Kutiyattam performers from other families regularly encounter dismissive attitudes from extended family members who no longer consider Kutiyattam a worthwhile endeavor. The wider valuing of the art by Guru Mani's extended family is thus relatively rare. One difference from other hereditary families that garners criticism is that most members of Guru Mani's family have pursued outside occupations to support themselves while continuing their hereditary legacy. Many have become teachers—Nambiar-ashan taught for decades at Kerala Kalamandalam, most of his siblings became Sanskrit and Hindi schoolteachers, and two of his children entered the teaching profession. Among Nambiar-ashan's siblings, his youngest brother P. K. Raghavan Nambiar is the only one who left the art for a longer period when he followed his father's order to join the army. I saw him publicly share this story with regret, explaining that he left only out of obedience to his father; the decades of separation had obviously been painful for him. Upon his retirement, he returned to the neighborhood, the family, and the art, and his wife Kalakkath Sathyavathy Nangiaramma now regularly performs her own matrilineal temple duty of Nangiarkoothu nearby.

Historical Context

What Nambiar-ashan calls "this area" is the Malabar region in northern Kerala, where his matrilineal family has lived for generations and which was ruled by the Zamorin of Calicut (Kozhikode) from roughly the twelfth to eighteenth centuries CE. Following the invasion by Haider Ali of Mysore in 1766, his son Tipu Sultan invaded Malabar in 1783. Led by Muslim rulers from a neighboring land, these incursions represented a cosmopolitan encounter of a particular kind—invasions by a foreign power at a time when India was composed of hundreds of varied kingdoms and principalities, each with distinct cultures. Tipu Sultan is known to have wrought such violence and destruction in Calicut that the Zamorin was forced to send his family south for safety. Dispossessed of his kingdom, the Zamorin set his palace on fire and perished in the flames, an event widely acknowledged as the end of the Zamorin's centuries-long rule as the most powerful king in Kerala (Menon 2019).[13] In this section, I explore the historical context before Tipu Sultan's invasion as well as its subsequent consequences. In the process, I demonstrate how Kerala was a cosmopolitan nexus of world trade in the period considered here, roughly the fourteenth through early nineteenth centuries CE. I focus in particular on the rise and fall of the Zamorin, often called the "lord of the sea," who was an important patron of Kutiyattam.[14]

The Zamorin ruled much of the area known today as the Malabar district of northern Kerala state. According to various versions of the *Keralolpatti*, he represented one of four ruling lineages to whom the last high king of Kerala, Ceraman Perumal, entrusted his kingdom after converting to Islam and leaving for Mecca.[15] According to the version of the Keralolpatti that depicts the history of the Zamorin's family, Perumal was originally a local chief of the landlocked Eranad (originally Eralanad) who forgot to give land to the Eranad brothers while dividing his kingdom. Upon realizing his mistake, Perumal gave them a small tract of land on the sea (Calicut) and granted them several rights: the right to rule as the matrilineal house/lineage of Netiyirippu, the right along with Muslims to navigate the seas, and the right "to die, kill and annex" with the sword he bestowed on them (Haridas 2016, 28).[16] This legendary right, purportedly given by the last high king of Kerala, was used by the Zamorin's family to justify conquering and annexing the lands of neighboring lords.[17] The Zamorin eventually expanded his kingdom across much of Kerala, at one point covering most of north Kerala and stretching eastward to Palakkad and southward to Kollam (Quilon), with all of the resident chiefs and even the king of Cochin as his vassals (Menon 2019).

The Zamorin's increasing power was fueled by the rise of Calicut as one of the most influential ports in medieval India, which Prange (2018, 159) describes as "the principle hub of trade not only on the [Malabar] Coast but across the entire western Indian Ocean." The port of Calicut was dominated by Chinese, Arab, and local Muslim (*Māppiḷa*) traders and came to eclipse the port of Kollam in the South, which was dominated at the time by local Christian and Jewish traders. Ibn Battuta, a fourteenth-century Moroccan traveler, wrote that he had seen no port equal to Alexandria in Egypt except Kollam and Calicut in India and Zaytun in China (Gibb and Beckingham 2000, 46). He described Calicut as "one of the chief ports in Mulaybar (Malabar) and one of the largest harbours in the world . . . visited by men from China, Sumatra (Indonesia), Ceylon (Sri Lanka), the Maldives, Yemen and Fars (in Iran) and in it gather merchants from all quarters" (quoted in Prange 2018, 234). Ibn Battuta attributed Calicut's popularity to the fact that the Zamorin did not confiscate goods from ships that strayed into port, as was customary in other places. Merchant trust was fundamental to Indian Ocean trade at the time, and Prange (2018) argues that the Zamorin's protection of original ownership of goods was the crucial element that contributed to the rise of Calicut in this period, as it caused merchants across the Indian Ocean to trust that their goods would be safe there. Over one hundred years later, Muslim traders still considered Calicut a safe haven, and late sixteenth-century Muslim chronicler Zain-ud-Din Ma'bari described how the Zamorin favored Muslims "above all foreigners" (Alam and Subrahmanyam 2007, 57).[18]

The Arab dominance of the spice trade, especially with Europe's increasing dependence on pepper, prompted Europeans to seek their own route to India. In fact, Christopher Columbus's famous voyage of 1492 was not intended to seek an alternate route to India but to find "the land of pepper," meaning Kerala (Prange 2018, 212). Equal motivation for these voyages of discovery was the search for the legendary Christian king of the East, Prester John, who had supposedly promised to support the Crusades with his vast riches.[19] Vasco da Gama's "discovery" of India upon his arrival in Calicut in 1498 opened the door to centuries of European imperialism in the region. Whereas commerce with earlier traders had been on equal terms, Europeans demanded trade monopolies, enforced through violence. Throughout the sixteenth century, as Prange (2018, 159) observes, Calicut became "a focal point of resistance against Portugal's imperial project in the western Indian Ocean." In his attempts over the next few centuries to rid his kingdom of the Portuguese, who were allied with the neighboring king of Cochin, the Zamorin formed alliances at various times with the Egyptians, Ottomans, Dutch, and British and eventually waged war against the French and his former allies the Dutch as well (Menon 2019). According to Duarte Barbosa (1812), an early-sixteenth-century Portuguese traveler who lived in Kerala for over a decade as a Malayalam interpreter, the Portuguese believed that, without their intervention, the Zamorin would have extended his rule to the whole of Kerala.[20]

With the Zamorin's coffers and forces depleted from endless wars, the 1766 invasion of Calicut by Hyder Ali was the last straw, marking the end of his effective rule and the beginning of nearly thirty years of intermittent Mysorean rule (Menon 2019). Hyder Ali's invasions disrupted the social, political, and economic fabric of Malabar and caused many people to leave their homes and flee southward to other kingdoms.[21] When Ali's son Tipu Sultan came to power and marched into Malabar in 1783, he widely destroyed Christian churches and Hindu temples, plundering them to finance his wars and disregarding the local rules of warfare that recognized temples as sanctuaries for cornered soldiers. The fear apparent in Nambiar-ashan's narrative of continuing temple performance makes perfect sense in light of what was happening at the time, as this would have involved great danger.

Continuing his campaign southward, Tipu Sultan attacked the Kingdom of Cochin and tried to march on the Kingdom of Travancore, but British forces intervened to defeat him on behalf of their ally, the king of Travancore.[22] The terms of Tipu Sultan's surrender in the Treaty of Seringapatam gave the English East India Company complete control of Malabar in 1792, downgrading the next Zamorin to a landlord receiving a pension that could be taken away if he ever acted against their interests.[23] After this momentous event, the Zamorin ruled in name only (Haridas 2016). The incursions of the Mysoreans into Kerala thus led to the direct rule of the British in Malabar, and the extensive road system that Tipu Sultan constructed to help his troops move through the heavily forested territory later aided British domination (Menon 2019). As the next section details, the king of Travancore noticed the consequences of the Zamorin's unsuccessful wars against European powers and decided to ally his kingdom with the British, advising his successors to do so as well.[24] The next legend I discuss describes a nineteenth-century encounter between a Kutiyattam actor and the British Resident of Travancore.

What was Kutiyattam's role in relation to the cosmopolitan world of the Zamorin? The Zamorin patronized Kutiyattam for generations, at least until the mid-twentieth century. Jayachandran Vellodi, born in 1941 into one of the branches of the Zamorin's family, told me of his childhood memories of Nambiarashan's father, Mani Madhava Chakyar, performing at the temple of his palace home in Kottakkal. Like his contemporaries, the Zamorin used the temples and associated elite culture as a way to legitimize his power, styling himself as the protector of Brahmins and cows and aspiring to become the overlord of all Kerala through his takeover and sponsorship of the famed Māmāṅkam festival. An event of great economic, social, and political importance, Mamankam attracted attendees and traders from across greater India and the world (Haridas 2016).[25] As Haridas (2016, 169–170) describes, palace records from the time show that Kutiyattam was part of the entertainment at Mamankam and other temple festivals. One eighteenth-century record describes the Zamorin using Kutiyattam to tie his rule directly to the god-king Rama. Indicating that it was perhaps a regular occurrence, the palace records describe the fifteen-month performance of Sri Ramayanakoothu at Ponnani Vairanellur palace from October 13, 1728, to January 12, 1730. This was a rare performance of the entire *Ramayana* at once, and the records provide a detailed description of the last day of performance, where Rama is crowned king (*valiya abhiṣekam*).

I summarize Haridas's (2016) translation of this passage: immediately after the fifteen-month-long Kutiyattam concluded, the Zamorin adorned himself with royal ornaments. Accompanied by parasols on long staves and a white fly whisk, along with the sounds of a conch being blown and eight mortars fired, the

Figure 26. Royal procession by Ammannur Rajaneesh Chakyar in *Hanumaddoothankam* of Bhasa's *Abhishekanatakam*. Photo by author.

Zamorin proceeded to the stage, the path before him ritually cleansed by two maidservants. Once onstage, he took the actor's sword and imagined himself as the escort to Lord Rama, who had been played by the Chakyar. Announced by a volley of musket fire, the Zamorin then led a procession of the Chakyar actor and a musical ensemble to Vairanellur temple. Upon arrival, the Zamorin handed his sword to a retainer and entered the temple with the Chakyar, worshipping the deity and paying an offering (*dakshina*) to the priests. Still dressed as Lord Rama, the Chakyar then presented the Zamorin with what is known as the arrow of Rama (*Rāmaśaram*). In return, the Zamorin presented the Chakyar who had played the lead role, named in palace records as "Koyappa Nāṟāna Cākyār," with one thousand measures of husked rice. The Zamorin also presented offerings to other Chakyars and Nangiars involved in the performance. Afterward, the Zamorin emerged from the temple holding the arrow of Rama, mounted a palanquin, and proceeded to the Thrikkavu goddess temple accompanied by a musical ensemble. There, he dismounted the palanquin, entered the temple to present money and other offerings to the deity, and continued his journey to the Vaikunda Perumal temple, where he also worshipped the deity, presented offerings, and then, from the eastern gateway of that temple, mounted the palanquin and returned to his palace (Haridas 2016, 170).[26]

Haridas (2016, 171) lists the ways the Zamorin used Kutiyattam to legitimize his royal power: (1) portraying the escort of Lord Rama as a virtuous act and, by association, characterizing the loyalty of local chiefs to the Zamorin as that of loyalty to the Lord; (2) making local chiefs eligible to escort Lord Rama given that the Zamorin escorted him; and (3) implying that the Zamorin, as Lord Rama's escort, represented the highest authority on Earth. Kutiyattam therefore served an important role for the Zamorin—squarely situated in the elite temple culture that he sponsored, that Tipu Sultan sought to destroy, and for which Nambiar-ashan's relatives risked everything.

Legend 2: The Chakyar, the Englishman, and the Dog

Figure 27. Sooraj Nambiar as Shankukarna with Kalamandalam Narayanan Nambiar on mizhavu. Photo by author.

The annual Kutiyattam festival at the Ammannur gurukulam, which I am currently in Irinjalakuda to attend, has been hosted the first twelve nights of January since 1987. Audience members regularly come from all over Kerala, India, and the world, reflecting the wide sphere of influence enjoyed by the gurukulam and Natana Kairali, Venuji's traditional arts organization. Today, I am sitting in the afternoon shade with Sooraj Nambiar, who we met in chapter 3. A young nonhereditary actor and instructor at the gurukulam, he belongs to the second group of students to study with Guru Ammannur Madhava Chakyar at the gurukulam in the 1990s. Sooraj has performed all over India and the world and has participated in several world theater exchanges with diverse international artists.[27] Sooraj is quiet and thoughtful, a deep thinker who always seems to speak with intention. He is graceful onstage and usually plays the hero, but over time, he has grown to play the more complicated antihero as well. When I watched him take the role of the demon-king Ravana years later at the same festival, a fellow American could not believe that the lanky actor had played the role, telling me, "He had such a powerful presence that I thought the role was played by a more physically imposing actor." Like Dr. Jayanthi, Sooraj has a talent with words. When I ask him about legends, he tells me that while studying with Guru Ammannur, he loved to listen to the stories his guru and Venuji so loved to tell. I ask him to tell me a few, and he launches into a lively storytelling session.

> In this family, there was Ammannur Parameswara Chakyar. At that time, there were three native kingdoms: Travancore, Cochin, and Malabar. There was a king who loved Kathakali [dance drama], and had artists on staff. He called Parameswara Chakyar there to teach one of his Kathakali artists, Easwara Pillai Vicharippukar, who was a bookkeeper, it's a big position. He was a great Kathakali artist, and this Chakyar was called there to teach him. When Chakyar was staying there, he used to go to the beach in the evenings to wander. At that time, British rule was going on, and a British official was there with his wife, walking his dog on the beach. When this dog saw people, it would bark and go over to them. He didn't bite, but he would frighten them. So he was barking and frightening people, and this couple was enjoying that.

Sooraj stops to chuckle and then continues: "This dog went up to the Chakyar, barking, so he took a stone and threw it, and the dog ran back yelping. The people thought that the Chakyar had thrown the stone, but he didn't, he was just acting. Nothing happened to the dog." He pauses, raising his eyebrows for emphasis.

> So the couple went to the king and complained that the Chakyar attacked their dog, and demanded the king punish him. At that time, you know, they were able to demand that, as they were the ones really ruling. So the king sent for the Chakyar and the Englishman said, "This is the man." The king asks Chakyar, "Did you do that?" He said, "No I didn't, I was just acting." The king understood he was just acting, but he told him, "Yes I understand you were acting, but I cannot make them understand that, so you must do so." The Chakyar turned to them and said, "I was just acting," but they said, "No, that can't be true, because it's a dog. He doesn't know any treatises of theater, how can you make him understand?"

Sooraj pauses to laugh again, more enthusiastically this time, obviously enjoying the thought of a canine theater connoisseur. Still smiling, he continues:

> So Chakyar said then, "To make you understand, let me do one thing," and Chakyar tightened his cloth into position. With his eyes he made a mountain, took it, and threw it at the man. The man fainted. He fainted! His wife was sitting farther away, so she saw this. When he [the Englishman] got up, then he finally understood what acting was.[28]
>
> And actually, this is the concept of acting also. This is the difference. Yes there is the question of contemporary and traditional, yet this is the main difference. I don't know much about contemporary theater, but I have seen things. Our concept is that acting is very stylized, the movements and mudras are stylized, but the result is very realistic. But in contemporary theater—he again chuckles—their acting is very realistic, but they want to make the result very stylized.

Meaning and Analysis

This personal legend is commonly known among the Kutiyattam community, and I heard and recorded several versions of it during my time in Kerala. Some narratives tell of a large imaginary stone thrown at the Englishman. Others describe throwing Mount Kailasa, reenacting a famous scene whereby the actor, as the demon-king Ravana, throws the sacred Himalayan mountain with the god Siva and his consort Parvathi sitting atop it.[29] Whereas all of the versions I encountered imply that the Englishman does not believe a dog could be duped by acting alone, Sooraj's version is the only one I saw where the Englishman makes the humorous observation that a dog could not possibly understand theater treatises. While many versions have the Englishman complain about the Chakyar at the royal palace, some skip this detail and have the Chakyar demonstrate his acting ability right there on the beach.

Many of the versions I encountered do not identify the king in the tale, and only a few include the king hiring the Chakyar to train a Kathakali actor. In some versions, the king does not appear at all, and the interaction takes place only between the Englishman and the Chakyar. Most narrators identify the main character as Ammannur Parameswara Chakyar or, more generally, as an Ammannur Chakyar, although some tell of an unnamed Chakyar. It is interesting to note that not a single version gives the identity of the Englishman, although some describe him as a British official, as did Sooraj. Most narrators do note that the legend is part of Sankunni's well-known multivolume book of legends, *The Garland of Legends* (*Aitihyamāla*). He is thought to have collected these tales in the late nineteenth century, publishing the first volume in 1909 and seven more volumes thereafter. Sankunni's full name was Kottarathil Sankunni, with *Kottarathil* meaning "of the palace," which clearly indicates his position in the employment of the Travancore royal family.

When I ask Sooraj where he learned the tale, he replies that he first read it in the *Aithihyamaala* legend collection. While the version published by Sankunni is similar to the version we see Sooraj narrate, it differs in significant ways. Sankunni's version sees Parameswara Chakyar throw a large stone instead of a mountain and identifies the other characters as King Marthanda Varma of Travancore, the British Resident at the time, and the Kathakali actor Easwara Pillai Vicharippukar. The timeline in Sankunni's published version differs a bit, describing how Parameswara Chakyar was first summoned to teach Pillai years earlier when Marthanda Varma was still the crown prince; it does not explain why he was summoned at the moment of the tale.[30] Sankunni also provides several more details, including that "a battalion of British soldiers and other officials also stayed in and around the palace" and that the English Resident's pet was a "giant sized dog that looked like a lion." He notes that the local people were "petrified" of the dog, but does not describe the Resident and his wife enjoying their fear. He also does not depict the king siding with the actor against the Englishman as does Sooraj, instead simply asking the Chakyar to prove his innocence before the court.

The litmus test of folklore is evaluating whether an item displays "multiple existence and variation," which indicates whether it is or has been in oral circulation, much like the well-known game of telephone where the narrative reliably changes as it passes from person to person (Dundes 1999). The different versions of the legend I encountered indicate that it is in current oral circulation, meaning that even though artists generally cite Sankunni's work as the original source, it is still being told and retold via word of mouth. It is unclear whether the legend has been actively told by the community all along, or if it reentered oral circulation after its early twentieth-century publication. From a folklorist's perspective, however, this detail is unimportant. The important point is that we know it is currently in active circulation, which indicates that it is meaningful for its community of tellers today.

What does this legend mean for tellers today? Like Nambiar-ashan, Sooraj interprets the tale just after finishing his storytelling. This involves a reflection on the nature of acting. Sooraj tells us that although Kutiyattam acting is highly stylized, it produces a realistic effect, in the process taking the opportunity to poke a bit of fun at contemporary theater. In this case, Kutiyattam acting is so believable that it convinces even a dog. When I ask Sooraj more pointedly what he thinks the story means, he reiterates: "It is very simple—it means that no matter how stylized your acting, the audience experiences it realistically." Most Kutiyattam artists I have asked this question have told me that the tale demonstrates the "histrionic" acting skills of the Chakyar, or Kutiyattam more generally. Sooraj's response, while not directly praising the actor's skill, nevertheless recognizes his acting prowess, for as those familiar with stylized forms of theater know, it is no small feat to translate stylized acting into realistic experience.

Artists generally consider this narrative related to others that recount the amazing acting feats of actors and actresses of yore. A story often shared with me in relation to this one involves a Chakyar from the same family—Ammannur Ittiyamman Chakyar, who is said to have possessed a similar power to fool the spectators' eyes. One legend tells of Ittiyamman Chakyar convincing a visiting Brahmin into believing that, as he flicked his hair during a dip in the temple pond, a few drops of water landed on the Brahmin. The enraged Brahmin, thinking himself thus polluted, notices upon closer inspection that the Chakyar has no hair and realizes this must be the famed Chakyar he had come looking for.[31] Another widely known legend about the same actor—although he is not always named—is often referenced to demonstrate the impressive skills of actors in the past. This is the story of the "flying Chakyar" (*paṟakunna Cākyār*), which tells of a Chakyar who performed the role of the eagle king Garuda, flying through the air held up by dozens of strings deftly manipulated by an expert Nambiar.[32] Today, no one knows exactly how the scene was performed, but it is often cited as evidence of the artistic heights that Kutiyattam reached in the past.[33] In 2013, Kalamandalam Girija re-created the scene in a large production in Thrissur that used a crane to help Garuda, played by Kalamandalam Jishnu Prathap, fly through the air.

Legends that tell of past Kutiyattam acting feats tend to focus on Chakyar actors, but they occasionally recognize the talent of Nangiar actresses as well.

The legendary "floating Nangiar" (*oḻukunna Naṅṅyār*) is similarly well known. It is connected to the figure of the flying Chakyar by the proverb "If seen, the flying Chakyar and the flowing Nangiar must be venerated" (*paṟakunna Cākyārum oḻukunna Naṅṅyārum kaṇḍāl tōḻanam*) (Nangiar 2018, 74).[34] This refers to a legendary scene in the play *Tapati-samvaranam* in which a Nangiar actress, as the heroine Tapati, successfully enacts floating in water onstage. It is said that multiple parallel strips of undulating cloth were used to produce the effect. As with the flying Chakyar scene, Kalamandalam Girija revived this scene onstage in 2016, drawing on oral tradition by tying strips of cloth to two poles to reproduce the effect of the flowing water. When I asked Usha-teacher about the proverb, she explained that it is used to teach students about the powerful acting skills of Chakyars and Nangiars of the past. Teachers use the proverb to convey to students that they should always strive to excel in their acting. Usha-teacher shared that she sometimes uses the proverb to calm students' stage fright, urging, "If they were able to perform without fear, even sometimes without an audience, so can you." Usha-teacher also recalled Kalamandalam Girija, one of her own teachers, citing the proverb during class to demonstrate that Kutiyattam has a long tradition of actresses playing powerful roles.

Another legendary Nangiar feat involves the hanging scene (*keṭṭiñāḻal*) of the character Malayavathi in the second act of Harshavardhana's Buddhist play *Nagananda*, in which an actress falls, twisting violently to the floor while gripping a noose around her neck.[35] In an earlier section, we saw Dr. Jayanthi recount how Nambiar-ashan's maternal grandmother, Nangeli Nangiaramma, took immense risk to perform the scene repeatedly. The last Nangiar in living memory to perform the scene within a temple context was Nambiar-ashan's eldest sister Thankamma Nangiaramma.[36] The scene was revived in the early 2000s, and I had the pleasure of seeing the young hereditary actress Aparna Nangiar perform it with the Ammannur gurukulam in 2009.

While Usha Nangiar (2018) provides several additional examples of legendary Nangiars in her exploration of talented Nangiars of the past, the final legend I discuss tells of a famous Nangiar responsible for upholding the acting tradition of the Ammannur family.[37] It is well known that the line of tradition would sometimes be broken historically, leaving a family with no one to teach the next generation. When this happened, the family in question depended on training from other families to continue the tradition. This particular legend details how, after the death of Itiyamman the flying Chakyar, there was no one to train his grandnephew, later known as Ammannur Valiya (senior) Parameswara Chakyar. To continue the Ammannur tradition, he was sent to study for eight years with a famous Nangiar actress in the town of Chengannur (Nangiar 2018). This actor is later known to have trained his nephew, Ammannur Cheriya (junior) Parameswara Chakyar, the same actor who triumphs over the Englishman in the legend just described.

Legends of the artistic prowess of Kutiyattam artists of yore bring the past actively into the present through both their narration and references in conversation in the form of the proverb mentioned above: "The flying Chakyar and flowing Nangiar must be venerated." The tales forge and solidify a continuity of artistic skill within the community that touches all contemporary artists, both hereditary and nonhereditary. They provide heroes and heroines for artists to emulate and artistic heights for artists to aspire to, inspiring artistic excellence and the re-creation of these feats in the present. For all listeners, they offer counternarratives to what is widely considered the decline of the art in the twentieth century, reduced to temple ritual and stripped of its artistic power. Artists use these tales to assert that Kutiyattam was not always an art in decline and that artistic excellence is central to the art's past, present, and future. In doing so, as in Henry Glassie's (2003, 176) well-known definition of tradition, artists actively "creat[e] the future out of the past."

Reading Resistance

To contemporary Kutiyattam artists, the legend of the Chakyar, the Englishman, and the dog evokes the incredible acting feats of Kutiyattam artists of the past. To a folklorist, however, the tale, in which an underdog gains the upper hand over a British official, evokes resistance to colonial domination. When viewed in this light, what may it reveal? We see an illustrious actor hired by the king to train the royal Kathakali dance drama troupe. After a hard day's work, the actor goes to the beach to enjoy his evening. While minding his own business, he is accosted by an aggressive dog and takes steps to defend himself. To provide some social context, even today, pet dogs in Kerala are unusual; most dogs one encounters are street dogs that still widely inspire fear. Contemporary audiences would thus identify with the fear the actor experiences in this encounter. When the English dog owner accuses the actor of harassment, the Chakyar professes his innocence to the king, who believes the actor is telling the truth. While the king knows of the Chakyar's acting skills because he hired him to train his Kathakali troupe, he communicates that the actor must prove this to the Englishman. In this act, the king indicates where the real power lies. We thus see both actor and king at the mercy of the British official. While a king's word is generally the law of the land, in this scenario, he is virtually powerless in the face of the Englishman's wrath.

The Englishman, however, is not depicted favorably. He and his wife are portrayed as taking pleasure in frightening innocent bystanders with their pet. When he thinks that the Chakyar has thrown a stone at his dog, even though it was obviously done in self-defense, the Englishman reacts with rage, demanding that the actor be brought before the king and punished. Embedded in this demand is the Englishman's assumption of power over local citizens and the king himself. As the inability to control one's anger is viewed with considerable disapproval in Kerala, the Englishman's rage and desire for revenge further serve to cast him in a negative light. His demand that the actor be punished for throwing a stone at a dog would also strike audiences as unreasonable or even ridiculous. The Englishman's unjust, unsavory character functions to make the Chakyar's victory over him all the more sweet. The actor thus emerges as a victorious underdog in the tale. The legend concludes with the actor in a position of power over the Englishman, who is subsequently forced to apologize and admit to the actor's unparalleled powers of acting. Although we hear no more of the king, we can imagine his satisfaction in seeing the smug British official brought to his knees, both literally and figuratively.

When I followed up with artists to ask if the victory of the Chakyar over the Englishman could be read as resistance to the British, most were unconvinced. In the archives of the Sangeet Natak Akademi, however, I discovered an instance when an actor reacted to the legend in a way that supports an interpretation of resistance. In a 2006 video-recorded interview with Ammannur Parameswara Chakyar, the interviewer asks about family legends. When he mentions his illustrious nineteenth-century namesake, the interviewer comments, "He sure scared that Englishman, didn't he?" (*Saippinŭ pēṭippichallē*), and they both chuckle with obvious glee.[38] The combination of this comment with their laughter hints at an element of resistance to and perhaps even contempt for British authority in the tale, engendering a humorous satisfaction in turning the tables of power and making the Englishman look like a fool.

Dr. Ammannur Rajaneesh Chakyar, grandnephew of Ammannur Madhava Chakyar as well as actor and instructor alongside Sooraj at the Ammannur gurukulam, paused thoughtfully when I asked him this same question. He reflected that many British people at the time did not accept the power of Kutiyattam acting and demanded to see it demonstrated in real life. He mentioned that he had heard another similar tale but could not guarantee it was true, as it was not part of Sankunni's legend collection. Rajaneesh began:

> At Thirunakkara temple in Kottayam district, a Chakyar was coming in the costume of the god Hanuman, on the first day of *Anguliyankamkoothu*.

> A Britishman asked him, "Hanuman is only a monkey, how much power does he really have?" So the Chakyar said, "We get his power when we perform, not from the costume." The Britishman challenged him, "Then show me his power." He ordered locals to tie the actor up with metal chains. He told Chakyar, "You prove your power, the power of Hanuman." The Chakyar accepted the challenge, and started praying to Hanuman in that temple for forty-one days. He received Hanuman's blessing, who told him to go ahead with the challenge and that the chains would break at that time. So the Chakyar did this. Every chain broke, and Chakyar jumped like Hanuman jumping across the sea. The Britishman was sitting outside, as he could not come inside the temple at that time [due to restrictions against non-Hindus]. In front of the temple there was a large banyan tree. When the Chakyar broke all of the chains, he made the deafening sound of Hanuman, and after one second the banyan tree fell down. The banyan is a very big tree, and in that moment, the Britishman . . .

Rajaneesh laughed heartily and continued, "He fainted. He wasn't killed, he just fainted from fright." I joined in his laughter, and asked if the Englishman had seen him jump. Rajaneesh explained:

> He saw the Chakyar jump from the top of one space to the stage of the koothambalam. While jumping he broke off his chains and made the sound, and at the same time the banyan tree fell down outside the temple. That is the connection, it was Hanuman who jumped down from there. After that, the Chakyar stopped performing. For the rest of his life, he only taught. We heard it like that. Some British people did not accept the power of acting. I'm not speaking of the extra human or supernatural power, but the power of acting. And whoever didn't accept it, they accepted it like this.

He laughed and said: "Only through seeing it with their own eyes, they accepted it." Rajaneesh laughed heartily and said that he had heard two or three stories like this.[39] He told me that when performing for people watching Kutiyattam for the first time, artists like himself take "power and inspiration" from the story. He mused, "But nowadays acting is global; it is spread all over the world. Now it is different. At that time, the British were ruling and thought they were superior to everyone else, but nowadays it has changed." As a young artist who has performed all over the world from Japan to France to Mozambique, Rajaneesh was subtly conveying that the power of acting is no longer doubted as it once was, at least by those outside of India.

Figure 28. Margi Sajeev Narayana Chakyar as Hanuman. Photo by author.

This legend repeats the theme of an Englishman doubting the power of Kutiyattam acting and fainting from fright when the actor demonstrates it to him. This Englishman is similarly confrontational and in a position of power, ordering the locals to do his bidding against the Chakyar. He is similarly brought to his knees by the Chakyar's acting, as the Chakyar's divine sound causes the large banyan tree to fall. However, there is more going on in this narrative than just defending the power of the art. The previous legend depicted a triumph over the Englishman by both the Chakyar and the king. In this, we see a triumph for the Chakyar, the god Hanuman, and, by implication, the Hindu belief that the Englishman belittles and doubts.

Folklorist Sadhana Naithani (2001a) explores how colonialism enlarged the repertoire of Indian oral folk narratives. She introduces the model of an "axis jump" in nineteenth-century Indian folklore that reveals how the colonized perceived their colonizers. As she explains, the colonial folklore archive largely represents the viewpoints and agendas of colonizer collectors, while the voices of the colonized folk themselves are much more difficult to find.[40] Naithani tells of discovering archival examples of North Indian folklore that reveal these folk perspectives. She asserts that although they are few in number, these items of folklore are significant and "remarkably consistent" in their viewpoints.

Naithani examines colonial-period rumors that reveal a perception that the British sought to inflict murderous harm on the population. These rumors include an Englishman hired by the British government to capture and cook young Indian boys for medicine or to collect human heads for the British Museum, and British census-taking intended to count children they planned to bury in bridge foundations or adults they planned to force into fighting their wars. As Naithani (2001a, 186) states, "These tales reflect an extreme mistrust of the colonial government, its officials and its measures [and] . . . their power as communication cannot be overlooked."[41] Naithani (2001a, 187) observes that these narratives contradict how British folklorists depicted the Indian folk and their lore—that Indian folklore was "ancient, spiritual, and traditional," untouched by European influence and without historical consciousness, and that Indians were "incapable of any literary conception and representation of their contemporary socio-historical reality." Naithani (2001a, 187) concludes by asserting that "instead of being passive bearers of a repertoire of tradition, the narrators emerge as self-conscious subjects whose narratives performed multiple functions in social communication. They were carriers of change and growth; as such, they did not possess live traditions so much as have a live relationship with tradition."

These legends about Kutiyattam actors encountering Englishmen are additional examples of how the Indian folk actively incorporated their contemporary experiences into narrative traditions. They are rare examples of the "axis jump" of folk commentary on British colonizers, but unlike Naithani's archival examples, these are still in active circulation.[42] The narratives we see here, however, reflect a very different relationship with the colonizers. Whereas much of the rest of India, including Malabar, came to be directly ruled by the British, the Kingdom of Travancore where these legends take place maintained a degree of sovereignty. As a princely state, it was directly ruled by its kings or queens, although the British claimed ultimate authority in matters that concerned them via a British Resident.[43] In these legends, we do not see the British portrayed as mass murderers with ultimate power over the lives and deaths of the local people. Instead, they are depicted as arrogant, callous, and demanding, conscious of their power over the king and the local population. The deeper impression we get of the folk attitude toward the colonizers here is one not of fear but disdain.

While contemporary Kutiyattam artists generally fail to read resistance into these narratives, resistance was most likely an easily recognizable subtext at the time. Humor is a widely employed tool of resistance, a "weapon of the weak" (Scott 1987) against the powerful, and this narrative serves to take the British down a notch by having a laugh at their expense.[44] Everyday storytelling forms like these become what Scott (1990, xii) terms "hidden transcripts" that oppressed groups transform into a form of resistance, representing "a critique of power spoken behind the back of the dominant." At a time when British influence was largely resented, the main message of the tale would have been that the actor made the Englishman look like a fool. Leela Prasad (2020, 7) introduces the figure of the "audacious raconteur" in colonial India, a skillful narrator who openly and "audaciously challeng[ed] the ideological bulwark of colonialism." While oppressive power serves to "other" fellow human beings, as Prasad (2020, 159) asserts, audacious narrators maintain a "counter-hegemonic sovereignty" that, among other things, "refuses labels or paradigms that belittle." In his blatant insubordination against the British colonialist, the actor in our tale becomes an audacious raconteur whose nonverbal narration rejects the oppressor's belittling of his knowledge and art.

While Prasad (2020) suggests an opposition between storytellers who employ "hidden transcripts" (Scott 1990) and the figure of the "audacious raconteur," our case at hand evidences overlap between the two; not only is the actor in our legend an audacious raconteur, but those who subsequently tell his story are as well. Even when told as a hidden transcript within the community, legend tellers celebrate the actor's bold insubordination and similarly reject the British devaluation of their knowledge and art. They, too, "own and control indigenous narrative space" in a way that challenges colonial power and ideology (Prasad 2020, 13). And they, too, even more than the hero of the tale they tell, "demonstrate that colonial knowledge about India was hollow because it tried to erase what could not be erased: an ethos of oral culture, ties of kinship, and varieties of past-consciousness" (2020, 13). Nowadays, the main takeaway of this tale is the greatness (*kēmam*) of the Chakyar's acting. As the meaning folklore holds for communities of tellers and practitioners inevitably changes over time, it makes sense that the more subversive meanings of the tale would have faded away as British domination became an increasingly distant memory. Yet, even in present-day narrations of the legend, storytellers demonstrate the importance of oral narrative, the value of kinship and community, and a connection with the past in ways that continue to defy colonial assumptions about India, even if unintentionally.

Historical Context

This legend is situated within the historical context of nineteenth-century British dominance over the princely state of Travancore, in a cosmopolitan encounter of domination similar to that described in the Tipu Sultan legend. As a Kutiyattam actor or actress would query in performance: How did this come to be? We saw in the last section that the Zamorin's endless wars began to take a toll on his northern Malabar kingdom by the early to mid-eighteenth century. This left an opening for the rise of the southern Kingdom of Travancore, which at the time was known as Venad. As rulers of a kingdom near the southern tip of the Indian subcontinent, the Venad kings had long been vassals to other kingdoms such as the Vijayanagar and Mughal Empires as well as subservient to their own powerful aristocracy.

With the 1729 crowning of Marthanda Varma, the balance of power shifted (Pillai 2015). A self-proclaimed enemy of the aristocracy, Marthanda Varma is credited with ending the feudal era and ushering in a modern age in Kerala, characterized by a centralized royal state (Menon 2019). By the mid-eighteenth century, Marthanda Varma had driven the Dutch out of the region and expanded his kingdom across most of southern Kerala.[45] As Bayly (1984, 186) has described, "Raja Martanda Varma began his career as ruler of the tiny royal domain of Venad: in less than 20 years, from 1734–1752, he swept away every one of the old chiefdoms in the southern half of Kerala [and] in their place he carved out a war-state which closely resembled the new warrior domains of north and central India." Having observed the result of the Zamorin's wars against European powers, Marthanda Varma is said to have told his heirs on his 1758 deathbed to maintain their friendship with the English East India Company at all costs (Pillai 2015). Pillai (2015, 19) has characterized this friendship as one that led the monarchy to "constantly reconcil[e] its dynastic prerogative with the demands of its colonial masters."

As we know, it was only with the aid of the British that Travancore was able to defeat the advancing forces of Tipu Sultan, and the resulting treaty gave the British direct control over Malabar in the North. In subsequent treaties, the Kingdom of Cochin, which under the Portuguese had been the first colonial settlement in India, became a tribute-paying vassal to the East India Company. Similarly, Travancore agreed to recognize British supremacy in foreign affairs and pay the expenses of the war against Tipu, which it could ill afford (Menon 2019). A mere decade later, the kingdom lost complete political freedom with the forced treaty of 1805, which allowed the British to intervene in Travancore's internal affairs via the British Resident. As a result, the royally appointed chief minister (*dewan*) of subjugated Travancore joined forces with the chief minister of subjugated Cochin in 1809 to lead a failed rebellion against the British. Known as the rebellion of Velu Tampi, it is widely recognized as one of the earliest rebellions against the British in India.[46] The failed revolt resulted in the demilitarization and further subjugation of Travancore, with the British installing a nonnative chief minister for the next fifty years. Rather than serving the king or queen as the position required, the chief minister of Travancore came to serve the British Resident instead (Pillai 2015). Sankunni identifies the king in our legend as the nineteenth-century Marthanda Varma II, so this would place the events of the legend sometime during his rule from 1840 to 1860. Contextualized in a historical moment when the British Resident had enormous power over the king, the undertones of resistance in the legend I propose here become not only plausible but likely.

Legend 3: How the Ammannur Chakyars Came to Moozhikkulam

Figure 29. Margi Sajeev Narayana Chakyar in Chakyarkoothu. Photo by author.

It is a quiet afternoon at Margi, disturbed only by the occasional falling coconut striking the metal roof overhead. I am sitting with Margi Sajeev Narayana Chakyar, whom I know as Sajeev-ashan, and we are discussing the Chakyar's special power of critique. Sajeev-ashan tells me that the art's *vidushaka* jester "tells both truths and faults," a phrase he attributes to the historic king Kulashekhara and his minister Tholan. He explains that this refers to the Koothu vidushaka, not the Kutiyattam vidushaka, because the latter is restricted by his role as a character in a play. As an all-powerful storyteller rather than a specific character, the Koothu actor has greater freedom in performance. Sajeev-ashan tells me, "When kings ruled, people didn't have the freedom to speak about the king's mistakes, as they do today. But during Koothu, by disguising the king's errors within well-known stories, Chakyars could speak out. And not only about kings, about anyone or any problems in society."

Establishing a continuity with the past in performance, he continues, "We still do this today. When I perform Koothu, I criticize things happening today, but not directly. I do this through metaphor, in a hidden way, but the audience still understands. That way, I can't be said to have directly criticized anybody." He smiles and raises his eyebrows for emphasis, then continues, "Like that, audiences in those days understood the Chakyar's critique." Sajeev-ashan pauses briefly and then launches impromptu into the following tale:

> There's a reason why the Ammannur family left Pattambi for Moozhikkulam. At that time, the ruling king, I think it was the Zamorin—it was in the Malabar area so it was either the Valluvanad king or the Zamorin, I don't know exactly. So the ruling king killed a Namboodiri (Kerala Brahmin) whose house name was Manthitta. We refer to Namboodiris using their house names, so he was called Manthitta. This Namboodiri had done something the king didn't like, so the king had him burned to death in a big oven.

I gasp, and Sajeev-ashan raises his eyebrows in amusement and nods, acknowledging the brutality of the act. He continues:

> Everyone in that house knew about it, but no one was prepared to say anything as they would meet the same fate. But when the Chakyar performed his Koothu, he said something. The king was in the audience, everyone was there. The story the Chakyar told was about the Pandavas' exile wandering the forest [i.e., the main characters in the *Mahabharata*].
>
> The Chakyar brought the issue to light questioning as though he was Dharmaputra asking Bhima, "Hey, what is that smell? Doesn't it stink like burning mango tree bark?" The word for mango tree bark [*māntōṭŭ*] sounds like Manthitta. So he asked, "Who burnt the mango tree bark in

the oven? Oh! He should not have done it, it was very wrong to do. What a horrible smell it has. Oh! Can you not all smell it?" He asked the audience this several times while pointing at them. Like that, they understood that he was talking about what the king had done to the Manthitta Namboodiri, but still no one spoke out. The king realized that the Chakyar had announced his misdeed publicly, and was very upset.[47]

The king sent a servant to tell the Chakyar he should come see the king in his palace after the Koothu finished. But the servant told him, "Don't go, or else the king will kill you too. Leave this place immediately." So that night itself, without anyone knowing, the Chakyar left with his family and all of his possessions. That is how he came here to Moozhikkulam.

Here there was a different king, the Travancore king, so the Zamorin could not do anything. When the Chakyar arrived, he told the king here what had happened, and the king gave him shelter. That's how he came to Moozhikkulam. Like this, everything has a story behind it. This is the critique of the vidushaka—he speaks both truths and faults.[48]

Meaning and Analysis

As with our previous two storytellers, Sajeev-ashan explains the tale's meaning at the end of his narrative, emphasizing that it demonstrates the critique of the vidushaka. Unlike the last two legends, however, this one was not told at my request.[49] This storytelling session emerged in what folklorists would term a natural context, a "breakthrough into performance" during an everyday conversation (Hymes [1975] 1981). Although part of a recorded interview, Sajeev-ashan told the legend spontaneously to illustrate the Chakyar's role as a social critic. Rather than critiquing more mundane aspects of the king's rule, the Chakyar dares to publicly bring the king's murderous actions to light. As Sajeev-ashan stresses, the Chakyar as vidushaka is meant to speak "both truths and faults," and in this legend, he takes that mandate to its fullest extent. Perhaps unexpectedly, there is a shared theme with the Tipu Sultan legend above. As with Nambiar-ashan's maternal ancestor, Sajeev-ashan's paternal ancestor risks his life to fulfill his duty to bring injustice to light. We also see humor used as a form of resistance, as in the legend of the Englishman and the dog. Whereas the legend of the Englishman represents a form of indirect resistance, however, the Chakyar's resistance to the king here is both direct and confrontational.

The Chakyar's role is to engage in social critique of the powerful. His performance, often in the context of a temple festival, could therefore have been a formalized mechanism for historically diffusing dissatisfaction with those in power via laughter.[50] Folklore scholarship on festival, with its topsy-turvy nature that often employs laughter and play to turn power relations on their head, explores how these performances can serve as a formalized mechanism for the masses to let off steam, thereby helping to maintain social hierarchies.[51] While Koothu is often performed in the context of temple festivals, it was historically performed only for the social elite in a restricted temple context inaccessible to the masses. It would therefore have served to diffuse tension not among the masses but among a particularly small but influential group of people. With the king and other powerful figures willing to be the butt of the Chakyar's jokes, the laughter he provoked at their expense would have served to bring those figures down to the level of the other spectators. If they played along, the audience would perceive these influential people as good-natured and relatable. Even if they did not, this gave their social inferiors the rare chance to gain the psychological satisfaction of the upper hand, however fleeting.

I ask Sajeev-ashan if most kings welcomed the Chakyar's critique. He replies that some did, even righting their wrongs as a result. This prompts him to narrate a more recent encounter between an Ammannur Chakyar and a king in the early twentieth century, which he once heard Guru Ammannur recount to Appukuttan Nair, Margi's founder. This tale involves Ammannur Chachu Chakyar, a maternal uncle to Guru Ammannur renowned for both the humor and critique of his Koothu (Chakyarkoothu).[52] Folklorists would consider Guru Ammannur's storytelling an anecdote, as he lived at the same time as the tale's main character. When told by someone like Sajeev-ashan, whose lifetime did not substantially overlap with the person described, it becomes a personal legend.[53] Sajeev-ashan recounts that Chachu Chakyar pleased many kings and other powerful figures through his critique of them, including the recently abdicated Maharaja of Cochin, Rama Varma XV.[54] As Sajeev-ashan narrates,

> The king invited Chachu Chakyar to perform Koothu in Thrippunithura for five days. At 11am each day during lunch, the king instructed him, "Today I want you to perform this story, from this point to this point." He then had to perform Koothu from 3–6pm that day. That's how it was! Each day the king told him to perform a different story—one story one day and another the next. This continued for four days. He didn't have much time to contemplate how he would perform each day and yet he performed well. Nevertheless, the circumstances didn't allow him to showcase his abilities.
>
> On the fifth and last day when he came to eat lunch, the king told him, "Chachu, your Koothu has plenty of Sanskrit explanations, but it has no

> humor and hardly any critique." Critique is the reason why Koothu is performed, to point out mistakes, and the king said his performance had little critique or humor. Chachu-uncle [*ammaman*] replied, "It's because you've been deciding the story each day. Today let me decide my own story." So he was told to choose a story. The stories the king had chosen until that point, like Melpathur's Rajasuyam, were very tough. At that time, the *Ramayana* was easiest. Everyone who performed Koothu was able to do it—that's a special feature of the *Ramayana*.
>
> Chachu Chakyar decided to tell a story from the last part of the *Ramayana*, where Ravana and Rama have a face-to-face conversation. There's a verse where Ravana mocks Rama. After the battle ends, Ravana comes to Rama and tells him, "You're trivial, you have no greatness at all." This verse has many meanings, and he related all of these meanings to the king, connecting them to different things the king had done. At the time the British came, all of the kingdoms gave themselves up except for Cochin. But the British attacked, and the king was forced to abdicate. Everyone said he abdicated willingly, but in fact he was attacked. Chachu-uncle mentioned this in his Koothu, saying, "Rama, you say you left your kingdom and went to the forest in exile willingly, because your father told you to, but in fact you were forced to leave, weren't you? Did you willingly resign, or were you forced to?" He asked this of the king, looking directly at him.
>
> After the Koothu finished, the king awarded him a *veerasrinkala* [*vīraśr̥ṅkhala*, a golden "bracelet of honor" awarded for outstanding performances]. The five days of Koothu was a test to see if he deserved a *veerashrinkala*.[55] Like that, there were kings who received criticism well, but it often led to anger.[56]

These legendary tales bring to life the historical right of Chakyars to criticize kings and other elites for today's audience and provide a sense of the stakes of performance. Whereas the king in the first legend is enraged by the Chakyar's critique, the king in this tale rewards it. In both narratives, we see the actor engage hard-hitting and serious topics in a way that reveals his courage and wit. Out of all the Koothu performances I have seen, the one that stands out likewise tackled a sensitive topic, making the audience laugh harder than I have ever seen in Kerala. It was just after the 2008 attacks in Mumbai. The Kutiyattam Kendra was hosting a festival in Trivandrum for college students from across the state to learn about the art. Sajeev-ashan was onstage for a brief thirty-minute Koothu performance, and I understood enough to know that he was talking about the attacks. Kutiyattam and Koothu audiences generally tend to be older, but this primarily younger audience was erupting in belly-shaking laughter every five minutes. Although I could not understand everything Sajeev-ashan said due to the highly Sanskritized, literary Malayalam he spoke, it was entertaining to simply watch the interaction between the actor and his audience. Sajeev-ashan addressed a topic that was heavy and hard hitting, just as Chachu Chakyar did, to a resoundingly positive response from his audience.

Shifting gears to consider the legend's performance in terms of the teller's identity, Sajeev-ashan's storytelling offers a window onto wider shifts within the matrilineal family system (*marumakkathayam*) in Kerala, which Arunima (2003) notes is the only kinship system in the world to have been intentionally abolished.[57] Sajeev-ashan inherited his status as a Pothiyil Chakyar matrilineally from his mother. His father, Padmasree Moozhikkulam Kochukuttan Chakyar, belonged to the Ammannur family. According to the matrilineal family system and rules of hereditary performance, Sajeev-ashan is not considered an Ammannur family member and thus not allowed to perform in temples where the Ammannur family holds hereditary rights. Within this kinship system, the maternal uncle plays the formative role in raising his sisters' children, with all maternally related family members residing together matrilocally in the matrilineal home (*tharawad*).[58] Women did not live with their husbands, and fathers played little or no role in their children's lives. As Sajeev-ashan explained, "In the Chakyar family tradition, the maternal uncle (*ammaman*), not the father, is the head of the family. Uncle is the one who teaches the children and does everything, not Father. The father is just the producer, one day only," he chuckled.

Sajeev-ashan's upbringing in Moozhikkulam in the 1960s and 1970s tells a somewhat different story, however, one that reflects the complex negotiations undertaken by many Kerala families within the matrilineal system throughout the twentieth century. Sajeev-ashan grew up living patrilocally with his mother and father, not his maternal uncle, as tradition dictated. And it was his father, an Ammannur Chakyar, who raised him and trained him in Kutiyattam. Due to changing legislation and social mores, fathers took on increasing importance in matrilineal families in twentieth-century Kerala.[59] While matrilineal families were previously both matrilineal and matrilocal, some fathers began moving in with their wives' families instead of staying in their own family homes. Many other families became patrilocal, with wives moving after marriage from their matrilineal joint family homes to their husbands' homes and raising their children there, as was the case with Sajeev-ashan's and Nambiar-ashan's families.[60] In these contexts, fathers assumed responsibility for financially supporting and educating their children.

Sajeev-ashan's story about his father's maternal uncle highlights the importance of his father and his father's family in his own life. Sajeev-ashan even refers to Chachu Chakyar as *ammaman*, meaning "maternal uncle," which describes his father's relationship with the guru. Through these legends he shares about the Ammannur Chakyars, Sajeev-ashan's storytelling reveals his close identification with his father's family. It also reveals how changes to the matrilineal family system in Kerala manifest in the context of everyday lives and relationships.

Sajeev-ashan lives patrilocally with his wife and daughter, a common family constellation today among Chakyars, Nambiars, and Nangiars of his generation and younger. This living arrangement correlates with the rise of the nuclear family and the increasing importance of the father in traditionally matrilineal Kerala communities, as described above. Regarding kinship naming practices, *Chakyar* refers to male members of a particular caste. Changing social norms in an increasingly communist Kerala led many in Sajeev-ashan's generation to discard caste names, although some Kutiyattam community members retained the caste names that simultaneously function as artistic titles. Among the generation of Sajeev-ashan's teenage daughter, however, the practice of inheriting caste/family names matrilineally has begun to change to a patrilineal model. Whereas these caste-cum-artistic titles were traditionally only inherited through the mother, there is now a rising trend of these names passed through the father.[61] In Sajeev-ashan's case, his daughter has taken Chakyar as her surname. This defies not only the traditional matrilineal model of naming but its gendered norms as well.[62] Because her mother is from a different community, she is not recognized as a hereditary Kutiyattam performer, nor is she permitted to perform in hereditary temple venues. Kerala temples, renowned across India for their conservatism, have largely continued to refuse performances by anyone not born into the art according to matrilineal rules of inheritance, with few exceptions. As previously discussed, naming practices have been contentious in contemporary Kutiyattam, and this newer trend among some hereditary families is no exception.

Returning to an analysis of the legend, from a content perspective, it explains how the Ammannur Chakyar family fled the Kingdom of Calicut for the Kingdom of Travancore and ultimately settled in the town of Moozhikkulam. As Sajeev-ashan notes, "Like this, everything has a story behind it." Forced to flee a murderous king enraged by the Chakyar's criticism, the actor takes shelter under the protection of a new king. Ramavarma (1978) describes a similar legend that tells of the Koypa/Painkulam Chakyar family fleeing the Kingdom of Calicut in fear. In this legend, the Zamorin actually kills the offending Chakyar in the middle of his performance and confiscates the family's lands for daring to criticize his governance.[63] Fearing further repercussions, the family flees the kingdom to Pandalur and eventually moves to Painkulam in the Kingdom of Cochin where they still reside.[64] As Johan (2014, vol. 1, 277–278) reports, however, Kalamandalam Rama Chakyar, who belongs to the Painkulam family, doubts that the Chakyar was actually killed midperformance.

To complete the story of the Ammannur family's migration, a branch of the family later migrated to Irinjalakuda in the Kingdom of Cochin to be near a temple where they regularly performed.[65] Part of the family's Irinjalakuda branch, Dr. Rajaneesh Chakyar surmised that the legend of how his family came to Moozhikkulam is around four hundred years old. He revealed that his ancestors never returned to the Zamorin's kingdom and that they relinquished all of their hereditary performance rights in the area. It was only in the late twentieth century that the family's performance in the region resumed. Local priests near Pattambi, where the family originated, determined that the temple deity was displeased that performances there had ceased. To rectify this, the priests invited Rajaneesh's uncle, Ammannur Parameswara Chakyar—the same figure we saw chuckle about the Englishman in the last legend—to resume performances there. Rajaneesh first performed there himself around 2010 and told me he was curious to learn more about his family history after so many years of hearing this story. Upon asking a local Namboodiri Brahmin family, he discovered that locals still tell the tale of how his family was forced to flee and can still pinpoint the exact location of his family's ancestral land.

Historical Context

In the centuries immediately before Indian independence, Kerala comprised three main administrative entities: Travancore, Cochin, and Malabar. In the late eighteenth and early nineteenth centuries, the Kingdoms of Travancore and Cochin became princely states under indirect British control, ruled by their royal families but with any major decisions subject to British approval. In contrast, as stipulated in the British treaty with Tipu Sultan, Malabar came under direct British control as part of the larger Madras presidency, and the Zamorin lost all political power. In the legend of the Chakyar telling both truths and faults, an actor from the Ammannur family flees the Malabar kingdom of Calicut for the Kingdom of Travancore. Fleeing angry kings, however, was not the typical form of cross-border circulation at the time. Historical circulation among the Kutiyattam community more commonly happened because of performance obligations. Just as artists travel regularly throughout the length and breadth of Kerala state today, artists did so historically as well. I argue that this travel constituted a form of regular, cosmopolitan border crossing in the days before Kerala statehood, despite a distinct Kerala regional identity that Veluthat (2018) states had arisen by this period.[66]

Nambiar-ashan, whose description of his childhood appeared in the first section, recalled how he traveled extensively to perform Koothu and Kutiyattam with his family for up to nine months a year. Hereditary performance rights did not align perfectly with the geographic boundaries of historical kingdoms, and artists often had to travel across borders to perform. This was increasingly the case as the number of Chakyar and Nambiar families dwindled over time. The remaining families often assumed the performance duties of those who could no longer fulfill them, thereby expanding the geographic scope of their performances.[67] As kingdom borders changed with local conquests, artists likely also found themselves crossing borders where none had previously existed. Despite these changing political borders, the administration of temples often remained the same (Haridas 2016).[68] This means that if a temple was under the sponsorship and protection of one ruler, that ruler typically maintained sponsorship of the temple even if the land surrounding it was annexed into a different kingdom.[69] The internal affairs of temples, many of which included annual Koothu and Kutiyattam performances, would have therefore remained relatively stable over time, resulting in minimal disruption to wider Kutiyattam performance.

Most performances fell into the category of hereditary temple obligations (*adiyanthirakoothu*). However, artists occasionally performed upon special invitation by wealthy patrons in a genre of performance known as *visheshallkoothu* (*viśēṣālkkūṭṭu*). One type of *visheshallkoothu* involved an individual actor invited to perform, as in the example of Chachu Chakyar performing for the king of Cochin. Another type, usually also sponsored by a king, involved a group performance with the best actors from across Kerala. The king of Cochin was known to regularly sponsor this type of performance, inviting the best actors from all families to perform together where he resided in Trippunithura.[70] As in the example above, he would specify the drama and assign the acting roles only on the morning of each day of performance. The invited actors and actresses thus required the skill to perform different dramas and roles impromptu. Competition in these performances was fierce, with the best performers awarded the coveted *veerashrinkala* golden bracelet prize. Dr. Rajaneesh Chakyar characterized these performances as involving the "superstars" of the day engaged in a "healthy type of competition," as most families were related. However, I heard of one competition that was not good-natured. Dr. Jayanthi told me about one of the last times the Maharaja of Cochin sponsored this type of group performance in the early to mid-twentieth century. During backstage preparations, someone surreptitiously added chili powder to her grandfather Mani Madhava Chakyar's eye makeup. Celebrated for the expressiveness of his large eyes, she told me, this was done to ruin his performance before the king, thus giving the other actors an advantage in their bid for the coveted *veerashrinkala* prize.

This final section differs from the previous two in that it features kings from all three major kingdoms associated with Kerala's preindependence political organization: a critique-averse Zamorin, a king of Cochin who welcomed criticism, and a king of Travancore who provided safe haven. As Kutiyattam artists historically interacted with these kings as their patrons, the differences among them are still discussed today. Dr. Rajaneesh Chakyar told me that while the Zamorin is well known for his focus on conquering neighboring lands, the kings of Cochin and Travancore are known for their arts patronage, regularly inviting the best actors for special performances. "That's what I heard," he said. "Kochi [Cochin] and Travancore concentrated on the aesthetics of our language and art forms; the kings enjoyed these things and devoted time to them." Notably, the Zamorin is still widely known for his militarism today, although his conquering activities stopped in the late eighteenth century. Within the Mani Chakyar family, who now holds the performance rights for most of Malabar, however, the Zamorin *is* known for his arts patronage and in particular for his regular sponsorship of their forefather Mani Madhava Chakyar in the twentieth century. To some extent, modern descriptions of these historical kings seem to reflect Kutiyattam family memories of past interactions with them, memories that legends play a primary role in sustaining.

Digging a bit deeper, Rajaneesh attributed the Zamorin's intolerance of criticism in the last legend to the ruler's preoccupation with political domination at the time. The setting of the tale reinforces this perception because it takes place in Valluvanad, a kingdom that the Zamorin conquered large parts of in the late thirteenth century CE. Interestingly, the *Keralolpatti* frames the Zamorin's takeover of Valluvanad as the result of following a holy man's advice to ensure the prosperity of his lineage, including sponsoring Kutiyattam and *Paṟakkumkūttu* (flying Koothu).[71] Rajaneesh compared the king of Cochin's relationship with criticism, saying, "The Kochi King was not like that. Our ancestors always criticized him. They could criticize him *the most* and he would only laugh. Chachu Chakyar, Ammannur-ashan's ashan, criticized him a lot and afterward still got the *veerashrinkala* golden bracelet. The Zamorin wasn't like that. After we left, we never returned to the Zamorin's lands." He laughed. "But now there's no Zamorin, it's all the government of Kerala. We respect the Zamorin; we now perform there. The Mani family took over our performances, and if they were unable to perform, we would sometimes fill in for them."

As the setting of the tale demonstrates, although wider conceptions of pre-independence Kerala today are largely dominated by these three kingdoms, the historical reality was more complicated. As we have seen, the legend is set in Valluvanad, which was part of the Zamorin's domain at the time. Valluvanad had its own ruler, however, one of a number of minor kings throughout Kerala's history (Menon 2019). Bayly (1984, 181) describes pre-1740s Kerala as "a patchwork quilt of shifting chiefdoms and principalities" with rulers similar to Indonesian "port kings" who controlled a coastal or river port and the surrounding areas but not the hinterlands.[72] She describes the rise of several rulers with access to the best harbors or spices—and thereby to tax revenues from Indian Ocean trade—characterizing their claims to kingship as "little more than a vague suzerainty over lesser local lords" that was focused not on outright conquest but the establishment of ritual authority through the building and sponsorship of temples and shrines (1984, 181). Menon (1999) notes that this lack of penetration into the hinterlands meant the kings could not collect land tax, and their influence in the hinterlands therefore relied on the allegiance of powerful landowning households. Haridas (2016, 312) has similarly characterized the rulers of medieval Kerala—including those of Calicut, Cochin, Valluvanad, Kolattunad (Cannanore), and Venad (later Travancore)—as "little kings" of "little kingdoms" whose position and social status were continually contested. He characterizes these "little kings" as being in a state of constantly shifting alliances and conflicts with each other in a contest for supremacy to become a "great king" on par with the last high king of Kerala, Ceraman Perumal.

Interestingly, in the *Keralolpatti*'s description of the last Perumal high king partitioning his territory before departing for Mecca in the twelfth century CE, Valluvanad inherited the coveted right to host the great Mamankam festival, a ritual celebration of the former high kings of Kerala. Taking place only once every twelve years over a thirty-day period during the bright phase of the moon, whoever controlled the festival was conceptualized as the symbolic ruler of all Kerala (Haridas 2016, 209).[73] The Kerala State Department of Archaeology describes the festival as "an occasion of cultural and communal harmony" in which "various forms of sports events, martial arts, intellectual contests, cultural activities, rituals and folk art performance [*sic*] were performed on every nook and corner of the vast and wide sandy shores of Bharathapuzha [Nila river]."[74]

As described earlier this chapter, the Zamorin's takeover of Mamankam reflected his political aspirations to be Kerala's high king. In the centuries after the Zamorin conquered the area where the festival took place, the king of Valluvanad famously sent squads of suicide warriors (*cāvēr*) to kill the Zamorin and regain control of the festival.[75] Within the festival's ritualized context, whoever killed the ruler would assume power, but the Valluvanad warriors never succeeded. The Mamankam festival plays a large role in the historical imagination of Kerala today, with several well-known folk ballads commemorating the bravery of these suicide warriors and multiple "Mamanka Smarakam" (Mamankam Memorial) heritage sites protected by Kerala state. More recently, a blockbuster film titled *Māmāṅkam* (dir. M. Padmakumar) played in theaters across Kerala in late 2019 and early 2020, telling the story of the festival with rich historical reconstructions from the perspective of the *chaver* suicide warriors.

This chapter has described the Zamorin's use of culture to legitimize his rule in a number of ways.[76] The political symbolism of the Mamankam festival where Koothu and Kutiyattam were performed projected the Zamorin as the ruler of all of Kerala.[77] He also used Kutiyattam in the eighteenth century to demonstrate the divine sanction of his rule, casting himself in the role of Lord Rama's personal escort. Haridas (2016, 224) observes that the Zamorin's sponsorship of temples and temple-based cultural activities were "statements of power" aimed to legitimize the Zamorin's rule. Haridas (2016, 231) also asserts that patronage of scholars became a way for rulers to "control the ideology of the elite class" and refers to an instance in the fifteenth century, noted by Ayyar, where the Zamorin publicly humiliated two poets who dared critique him.[78] If this instance is indicative of a larger trend, Haridas (2016, 241) argues, "it implies the king's right over the scholars and ultimately control of scholarship."

When performing Koothu historically, the Chakyar was not only an actor but also a scholar, deftly translating scholarship for the audience while commenting on current affairs and sometimes even performing his own poetic compositions.[79] Royal censorship of Chakyars must therefore be viewed in the same light as censorship of scholars—as a means to control the opinions of the elite. In the final legend of this chapter, the Zamorin plans to kill the Chakyar for his critique despite the Chakyar's well-established right to criticize those in power. In addition to the historical example of the Zamorin humiliating critical poets and the briefly mentioned legend in which he supposedly kills a Chakyar midperformance, this indicates a policy in Calicut whereby, perhaps for a time, patronage of the arts and scholarship was strictly a way to legitimize political power, with any criticism perceived as a direct threat to royal authority.[80] We may never know if this is true; however, these examples point to a wider perception of such a policy despite a lack of historical evidence.

This political use of culture aligns with what Bayly (1984, 189) noted was happening in Cochin and Travancore as well, where these kingdoms' eighteenth-century rulers "constructed an entirely new court culture and new rituals of state which served to assert and dramatize their assumption of sovereignty." In fact, Bayly characterizes eighteenth-century Kerala as a period of greater upheaval than any time since the dissolution of the Chera dynasty in the twelfth century. Focusing on Cochin and Travancore, she attributes the rise of the modern state in Kerala to this period. She firmly contextualizes this rise within wider processes of state formation across eighteenth-century India, which entailed fundamental changes to most societal institutions at the time.[81] As part of state-building, the patronage of art, poetry, and scholarship was a priority for the kings of the newly centralized Travancore and Cochin. These kings became known for their lavish patronage of temples and Hindu learning as well as for introducing new festivals, a characterization that aligns with how Kutiyattam community memory portrays them today (Bayly 1984).

According to the oral tradition of the Ammannur Chakyar family, what appears to distinguish the kings of Cochin and Travancore from the Zamorin of Calicut is their tolerance and even reward of criticism. As mentioned above, however, the Mani Chakyar family has more favorable impressions of their former patron, the Zamorin. It is important to note that, while Sajeev-ashan equates the murderous king of Valluvanadu with the Zamorin in the above legend, he admits that he is not entirely sure. The connection becomes more dubious in a broader perspective, with multiple versions naming different rulers. K. P. S. Menon (1994) attributes the murderous act to the king of Vellatra, while Venu (1988) ascribes it to the local king of Valluvanadu (Valluva Konathiri). S. Rajendu, a historian of both Valluvanadu and Nedunganadu, attributes the act to the local king of Nedunganadu.[82]

Let us examine Rajendu's (2012, 289) published version of the tale, as follows: "The Manthodu Namboodiri happened to hear about the local king's amoral trysts during the nights of a festive season. When the king's henchmen heard about this, they burned the Namboodiri alive in a firewood stove. During a Koothu at the Nedunganad Thali situated in the bazaar area of Pallippuram, the Chakyar during his narrative act asked the king directly, 'What is the burning smell of the mango tree bark?' It is said that, following his narration, and still in full costume, the Chakyar swam across the Bharatapuzha [Nila] river and obtained refuge in the kingdom of Cochin."[83] We can see that Rajendu's version encompasses a threefold variation, not only of the offending king—here the king of Nedunganad—but also of the king providing refuge and the victim's family, the Manthodu instead of Manthitta Namboodiri family. Due to the ever-changing nature of legends and communal memory, we will never know for sure. Based on S. Rajendu's research, however, it appears very likely that the murder of the Namboodiri—considered one of the greatest sins possible—and the intended murder of the Chakyar who brought this to light, were most likely committed by the king of Nedunganadu, a lesser king under the larger suzerainty of the Zamorin. From what we have seen here, it seems that the Zamorin dominates Kerala's historical imagination as the primary ruler associated with the Malabar area, attributed over time even with deeds he likely did not commit.

Conclusion

As shown throughout the chapter, these three aithihyam legends offer a lens onto Kerala's cosmopolitan history through descriptions of cosmopolitan encounters and circulation in Kutiyattam's past. A perhaps less obvious theme these tales share is resistance to authority. The first two narratives showcase a resistance to foreign authority—to Tipu Sultan, a Muslim ruler from a neighboring land with a different language and culture, and to the British, from a land far across the sea. In the case of Tipu Sultan, this resistance is to a foreign authority imposed by military force, and in the case of the British, by threat of military force already clearly demonstrated in other areas of the subcontinent. The third legend, however, describes a resistance to a royal abuse of power by a native king. This comes in the form of the king's secret murder of a Brahmin, a group that kings generally did not have the authority to prosecute. The actor in this legend evidences a twofold resistance: a direct form by publicly calling out the king's abuse of power during performance, and an indirect form by secretly fleeing the kingdom to avoid the king's wrath. These tales of resistance all involve a feat of courageous risk-taking. In the case of the tale involving Tipu Sultan as well as that of the murderous king, this risk-taking is self-evident, with actors risking life and limb to fulfill their duties to perform and, as part of performance, to critique. Risk-taking may seem less apparent in the tale of the Englishman and the dog, yet when the actor chooses to enact a scene in which he throws a large object at the colonialist, he takes a calculated risk. In performing this symbolic act of aggression, the Chakyar protagonist risks further angering the already enraged Englishman and incurring some form of punishment as a result. His triumph over the Englishman thus comes at a potentially high price.

One of the fundamental assumptions within folkloristics is that folklore is a window onto a community's culture and values. As stressed above, if narratives are told today, this means that they hold meaning for their contemporary community of tellers. When narratives tell of the past, they reveal more about how people in the present interpret and relate to the past than about the past itself. Wider approaches to the historical imagination acknowledge that the past is inescapably viewed through the lens of the present. Renowned Kerala-based historian Kesavan Veluthat (2009, 134) has noted that the history of any society offers a window onto the contemporary concerns of that society, as it reveals which events of the past they consider more important than others. A protegée of Veluthat, Haridas (2016, 251) has similarly stated that in the process of history writing, "the present looks at its past . . . to serve a specific purpose." In this case, Haridas is referring to an eighteenth-century "present," in which history was used to justify the Zamorin's rule. As folk narratives circulate orally over time, the narrative present, its relationship to the past, and the associated meanings narratives hold for their tellers are constantly in flux. These shifting meanings underscore the importance of the methodology of asking tellers what their particular narratives mean to them as a way to gain insight into their social function and meaning.

What current community values and visions of the past do these legends reveal? Let us start with what they reveal about the past and Kutiyattam artists' perceptions of the past. As I have argued here, the personal legends we see in this chapter are examples of nonofficial or vernacular histories, histories from below that provide a nonruling perspective of Kerala's past.[84] These are not subaltern or nonelite histories because the Kutiyattam community has always had elite status and close ties with those in power. However, they offer glimpses beyond official, top-down histories. Tellers assert that these legends represent accounts of the lives of Kutiyattam artists of yore, and, as we have seen, the details of each legend generally align with official historical events, personages, and chronologies. We cannot be certain of their historical accuracy, just as Usha-teacher defined the aithihyam genre by its historical uncertainty—its description of events that occurred just long enough ago that we cannot really be sure they happened in the way the tales claim they do. Despite this uncertainty, however, we also cannot discount them. I argue that these narratives are a rich resource for filling in the everyday gaps of wider records of Kerala's cosmopolitan history. Artists generally claim them as truth, and it is this belief in their truth value that informs how Kutiyattam artists relate to their past as part of the process of placing themselves in the present.

As legend scholarship emphasizes, belief always plays a primary role in these types of narratives. As Dégh and Vázsonyi (1976, 119) write, legends provide an opportunity to express an "opinion on the question of truth and belief" whether narrators and listeners believe them or not. Oring (1986, 125) further observes that, in the process of legend narration, truth must always be at least "entertained, even if that truth is ultimately rejected."[85] In their aithihyam narration, Kutiyattam artists overwhelmingly claim these tales as true, although I encountered a few exceptions. For example, one hereditary artist expressed doubt that the dog in the legend of the Englishman would have actually been convinced through acting alone that he had been hit by a stone. Rajaneesh Chakyar, on the other hand, asserted that the legend of the Englishman and the dog is definitively true because it is included in Sankunni's famous legend collection, *Aithihyaamaala*. He described the published tales as accounts of "exclusive personalities at the time [nineteenth century]" such as magicians and kings, and emphasized that "they are not belief; they actually happened." His confidence in the truth of the legends, he explained, is based on the temporal closeness of the collector Sankunni to the recounted events in the tales. He did make clear that he could not guarantee the truth value of the legend of the Englishman and Chakyar at the Hanuman temple, as it is not included in Sankunni's collection. The tale of the Englishman and the dog was the only narrative of the three examined here in which I observed elicit discussions of truth and belief. The other two legends were told by senior gurus as historical truth in a manner and context that left no room for doubt or dispute.

Truth value and historical accuracy aside, what these tales definitively reveal is a contemporary historical consciousness that takes Kerala's rich cosmopolitan history for granted. In these tales, Kutiyattam artists reckon with foreign sultans, encounter English colonialists, and regularly cross political borders to interact with rulers of various Kerala kingdoms. The tales clearly show that Kutiyattam artists were historically part of a cosmopolitan world. Spanning approximately the sixteenth to nineteenth centuries, these legends reveal one historical period of Kutiyattam's multiple cosmopolitanisms over time. Despite the remarkable history of these legends, however, storytellers often regard the cosmopolitan details and settings as not particularly noteworthy—they are simply part of their history. These details are not what matter the most in contemporary tellings and interpretations; they simply set the stage for the heroic actions of the main Chakyar characters.

The current meanings of the tales are thus not about cosmopolitanism but other values important to the contemporary Kutiyattam community—ensuring the continuity of tradition and communicating Kutiyattam's power of artistic expression. The aithihyam legends are didactic, narrated in order to transmit these values to others through lessons from the past. In terms of the continuity of tradition, they describe artists of previous generations risking their lives to fulfill their performance duties. In the process, the heroes of these tales ensure the continuity of Kutiyattam along with their own artistic integrity. The didactic nature of these stories is evident in both their narrative contexts and interpretations. In the legend about performing in the time of Tipu Sultan, Nambiar-ashan describes how his uncle narrated the tale as a lesson that he must continue to perform, even in times of uncertainty. When Nambiar-ashan told me the tale, however, it served a different function—to teach me about his family and wider community's intense dedication to ensuring that the art survived the ages. Similarly, Sajeev-ashan narrated the tale of the Chakyar confronting a murderous king to demonstrate the duty of the *vidushaka* to tell "both truths and faults" at any cost. In this performance context, the story's most obvious function—to explain how the Ammannur family came to settle in the town of Moozhikkulam—was secondary. In the legend of the Englishman and the dog, a second community value emerges—communicating the artistic power of Kutiyattam to others. The most widely known story of the three, this aithihyam serves to convey the power of Kutiyattam acting. Along with related tales of the wondrous acting of Kutiyattam artists of yore, this narrative is circulated today to teach audiences that incredible artistic feats are an important part of the art's history and that the contemporary Kutiyattam community places great value on its deep-seated tradition of artistic prowess.

As I mentioned above, narrative connections with the past reveal present claims to community membership. In this chapter, both hereditary and nonhereditary Kutiyattam artists have narrated these tales, each claiming these pasts in some way as their own. For nonhereditary artists like Sooraj, this past is peopled by artistic ancestors and represents a long line of theatrical tradition of which he is a contemporary inheritor and teacher to future generations. For hereditary artists like Nambiar-ashan and Sajeev-ashan, this past encompasses all of the above but adds a familial connection. This connection, in which artistic ancestors are simultaneously hereditary ancestors—great-uncles, grandmothers, fathers, and mothers—leads to a different sense of inheritance. Sajeev-ashan once told me that his father and uncle performed Koothu in the Moozhikkulam temple every year for forty-one days, remarking, "This is in our blood."

Regardless of whether these ancestors are familial or not, in telling these tales, artists assert and reinforce their community membership and artistic inheritance by teaching the lessons of these tales to future generations. In each moment of a legend's telling, the past becomes alive in the present, creating a bridge of affinity and identification between artists in the present and those in the past. Each time a legend is shared with junior artists, the telling simultaneously functions as part of the latter's initiation into the "collective memory" of the community (Halbwachs 1992). As Guha (2019) asserts, oral narration is one of the oldest and most widespread ways of representing and transmitting memory around the world. It is more democratic and durable than even the texts created by scribes and other memory specialists. Guha considers the "narrative past" one of three types of pasts—the grammatical past, the narrative past, and the historical narration of the past—that, when propagated and spread, become social memory. As Zerubavel (2004, 3) has noted, "Acquiring a group's memories and thereby identifying with its collective past is part of the process of acquiring any social identity, and familiarising members with that past is a major part of communities [sic] efforts to assimilate them."[86] In telling these aithihyam personal legends, artists actively sustain the community's collective history as guardians of memory carrying the Kutiyattam community into the future.

Notes

1. In the Sanskritic vernaculars, a similar true and false distinction is made between *kathā* and *kahānī*, the former a religious story believed to be true and the latter a fictional, secular tale (Narayan 1989, 39), and between *kīssās* (myths and legends) and *kahānīs* (Wadley 1986, 199). This query is inspired by Dan Ben-Amos's (1969) famous call to explore emic categorizations of folklore.

2. See also Oring 1986.

3. Legend transcriptions in Malayalam are available upon request.

4. For an example of how the interpretation of narratives by tellers and listeners may conflict with academic analyses, see Lowthorp's (2014) study of the Irish Kerryman joke.

5. As Dundes (1966, 506–507) emphasizes, "*Folklorists must actively seek to elicit the meaning of folklore from the folk*" (emphasis in original).

6. See Rao, Shulman, and Subrahmanyam 2001; Veluthat 2009; and Guha 2019.

7. Guru P. K. Narayanan Nambiar sadly passed away at ninety-six in late 2023.

8. They performed at the Madras Academy of Music upon Dr. V. Raghavan's invitation; see chapter 6 for more.

9. See chapters 5 and 6 for more details.

10. Although he does not identify a specific individual by name, Nambiar-ashan considers the legend's protagonists his ancestors, making this a personal legend. Some may disagree.

11. Nambiar-ashan's younger brother P. K. G. Nambiar relayed a legend involving Kutiyattam performance at Triprayar temple, where his family has hereditary rights. When the Chakyar found himself performing to an empty hall, the temple deity spoke, reassuring him not to be upset because the deity was always watching. This is told to explain why the stage at this temple is unusually placed directly in front of the deity's *mandapa* (pavilion).

12. In a 2006 interview, Dr. C. K. Jayanthi's paternal aunt, eighty-five-year-old Kochampilly Thankammu Nangiaramma, revealed that her maternal grandmother mentioned here, Kutty (Nangeli) Nangiaramma, performed the scene seven times; see SNA 2006b.

13. See also Haridas 2016; Pillai 2015.

14. The Malayalam term for Zamorin is *Sāmūtiri*. Often speculated to mean "lord of the sea," Manmadhan (2020) discusses other potential etymologies.

15. Belonging to the lineage (*svarūpam*) Eranad, alternatively known as Netiyirippu, the other three lineages this version of the *Keralolpatti* entrusts with Kerala's rule are Kolattiri (Cannanore), Venad (Travancore), and Perimpatappu (Cochin) (Menon 2003, 91). See Prange (2018, 93–110) for more on this version of the narrative and related period politics.

16. Summarized and translated by Haridas from Gundert's (1868) *Keralolpatti*. Zamorin family member and vernacular historian Ullattil Manmadhan disagrees with the above, clarifying that the departing Perumal bestowed only the right to "kill and annex"—the Nediyirippu rights existed previously and trade rights belonged to the ruler, but he did not actually navigate the seas (pers. comm., January 16 and 18, 2021).

17. As Prange (2018, 284) writes, the last high king served as a "virtual overlord for Malabar's various 'little kings,' who could call on him as a source of legitimation". Frenz (2000, 162) compares this use of Cheraman Perumal in Kerala's history with that of Charlemagne in European history.

18. The 1607 Arabi-Malayalam poem *Muhyiddin Mala*, describing a battle between the Portuguese and the Zamorin's Muslim and Hindu forces, also claims the Zamorin loved Muslims above all other subjects (Sutton 2015, 78). There are several foreign accounts of the Zamorin; see Alam and Subrahmanyam 2007, Barbosa 1812, and Nieuhoff 2003, among others.

19. I would like to thank Ullattil Manmadhan for pointing this out. The legend of Prester John, which persisted throughout Europe from the twelfth to eighteenth centuries, must be seen within a "larger narrative of Christian global expansion . . . [as it] proferred an expectation that the known world would succumb inevitably to the will of a global Christendom" (Taylor 2014, 446); see also Manmadhan 2016.

20. See also Prange 2018, 44. Barbosa lived in both Cannanore and Cochin.

21. Menon (2019, 248–251) describes how the Mysorean invasion led to significant lasting changes in Malabar society. One was a new tax system that circumvented landlords by collecting tax directly from tenants, giving lower castes greater dignity and voice. Muslim favoritism during this period also led to tensions between Muslims and Hindus and, when discontinued by the British, sparked the nineteenth-century Mappila uprisings. See also Menon 1999.

22. The royal family still proudly displays Tipu Sultan's captured personal standard in processions at the Sri Padmanabhaswamy temple in Trivandrum (Pillai 2015, 562).

23. This pension or privy purse was known as *malikhana.*

24. See Pillai 2015.

25. Begun by the Perumal high kings of Kerala, Mamankam was a religious and political festival held every twelve years until 1755. There are a number of accounts of Mamankam from visiting foreigners at the time.

26. See Haridas (2016, 170) for a more detailed summary. Ammannur Rajaneesh Chakyar performed Rama's coronation on the temple stage for the first time in one hundred years in 2017 at Koodalmanikyam temple, Irinjalakuda.

27. See Venu 2002 for more details.

28. For other versions, see K. P. S. Menon 1994, 132; Venu 1988, 15–16; 2002, 37.

29. See Venu 2002, 37 for an example of the latter. K. P. S. Menon (1994, 132) claims that the Chakyar actually threw the stone at the Englishman.

30. Another legend in the collection titled "King Uthram Tirunal Marthanda Varma and His Kathakali Troupe" describes this earlier event.

31. See also Venu 1988, 14–15; 2002, 36–37.

32. This scene is from the fourth act of Harshavardhana's play *Nagananda.* The scene entails Garuda swooping down from the top of a hill to pick up Jimuta Vahana, who is lying on the ground. For more information, see K. P. S. Menon 1994, 130–131; Venu 1988, 14. The Nambiar is sometimes identified as Kunjan Nambiar.

33. Venu (1988) provides a description, although the source is unclear.

34. Usha Nangiar (2018, 74) cites this proverb in English translation. Salini Harikrishnan kindly provided the original Malayalam proverb. Everyone in the Kutiyattam community is familiar with these legends as narratives, often simply referenced as the "flying Chakyar" or "flowing Nangiar."

35. Mani Madhava Chakyar details the special responsibilities that a Nambiar traditionally had in addition to his regular duties, including "tightly twisting the cloth for representing the hanging of the heroine in *Nagananda,* 'holding the string' in 'Parakkum Kuttu' in *Nagananda,* and warping the threads in 'Ozhukilankam'" (The Act of Drowning) (1994a, 51). He states that "these scenes, unless done with care and precision, are fraught with danger" (1994a, 51).

36. See Dr. P. Venugopalan's video-recorded interview with Kochampalli Thankammu Nangiaramma, SNA 2006b. She describes performing several roles before marriage, including the hanging scene at age fourteen or fifteen, and after marriage only playing the *kuzhithalam* cymbals and reciting Sanskrit verses onstage.

37. In addition to those mentioned previously, Usha Nangiar (2018, 95, 259) includes the well-known legend that explains the origin of Nangiarkoothu, namely, that King Kulashekhara was so enamored of the skills of one Nangiar that he married her and created the solo performance of Nangiarkoothu for her. Another involves Pappi Nangiar, who married into the royal family of Kochi and taught acting to the famous Kathakali actor Itteeri Paniker; see Nangiar 2018, 259–260 and K. P. S. Menon 1994, 139–140 for more examples.

38. The interview is available in the Sangeet Natak Akademi archives in New Delhi. Titled "Interview with Ammannur Parameswara Chakyar," it was conducted by P. Venugopalan on April 14–15, 2006; SNA 2006a.

39. Interestingly, Manmadhan (2018) describes how Englishmen were widely believed in India to have descended from Hanuman, and he hypothesizes a possible connection between this and Kathakali's Hanuman costume.

40. See also Naithani 1997, 2002.

41. Korom (1989, 61) similarly notes that themes of British exploitation arise frequently in Bengali folklore.

42. Another example is folk songs in North Kerala that celebrate the eighteenth-century minor king Kerala Varma Pazhassi Raja of Kottayam (Wayanad district). Betrayed by the English East India Company whom he had helped defend from Tipu Sultan's forces several times, he fought the British for over a decade using guerrilla tactics in a series of confrontations known as the Cotiote War. He was killed in an 1805 ambush. British general Arthur Wellesley, celebrated for his guerilla tactics that led to victories over Napoleon in Spain, spent years in Malabar unsuccessfully fighting Pazhassi Raja. Kerala historians attribute the tactics he learned from his battles with the Kottayam king to Wellesley's ultimate success at Waterloo (Menon 2018). For more about Pazhassi Raja, see Menon 1999. The 2009 film made about him, *Kerala Varma Pazhassi Raja* (dir. T. Hariharan), was the highest-grossing Malayalam film ever produced until that point.

43. The Kingdom of Cochin was also a princely state along the same model.

44. For more on the link between humor and resistance, see Dundes 1971; Oring 2004; Stokker 1995.

45. He defeated the Dutch at the Battle of Colachel in 1741, widely celebrated as the first Indian power to defeat a European naval force (Pillai 2015). The Indian Army celebrates this victory today (Special Correspondent 2010). After the Dutch surrender, former Dutch commander Eustachius De Lannoy went on to train Marthanda Varma's army; see De Lannoy 1986.

46. See Sobhanan 1978.

47. I would like to thank Ullattil Manmadhan for aiding this translation and pointing out that mango tree firewood is often used for cremating the dead.

48. For other versions, see K. P. S. Menon 1994, 130; Rajendu 2012, 289; Venu 1988, 13.

49. See Haring 1972 for issues surrounding soliciting tales via interview versus in context.

50. For further legends of the Chakyar's critique of the powerful, particularly kings and Namboodiri Brahmins, see Johan 2014, vol. 1, 277–278.

51. For example, see Abrahams 1987.

52. Born Ammannur Parameswara Chakyar. Chachu was a nickname.

53. Chachu Chakyar died in 1967, three years after Sajeev-ashan was born (Madhu and Nambiar 1994). See Cashman 2008 for the difference between the genres of anecdote and personal legend.

54. Popularly called the Abdicated Highness, King Rama Varma XV ruled Cochin from 1895 to 1914. Pradeep 2015 attributes his abdication to pro-German politics and ill health.

55. See Paulose 2006, 147–148 and Venu 1988, 2002 for Chachu Chakyar's additional points of critique. Sajeev-ashan remarked that Chachu Chakyar used the verse to criticize several acts of the king, including adjudicating the well-known court case of Kuriyedathu Thaatri, a Namboodiri woman accused of adultery with dozens of powerful men. This excommunicated many Namboodiris, including any children fathered after the discretion occurred, in a process known as a caste inquisition (*smārttavicāram*), whereby Namboodiri children were "demoted" to Chakyars, Illodammas, Nambiars, or Nangiars. Painkulam Narayana Chakyar explained that his Painkulam (Koypa) Chakyar family gained new members this way sometime in the last few centuries. See A. M. N. Chakiar 1999 and Nilayamgode 2011 for autobiographical accounts of demotion to Kutiyattam castes as a result of the Thaatri case. See Johan 2014, vol. 1, 147–159 for a description of other cases of known conversions to the Kutiyattam community.

56. For other versions, see Johan 2014, vol. 1, 277; K. P. S. Menon 1994, 132–133; Paulose 2006, 147–148; Ramavarma 1981, 2–6; Venu 1988, 17–20; 2002, 39–41.

57. For more information on *marumakkathayam*, see Fuller 1976; Gough 1955, 1959, 1978.

58. See Johan for more on this kinship system among Chakyars (2014, vol. 1, 65–83, 88–97) and genealogical charts of Chakyar families (2000, 2014, vol. 3, 24–28). See G. K. Nambiar 2010 for genealogies of all Chakyar/Illodamma and Nambiar/Nangiar families.

59. See Arunima 2003 for early twentieth-century legislative and social changes concerning matriliny in Kerala, and Jeffrey 2004 for later twentieth-century changes.

60. We see both processes at work in Nambiar-ashan's family, which unusually led to children of several generations residing and having close relationships with their fathers for over a century. It began when Mani Madhava Chakyar's maternal uncle, Mani Parameswara Chakyar, moved to his wife's home in Killikkurrissimangalam, and he subsequently followed suit.

61. See Johan 2014, vol. 1, 83–87; 2017b, 37 for more details.

62. Sajeev-ashan's nephew, whose mother is also from a different community, has done the same.

63. According to Ramavarma 1978, this involved Koypa Kandar (Nilakanthan) Chakyar being killed at Govindapuram koothambalam for

presenting a work of Chennas Narayanan Nambudiripad criticizing the king's "misgovernment."

64. K. P. S. Menon's (1994, 139) version of this legend varies in many ways: naming the Chakyar killed as Kandar's brother, Koypa Chattaru (Sastrasarman) Chakyar, and stating that the family left Vanneri first for Trikkalloor, only later going to Pandalur. He also notes that the family left for Painkulam in 1790–1791 during the "social disturbances" in Eranad, ostensibly caused by Tipu Sultan.

65. This occurred in 1874. The main branch of the family today resides in Irinjalakuda.

66. Veluthat (2018) argues that Kerala became identified as a distinct region by the sixteenth century CE.

67. See P. R. Chakyar 1994 for a list of all eighteen original Chakyar families, including which families took over the duties of those whose line died out, and which merged with others. Chakyar families dying out is not the only way that other families gained new performance duties. As P. R. Chakyar (1994) and Johan (2014) note, some Chakyar families merged with others over time, automatically taking over their duties. Some families were awarded the duties of others who had fallen out of political favor or were awarded new duties through political favor (Johan 2014, vol. 1, 176–181).

68. The Zamorin was a major exception to this, having a particular interest in controlling temples.

69. See Tarabout 2009 concerning competing claims over Annamanada temple and its lands.

70. Rajaneesh noted that this took place in the Sri Poornathreyeesa temple in Thrippunithura.

71. See Menon 2003, 78–80.

72. Veluthat 2009, 262–264, 268 describes various local nodes of power, including petty chiefs, Brahmin villages, non-Brahmin autonomous areas, and landed magnates, either temples or individual "lords."

73. See Haridas 2016, 261–292 for more details about the festival.

74. Quoted from an introductory sign at the heritage site of Changampally Kalari, part of Kerala state's protected monument complex known as Mamanka Smarakam (Mamankam Memorial).

75. See Bayly 1984 for a discussion of different types of *chaver* in medieval Kerala.

76. For a deeper exploration of the Zamorin's political approach to culture, including his sponsorship of Krishnanattam, see Haridas 2016, especially 231–292.

77. See Haridas 2016, 275.

78. This incident is likely a legend, as Ayyar (1938, 301) notes that it happened "according to tradition" and involved famed scholars Chennas Namputiri and Mullapalli Nambudiri.

79. See Goren Arzony 2019, 311.

80. Veluthat (2009, 141) observes that Zamorins were keenly aware that their caste status was inferior to other Kerala kings. See also Haridas 2016, 163, 313.

81. Bayly (1984, 178) notes that Hindu rulers in Travancore and Cochin implemented "thorough-going changes in military organization, in the machinery of state, in caste leadership and in the structures of court culture and religious life throughout their domains."

82. Rajendu's attribution hails from a 2021 conversation that Ullattil Manmadhan, connected to the Calicut royal family, had with him. As Manmadhan conveyed to me via email, Rajendu explained that Koppam village in Pattambi subdistrict, where the Ammannur family home was situated, was in those times part of Nedunganad. He is therefore certain that the Nedunganad raja was the king involved in the Ammannur story, not the Zamorin or the Valluva Konathiri (also known as the Vellatri or Velathiri). He also reported that the Namboodiri involved was from the Manthodu Namboodiri home, not the present-day Manthittta Namboodiri home, mentioning that his legend passage is based on multiple oral testimonies (email communication, January 18, 2021).

83. See also Rajendu 2016, 83–84, n. 224. I would like to thank Ullattil Manmadhan for bringing Rajendu's work to my attention, assisting in its translation, and inquiring with Rajendu as to the king's identity.

84. Rao, Shulman, and Subrahmanyam (2001, 11) have also queried whether the alternative forms of history that they discuss constitute a "history from below."

85. See also Cashman 2008.

86. See also Guha 2019.

5

KERALA, COMMUNISM, AND HERITAGE

Reinventing Tradition at Kerala Kalamandalam

Figure 30. Kalamandalam Shivan Namboodiri as Ravana. Photo by author.

The warm hues of the late afternoon sun flood the room at Margi where Usha-teacher and I sit chatting after the students leave, awaiting our daily afternoon chai together. Teacher's jolly, outgoing husband, Joby-chetan, usually brings chai and snacks from a nearby tea stall during his afternoon breaks, often sweeping into the room with a greeting that playfully mimics my accented Malayalam—"Namaskāram namaskāram." Carrying a metal canister of piping hot chai in one hand and a newspaper-wrapped bundle of fried snacks in the other, he brings an array of tasty Kerala snacks—breaded sweet plantains and green chilies fried in coconut oil, golden-hued savory doughnuts dipped in coconut chutney, or, my personal favorite, crispy balls of fried onions and dough that melt in your mouth, one crunchy bite at a time. Today, however, Joby-chetan is running errands, so Usha-teacher and I set off on foot toward a nearby tea stall. We head through the narrow, shaded alleyways surrounding the temple adjacent to Margi where Namboodiri (Kerala Brahmin) and other upper-caste families associated with the temple live in their small, tightly packed homes, with beautifully intricate *kolam* patterns drawn daily in white chalk or rice flour before their front entrances. The air is heavy with the sweet smell of frying coconut oil, and our eyes are met with various arrays of brightly colored clothing hung to dry in the sun. Neighbors warmly greet Teacher along the way, sometimes jokingly urging their children, who shyly protest, to accompany me back to America.

Emerging out of the quiet alleyway onto the main road, Kerala's public sphere is on full display. Prominent movie posters and placards featuring photos of local children earning the highest school marks dot the walls of shops and businesses. Alongside these are various political posters and graffiti, some calling for the general strike that recently shut down all transportation and movement in the state. Particularly noticeable to an outsider such as myself are the many communist symbols on display. At a nearby junction, several flagpoles fly large cherry red flags featuring white hammer and sickle symbols alongside the acronym "CPI(M)," which stands for the Communist Party of India (Marxist), a main political party in Kerala. I notice that many of the nearby electricity poles are painted with the iconic image of Che Guevara alongside the acronym "DYFI" (the Democratic Youth Federation of India), the youth wing of the CPI(M). Kerala is widely known for electing the world's first large-scale democratic communist government in 1957, and the Left continues to be a dominant political and social force in the state today.

We spot a busy tea stall next to the political paraphernalia with clusters of men socializing over chai, coffee, and snacks. We opt for our preferred stall, a quieter, less male-dominated space where we can sit and take our time. The friendly tea maker smiles his affirmation of our order and dramatically pours the chai back and forth from a considerable height before handing us the hot liquid. We choose a table in the back and wait for our chai to cool, watching the thick puffs of steam wafting into the air before daring a sip. After discussing recent happenings, I ask Usha-teacher a question I will eventually ask all Kutiyattam artists I interview, namely, "Teacher, do you consider Kutiyattam a Keralan, Indian, or global art form, and did your opinion change before versus after the art's UNESCO recognition as intangible cultural heritage?"

I try to articulate my motivation behind asking this question, observing that Kutiyattam is no longer confined to the temple stage and is now performed on public stages all over Kerala, India, and the world. Explaining that I would like to explore how exposure to these larger arenas has affected the identity of Kutiyattam artists, Usha-teacher interrupts me, laughing, "You mean how they *tried* to affect our identity, but it didn't work!" She then states matter-of-factly, "Kutiyattam is Kerala's tradition." She continues by describing what she views as the uniqueness of Kerala, saying, "Even if it is a part of India, Kerala's culture is special, with its customs and rituals. In other places you can enter temples normally, but here you can only enter after purifying yourself. . . . And Kerala has a special beauty. In India if you go to each place, the atmosphere changes significantly. When you go to the north, east, west, it is really hot and really cold. . . . Kerala's culture is special, because Kerala's atmosphere is nice, everyone likes it—it is not too hot, not too cold." Kerala is, in effect, just right.

Since the second half of the twentieth century, Kutiyattam has been embedded in several realms of official identity construction—Kerala state; the Indian nation; and, through UNESCO designation, the world. Yet for Usha-teacher, as for most artists today, the region persists as the primary site of her artistic identity. While answers to my question varied, the overwhelming majority of artists responded that Kutiyattam is a "Kerala art form," with several further emphasizing their position with phrases like "It is *definitely*" or "*only* a Kerala art form." Sindhu-chechi (Kalamandalam Sindhu) even repeated that Kutiyattam is "*only* Kerala's" (*Kēraḷattinde mātram*) in ten different ways, just to make sure I completely understood her.

What does it mean for an art form to *belong* to Kerala? How did a temple art performed exclusively by and for the caste elite across multiple regional kingdoms over nearly one thousand years come to be conceptualized as *belonging* to the region, and its people, as a whole? And, perhaps most intriguing, how did an elite temple art come to represent the official heritage of a communist state? Within a framework that considers how the rise of democratic communism in Kerala paradoxically led to the creation of a regional heritage canon that embraces elite upper-caste arts, this chapter examines Kutiyattam's twentieth-century reinvention at the Kerala Kalamandalam state performing arts institution. Centered on reimagining the production of plays and women's roles onstage through discourses of beauty and democratization, I consider the caste and gender dynamics of the art's reinvention for local communist audiences. Exploring the efforts of Guru Painkulam Rama Chakyar to make Kutiyattam simultaneously more "*bhangi/bhamgi*" (beautiful) and *less elite* in order to appeal to communist audiences, my study offers a significant contrast to those detailing the "sanitization" of women's bodies-in-performance in other classical Indian arts, made to embody a newly imagined upper-caste Indian nation. At the same time, I move forward Peterson and Soneji's (2008a, 2008b) push to expand the historiography of South Indian classical performing arts beyond the "elite nationalist project" to focus on the region.

~

Communism and Regional Heritage in Kerala

Figure 31. Communist public imagery in Kerala. Photo by author.

History of Communism in Kerala

Twentieth-century Kerala experienced immense social, economic, and political upheavals that transformed its "rigid, closed, and compartmentalized society" into a socially and geographically mobile, highly educated, and politically active population (Jeffrey 1992). Jeffrey (1992) names the destruction of the region's matrilineal joint family system, the spread of formal education and literacy, rising political activism, and an increasing cash economy as primary factors behind the rise to power of the Communist Party in Kerala. During this period, communism was a cosmopolitan ideology that inspired people around the world to translate its principles into political action in vastly different ways. In Kerala, political activists transformed these cosmopolitan ideas into democratic political practice, resulting in the first large-scale democratically elected communist government in the world. Drawing on the writings of EMS Namboodiripad (henceforth EMS), this section considers the rise of Communism in Kerala. The "undisputed leader and theoretician of the communist movement in Kerala," EMS was the state's first chief minister from 1957 until the Indian central government disbanded his communist ministry in 1959 (Devika 2010, 802).

At the turn of the twentieth century, Kerala had the strictest caste system in all of India, with some castes not only "untouchable" but "unseeable" as well. If a high-caste individual appeared on the road, lower castes (known as Dalits) were expected to run away, upon pain of death, until they had reached a prespecified distance. Caste inequality, intimately tied to social and economic inequality, was the most important issue of the times, and a number of caste-based movements sprang up that advocated for reform. Among the most influential of these was the lower-caste Ezhava reform movement led by Sri Narayana Guru and his association, the SNDP Yogam. Founded in 1903, this movement sought to abolish untouchability and gain political recognition (Lukose 2006). Guided by Narayana Guru's famous motto "One caste, one religion, one God for Mankind," the activists of the SNDP Yogam tirelessly advocated for the civil rights of the Ezhava, and still do today. Among the movement's greatest achievements was gaining entry for Dalits into Hindu temples, previously only accessible to higher castes. Their iconic *satyāgraha* (nonviolent resistance) campaign at Vaikom temple from 1924 to 1925 gained national attention and support from Mahatma Gandhi and became the first step toward the goal of temple entry by advocating for the right of Ezhava to use the roads surrounding temples (Jeffrey 1976). While a failure in the short term, the campaign ultimately led to temple entry proclamations across Kerala beginning in the mid-1930s that threw open temple doors to all Hindus.[1] This inspired young activists who would later play an important role in Kerala's communist movement. A young activist himself at the time, EMS notes that the anti-high-caste movements of Kerala's lower castes significantly led him toward leftist ideas (Namboodiripad 2010a, 105).

Dilip Menon (1994) argues that the success of Communism in twentieth-century Kerala was ensured by its self-promotion as a doctrine of not only economic and social equality but also caste equality. Early Socialists in Kerala, many of whom later became Communists, sought a secular culture that would enable them to transcend caste and religious identities.[2] As EMS observes, "The development of the democratic movement (in Kerala) is bound to be linked with the organized struggle against caste-Hindu domination" (Namboodiripad 2010a, 107). Devika (2010, 805) specifies that "because demeaning caste practices were so closely entangled with feudal hierarchy in Kerala, struggle against the latter was well-nigh impossible to conceive without struggle against the former." Lower-caste movements in early twentieth-century Kerala made the link between knowledge and power explicit and, as a result, focused on increasing literacy. D. Menon (1994) notes that a new culture emerged around reading rooms established by caste associations—and, later, trade unions and political associations—across Malabar.[3] In these, the communal drinking of tea and coffee accompanied the communal reading of newspapers, where one person would read aloud while the others listened and then discussed. As tea and coffee were newly introduced beverages, there were no existing taboos on sharing them between castes. This fostered an environment of solidarity across caste boundaries, with the reading rooms becoming "central to socialist organization in the villages" (1994, 150). As D. Menon (1994, 147) states, "Through the readings rooms, newspapers and tea shops a whole new world was imagined, and discussions built up a collective memory of organization."

At the time, Gandhi and the Indian National Congress (Congress Party) were not willing to associate caste inequality with unequal social and economic realities. Instead, they located the problem of caste inequality in physical difference—in degrees of cleanliness and uncleanliness—thereby pushing the increasing numbers of Kerala's social justice–minded citizenry away from them and toward the Communist Party of India (CPI), whose Kerala unit was founded in 1939 (D. Menon 1994, 85).[4] As EMS reflects, "The Marxist call, 'workers of the world, unite,' inspired us all. We, therefore, did not allow the caste, the communal or any other consideration to stand in the way of the workers' unity against the capitalists, the peasants' against the landlords, other sections of the working people for their own demands—all of them against British imperialism and autocratic rule in the princely states" (Namboodiripad 2010a, 107). Yet the national CPI was accused of being antinationalist for supporting the "sectarian" causes of oppressed castes and religious minorities. The CPI was again accused of being antinationalist when, initially "rallying the people behind the Soviet Union and other forces of the world revolutionary movement, even while fighting British imperialism," the party came out against the Quit India movement after the Soviet Union entered World War II as a British ally (2010a, 116).[5] The CPI's shift from opposing World War II as an "Imperialist War" to supporting it as a "People's War" led to the British legalization of the Communist Party in 1942 (Gupta 2006). Before this, the CPI had been an illegal underground organization, with its leaders across India, including Kerala, regularly jailed.[6]

The newly established Kerala branch of the CPI asserted leadership in the United Kerala (*Aikya Kēraḷam*) movement as it reached its height in the early to mid-1940s, claiming "the moral authority to speak for Kerala's linguistic unity and national identity" (Devika 2010, 801).[7] Aiming to combine the three Malayalam-speaking areas of Travancore, Cochin, and Malabar into one political unit, the movement had to contend with the Dravidian nationalist movement in the neighboring area of present-day Tamil Nadu state. Exemplified by the motto "Divide on the basis of language, unite on the basis of race," the Dravidian nationalist movement sought to create a separate nation that would unite the Dravidian language–speaking regions of South India, including Malabar (Menon 2006). Based on an Orientalist-constructed idea that Dravidian language speakers constitute a distinct "Dravidian" race, this racial identity was constructed against a North Indian "Aryan" racial identity composed of Indo-European language speakers.[8] Creating a Brahmin/non-Brahmin opposition, the movement conceptualized the upper-caste Brahmin as an ancient "invader" of South India who forcefully imposed the caste system on existing egalitarian models, placing himself at the top of social and religious hierarchies. Viewing Brahmins as symbols of North Indian imperialism, Dravidian nationalists sought to expel all Brahmins from South India. For proponents of the United Kerala movement attempting to define their own political identity as Malayalam speakers, the Dravidian nationalist movement appeared to border on "regional imperialism" (2006, 40).

To counter the Dravidian critique, EMS, himself a Namboodiri Brahmin, wrote a Marxist history of Kerala that engaged in what Menon (2006) characterizes as a deliberate misunderstanding of Marxism for the political purpose of imagining a regional Kerala unity undivided along Brahmin/non-Brahmin lines. In his *Kerala, the Motherland of the Malayalis* (*Kēraḷam, Malayāḷikaḷute Mātṛubhūmi*), EMS ([1948] 2017) argues that, through their introduction of the caste system, Brahmins played a pivotal role in furthering the historical development of Kerala's productive forces and regional culture *in cooperation with*, rather than in opposition to, the Dravidian culture already present. As Menon posits (2006, 44), EMS thereby "recover[ed] a role for the nambudiri as the prime mover in the economic and social transformation of the region," facilitated through adapting Marxist thought. Drawing on a wider sentiment in Kerala at the time that patrilineal monogamy within the nuclear family represented "progress," while matrilineal polyandry within the joint family represented a "primitive" past, EMS (1952) also suggested that Brahmins introduced a "patriarchal" model to Kerala that allowed its society to progress away from "matriarchal" family forms. He thereby conceptualized Brahmins and their caste-based culture as part of a past that was a necessary stage in a linear model of Kerala's historical progress and inevitable modernization. In 1956, the national States Reorganization Act established the united Malayalam-speaking Kerala state that the Communists had desired. In 1957, EMS led the Communists to victory in the first state election, becoming Kerala's first chief minister.

The next several decades, however, would be politically tumultuous, often intertwined with the fate of Communism on the world stage. This first political victory was short-lived, with EMS's communist ministry dismissed by the president of India in 1959, mainly due to the anticommunist operations of the CIA and the US Embassy in India (Ajayan 2017). To accomplish their goal of "install[ing] a non-communist stable government in Kerala to meet the dangers of communism in Asia," these US agencies provided substantial funding to a block of political parties opposing the CPI in Kerala's 1960 election, known as the United Front (2017, 212).[9] Among the accusations that the United Front leveled against the CPI was its antinationalist "extraterritorial loyalties" to other communist nations (2017, 212). While the United Front won the election, many prominent Communist leaders retained their legislative seats, and the Communist Party ended up winning a greater number of votes than in 1957, demonstrating that the party's power had not diminished.

Various unstable political coalitions characterized Kerala politics for the next two decades, yet the state had a communist chief minister during all but six of those years. At the national level, internal party disputes over international issues like the Sino-Soviet split, "de-Stalinization" in the Soviet Union, and the Sino-Indian border dispute led to a party split between the rightists, who remained in the CPI, and the leftists, who formed the CPI(M).[10] The latter quickly became the dominant party both in Kerala and nationally. Representing the CPI(M), EMS returned to lead the state government from 1967 to 1969, overseeing the important Kerala Land Reforms (Amendment) Act of 1969. Considered among the most radical and successful in South Asia, the act abolished tenancy and resulted in a large-scale redistribution of land rights (Franke and Chasin 1994). According to Devika (2010), however, the gains accrued mostly to the intermediate and upper castes, who became the state's new elite.

From 1982 onward, the status quo became a steady power shift every five years between two political coalitions—the Communist-led Left Democratic

Front (LDF) and the Congress-led United Democratic Front (UDF), with the latter generally leaning left to appeal to the wider Kerala electorate. This predictable power shift was broken in Kerala's 2021 election when the LDF won an unprecedented second term that many have attributed to its highly lauded response to the coronavirus pandemic; it is unknown what this may bode for the future of leftist politics in the state.

The long-standing dominance of communism in Kerala sparked the celebrated narrative of "egalitarian developmentalism" that views the state as a model for development both in Kerala and worldwide, rendering ongoing caste inequalities invisible. Devika (2010, 802) describes a "secularized casteism" dominant in Kerala today that developed "in and through precisely the powerful anticaste struggles by communists since the 1930s, which destroyed the traditional caste order, . . . [yet] the 'disappearance of the landlord class' is not the same as the disappearance of caste as an axis of political power in modern Kerala." As she poignantly asserts, "The exclusion of Dalits was not an accident in the history of left politics and developmentalism in Kerala, but was connected to political strategy advantageous to the largely upper- or middle-caste elites" (2010, 815). Predominantly upper-caste communist leaders in Kerala like EMS strategically used their caste privilege, thereby assuming a "moral right" to transform the lower castes into "caste-neutral, 'working-class poor'" (2010, 806).

Regional Heritage and Identity

In 1999, Kerala was recognized by *National Geographic* magazine as a "paradise found" among the world's "50 Places of a Lifetime," marking the success of the state's tourism brand "God's Own Country."[11] With over three million views, a 2015 official tourism video on YouTube titled, "Experience Kerala, God's Own Country" showcases vibrant images of Kerala's natural and cultural heritage (Kerala Tourism 2015). Alongside images of Kerala's iconic natural beauty—sparkling beaches, forests of palm trees, and verdant mountains—the video features Kerala's colorful cultural heritage, including a smiling Sindhu-chechi in Kutiyattam's female costume. Among the art forms on display, the most prominent are Hindu: Kerala's three official classical arts—Kathakali, Kutiyattam, and Mohiniyattam—and the upper-caste women's folk dance Thiruvathirakali. Taken as a whole, the video projects images of Kerala's heritage to the world—full of natural and cultural wonders; majority Hindu yet celebrated for its interfaith harmony; and, reflecting the state's well-known radical politics, set to a soundtrack celebrating folk songs despite visuals that privilege upper-caste Hindu "classical" arts.

It may seem paradoxical that a state known for its democratic communism prominently features elite temple arts as part of its official heritage today. In the context of a communist movement led predominantly by upper-caste leaders, however, it begins to make more sense. As Menon (2006, 62) describes, "Coming at the end of a redefinition of politics in Kerala, though the rightful place of the 'working classes' was established, the culture of new Kerala was defined in terms of the culture of the caste Hindu." This section considers how the rise of democratic communism in Kerala directly fostered the creation of a regional heritage canon that fully embraces and celebrates upper-caste Hindu arts.

Heritage is conceptualized as a politically situated cultural practice that frequently promotes a state-sanctioned "consensus" view of history and, in the process, masks its own involvement in the production of power, identity, and authority (Smith 2006). As David Harvey (2005) suggests, heritage is a process concerned with the legitimization of power in both national and other cultural and social identities. Folklorists have paid special attention to the relationship between heritage and a number of subnational identities, including regional and local identities.[12] In contemporary India, discourses of local and regional identity politics have been increasing sites of contestation, often centered around the performing arts as particularly powerful reference points, and Kerala is no exception.[13] The contemporary (re)imagining of Kerala we explore here is rooted in what Bayly (1998) terms "old patriotisms" of regional bodies in India that themselves help to facilitate nationalism in the context of the modern Indian state.

According to John (2006, 234), "The land of Kerala, from very ancient times was geographically, linguistically, ethnically and culturally a single cohesive unit," and Malayalam speakers in these areas maintained a common cultural identity despite various political demarcations throughout history. While this problematic statement ignores the vast historical and present-day linguistic, ethnic, and cultural diversity of the region, it represents a widespread contemporary "national" imagining of a Hindu Kerala rooted in a deep past. Non-Hindu cultural forms tend to be excluded from the state's heritage, yet the state tourism department recently began promoting Kerala's Jewish and Christian built heritage as tourist sites while continuing to exclude Muslim built heritage.

Kerala's two foundational myths, which Thomas (2018) terms *mythistories*, contribute to this perceived deep-rooted national imaginary via the figures of Parashuram and King Mahabali. As detailed in the *Keralolpatti*, Parashuram, an incarnation of the Hindu god Vishnu, lifted Kerala from the sea by throwing his axe from Kanyakumari to Gokarna, giving the new land to the Namboodiri Brahmins he had brought from the North to rule. Veluthat (2004b) argues that this creation myth marked the emergence of a pan-Kerala identity that was upper caste, Brahminical, and Sanskritic during the Cera Kingdom (800–1124 CE). He considers the myth of Parashuram, which explains the divine establishment of Brahmins in Kerala by the god Vishnu, a political tactic used to justify new Brahminical dominance in a formerly Buddhist land (Veluthat 2004a). Since its inception, the myth has consistently justified ongoing Brahminical dominance in the region.

The myth of King Mahabali, on the other hand, details the origins of Kerala's annual Onam festival, which the state government declared "Kerala's National Festival" in 1961 because the people of the new state "were yet to feel a common 'Kerala-ness'" (Tarabout 2005, 199).[14] King Mahabali is a legendary non-Brahmin *asura* (demon) king who ruled all of Kerala in a mythical golden age characterized by "no quarrels, no cheating, no robbery, and no gossip, [when] there were no castes, and everyone was equal" (Osella and Osella 2000b, 141). Jealous of this harmony on Earth, the gods sent Vishnu incarnated as the Brahmin dwarf Vamana to punish Mahabali by tricking him into giving away his kingdom and then banishing him to the underworld. Granted one boon—the chance to visit his people once a year—the Onam festival celebrates the beloved king's annual return. As Kalidasan (2015, 104) suggests, "The cultural practices around Onam, Kerala's most popular festival, presupposes a common ancestry, a common myth of origin and a common 'civilization' for all people of Kerala . . . centred around a visiting king during whose reign the ideals of contemporary democratic practices and the policies that a welfare state dreams to achieve had all been achieved."

Though the two myths conflict, they are promoted side by side as dual narratives of Kerala's origins. While generally rejecting the figure of Parashuram, leftist politics in Kerala have widely embraced Mahabali. Osella and Osella (2000b) describe how the Kerala CPI appropriated the image of King Mahabali and universal equality as part of its United Kerala campaign. In his writings, EMS locates the kingdom of Mahabali, *Mavelinadu*, as part of the future his party was creating, stating that "a new Kerala in which equality and freedom reign, in which poverty and unemployment will be unknown, will begin to emerge. That *Mavelinadu*, which exists only in our imagination, will become a reality in the 20th century" (Namboodiripad [1946] 1999). Today, the state government still widely promotes the connection between the return of the egalitarian, non-Brahmin king and the modern welfare state, regularly initiating a number of social welfare schemes during the Onam festival season and establishing a government-owned, fair-price grocery store chain known as the "Maveli stores" (Kalidasan 2015).[15] State Onam festival celebrations today also liberally feature upper-caste temple arts such as Kathakali, Mohiniyattam, Kutiyattam, Nangiarkoothu, and Chakyarkoothu as a prominent part of the state's heritage canon. As J. Devika once observed to me, the state's Onam festival represents a significant achievement, successfully taken over from Hindus and converted into a "proxy celebration of the welfare state."[16]

The relationship between communist politics and the arts in Kerala was not always paradoxical. With the rise of the CPI in the late 1930s, Kerala's Progressive Literature Movement (PLM) emerged, its guiding principle conceived by EMS—that unlike in elite temple arts or Sanskrit literature, art should not exist for art's sake alone but for the sake of social progress (Mannathukkaren 2006, 138). According to D. Menon (1994, 149), the movement attacked the structures and values of traditional upper-caste society, condemning existing regional literature as "a product of 'feudal' culture written in languages alienated from the masses—Sanskrit and highly Sanskritized Malayalam." Progressive writers demanded a new literature, devoid of Sanskrit influence and royal or divine subjects, which would reflect the lives of ordinary people in a language that was their own (Menon 2006).[17] Upper-caste temple arts like Kathakali and Kutiyattam were likewise rejected as "subsidized by peasants but culturally restricted to the landlord," part of a general attack on high culture for its historical relationship with feudalism (2006, 60).

Joseph Mundassery, a major proponent of "art for art's sake" who would become the state's first education minister, led a split from the PLM (Mannathukkaren 2006). The dispute was resolved in his favor not long after, with EMS's determination that "both revolutionary content and aesthetically beautiful form are the products of the people" (Namboodiripad 1982, 420). As EMS articulated, "There is a common assumption that expressing an interest in the fine arts or developing a taste for it is not suited for a communist. Those communists who have an interest in kathakali, festivals and temple festivals often are embarrassed about admitting it. Today the circumstances are such that we have the opportunity to lead the renaissance in literature, music and the other arts" (Namboodiripad 1944, 6). A crucial shift that redeemed elite caste culture, this reconceptualization would determine the future of a leftist Kerala's regional heritage. As Devika (2010, 809) writes, "Even as traditional caste servitude was challenged, upper-caste culture and social norms were not only largely spared, but actually reclaimed as the 'unifying core' of Kerala's national culture."

In this process of reclamation, upper-caste arts and culture were consigned to the past by Kerala's Communist Party as part of its consolidation of a regional identity that, as we saw earlier, united Kerala by eschewing the

Brahmin/non-Brahmin divide polarizing other areas of South India. The crux of EMS's Marxist reinterpretation of history was his reconceptualization of Brahmins and their elite caste culture as part of a past that was a necessary stage in a linear model of Kerala's historical progress and inevitable modernization. This temporalizing strategy created a "usable past" whereby elite art forms such as Kutiyattam were assigned to a neutral bygone era and thereby taken up as emblems of Kerala's regional culture and heritage (Menon 2002).

Shankar, a homestay host who spent nearly four decades in the US, once enthusiastically told me about his experience visiting a local CPI(M) party member. Arriving at the office, the official told him, "Excuse me, I just have to go pray." With raised eyebrows, Shankar amusedly reflected, "A Communist! That's how Communism is in Kerala, the exact opposite of what Americans think it is!" Understanding my interest in classical arts, he further revealed that the local CPI(M) party secretary was a Kathakali drummer. Narrated with similar exuberance, he mused, "These things should be considered opposites, but here they're not. The Communist Party in Kerala had to compromise on religion and art, or else they would lose power. If you asked Kerala people to choose between a political party and the temple or arts, they would always choose the latter, there's no doubt."

Elite temple performing arts thus came to play a vital role in the state government's conscious assertion of a collective Malayali identity through its sustained sponsorship of cultural activities that focus on the performance of "traditional" Kerala art forms. As Osella and Osella (2000b) have argued, the continued government sponsorship of statewide Onam celebrations showcasing "traditional" art forms has aimed to construct an image of state unity and harmony, playing a significant role in the construction of Kerala's regional identity.[18] As a result, Mahabali's legendary golden age of equality is widely viewed as a legitimizing historical precursor of Kerala's contemporary politics. The state-sponsored Onam festival has since been renamed "Onam and Tourist Week," involving street parades and performing arts festivals in major cities throughout the state (Tarabout 2005).

In 2007, the Communist-led Kerala government established the Kerala Utsavam tourism festival, which showcased over one thousand performing artists in numerous locations over multiple months. Paradoxically, the vast majority of the audience-cum-tourist-consumers at government-sponsored tourism festivals like Onam and Tourist Week and Kerala Utsavam are Malayali, and proceedings are predominantly in Malayalam with no attempt made to translate for the non-Malayali tourist. Offered free of charge, the tourism element of these festivals appears to be a ruse, with the ultimate result being the ongoing cementing of regional identity through educating the Malayali public about "their" performing arts. With many seeing these art forms for the first time at these festivals, this parallels processes, as examined by Rajagopal (1999), of educating consumers into modern Indian citizenship through the medium of advertising. Kutiyattam has been showcased at both Onam and Tourist Week and Kerala Utsavam, with a strong emphasis on introducing Kerala audiences to an art the majority have never seen before. Thus bolstered by agendas of political mobilization, performing arts continue to inform Kerala's regional identity construction by reinforcing an imagined community of Malayalis both within and outside of Kerala in the wider national and international Malayali diaspora.

Guru Painkulam Rama Chakyar and Radical Reform

One of the main vehicles for the consolidation of Kerala's elite performing arts as regional heritage is Kerala Kalamandalam, the state performing arts institution, which opened a department of Kutiyattam in 1965. In this section, I take a deeper look at the period just before the art's inclusion at Kalamandalam to consider how the Kutiyattam community negotiated this tumultuous period in Kerala's history. In particular, I examine the radical efforts undertaken by Guru Painkulam Rama Chakyar, a pivotal figure who would later lead the newly formed Kutiyattam department at Kalamandalam, to adapt the art to the changing times.

As we have seen, early-to-mid-twentieth-century Kerala experienced intense upheavals, and these profoundly impacted the matrilineal, upper-caste, gurukulam-educated, landowning Kutiyattam community. As Narayanan (2005) details, the disintegration of Kerala's feudal-based agrarian temple society, the associated decline of temples as economic centers, and the increasing secularization that led to a loss of influence by temples and their associated traditions in the lives of everyday people, together sparked an economic crisis in the Kutiyattam community. Many temples stopped their Kutiyattam performances altogether, while those that continued did not increase remuneration to account for rising inflation. This eventually led to a situation, as is still the case today, where the cost for hereditary artists to fulfill their temple performance duties often exceeds their remuneration. These changing economic and social conditions, combined with the rise of cinema as a popular form of entertainment, also led to a sharp decrease in Kutiyattam audiences and patronage as well as the eventual loss of most families' main source of income due to land redistribution legislation. As a result, many members of Kutiyattam families sought other occupations, rejecting the existing agrarian order and becoming "agents of modernity in new forms of employment" like so many others in Kerala who came to associate their hereditary caste occupations with an increasingly distant past (Osella and Osella 2006, 571). This mass exodus further exacerbated the community's problems, leaving many families with no gurus to train their youth. This resulted in several generations of untrained or undertrained performers who knew just enough to fulfill their temple duties. As the social, economic, and political realities once assumed to be stable collapsed, Kerala's emerging communist movement was promoting a new egalitarian reality. In response to these changing times, two progressive members of the Kutiyattam community—gurus Painkulam Rama Chakyar and Mani Madhava Chakyar—fought to make the art more accessible and egalitarian, bravely enduring censure by the wider community. While I focus here on Guru Painkulam's impact within Kerala, I discuss Guru Mani's national impact in the next chapter.

Considered unthinkable at the time, Guru Painkulam's first performance outside the temple confines in 1949 has come to be widely celebrated by artists as revolutionarily necessary for the survival of the art form.[19] Though at the time he faced severe ostracism from members of his community, the guru is now widely characterized as the savior of Kutiyattam. I have heard various accounts of the circumstances surrounding this first performance outside of the temple, but here I draw primarily on Ramavarma's (1978) multipart article due to its rich imagery and detail. Ramavarma attributes Guru Painkulam's first performance outside of the temple to his 1943 encounter with Dr. Joseph Mundassery, a Christian radical literary critic and future communist education minister of Kerala who promoted the "art for art's sake" stance, as mentioned in the previous section.[20] Despite the temple entry proclamations of the 1930s and 1940s, which granted temple entry to all Hindus throughout Kerala, Mundassery was Christian and thus not allowed entry for Kutiyattam performances. According to Ramavarma, Mundassery began regularly meeting with Guru Painkulam after his Chakyarkoothu performances at Thrissur's Vadakkumnathan temple. The latter would recount the *prabandha,* or puranic story he had narrated that day, replete with details of his witty use of metaphor and wordplay to critique social and political events of the time. Mundassery eventually aired his grievances to Guru Painkulam by reportedly saying: "Are even young people like you thinking that this sublime form of art may be allowed to gradually decay in the dark interiors of temples? This rusty chain has to be broken. Otherwise, before long, this art will be lost entirely . . . Painkulam, you should bring this art form out of the temples. In the days to come, there will be more connoisseurs not inside the temple but outside them. Shouldn't they also be given a chance to enjoy this art?" (Ramavarma 1978, 7). As Ramavarma never cites his sources or claims to have personally witnessed this exchange, we must approach this account through his 1978 perspective. While we can reasonably assume that he took some degree of artistic license with his quoted text, Ramavarma's characterization of the temple as an artistic environment of decay and loss is significant. Through the words of Mundassery, he pits Kutiyattam and, by extension, temple-based Kerala society as being constrained by a "rusty chain" of religious orthodoxy in need of liberation by proponents of a democratic, civil society in which art forms such as Kutiyattam could be enjoyed by all. In short, he condemned Kutiyattam to decay and potential extinction if its artists did not adapt to new social conditions.

Ramavarma proceeds to justify the six-year gap between this 1943 encounter and Guru Painkulam's 1949 temple exit by characterizing the former as a time in which performing outside the temple was "totally unthinkable." He stressed that anyone doing so would never be allowed by "orthodox aristocrats" to perform inside the temple again, thereby losing their only means of income. Ramavarma contrasts this with the vastly changed environment of 1949 after Indian independence, when the power of provincial princes had substantially decreased, temple entry was guaranteed for all Hindus across Kerala, and most temples in Cochin and Travancore were under the control of the government-appointed Devaswom Board, leaving "no one to fear."

It was amid these changes that, as Ramavarma (1978) reports, Painkulam Rama Chakyar went on a pilgrimage in September 1949 to Kanyakumari, at the southernmost tip of India, to mourn the sudden death of his favorite nephew. On the return journey, he stopped at the Namboodiri Brahmin household of Cherupoyya Thekkekara Bhattathiri near Kottarakara, known for being Kutiyattam connoisseurs. The household insisted that the guru perform three days of Chakyarkoothu narration. Though he had his costume on hand, there were no Nambiar/Nangiar families in the area to accompany him on the *mizhavu* percussion and *kuzhithalam* cymbals, making it impossible for him to perform in the temple. Under the circumstances, Guru Painkulam decided to perform unaccompanied in the house itself, reportedly worried only about the reaction of his own guru, his sister's husband Ammannur "Chachu" Parameswara Chakyar. To allay these concerns, he decided to begin the performance with

Figure 32. Guru Painkulam Rama Chakyar as *vidu-shaka*. Photo by Clifford Jones, courtesy of Lizzette Thomason.

an invocation to Lord Parameswara that, through creative wordplay, also honored his guru: "May I 'bow' (*chachu*) my forehead to the lotus feet of Lord Parameswara and narrate the good story. O Great soul, may thy graces help me in finding the true way to ultimate bliss" (1978, 8). His orthodox guru, whose other two students only performed outside the temple in the late 1970s (Ammannur Madhava Chakyar) or never at all (Ammannur Parameswaran Chakyar), reportedly accepted the gesture in his understanding that "behind his disciple's endeavour was the aim to gain more popularity for these art forms" (1978, 8). While it seems doubtful that Chachu Chakyar actually reacted in such a way, it is significant that it is thus narrated, with an explicit understanding that Guru Painkulam's breaking of tradition was justified as a means to achieve the greater popularity and survival of Kutiyattam.

After this first performance, Guru Painkulam continued to present Chakyarkoothu outside the temple, with percussion accompaniment by

Chathakudam Krishnan Nambiar, at several schools, libraries, and colleges throughout Kerala. He persevered despite intense criticism from the Kutiyattam community, which purportedly resulted in some artists refusing to perform with him, as well as an attempt to banish him from temple theaters altogether (Gopalakrishnan 2004). To reduce such criticism, Guru Painkulam redesigned a slightly different costume for these performances, which only further fueled the opposition. He also significantly participated in the first public performance of Kutiyattam (in its dramatic form with several characters onstage), staged in August 1956 by All India Radio of Calicut before an invited audience at the Zamorin's royal palace, recorded for later broadcasting to the public. His troupe enacted a section of the *vidushaka*'s *puruppadu* as well as the first day's Kutiyattam of the first act of the play *Subhadradhananjayam* over the course of six nights.[21] Invited to attend this performance were nationally prominent Sanskrit scholar and art critic Dr. V. Raghavan and Sanskritist Dr. K. Kunjunni Raja. Only thirty years after Kutiyattam's first temple exit, Ramavarma (1978, 4) reflected on the changing times, writing, "Today people will laugh if they hear that once Chakyars considered it a grievous sin to perform outside the temple," thus attempting to stress the momentousness of this act within its own temporal context.

The emergence of Kutiyattam from the confines of the temple significantly fractured Kutiyattam into two spheres—the temple sphere and the public sphere—which have over time become synonymous with the blurred dichotomies of tradition/modernity, private/public, religious/secular, orthodox/progressive, and untrained/trained artists. As Lukose (2009) has noted, instead of representing a theoretical perspective, the dichotomy of tradition versus modernity emerges as significant due to its pervasiveness within a Kerala context.[22] I also found this the case with the above-listed binaries, made salient through their use by Kutiyattam artists. Kutiyattam today is predominantly performed by institutionally trained actors and musicians of various castes performing together in public venues. These post-1949 public performances have now assumed the unmarked normative category of Kutiyattam, whereas the annual temple performances that were once the norm are now marked as *adiyanthirakoothu*, loosely translated as "ritualistic performance." For many artists, adiyanthirakoothu has come to embody what they perceive as the ritualistic past of Kutiyattam. This reflects a temporalizing divide in which ritualistic temple performances come to represent the art's premodern past, while nonritualistic public performances embody its modern present in a complex ongoing negotiation of values.

In Search of an Audience: Kerala Kalamandalam, Aestheticization, and the Reinvention of Tradition

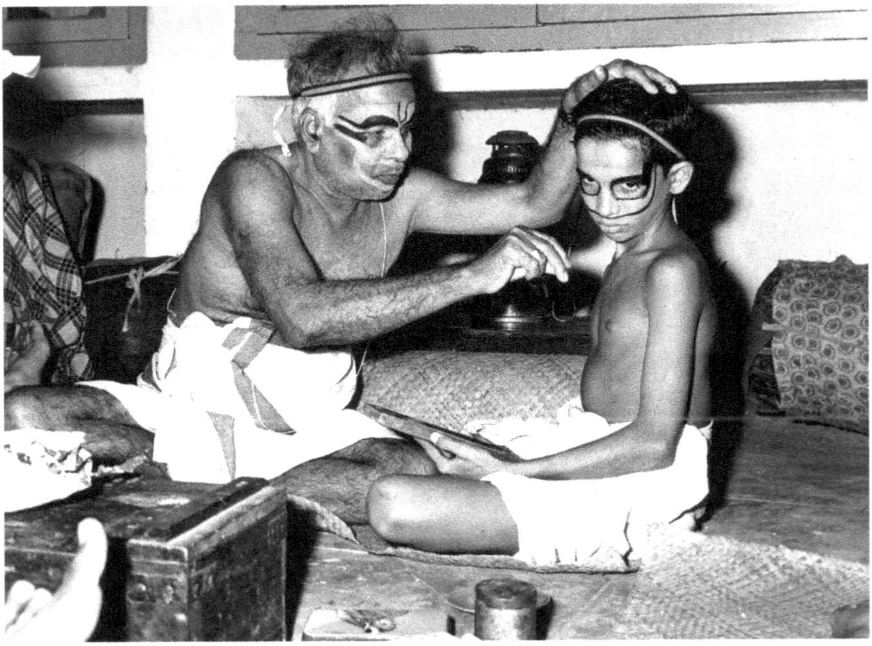

Figure 33. Guru Painkulam and student Painkulam Narayana Chakyar. Photo by Clifford Jones, courtesy of Lizzette Thomason.

It is a muggy afternoon, like most afternoons in Kerala outside of the monsoon season, when you can still hope for a cool gust of wind to relieve your otherwise constant state of stickiness. This afternoon, however, there is no hope of relief but to ignore the varied rivulets of sweat that slowly transform my body into a rivery, central Keralan landscape. I am sitting in one of the cement classroom blocks that dot the sloping campus of Kerala Kalamandalam. Class has finished. The students roll up their straw mats and start to file out of the room in bubbly excitement, headed toward the nearby girls' dormitory before their evening classes begin. I sit with Shylaja-teacher, one of the first nonhereditary students to study Kutiyattam under Guru Painkulam Rama Chakyar. A beloved guru of my own teacher, she is in a good mood, with an ever-sharp wit and ready laugh. We sit across from each other on wooden stools and begin our interview, chatting freely. I ask why she first wanted to learn Kutiyattam, and like so many other female Kutiyattam performers trained at Kalamandalam, she replies, "I didn't. I wanted to study dance, but after my audition, I was assigned to Kutiyattam. The choice was to study Kutiyattam or not join Kalamandalam at all. I was upset at first, but then I came to appreciate and love this difficult art form."

Wending our way through a variety of topics in the late-afternoon stillness of the open-air classroom, I ask about her guru: "Why did Painkulam Rama Chakyar *ashan* [guru] decide to bring changes to Kutiyattam?"

"To save (*samrakṣikān*) Kutiyattam," she replies. "As Nangiars, Nambiars, and Chakyars were all going for other jobs, *Ashan* believed that teaching non-hereditary members was better. Because of students like us, the art form grew."

A bit later, I ask about UNESCO, and Shylaja-teacher reflects, "You know, *Ashan* was the first UNESCO—without him, Kutiyattam would never have survived long enough to receive UNESCO recognition."

This section considers Kutiyattam's mid-to-late-twentieth-century re-invention at Kerala Kalamandalam under the progressive direction of Guru Painkulam Rama Chakyar, who strove to democratize the art, making it simultaneously more *bhangi* (beautiful) and *less elite* in order to appeal to wider communist-leaning audiences.[23] Founded in 1965, Kalamandalam's Kutiyattam department represented the first formalized financial support for the art since the dissolution of royal and temple patronage. Most significantly, as a state institution with a nondiscriminatory admissions policy, it served to democratize the Kutiyattam community, throwing open the doors to people of all castes to learn and perform the art. Guided by the ideals of equality and beauty carrying the art into the future, one of Guru Painkulam's core beliefs was that Kutiyattam should be open for all to learn, perform, and watch, irrespective of caste. While centering the democratization of performers and audience members, he radically reimagined play production and women's costumes and roles onstage and, together with Guru P. K. Narayanan Nambiar, revolutionized the art's soundscape.

Kerala Kalamandalam is a sprawling campus in the small town of Cheruthuruthy on the banks of the Nila River. It was founded in 1930 by celebrated poet Vallathol Narayana Menon with art lover Mankkulam Mukunda Raja for the promotion and preservation of Kathakali dance drama.[24] According to Zarilli (2000, 31), Kalamandalam was established to preserve Kathakali by promoting it as a symbol of Kerala regional identity as well as Indian national identity. Initially founded only for the promotion and training of Kathakali, Kalamandalam's later inclusion of art forms like Mohiniyattam and Kutiyattam helped to cement the state's classical arts canon. At first privately funded—built on land donated by the Maharaja of Cochin—the institution came under the control of the new Kerala state government in 1958 (Zarilli 2000). Modeled after the traditional gurukula educational system where students live alongside their guru with arts training incorporated into the routine of daily life, in the early days of the Kutiyattam department, male students lived with Guru Painkulam.

Currently, however, students live on or near campus in dormitories. While some teachers live on campus, the majority now live off campus and interact with students primarily during class time. Teachers recount a much more intimate relationship with their own gurus during their Kalamandalam student days, with interactions extending outside of class to expectations of cooking for their guru daily and other family-style obligations.

The 1965 opening of Kalamandalam's Kutiyattam department ushered in a period of both democratization and intense creativity and innovation in the art under state guardianship and the leadership of Guru Painkulam. It also marked the beginning of a close association with Kathakali. Borrowing heavily from Kutiyattam throughout its development in the sixteenth century, Kathakali in turn influenced Kutiyattam's reinvention at Kalamandalam, especially in costuming, makeup, and the rigorous *uzhichil* massages male students began undergoing.[25] While Kathakali and Kutiyattam are very different art forms, the differences are not always immediately apparent to the undiscerning observer. Among the most prominent differences are Kathakali's all-male cast versus Kutiyattam's mixed-gender cast, a musical storyline in Kathakali sung in Malayalam that accompanies the actors' dancing versus Kutiyattam's Sanskrit recitation, and the dominant mood of the former being heroism (*veera*), whereas love (*sringara*) and comedy (*hasya*) are more prevalent in the latter (Jones 1977).[26] Betty True Jones (1977, 12) observed that Kalamandalam's Kutiyattam students in the 1960s and 1970s were "in constant contact with the Kathakali students and teachers" (1977, 12). As longtime Kalamandalam art superintendent Killimangalam Vasudevan Namboodiripad recalled, "Rama Chakyar was very liberal—liberal means he was not narrow-minded. And he says what is good in Kathakali you can use in Kutiyattam too" (Bindu 2013, 153).

Nevertheless, Guru Painkulam faced intense opposition from many members of the Kutiyattam community for his role at Kalamandalam. Several tried to discredit his efforts by claiming that he was turning Kutiyattam into Kathakali. Many felt their own rights to temple performance threatened by his training of nonhereditary performers. As a result, the guru had to fight to find performance opportunities outside of Kalamandalam for his first non-Chakyar student, Kalamandalam Shivan Namboodiri, now considered one of the best performers of his generation. Despite the fact that he occupied a higher-caste position than Chakyars as a Namboodiri Brahmin, Shivan Namboodiri was widely shunned by the community. Even today, he recounts with intense emotion his rejection and his guru's fierce defense of him.[27] He told me of one such rejection in the early 1970s at a temple performance in Manjeri, which resulted in his guru boycotting the performance with the words "If my disciple is not acceptable to you, you are not acceptable to me."

Guru Painkulam's first male acting students were Shivan Namboodiri and his grandnephew Rama Chakyar in 1965, with his great-grandnephew Narayana Chakyar and Radhakrishnan joining later. He began teaching his first non-Nangiar student, P. N. Girija Devi, in 1971, with C. K. Shylaja (1973) and P. S. Sathi (1976) following thereafter.[28] In this early period, Mani Madhava Chakyar was one of the few Chakyars to actively support the department by encouraging his son P. K. Narayanan Nambiar, recognized as the best mizhavu drummer of his time, to accept the position as percussion instructor there in 1966. Guru P. K. Narayanan Nambiar—Nambiar-ashan, who we saw narrate the legend of Tipu Sultan in chapter 4—went on to revolutionize mizhavu on the Kutiyattam stage. His first mizhavu student at Kalamandalam was Unnikrishnan Nambiar, whom I later came to know at Margi as Unni-ashan, in 1967; the first non-Nambiar student, Eashwaranunni, arrived in 1972.

In stark contrast to Shivan Namboodiri, none of the other early students reported traumatic experiences associated with being nonhereditary performers. Kalamandalam Shylaja did recall Ammannur Madhava Chakyar once rebuking her by for being a nonhereditary Kutiyattam student.[29] While sharing the story, she acted out the role of the scolded child—her eyes widened and shoulders hunched exaggeratedly. She quickly relaxed into her usual laughter upon recounting her guru's reaction. Seeing his student reproached, Guru Painkulam quickly reassured her, "Don't listen to him. You are doing a wonderful job, keep up your studies." Shaking her head slightly from side to side with an intense affection and respect I have observed in all of Guru Painkulam's students, she remarked on the love and care he showed to his students. She believed the only consequence of her nonhereditary status was her inability to perform in *koothambalam* temple theaters. Like many nonhereditary Kutiyattam artists today, however, she claimed disinterest, saying, "Let the Chakyars have the koothambalams. There are plenty of other performance venues, why should I want to take that away from them?" Despite this indifference, she said she was lucky to have had the opportunity to perform in a koothambalam during the filming of the UNESCO application video, clearly valuing the experience.

In addition to training nonhereditary students, Painkulam Rama Chakyar's primary contribution at Kalamandalam was his conscious reinvention of Kutiyattam. In this reinvention, he emphasized an aesthetic ideal of beauty to make the art more appealing to the public. The term *aesthetic* has a long history in Western philosophy, from the Greek *aisthetikós*, meaning "perceptive by feeling," to the Kantian "disinterested, distanced, contemplative, and objectifying act of consciousness" (Mascia-Lees 2011, 3). I consider the aesthetic through Mascia-Lees's (2011, 7) concept of "aesthetic embodiment," which crystallizes Merleau-Ponty's (1964) aesthetic concept as a form of embodied knowing, defined as a "somatically-grounded, culturally mediated, affective encounter with the beautiful." Guru Painkulam led Kutiyattam's aesthetic reinvention by developing class syllabi, standardizing the strong Kutiyattam body-in-performance, re-creating the female costume, revitalizing female roles onstage, reconstituting music onstage, developing new and renewed choreographies, and shortening the repertoire to accommodate "modern" audiences with lower attention spans.[30] Artists today retrospectively narrate Guru Painkulam's efforts, controversial at the time, as necessary for adapting Kutiyattam to the radically changing times and wider, nonexpert audiences outside of the temple. While Guru Painkulam led the charge, Kutiyattam's reinvention, so central to the constitution of the public face of contemporary Kutiyattam today, was a collaborative venture with mizhavu guru P. K. Narayanan Nambiar, costuming and makeup maestro Kalamandalam Govinda Warrier and his student Kalamandalam Ram Mohan, art superintendent Killimangalam Vasudevan Namboodiripad, and American scholar Clifford R. Jones.

In a brief exploration of the concept *reinvention of tradition*, I begin with Hobsbawm's (1983) well-known notion of "invented tradition" from the classic text *The Invention of Tradition*. Hobsbawm (1983, 4–5) posits that traditions are most often invented "when a rapid transformation of society weakens or destroys the social patterns for which 'old' traditions had been designed . . . or when such old traditions and their institutional carriers and promulgators no longer prove sufficiently adaptable and flexible, or are otherwise eliminated." The most common critique of this concept is that all traditions are invented. Prickett (2009, 15) asserts that all traditions "are the product of some degree of self-conscious creation, and . . . *always* represent, to a greater or less degree, an attempt to appropriate a past which was ambiguous, dangerous, or even capable of interpretations subversive to the ideology of the creators of that tradition." As Ivy (1995, 21) points out, however, this stance still problematically relies on binaries between invention and authenticity, fiction and reality, and discourse and history.

Following folklorist Regina Bendix's (1997) classic text *In Search of Authenticity*, I reject any term that relies on a discourse of authenticity as rooted in a purportedly "pure" past and instead use the term *reinvention of tradition* along the lines of Schoepf (1992, 234) to mean the "reshaping [of] . . . 'tradition' to meet changing circumstances." Kutiyattam, an orally and mimetically transmitted, embodied artistic practice, is understood by its artists as undergoing inevitable and continuous adaptation throughout its history. Artists conceptualize their art as existing in an ever-shifting interplay with the contemporary world, part of a necessary process of artistic development led by innovative gurus throughout its history. When artists commonly assert that "Kutiyattam is not a museum piece," they highlight the dynamic nature of artistic practice, emphasizing that Kutiyattam has always adapted to changing times; that artists are foremost contemporary individuals who live and think according to their time; and that art, as a creative endeavor, *is meant to change*.[31] In making this statement, artists reject frequent attempts by the media and wider heritage discourses to frame Kutiyattam as a frozen relic of an ancient past.

Costumes, Acting, and Stage Production

Historically, a distinction was made between two types of Kutiyattam audiences: the *prekshaka* (*prekṣaka*) and *nānālōka*. The *prekshaka*, an elite audience of Brahmin connoisseurs sitting immediately next to the stage, could understand the subtleties of eye expressions and associated mudra hand gestures from their vantage point, while the *nanaloka*, or common audience, watching from farther away could enjoy the body language and dance movements. An ideal performance should please both types of audiences. Another historical distinction, still made today, was between *natyadharmi* (stylized acting) and *lokadharmi* (realistic acting). In his effort to popularize Kutiyattam for a wider nanaloka audience, Guru Painkulam focused on improving the techniques of the body, the mechanics of expression, and the beauty of the overall form. He adjusted several mudra hand gestures to become more lokadharmi for greater intelligibility. Through the institution of class syllabi and rigorous, daily training that stretched from four in the morning until eight at night, Guru Painkulam standardized the strong aesthetic Kutiyattam body—legs out-turned; elbows and arms perfectly parallel to the ground; and the core in a deep *aramandalam* bend (the basic Kutiyattam stance), with the center of balance close to the earth.

With the institutionalization of new standards for the Kutiyattam body at Kerala Kalamandalam, Guru Painkulam developed an aesthetic standard through which performance is now universally judged. This aesthetic ideal created a minimum professional body requirement for all artists regardless of where they trained, and it continues to guide performance and training interactions today, as shown by frequent artist evaluations of technique through the lens of beauty. As I mentioned in chapter 2, this process of standardization sparked discourses on style, with many equating the "old style" performed in the temple—a product of the home-taught gurukula system—with a poorly trained, ritualistic body, and the new "Kalamandalam style" with a rigorously trained, aesthetic body. Kutiyattam's first nonhereditary female students and longtime instructors at Kalamandalam explained the difference. As Kalamandalam Shylaja described, "After Kalamandalam, a system [*ciṭṭa/chitta*] emerged. You should place your legs like *this*, sit like *this*, raise your legs like *this*, keep your elbows raised. Before it was like *this*," and she exaggeratedly performed with her elbows down at her sides, chanting in a lackluster monotone with the corresponding hand gestures: "'Once upon a time [*eṅkilō panḍŭ*] . . .' This much was enough. There was no audience, right? It was for God, no?" She continued, laughing, "This much was enough for God!" She humorously mimicked again and stressed, "*We* perform for the audience." Kalamandalam Girija explained her understanding of the difference: "If I perform like this [holding her arms at a forty-five-degree angle to the ground], and you perform like this [arms parallel to the ground], this one [the latter], is a little more beautiful [*bhangi*]. You studied with *chitta*. I studied with my grandmother or mother, this much only, this is the difference. . . . With regular practice, more beauty comes. The rest is the same, the frame isn't different. So when instruction is less, it won't be beautiful, the elbows won't be held high enough. That is the difference."

Beauty was an overarching principle for the reformed hand gestures as well, and many artists demonstrated the "before" and "after" mudras to me, often seeking my confirmation that the reformed mudra was indeed more beautiful. Among others, the gestures for *I*, *my*, *demon*, and *palace* were reformed, and various additional case endings were distinguished. *Vishnu* and *Krishna*, formerly the same mudra with a subtle change of facial expression, were distinguished through hand positioning, with *Krishna* altered to imitate the playing of a flute as is performed in Kathakali. As one artist told me, Guru Painkulam made these changes "so that the local audience would recognize it is Krishna." He modified other performance details "for the sake of beauty" as well, such as his aestheticization of the *nityakriya* ritualistic dance episode with its songs, bringing both more consciously in line with Mohiniyattam dance standards that had been developed and fixed years earlier at Kalamandalam. Beauty at Kalamandalam became primarily equated with intelligibility, clarity, and standardization of form, strong agile bodies, visually appealing costumes, and the presence of women onstage.

Casassas (2012) has characterized Guru Painkulam as the "first stage director" in an art form that previously focused only on the creative freedom of each actor. In addition to the above, he modified the beauty and aesthetics of the stage, reinserting some female characters while further developing others. For example, Sita's character was erased from the stage at some point in Kutiyattam's

Figure 34. (*Left to right*) Kalamandalam *Bālivadham* with full cast of characters and Kalamandalam Krishnendu and Kalamandalam Athira in *Udyānavarṇana*. Photos by author. (In *Balivadhom* [*left to right*]: Kalamandalam Jishnu Prathap, Kalamandalam Rajeesh, Kalamandalam Achuthanandan, Kalamandalam Radhakrishnan, Kalamandalam Kanakakumar, and Kalamandalam Charu Agaru.)

history, substituted by the actor through a number of dramatic conventions.[32] The first among these was *keṭṭāṭuka* (hearing and acting), in which the Chakyar actor would pretend to listen to and then repeat Sita's lines onstage. A second technique involved the actor interacting with the oil lamp onstage instead of the female character, and a third had the cymbal-playing Nangiar recite Sita's lines from the side of the stage. Casassas (2012) notes that Guru Painkulam restored Sita to the stage, developed Lalita's character in *Shurpanakhankam*, and revived both Ajjuka and her friend in *Bhagavadajjukam* and Vijaya in *Toranayuddham*.[33] He similarly choreographed a new sequence, *Udyānavarṇana*, in which two female characters describe a beautiful garden together (see fig. 34). While aesthetically pleasing, *Udyānavarṇana* is largely devoid of content. Johan (2011a) has argued that this reintroduction of female characters onstage provided women with a largely decorative rather than dramatic role.

Several other characters were erased from the stage over time due to a lack of performers and resources. Guru Painkulam made an effort to bring all missing characters back to the stage, as in *Balivadham*, in which six characters now appear simultaneously (see fig. 34). He choreographed and rechoreographed several other pieces and revived others that had disappeared from performance altogether.[34] He taught each performance in unedited form to his students. As each extended over several days, he reduced their onstage production to two to three hours to accommodate "modern" audiences pressed for time.[35] Guru

Painkulam described his process during an interview with theater scholar Richard Schechner in 1976.

> I never felt it necessary to go out of the traditional form as far as the training is concerned, but when it is performed on the stage, I brought some changes to make it more enjoyable. . . . In the original form, there are some very long and dragging or slow-moving scenes when performing. Though I have taught the students here [in unedited form], I have edited it, leaving the important parts, so that people are able to enjoy it. For this particular reason, we now mostly deal with stories with dramatic importance. In the earlier days, one story was structured to last twelve to fifteen days, but today Kalamandalam is performing such stories in one to two days. For example, Balivadham (the killing of Bali) used to last five days, each day for three or five hours. The same story was performed in 2.5 hours in Ujjain and Ahmedabad. In Ottapalam we did it in 1.5 hours. By this, the actual story gets more importance. (Chakyar 1976)

One of Guru Painkulam's most celebrated innovations was his redesign of Kutiyattam's female costume and makeup, now accepted by all institutions. The redesign was a collaboration with costuming and makeup maestro Kalamandalam Govinda Warrier; Warrier's student Kalamandalam Ram Mohan; and American scholar Dr. Clifford R. Jones, a University of Pennsylvania PhD student at the time.[36] The earlier female costume, still occasionally used in temple performance today, consisted of a cone-shaped headpiece (*kūṭu*) made of natural materials with a bark base, a red fabric covering, and a silver-colored serpent ornament at the top (figs. 35 and 36).[37] It was decorated as each actress saw fit with coral-colored techi flowers (*tecchipūvŭ*) and various metallic ornaments of their choice. Constructed anew for each performance, this led to headpiece variation not only between actresses but also between performances. As the costume featured split skirts open in front, the actress maintained her modesty through limited movement onstage, generally standing in one place or staying seated. Red facial makeup made of natural pigments covered her face, with black kohl outlining her eyebrows, eyes, jawline, and sometimes her entire face. Using limited ornaments, most actresses wore their own gold jewelry—bangles and necklaces over a sleeveless fabric chest covering tied in the back (*gathrika*), leaving the stomach bare—and adorned their upper arms with three decorative white lines of rice paste. Kalamandalam Shylaja jokingly told me, "It was not beautiful!" She then mirthfully recounted a performance during the costume's transition period in which she, playing the heroine, got the "good" costume while her coactress, Kalamandalam Girija, was left to wear the "old" and, by implication, "bad" costume.[38]

Figure 35. (*Left to right*) Vasanthi Nangiaramma in bark-base headpiece and traditional makeup. Photo courtesy of Diane Daugherty. Kalamandalam Reshmi with Kalamandalam's reinvented headpiece and makeup. Photo by author.

Kalamandalam Ram Mohan illuminated many of the changes made to the Kutiyattam costume at Kalamandalam. A guru of Kutiyattam and Kathakali makeup and costuming, Ram Mohan-ashan sews the costumes himself and, upon receiving the wooden carvings from the carpenter, decorates them with gold foil and colorful stones. In contrast to the previous female headpiece, the new headpiece was explicitly made to be durable and reusable. Constructed from a special ayurvedic wood, it was modeled in both shape and size on the headpiece of Kathakali's Saraswathi character, which is rarely brought to the stage. The serpent adorning the apex of the headpiece was moved down to just above the forehead, and a number of natural or handmade decorations were replaced with manufactured ones for both convenience and durability (figs. 35 and 36). The ubiquitous techi flower, also known as the flame of the woods, was replaced with red woolen yarn. As Ram Mohan-ashan told me, "This flower, which used to be everywhere, is now difficult and expensive to get." He further recounted that due to availability and cost, bright gold aluminum foil acquired from Bombay by his guru Govinda Warrier came to replace a dull gold-colored lead foil produced by a family in Palakkad using ayurvedic materials and sealing wax, in a secret procedure they never divulged and was thus lost. Similarly, the naturally reflective mica stone previously used on the headpiece was replaced by glass, a substitution already made in the art's pre-Kalamandalam years. In the early years, Guru Painkulam insisted that the glass stones remain clear, but Ram Mohan-ashan revealed that he slowly introduced colored stones into the headpiece, which the guru then liked and accepted. As he emphasized, "This is not change, this is innovation." When I asked him to tell me about Guru Painkulam, he smiled. "He was both jolly and serious. He was a very nice man, always. Most of my works were approved by him." The collaboratively redesigned headpiece that Kalamandalam Ram Mohan played a role in creating is widely viewed today as a vast improvement over the earlier one, considered both more beautiful and durable.

Guru Painkulam redefined women's performance by emphasizing an active body. He changed former static poses to dynamic movements like jumping and taking high steps with raised legs.[39] As the split skirt could not accommodate this new activity without violating accepted notions of female propriety, Guru Painkulam replaced it with a full skirt and loose-fitting "pajama" pants underneath, similar to the Kathakali female costume. He modeled women's makeup on that of Kathakali as well, extending it past the jawline onto the neck, with added decorative rice paste dots along the eyebrows and optional curls at the hairline (fig. 35). Kalamandalam actresses further experimented with substituting the red vermilion and yellow *manayola* facial pigments with pancake makeup but shifted back toward natural materials in creating the mango-colored makeup that is standard today—layering a mix of yellow manayola and red oxide pigments on top of a pancake base with powder. While temple makeup had a reddish hue, Daugherty (1996, 2016) surmises this lighter shift also modeled the more naturalistic base makeup used for Kathakali female characters.[40] Other elements Guru Painkulam adopted from Kathakali's female costume are a headband with delicate silver pieces hanging just below the headpiece (*kuṛunira*), a mirrored belt (*oḍyāṇam*), and a choker to cover the bare neck. He also adopted a number of gold-foil wooden ornaments from the Kutiyattam male costume—shoulder pieces (*tōḷvaḷa*), large bangles (*vaḷa*), a large beaded necklace (*poḷūmpŭ*), and small ornaments tucked over the ears known as *chevipoo*, or "ear flowers." Large golden half orbs (*kuṇḍalam*) also replaced the flat silver disks that had previously covered actresses' ears (figs. 35 and 36).

Kalamandalam Girija and Kalamandalam Shylaja further changed elements of the women's costume after becoming teachers at Kalamandalam in the early 1980s. Kalamandalam Girija recounted the traditional rules for Kutiyattam costuming: "You should be able to see the lower part of your arms, your stomach,

Figure 36. (*Left to right*) Unknown Nangiar actress in female costume circa 1933 (Gilchriest Hatch 1933). Photo courtesy of Susan Marie Mathias. Kalamandalam Girija in contemporary costume. Photo by author.

your neck, and the lower part of your legs, for both men and women." By this time, Guru Painkulam had already lengthened the skirt and partly covered the neck with jewelry, but the stomach remained exposed. The two therefore decided to convert the costume's sari blouse into a full jumper that covered the stomach because, as Kalamandalam Shylaja joked, "Hey, you don't want to see our stomachs . . . our stomachs aren't so pretty!"[41]

Changing notions of propriety regarding the female body and dress had already been impacting Kutiyattam actresses for the better part of a century. Since the nineteenth century, a rising ideal of universal female modesty expressed through covered breasts and an increasingly covered body came to govern women's bodies and sexualities across Kerala. Up through the mid-twentieth century, women's dress in Kerala was distinctly tied to community identity and very literally embodied social divisions by caste and religion (Thomas 2018). Different castes as well as Jews, Muslims, and various Christians all had socially mandated dress. Dress standards prevented lower-caste women from covering their breasts in public and mandated that upper-caste women and men remove their upper-body clothing when entering the temple, with bare-breastedness viewed as a sign of subservience to God. In Kutiyattam and Nangiarkoothu, while Nangiar actresses wore a sleeveless piece of fabric (*gātrika*) that covered their breasts during performance, those playing cymbals on the side of the stage were customarily bare breasted.[42] In the nineteenth century, British missionaries played a large role in imbuing women's bare breasts, previously the status quo for many groups, with a sense of immorality. According to Devika (2007a), the practice of *covering* women's breasts had previously been considered immodest in Kerala temples, as it was associated with sexualized temple dancers who used the practice to eroticize the female body. A group of lower-caste Christian converts, the Nadars, first lobbied for the right to cover their breasts in public as part of the Breast Cloth Movement in early-nineteenth-century Travancore. As a result, the queen of Travancore issued an 1865 proclamation allowing all castes to cover their breasts in public.

The practice of female bare-breastedness at home and in the temple, however, continued in the Kutiyattam community and more widely in Kerala until the mid-twentieth century when caste-based clothing was rejected in favor of the secular North Indian sari. In fact, it is common today to see older family photos of bare-breasted grandmothers or great-grandmothers in homes across Kerala, in stark juxtaposition to the dress of the women who inhabit them. As Thomas (2018) argues, the choice by women throughout Kerala to wear the sari represented a homogenization of caste and religious identity into one single identity—that of gender—as bodies became recognizable through their clothing only as male or female. This fits a larger process of late nineteenth-century and early twentieth-century public discourse in Kerala that Devika (2007a) argues actively "engender[ed] individuals." As Devika explains, this discourse aimed to construct modern gender identities (e.g., man/woman) that would supersede caste and community identities. Over time, not only breasts but also shoulders, upper arms, and ankles all became associated with female immodesty. These wider changes profoundly impacted women in Kutiyattam, and the previous norm of bare-breasted cymbal players and sleeveless actresses in temple performances eventually changed to all women performers today wearing the sari blouse, regardless of venue. One hereditary actress told me that her mother had been asked by temple authorities to remove her blouse for performance as recently as the late 1960s, but she refused.

Guru Painkulam's innovations to women's costuming and makeup at Kalamandalam reflected these ongoing changes to women's dress in wider Kerala society. Today, they have been universally adopted by professional actresses on both public and temple stages. For nonprofessional Nangiar actresses performing on hereditary stages, the reception has been mixed. While some have adopted the Kalamandalam costume, others continue to use the less costly, naturally sourced one, maintaining the wide range of individual decorative styles that characterize the older costume. Throughout the 1970s and early 1980s, several costume variations mixed elements from both the older and newer costumes. Today, most overt costume variation has disappeared, although it is still possible to observe slight variations in the shape of the belt, color of the sari top, style of choker and earrings, and choice of decorative makeup flourishes. I have noticed that Kapila Venu, a young, nonhereditary actress, occasionally uses the old makeup style, with a red base and chin outlined in black, but this is not common.

Changes to the male costume have been less drastic (fig. 37). Kalamandalam Ram Mohan detailed many of the more subtle changes to the men's costume at Kalamandalam. As with the women's costume, the neck and stomach were covered, and natural elements such as flower and cotton garlands were substituted for longer-lasting red and white yarn garlands. While the makeup patterns for different characters have remained the same, men's makeup was brought in line with Kathakali by enlarging the *chutti* (*cuṭṭi*) rice paste beard through the use of paper and adding a *poṭṭŭ*, or decorative mark between the eyebrows for all characters instead of only a few.[43] Ram Mohan-ashan told me about what he believed was the first paper beard used in Kutiyattam. Previously formed by slowly building up layers of hardened rice paste along the jawline, the *chutti* beard easily crumbled. His teacher, Govinda Warrier, first put a paper beard on Mani Madhava Chakyar while doing his makeup for a performance at Kalamandalam.[44] This would have occurred before the opening of the Kutiyattam department when paper beards had been in vogue for Kathakali since World War II.

In terms of the male costume, Guru Painkulam extended the half-sleeves of most characters to the wrists, added Kathakali's large gold-foil wooden bangles (*vaḷa*) to smaller existing bangles (*katakam*), and substantially increased the size of the headpiece.[45] Gopalakrishnan (2016b, 39) notes that these changes to the sleeves as well as improvements on the *poynakham* skirt resulted from discussions between Guru Painkulam and Guru Kalamandalam Govinda Warrier, adding that Guru Painkulam also consulted with Kathakali guru Kalamandalam Padmanabhan Nair while improving Kutiyattam's costumes and aesthetics. Ram Mohan-ashan further explained how he himself had substituted fake fur jackets for several of the monkey characters as well—the earlier Hanuman jacket was made of white cloth stitched with cotton balls, that of Sugriva of black cotton, and that of Bali of red and black striped material. He further noted that Sugriva's headpiece (*makutham*) was formerly made of bamboo, describing how he had changed it to a black version of Hanuman's white headpiece, thereby discarding the bamboo.[46]

Figure 37. (*Left to right*) Unknown Chakyar actor in male costume circa 1934 (Gilchriest Hatch 1934). Photo courtesy of Susan Marie Mathias. Sooraj Nambiar in contemporary costume. Photo by author.

I noticed much less individual variation in the men's Kutiyattam costume than the women's. I was told that the actor Margi Madhu had added creative flare to his costume and makeup by using innovative forehead marks (*pottu*) for his characters as well as a permanent hairpiece usually used for only a few characters. Apart from this, there does not seem to be much variation in costume interpretation among actors except for the decorative woodwork of their ornaments, a modification determined not by actors but by the craftsman who constructs them. The men's wooden belt (*katisūtram*) and one particular headpiece (*vasikam*) feature Vyali, a mythical dragon often seen guarding the entrance to South Indian temples. Ramankutty Kothavil, the only carpenter in Kerala today who makes Kutiyattam costumes, carves each ornament as a unique piece of folk art. As he told me, "I do each Vyali differently. With each order I try to make it a little more beautiful than the last. The old Vyali's eyes were very small, you saw? Now I make them differently."[47] Ramankutty's father was originally commissioned by Guru Painkulam and Govinda Warrier

Figure 38. Three variations of Vyali on a Kutiyattam *vasikam* and craftsman/carpenter Ramankutty Kothavil making a Kathakali headpiece. Photos by author.

to make the wooden elements of Kutiyattam costumes—headpieces, belts, neckpieces, bracelets, and shoulder pieces. No one knew who had carved them earlier, so his father taught himself using old costumes as models while also incorporating innovations requested by the gurus. According to Ramankutty, Kalamandalam enhanced the beauty of the design by adding new details to the woodwork, such as floral flourishes.

The *pozhumbu* neckpiece, which currently has thick golden chains and pompoms hanging from it, used to consist solely of the wooden neckpiece. According to Ram Mohan-ashan, Guru Painkulam began this design by hanging four to five strands of beads; the necklace would have broken with more. Around 1972 or 1974, Ram Mohan-ashan added a full string of beads sewn to a fabric background as in Kathakali—now the standard—so that it would not break. Another variation is the *uttarīyam* sash, which used to be standard for the entire troupe. Artists have modified this over time by using individualized sashes in performance.

As Usha-teacher explained, these innovations in makeup and costuming were undertaken to enhance the beauty of Kutiyattam, with the goal of attracting new audiences outside of the temple. Part of the process of ensuring the

Figure 39. (*Left to right*) Comparing size between a contemporary and an older male headpiece and Kalamandalam Ram Mohan decorating a Kutiyattam headpiece. Photos by author.

art's wider appeal involved responding to new stage conditions, as Kutiyattam suddenly found itself on proscenium stages with very different conditions than temple stages. Ram Mohan-ashan clarified the difference: "In the koothambalam there were only oil lamps, so there was very little light. If the costumes had any problems, like the color was fading or something, it wasn't a problem because people couldn't see them well. But in Kalamandalam it is just like in theaters and other stages, there will be flat electric light, so the small faults will be seen by the audience. So we have to care more about the costumes and the characters' dress also."

Narayanan (2005, 36) beautifully describes the different circumstances of temple stage lighting, where "the soft, upward, yellow light of the lamp and the play of light and shade put the actors' costumes and makeup into high relief, exaggerating and enhancing their size, shapes and colours. With only the actors in the circle of light and everything else, including the musicians and the rest of the stage, in a shadowy penumbra, it produced an ethereal, larger than life quality to the performance." He points out that in contrast, new secular stages, with their increased lighting and greater size and distance from the audience, make the actor appear smaller onstage. Narayanan characterizes further innovations—brighter colors of costumes and makeup, a general increase in the size of costuming elements, and what he terms more expansive modes of acting and gestures—as attempts to adjust for this reduction in size in relation to the stage (2005, 41).

Music

One of the most significant contributions to the improvement of Kutiyattam's performance aesthetics at Kalamandalam was the reinvention of Kutiyattam music by mizhavu guru Padmasree P. K. Narayanan Nambiar, in collaboration with Painkulam Rama Chakyar. Whereas temple performance included a number of instruments onstage—the mizhavu drum, the edakka drum, the oboe-like *kurunkuzhal* (*kuṟuṅkuḻal*), and the *shanku* (*śamkhŭ*) conch shell—the latter two eventually disappeared from performance at Kalamandalam.[48] The sharp, high-pitched kurunkuzhal—generally played with no predetermined tune—dominated the soundscape when it was onstage, such as during the *akkita* hymns in the preliminaries to Kutiyattam performance. As scholar L. S. Rajagopalan (1994, 118) writes, "The *Kuzhal* player . . . often plays a series of notes which produce an unmusical or jarring effect. These mainly have no relation to the sentiments or action portrayed by the [actor]. . . . I for one, can never imaging [*sic*] that the originators of this wonderful art of Kutiyattam—who were so particular in the use of different *ragas* for different shades of the same *rasa*—would ever have allowed the indisciplined freedom that the *Kuzhal* player now appropriates to himself." Guru Painkulam insisted on including kurunkuzhal at Kalamandalam, with Kunhikrishna Pothuval—whom Kalamandalam Unnikrishnan Nambiar recalls as being especially talented—playing along in tune. After Pothuval's retirement in the 1970s, the instrument disappeared from the stage, with the mizhavu remaining the key element in the Kutiyattam soundscape and the edakka and *kuzhithalam* cymbals in supporting roles.[49]

The single-most important change to Kutiyattam music was Guru P. K. Narayanan Nambiar's revolutionizing of mizhavu percussion technique. Artists describe this innovation as having created a "coordination" or "synergy" (*yōjippŭ*) between actor and drummer that had not existed before. Several artists told me that drummers and actors never practiced together in earlier temple performances, performing virtually independently of one another. Due to Chakyar/Nangiar intermarriages in Guru Narayanan Nambiar's family, Chakyars, Nambiars, and Nangiars had lived together in his family household for several generations. He grew up observing family members—actors,

Figure 40. (*Left to right*) Chathakudam Krishnan Nambiar and Guru P. K. Narayanan Nambiar playing mizhavu in the late 1960s/early 1970s. Photo by Clifford Jones, courtesy of Lizzette Thomason.

actresses, and drummers—practicing together regularly. As the mizhavu guru at Kalamandalam, not only did he and his students rehearse with the acting students in combined *choliyattam* (*cōlliyāṭṭam*) practice, but they did so while sitting in front of the actors, thereby fostering a dialogue between actor and drummer that allowed for the subtleties of the acting to be conveyed through musical accompaniment.[50] Nambiar-ashan timed certain movements musically, and he drastically expanded the variety of rhythms (*tāḷams*) featured, with certain rhythms synchronized with certain sequences and emotional sentiments. He writes that the mizhavu player "has to be extremely cautious in providing the appropriate *mela* (accompaniment) using various *tāḷās* (rhythms) that perfectly harmonise with the gestures of the actor, the action, the *bhāvās* (sentiments) enacted and the different kinds of stylized movement" (Nambiar 1994, 111). Through these innovations, drummers became the voice for actors during long sequences of silent miming, enriching the performance by heightening the emotions conveyed in each scene. Many actors today say that the mizhavu provides vital emotional support for their acting. As one actress emphasized, "The mizhavu is the *most* important! . . . Without a good percussionist, the audience won't feel anything." Guru Painkulam once expressed similar sentiments to Richard Schechner, telling him, "[The mizhavu] gives power to the mudras while acting, otherwise they will have no life. Suppose one is acting the act of beating, drums will give it power. Even if the gestures are mild they get their life from the drummer" (Chakyar 1976).

According to Kalamandalam Easwaranunni (2001, 74), Guru Narayanan Nambiar's student and successor at Kalamandalam, "The whole visual richness of Koodiyattam is felt by the spectators only with the magical fingering of Nambiar on the Mizhavu." In an article written in homage to his guru, Easwaranunni describes another critical innovation by Nambiar-ashan, namely, the codification of *vaythari* rhythmic syllables in relation to specific dance and ritual movement sequences (*kriyas*) onstage.[51] Creating a "pre-determined rhythmic structure," Guru Narayanan Nambiar standardized the rhythms of numerous sequences like *maṟayilkriya*; the *nityakriyas*; and those for *Anguliyankam*, *Mattavilasam*, and others (2001, 72). He similarly set the *akkitas*, a sequence of invocational verses sung by the Nangiar sitting side-stage, to specific rhythmic scales and restructured the opening strokes on the mizhavu (*miḻāvŭ occappeṭuka*) in a simplified and standardized two-beat *ēkatāḷa* cycle (2001, 73).

Besides these critical developments, Guru Narayanan Nambiar, who has been called "a living encyclopaedia of Kutiyattam," has made several other important contributions to the art (Easwaranunni 2001, 72). He created an independent percussion ensemble called *mizhavil thayampaka*, modeled on Kerala's popular *tāyambaka* temple solo drumming genre, which helped increase the popularity of mizhavu outside of its original theatrical context.[52] *Mizhavil thayambaka* generally features three mizhavus playing shifting patterns of varying slow and fast rhythms, led by an improvisational soloist (fig. 41).[53] Cymbals such as *ilatāḷam*, *kuḻitāḷam*, or *cēṅṅala* keep the beat, while two supporting drums such as bass *chenda* (*vīkŭ ceṇda*), edakka, or *thimila* accompany them.[54] This laid the groundwork for mizhavu to be recognized in its own right across wider performance contexts, like in Roysten Abel's 2014 international theater production *The Kitchen*, which featured an orchestra of twelve mizhavus, and A. R. Rahman's 2018 Amazon Prime show *Harmony*, whose first episode, "Entering the Kalari," was devoted to the mizhavu playing of Kalamandalam Sajith Vijayan.[55]

Finally, Guru Narayanan Nambiar has also made a significant scholarly contribution, authoring books about the performance of *Mantrāṅkam* (1980) as well as a definitive manual of mizhavu history and performance (2005). One of his crowning achievements was the 1984 publication of an acting manual for Nangiarkoothu, compiled by meticulously collecting old palm-leaf Nangiarkoothu

Figure 41. Mizhavu *thayambaka* led by Kalamandalam Eashwaranunni (*center*). Photo by author.

manuscripts from hereditary families around the state, including his own. The publication of his *Śrīkṛṣṇacaritam Naṅṅyārammakūttu* (*Story of Srikrishna Nangiarammakoothu*) was a watershed moment that led to the full-scale revival of Kutiyattam women's solo performance during the 1980s and 1990s.[56] Guru Narayanan Nambiar thereby helped bring the original vision of Guru Painkulam, who apprenticed Kalamandalam Girija to the hereditary actress Kunjipilla Kutty Nangiar in the 1970s, to life.[57] Nambiar-ashan has also choreographed several productions for the stage, including all five acts of Bhasa's *Bālacaritam*, full productions of *Mantrāṅkam* and *Mattavilasam Kutiyattam* at Margi, and several Nangiarkoothu episodes.[58] More recently, he choreographed and wrote an *attaprakaram* (stage manual) for new Kutiyattam productions, including *Mallāṅkam* and an episode from *Mārkaṇḍeyacaritam* titled *Antakawadham*, which brought Shiva to the stage in costume for the first time.

Implications

The reinvention of Kutiyattam at Kalamandalam reflected larger processes of democratization and secularization across a newly communist Kerala, which significantly changed the face of contemporary Kutiyattam performance. The art's own democratization and secularization led to the fracturing of Kutiyattam into three types of performers: (1) the hereditary nonprofessional performer rooted exclusively in the temple, fulfilling familial and caste duties; (2) the nonhereditary professional performer rooted exclusively in the public sphere, generally not permitted to perform on koothambalam temple stages; and (3) the hereditary professional performer who moves between both temple and public spheres, actively negotiating between two simultaneous worlds of "traditional" and "modern" performance that coexist in contemporary Kutiyattam. These three types of Kutiyattam performers and accompanying discourses highlight the varying conceptions of tradition and modernity, private and public, and religious and secular that Lukose (2006) asserts characterize contemporary cultural politics in Kerala.

Guru Painkulam's reinvention of Kutiyattam through the lens of beauty-as-intelligibility recalls the notion of the aesthetic as well as Bourdieu's (1984) celebrated critique of Kant's formulation of the aesthetic as independent of social, political, and economic influence. In contrast to Kant, Bourdieu (1984) thought of aesthetic appreciation as a form of cultural capital vital to constructing class identity and maintaining its privilege through distinctions in "taste." As an exclusive temple art, Kutiyattam possessed elite cultural capital, demonstrated by its upper-caste artists performing in elite contexts inaccessible to lower-caste peoples and its use of Sanskrit, the language of the Brahminical elite. As we saw previously, Kerala's emerging communist politics initially rejected Brahminical cultural products, despite eventually embracing them as emblems of regional heritage. As Dr. C. K. Jayanthi, Sanskrit professor and granddaughter of Guru Mani, told me, "Everyone in Kerala thought that Sanskrit was bourgeois, so it should be neglected . . . Brahminical traditions, Sanskrit traditions were really strong in Kerala, like Kutiyattam and the Vedas. But after independence, all of this disappeared. People said, 'You can't do that, you shouldn't go to the temple,' it wasn't okay, religion wasn't okay, Sanskrit wasn't okay, the Vedas weren't okay, Namboodiris weren't okay, everything wasn't okay." As Jones (1977, 12) similarly describes in mid-twentieth-century Kerala, "The growing lack of interest in Sanskrit as the most esteemed language of culture had reduced [Kutiyattam] audiences in an alarming way."

Kerala's cultural heritage ultimately came to be defined in terms of elite, caste culture now accessible to all. Intending to make the art more intelligible and appealing to wider audiences, Guru Painkulam's efforts toward Kutiyattam's standardization and beautification at Kalamandalam were, I argue, attempts to shed some of its elite cultural capital in order to adapt to an increasingly egalitarian-minded public—in effect, to make the art less elite. While he radically changed performance to focus on nonhereditary bodies performing in nonhereditary contexts, as we saw above, Guru Painkulam also greatly limited the use of Sanskrit, reducing previously twice-chanted Sanskrit verses to a single recitation. Yet even this decreased use of Sanskrit is perceived as a barrier to accessibility, especially combined with intricacies of performance that require a time commitment to truly understand. As a result, there is a widespread conception that Kutiyattam is a difficult art form to understand, limiting its audience appeal today.

Kutiyattam's reinvention also significantly resulted in shifting the majority of performances to Kerala's public sphere.[59] Governed by increasingly compressed notions of time, artists today lament that Guru Painkulam's initial editing of performances down to three hours for public stages has been pushed to contemporary extremes of what they call "capsule" performances. One artist expressed exasperation as he shared how he turned down the request of a potential patron who asked him, "Can you do a Kutiyattam in ten minutes?" Keeping in mind that costume and makeup preparation require around three hours, such requests border on the absurd. This wider secularization and recontextualization of the art in the public sphere have also led to some artists abandoning the traditional rules of purity and impurity associated with Kutiyattam as a temple art. Several Kalamandalam-trained actors, for example, no longer tie the red thread around their forehead before performances.[60] The thread symbolizes the actor's transformation into the liminal space of the character; after tying it, the actor will theoretically remain pure even upon the death of a family member, allowing them to finish a performance despite the pollution that death brings. As Kalamandalam Shylaja explained, "If you tie the red thread, you need to do it in a pure (*shudhamayitte*) way. If not, it has no meaning and is a great sin. Everything in Kerala is impure, so why should we unnecessarily commit a great sin?" This view of the public sphere as impure and thereby sacrilegious serves to reinforce the divide between hereditary temple performances and public performances.

In addition to wider shifts from hereditary to nonhereditary performers and from religious to secular performance contexts, Betty Jones (1977) observes another shift taking place: from a focus on the actor's scholarly training to an emphasis on his physical and theatrical abilities. Jones (1977, 9) notes that fifty years before her writing in the 1970s, "the emphasis was indisputably on the Cākyār as Sanskrit scholar," reflecting the expectations of audiences with erudite Sanskrit knowledge. As she describes, "Sanskrit lessons, the teaching of the rāgas for recitation, and of Sanskrit and Maṇipravāḷam verses, proceeded with more regularity, but the physical training tended to be less rigorous. Although the young Cākyār learned all of the prescribed movements, his execution of them was not of the same high order as his scholarship and recitation" (1977, 9). Jones (1977, 14) continues by posing a question about the changes she has observed at Kalamandalam, namely, "Can the students who are being trained today, with so much more emphasis on their physical training, attain the time-consuming high level of scholarship for which their predecessors were famous? Is it possible within a lifetime to memorize thousands of shlokas from Sanskrit epics, kāvya, prabhanda, campū, and miscellaneous literature, and also to attain the proficiency and artistry which they are attaining in the physical sense?" Due to decline in the prestige and appreciation of Sanskrit in Kerala, she concludes that the trend of emphasizing the theatricality of the physical form over Sanskrit scholarship would likely continue.

The last major progressive change attributed to Guru Painkulam at Kalamandalam is the art's first international tour. He led the Kalamandalam Kutiyattam troupe to Poland and France in May 1980, at a time when orthodox Hindu communities believed that crossing the ocean was blasphemous. Shortly after the troupe's return, Guru Painkulam tragically passed away.[61] The tour was coorganized by Milena Salvini, director of the Centre Mandapa for the promotion of South Asian performing arts in Paris and organizer of Kalamandalam's first international Kathakali tour to Paris a decade earlier, and Dr. Maria Krzysztof Byrski, professor of Indology at Warsaw University and the first foreign Kutiyattam student under Guru Mani nearly two decades earlier. The troupe performed in Paris to packed audiences and in Poland at the Warsaw International Dance Festival. This first tour, highlighted in a 1980 issue of *UNESCO Features*, was partly funded with assistance from UNESCO's International Fund for the Promotion of Culture. This placed Kutiyattam on UNESCO's radar and foreshadowed its later international recognition. Most importantly, the tour initiated Kutiyattam's participation in global flows of performance that would greatly impact the art and its audiences through the present day.

Gender and Caste in Contemporary Kutiyattam

The above innovations at Kerala Kalamandalam in the mid- to late twentieth century served to redefine gender and caste relations in Kutiyattam. Today, the majority of professional actors and acting students are women, and more than half of all professionally trained Kutiyattam artists, including mizhavu drummers, are nonhereditary performers. As in broader Kerala society, however, despite a wider egalitarian ideal from decades of communism, caste inequality has not disappeared but simply transformed. In this section, I explore how gender and caste have intersected in divergent ways in the lives of contemporary Kutiyattam artists.

On my most recent trip to Kalamandalam in January 2020, many things had changed since the six months I spent there in 2009–2010. Kalamandalam Girija and Kalamandalam Shylaja retired, Margi Sathi tragically passed away, and several former graduate students are now primary instructors. Sindhu-chechi is also now teaching there as a temporary instructor—she left Margi several years ago for Kalamandalam's better salary and to be closer to family. As I walk uphill through the sprawling campus, I feel excited to see old friends and catch up. The familiar cacophony of drumming fills the air as percussive beats stream out of open-air classrooms. Approaching the boys' classroom for Kutiyattam acting, I see only two students—a young Malayali teenager and a Spanish student in his twenties. The instructors are chatting outside.

After an enthusiastic reunion, Kalamandalam Kanakakumar, who recently secured a permanent teaching position after nearly a decade of trying, updates me on the state of Kutiyattam admissions. He tells me that the existing trend of greater numbers of female (*streevesham*) than male (*purushavesham*) acting students has increased exponentially. Displaying the numbers on his fingers for emphasis, he tells me that there are currently a grand total of five *purushavesham* students—one first year, two second years, one third year, and one fourth year—compared to a whopping forty-three *streevesham* students. It becomes obvious that women are the future of Kutiyattam as I tour the packed girls' classrooms around campus, expertly led by instructors such as Kalamandalam Krishnendu. After many years, she is still hoping to secure a permanent teaching position there, but Kalamandalam has not opened any.[62] Finally climbing to the very top of the hill, I visit a mizhavu classroom led by another old friend, Kalamandalam Sajith Vijayan, who smiles upon my arrival. Among other updates, he tells me, "Nowadays, actually the ladies are doing most of the work in everything, most of the programs and new stories."

Indeed, the strong emphasis at Kalamandalam on the reinvention of Kutiyattam's female costume, the revival of women's roles onstage, and the revival and development of Nangiarkoothu sparked a renaissance in women's performance that has lasted from the mid-1980s through the present day. While the hereditary actresses Usha Nangiar and Dr. Aparna Nangiar are among the most well known in the field today, the majority of actresses in contemporary Kutiyattam are nonhereditary performers. Fully embraced and celebrated, nonhereditary women artists represent many of the stars of the contemporary Kutiyattam stage. Upon closer examination, however, it becomes clear that, although never discussed, the vast majority of contemporary nonhereditary actresses come from upper-caste backgrounds.[63]

As with Kutiyattam actresses, nonhereditary artists form the majority of mizhavu drummers today, but unlike actresses, they are more caste-diverse. As with other nonhereditary artists, nonhereditary drummers are barred from performing in hereditary temple contexts.[64] I never personally observed caste discrimination against drummers or conversations about it, but this does not mean it never happens. I did observe discrimination against drummers vis-à-vis actors and actresses. Mizhavu drummers consistently receive lower institutional salaries and lower remuneration for performances than do actors and actresses even though, as several drummers told me, their rigorous performance is so strenuous they sometimes urinate blood the following day. In wider performance circuits, actors and actresses are generally treated as stars, with drummers often sidelined, despite the seminal role that everyone acknowledges they play in performance. Kapila Venu once mentioned a performance elsewhere in India where she, the actress, was provided a room at an upscale hotel, while the drummers were given third-rate accommodations. When she insisted that the drummers be given equal accommodations, the organizers relented. This hierarchy of actors and actresses privileged above drummers seems to parallel the art's strictly hereditary days, although in a slightly different form. In speaking to Nambiar/Nangiar families, I learned about a distinct hierarchy in earlier days that placed higher-caste Chakyar actors above Nambiar drummers and Nangiar actresses who, with less power and agency, were subject to Chakyar authority. In contemporary power constellations, actresses have joined actors in terms of power and recognition in the performance context, while drummers have been left behind.

Actors represent the group of Kutiyattam performers today generally least welcoming to nonhereditary performers.[65] Kutiyattam acting continues to be dominated by hereditary Chakyar actors, many of whom still control much of the art's knowledge. This includes knowledge of extended, unedited performance pieces as well as access to palm-leaf dramatic manuscripts, which they are generally unwilling to share with nonhereditary artists. As half-Brahmins, the continued dominance of Chakyars today can be positioned within a wider dominant framework of Brahminical patriarchy. In the early days, even students with a caste status higher than Chakyars, such as Kalamandalam Shivan Namboodiri, experienced discrimination. Among a later generation of nonhereditary actors who studied at Kalamandalam under Guru Painkulam's students, some claim that Chakyar instructors consistently favored Chakyar students, including teaching them unedited performance pieces withheld from nonhereditary students. Overall, it has been much more difficult for nonhereditary actors, as compared to actresses, to find success in terms of performance opportunities, stage recognition, and permanent institutional teaching positions.[66] However, the Kutiyattam actor has retained a definitive degree of privilege. For example, despite extremely low numbers of *purushavesham* students at Kalamandalam, the only permanent teaching positions that have opened in over a decade are for male Kutiyattam acting instructors. Mizhavu and *streevesham* Kutiyattam instructors have been waiting nearly a decade for positions to open in their areas of specialty. Despite several retirements years ago, these positions have remained unfilled, with instructors instead hired into temporary annual contracts.

Kutiyattam and Communism

Returning to Kerala's communist politics, I asked artists, "What is the relationship between Kutiyattam and Communism?" This question surprised most artists, who generally answered after a slight pause, "There's no relation at all." Many of them went on to explain that artists are supposed to avoid politics. As Usha-teacher proudly told me, "I teach everyone, regardless of what political party they or their parents belong to."

What emerged from these conversations is the idea that being political in Kerala means being an official party member active in party activities. Artists are subject to the funding whims of constantly shifting political winds and for their own well-being are expected to be nonpartisan. As we have learned, for the past forty years, the political coalitions ruling the Kerala government have predictably shifted every five years between the leadership of the CPI(M) and the Congress Party. Most Kutiyattam institutions, including Kerala Kalamandalam, are dependent on funding from the ever-changing Kerala government. As the political winds change, so do the upper administrators at Kalamandalam, who are appointed by the ruling party.[67] Any permanent hires must be approved by the current ruling coalition, and for an artist who may find himself on the wrong side of the political spectrum during a once-in-a-lifetime job opportunity, the results could be disastrous. It is therefore prudent for artists to remain politically neutral by refraining from party membership.

Sympathizing with one party or another, however, is acceptable. In fact, I was told that traditional artists of both folk and classical arts in Kerala are generally sympathetic to the Communist Party. Kalamandalam Ram Mohan-ashan assured me, "Classical artists are all followers of communism." He paused, and then added, "Well, *most* of the classical artists are, but they're *not* party members." Considering Guru Painkulam's strong principles of caste equality, radical for a Chakyar at the time, I wondered if he had such sympathies as well. Ram Mohan-ashan confirmed my suspicions, saying, "Painkulam Rama Chakyar was a follower of the Communist Party. He was a friend of EMS and Mundassery. When the Communist Party was banned, people hid EMS in houses in villages, people from all groups. Rama Chakyar and EMS' homes were near to one another." He enthusiastically continued, "At that time, they were a gang of friends—EMS, Rama Chakyar, Mundassery, Kuttykrishnan Marar, they were all friends and used to meet regularly. Killimangalam Vasudevan Namboodirippad also, but he was young at the time.[68] Kuttykrishnan was a Sanskrit teacher at Kalamandalam at Vallathol. And Rama Chakyar was appointed in 65, by the EMS government."

When I inquired further, several junior artists at Kalamandalam confirmed that they had heard of Guru Painkulam's communist leanings. Some had also heard that he was friends with Achutha Menon, an influential communist leader of the CPI and chief minister of Kerala for nearly a decade. Painkulam Narayana Chakyar verified that his great-granduncle had been close friends with both Achutha Menon and Joseph Mundassery. He further told a tale of Guru Painkulam performing Chakyarkoothu at a large communist conference in the 1960s, and there making fun of A. K. Gopalan, another prominent communist leader. He revealed that in addition to Joseph Mundassery's encouragement, Achutha Menon had also encouraged and supported the guru to perform outside of the temple. At the mizhavu classroom, Kalamandalam Sajith Vijayan told me, "Painkulam Rama Chakyar was a great friend of these people. They would meet and discuss, so maybe he got some ideas from them. Chakyars were very conservative, so it takes a Chakyar with an open mind to do what he did here."[69]

Turning to written accounts, Johan (2014, vol. 1, 72) has characterized Guru Painkulam as a "communist activist" who was the only prominent guru at the time to marry outside of his caste, taking a Nair wife. Theater scholar and director Herbert Blau (1992, 35) has likewise written what appears to be a telling account of the guru: "Some years ago in a project in which we were exchanging performance techniques . . . I asked the leader of the Kutiyattam dancers, a gentle scholarly man, how he felt about what was happening in the form now that it is no longer in the sanctuary of the temple. 'It is very sad,' he said, 'but then, you know, I am a Marxist too.'"

In terms of wider governmental support for the arts, most artists I spoke to agreed that while the CPI(M) and the Congress Party have both been supportive of the arts, the CPI(M) has given slightly more support. Some thought that they were equally supportive. Others stated that the CPI(M) was substantially more supportive, describing it as the party that generally initiated new arts funding schemes, whereas Congress would simply continue them.[70] One artist insisted, "Communism supports the arts much more, the other simply continues it grudgingly," humorously enacting having to yank money out of someone's hands. He then offered a commentary on the Hindu nationalist party, the Bharatiya Janata Party (BJP), whose support is still low in Kerala but gaining steadily: "But the BJP is bad, they are favoring the Brahmins. Being a Brahmin is only an idea."

In terms of more concrete examples of communist financial support of Kutiyattam over the years, Ram Mohan-ashan told me that the koothambalam theater at Kalamandalam was approved, granted, and paid for in the 1970s by Achutha Menon while chief minister of Kerala, with Appukuttan Nair hired as the chief engineer at the same time he was managing Margi.[71] He also mentioned that the communist government paid for a complete set of new Kutiyattam costumes in the early years of the department and that it granted more permanent teaching posts. "At least it's my understanding that the communist government did all of this," he told me. The CPI(M)-led government also presided over the two recent Kutiyattam *purushavesham* teaching hires at Kalamandalam, which had been stalled for years.

To explore the official position of the communist-led government, in February 2020 I visited the Kerala state Directorate of Culture in Trivandrum, located in the last palace built by the king of Travancore. As I entered the dirt courtyard from an unassuming side road, I was met with an imposing two-story building that seemed straight out of nineteenth-century Europe. Its impressive columns stood twenty-five to thirty feet tall, adorned with carved tendrils of winding ivy and flanked by two massive balustraded staircases capped by delicately carved cherubs. There, I met the director of culture, T. R. Sadasivan Nair, and asked if he believed that Communists had supported arts more than other parties in Kerala. He replied, "Leftists have always had a very favorable approach to art and culture. They cleverly know how fast art and culture can propagate their ideas. Art can take their ideas to the people." His comment made me think of Thoppil Bhasi's iconic play *You Made Me a Communist* (*Niṅṅaḷenne*

Commūnistākki), which, along with other political plays performed in villages throughout mid-twentieth-century Kerala, helped bring Communism to the masses.[72] The director smiled, continuing, "This is the only place in India with a scheme system for culture at the state level, perhaps the only place in the whole world! This is a very big commitment on the part of communist leadership. It is only because of the left government that the Directorate of Culture was strengthened. Before, money went directly to the academies and Kalamandalam; now it goes to the Directorate for schemes." His assistant nodded his affirmation, showing me a leaflet with the new cultural funding schemes this government had initiated in its most recent tenure since 2016.

One of the funding schemes in the leaflet was a program many young Kutiyattam artists had mentioned, the Diamond Jubilee Junior fellowships, created as part of the state's 2017 Diamond Jubilee celebration commemorating sixty years since the Communist government first came to power in Kerala. The officer in charge of the scheme noted that it supports one thousand young artists from forty-five different art forms, including Kutiyattam. In collaboration with the state and local *panchayat* (village council) governments, each artist receives Rs. 15,000 per month for two years in order to teach free classes to local students irrespective of caste or age, culminating in an end-of-course performance.[73] He proudly revealed that fifty thousand people were currently being given arts training across the state, with the goal of teaching the public how to understand these art forms, "so that at the least they can peacefully watch them for one or two hours." One of his assistants chimed in, "Common people are not interested in art, so we promote it." The directing officer agreed, "This government are pioneers [*sic*] in art and culture."

He explained that the Diamond Jubilee fellowships have three aims: (1) to give financial support to young artists under the age of thirty-five, (2) to popularize many art forms of Kerala, and (3) to engage young people and counter the negative influence of social media. Elaborating on the third point, the officer explained seriously, "Social media is constructive as well as destructive, but the youth can't judge correctly which is which. This program was implemented to counter the evil effects of social media. For the past five to six years, the younger generation is under the influence of these kind of negative impacts—social media, alcohol, drugs. But a person who loves art cannot stray from the right path." He continued:

> Art directly affects the heart. Other forms can affect the intellect, but feelings come from the heart. If we can provide something that goes directly to the heart, we can help them become good human beings. These days, if

> there is an accident and someone is hurt, people will simply stand around taking videos before they will call for help. An art lover cannot stray from the right path, but a person with intellect can still be cruel. Like that, making a positive change in society is an indirect aim of the scheme. Through art we can inculcate values of life to the younger generation.

I was struck by the poetic nature of his response. "Is this the official stance of the party?" I asked.

"Yes," he replied.

The CPI(M)'s aim to foster future art lovers, conceptualized as those "on the right path," is also an effort to foster future good citizens. Combined with the director of culture's comment that leftists "cleverly know how fast art and culture can propagate their ideas," we must contextualize the scheme as part of a wider political agenda. Belonging to a larger push toward a neoliberal "individualist model" of arts funding, J. Devika has called the scheme "a dole to artists to guarantee their votes in the future."[74] At the same time, we must consider it within the larger context of an unprecedented financial crisis in the Kerala government, set in motion by the BJP-led central Indian government.[75] With Kerala state a bastion of resistance against the central government's Hindu nationalist initiatives, most notably the Citizenship Amendment Act of 2019, which legislated discrimination against religious minorities, some see the punitive financial penalties levied by the central government against Kerala state as political retribution. Though a newer iteration, this forms part of a longer history in which an earlier anti-left central government repeatedly manipulated food supplies and finances to Kerala to "undercut left-wing governments" (Franke and Chasin 1994, 20). Whatever the current political climate may be, it is clear that the Kerala CPI(M) has long considered the support of traditional arts in its best interest as part of shaping its regional citizenry, and that there is an undeniable history of its support for Kutiyattam.

Conclusion

In this chapter, I have explored how the rise of democratic communism amid wider social, cultural, and economic changes in twentieth-century Kerala has deeply impacted contemporary Kutiyattam, catalyzing the art's reinvention at Kerala Kalamandalam and positioning it within wider discourses of regional heritage. In adapting the art to the changing tastes of increasingly diverse, communist-leaning audiences, the reinvention of Kutiyattam is a perfect example of the intimate connection between bodies and sociopolitical worlds. The changes to the Kutiyattam body-in-performance instituted by Guru Painkulam at Kalamandalam mirror wider changes in both the social body and the body politic in Kerala.

Drawing from the work of Marcel Mauss (1936), anthropologist Mary Douglas ([1970] 1973) suggests that the physical body is a microcosm of society. In her essay "The Two Bodies," Douglas ([1970] 1973, 93) argues that there is a constant exchange of meanings between the social and physical bodies that continually reinforces the category of the other. The social body "constrains the way the physical body is perceived," while the physical body, "always modified by the social categories through which it is known, sustains a particular view of society." Anthropologists Nancy Scheper-Hughes and Margaret Lock (1987) propose a third body, that of the body politic, which regulates physical bodies via political and legal means. Of these three interrelated bodies, Scheper-Hughes and Lock consider the body politic the most dynamic in suggesting why and how certain bodies are socially produced.

For centuries, Kutiyattam had been situated exclusively within a hereditary temple context that was a realm of "habitus" where art, work, and life were inseparable (Bourdieu [1980] 1990). This chapter has detailed the art's separation from its hereditary sphere of everyday life as the habitus of Chakyars, Nangiars, and Nambiars alongside its increasing professionalization and reinscription in a democratized, nonhereditary public sphere governed by new social and political ideals of equality. At Kalamandalam, the body was shaped, aestheticized, and standardized to appeal to new left-leaning audiences, leaving the art unalterably changed. Its democratization at the institution, with training and performance opened to nonhereditary performers for the first time, mirrored Kerala's emergent public sphere in which occupation, schooling, religion, and the physical spaces in which citizens could move their bodies were no longer restricted by caste.

At the same time, Kutiyattam became implicated in an upper-caste performing arts heritage formulated by the Communist Party to represent Kerala's emergent, subnational identity. At Kalamandalam and on state festival stages, the Kutiyattam body became an emblem of state heritage through processes of institutionalization, democratization, and professionalization, embodying wider social and political processes actively shaping an emergent Malayali identity. These processes did not fully transform the art, as they did not fully transform Kerala society, leaving caste hegemony and Kerala's conservative temple culture largely intact.[76] As we have seen, despite the Communist Party's egalitarian ideology, its mainly upper-caste leaders have tended to reinforce Hindu caste culture and hierarchies over time.

Communist leadership in the construction of Kerala's subnational identity sparked the well-known narrative of the state's unique social development, characterized as "egalitarian developmentalism," which brought the state international acclaim (Devika 2010). Kerala's high levels of social development combined with low levels of economic development led economist Amartya Sen to famously declare the state a model—the Kerala model—for "third-world" development worldwide.[77] As the Kerala model has become increasingly unsustainable, however, many have come to regard it as a failed project, a utopia-cum-dystopia characterized by "corruption, moral laxity, stagnant economy, widespread unemployment, high suicide rates, alcoholism, indebtedness, increasing violence against women and, more recently, AIDS" (Sreekumar 2007, 43). Yet the narrative of Kerala's exceptionalism persists and forms an integral part of the region's identity today. According to J. Devika, the current challenge for Kerala scholars is the "ongoing struggle of reimagining the local, destabilizing developmentalist subnationalism."[78]

Along these lines, Bose and Varughese (2015, 11) challenge the prevailing "nationalist-Marxist" model of Kerala modernity by emphasizing the "'globality' of the region—a sense of being connected to and participating in the world through multiple channels and pathways." Their model emphasizes Kerala's regional modernity as a rhizomatic assemblage that lacks a fixed genealogy, with multiple points of entry and diverse space-times.[79] Bose and Varughese (2015, 10) propose three elements to this approach:

1. an understanding of the region as not completely determined (both methodologically and historically) by the nation;
2. an emphasis on the "region" as not a given, pre-discursive, homogenous and inert domain, but internally multiple and constantly de-re-territorialised, and;
3. its existence as part of and contributing to the global modernity.

In this chapter, I have positioned Kutiyattam within the nation-building efforts of communist politicians in Kerala seeking to construct regional identity and heritage. It may seem, therefore, to reify the Marxist-nationalist model of Kerala modernity that Bose and Varughese (2015) convincingly argue is too limiting, representing just one tale of many Kerala modernities. Stepping back to consider *Deep Cosmopolitan*'s larger focus on Kutiyattam's multiple cosmopolitanisms over time, however, I explicitly situate this narrative within a larger cosmopolitan framework of global communism. In so doing, I challenge the nationalist model by highlighting Kerala's relationship with wider global modernities.

While communist mass politics in Kerala have focused primarily on local issues, they have done so with explicitly global aims, exemplified in the slogan "workers of the world unite." As Jussy (2005, 33) observes, "Inspired and influenced by the revolution in the Soviet Union, the Left movement in India and in Kerala drew from their experiences." The movement not only drew from Soviet experiences but also actively engaged in a global communist imaginary through sustained ties with the Soviet Union. As noted earlier, the CPI was founded in the Soviet city of Tashkent by Indians trained in Moscow, and the party was often accused of antinationalist sentiment due to its international ties (Namboodiripad 1994, 8). In particular, it had long-lasting ties with the Third International, a.k.a. the Communist International (Comintern), a Soviet-controlled international organization that advocated for world revolution and claimed to represent the collective will of communist parties worldwide (Gupta 2006). EMS, as "one of the pioneers of the Communist movement in India," was deeply embedded in these networks both nationally and internationally, from his base in Kerala (Jussy 2005, 33).

From a cultural perspective, close ties with Soviet Russia are evident in the prevalence of Russian literary works in Kerala. Sanjeev (2011) writes that more Russian works have been translated into Malayalam than any other Indian language, and Russian comes second only to English in terms of foreign language literature in Kerala. This includes children's literature, with books of vibrantly illustrated Russian folktales popular among Malayali children during Sanjeev's childhood in the late 1970s and early 1980s, as well as Soviet periodicals such as *Soviet Land* and *Soviet Women* (2011). As he further observes, it is likely no coincidence that the first biography of Karl Marx in an Indian language was published in Malayalam in 1912. In terms of the wider culture of naming in Kerala, while less common today, it is not unheard of to encounter individuals with names such as Stalin.[80] These wider global imaginaries have thus not only dominated the world of politics but also permeated the realm of everyday life, clearly situating Kerala in a wider web of global communist political, social, and cultural imaginaries.

To conclude the chapter, I consider the reinvention of Kutiyattam in relation to the wider phenomenon of the reinvention of Indian classical dance. Despite the regionally specific histories of each dance form, scholarship on the topic typically emphasizes implications for Indian national identity. Many equate the reinvention of contemporary Indian "classical" dances with the "sanitization" of tradition and, more specifically, the sanitization of women's bodies-in-performance that came to embody a newly imagined upper-caste Indian nation for middle-class consumption (Chakravarti 1989).[81] Sanitization and adaptation became synonymous with classicization, with many forms striving toward a greater affinity with ancient Sanskrit texts, particularly the *Natyashastra*. With Sanskrit the ultimate marker of classicism, Kutiyattam, as the performance of ancient Sanskrit plays onstage, is generally considered a direct link to a classical, pan-Indian past. As a result, Kutiyattam was not constrained by the same classicizing aspirations as other art forms of the time.

The reinvention of Kutiyattam offers a meaningful contrast to this wider landscape, as it focused on the regional specificities of a communist Kerala rather than a nationalizing India. Guru Painkulam reimagined women's costumes and roles onstage, as did most classical dances throughout India. However, neither of the common efforts at the time to make forms more elite—the sanitization of women's bodies-in-performance and the Sanskritization of form—was undertaken at Kalamandalam. In fact, the opposite was true: to ensure a future for Kutiyattam at a time of unprecedented upheaval, Guru Painkulam decided to reshape the art to appeal to new caste-diverse, left-leaning Kerala audiences. He did this by aestheticizing the art while making it less elite through processes of democratization, condensation, curation, and decreased use of Sanskrit. My focus here on the regional specificities of Kutiyattam's reinvention moves forward a "critical turn" in the study of South Indian classical performing arts, namely, Peterson and Soneji's (2008a) call to push beyond the elite nationalist project to explore Indian regional histories. Returning to the strong sense of regional belonging among Kutiyattam artists at the beginning of the chapter—that Kutiyattam belongs *only* to Kerala—it is now possible to connect this sentiment to successful communist efforts in the state to consolidate a Malayali subnational identity. This wider attitude is particularly evident in polls demonstrating that a much higher percentage of people in Kerala than in other Indian states agree with the statement "We should be loyal to our own region first, and then to India" (Singh 2010, 287).

Notes

1. In 1936 for Travancore and 1947 for Cochin and Malabar.
2. For more on communism in Kerala, see Jeffrey 1992; D. Menon 1994; Namboodiripad 2010a; Nossiter 1982.
3. This also occurred across Kerala more widely.
4. The CPI was founded in the Soviet city of Tashkent in 1920 (Namboodiripad 2010b, 228).

5. See also Mannathukkaren 2006, 143–144.

6. For party leader accounts of Kerala's underground years, see Gopalan 1973 and Namboodiripad 1994, 59–69. Arrests decreased after 1942.

7. They likewise engaged in the "hegemonization of the movement for linguistic unity among Malayalam-speaking regions" (Devika 2010, 801).

8. See Barnett 1976; Caldwell 1856.

9. The United Front consisted of the Congress Party, the Praja Socialist Party, and the Muslim League.

10. For more details, see Lahiri 1997.

11. See Madhukar 2013 for the brand's origins.

12. For example, Hufford 1994a, 1994b.

13. See also Diamond 1999; Seizer 2005; Weidman 2006.

14. Before *Aikya Kerala*, a homogenous language and culture was likewise unavailable (Devika 2007b; see also Radhakrishnan 2015).

15. Kalidasan (2015, 110) argues that *Mavelinadu* is an "active force behind the policies of the modern state," with parallels between Mahabali and the annual return of Kerala's numerous Gulf migrants.

16. Conversation with J. Devika, February 6, 2020.

17. Standard Malayalam was fashioned from elite Nair and Namboodiri caste dialects, problematizing the notion of Malayalam as the language of the people (Sanjeev 2011).

18. See also Zarilli 1996.

19. The date, 1949 or 1951, is uncertain. For more details, see Moser 2008, 52–53; 2013a, 252–253.

20. I would like to thank Virginie Johan for bringing this article to my attention and providing a copy translated by M. V. Narayanan.

21. Performers: Vidushaka—Painkulam Rama Chakyar; Dhananjaya—Painkulam Damodara Chakyar; Subhadra—Chathakudam Komalam Nangiar; Mizhavu—Chathakudam Krishnan Nambiar; Thalam—Chathakudam Kunjukutti Nangiar, as referenced in Ramavarma 1978.

22. See chapter 6 for colonial connections to the tradition/modernity binary and how such conceptualizations manifested in the Indian nation's early years.

23. For a brief summary of the changes, see Gopalakrishnan 2016b; Lowthorp 2020, 34–36; Oberlin 2016.

24. For more on Kerala's classical icon, see Gopalakrishnan 2016a and Zarilli 1984; on the founding of Kalamandalam, see Daugherty 2019.

25. Mani Parameswara Chakyar first added massages to Kutiyattam training for use on his nephew Mani Madhava Chakyar (Bhargavinilayam 1999, 69).

26. For an in-depth comparison of Kutiyattam and Kathakali, see Jones 1977.

27. While I heard this story firsthand, it can also be found in the documentary *The Master of Valour: Kalamandalam Sivan Namboothiri* (C-DIT n.d.).

28. These artists' professional names are Kalamandalam Shivan Namboodiri, Kalamandalam Rama Chakyar, Painkulam Narayana Chakyar, Kalamandalam Radhakrishnan, Kalamandalam Girija, Kalamandalam Shylaja, Margi Sathi, Kalamandalam Unnikrishnan Nambiar, and Kalamandalam Eashwaranunni, respectively. Kalamandalam's first female student was Rukmini Nangiar, from 1967 to 1971. Sathi's elder sister Devaki studied Kutiyattam from 1976 to 1977 or 1978, tragically passing away of rheumatic fever (Daugherty, email communication, September 6, 2021).

29. She similarly narrated how, when Guru Ammannur became a Kalamandalam instructor after Guru Painkulam's death, he told students everything they were doing was wrong. When Guru Mani took over the following year, he gently told them to continue as their guru had taught them.

30. For more on Kalamandalam's Kutiyattam syllabus, see Sharma 1994. For a detailed description of Guru Painkulam's training, see Sowle 1982.

31. Wilcox (2018) notes a similar concept at work within Chinese traditional music and dance.

32. See Rajagopalan 1997.

33. See also Daugherty 2019, 593–594.

34. These include *Shurpanakhankam*, *Jaṭāyuvadham*, *Tōraṇayuddham*, *Bhagavadajjukiyam*, *Kalyāṇasaugandhikam*, the first act of *Subhadradhananjayam*, the fourth act of *Svapnavāsavadattā*, *Naganandam*'s second and third acts, and *Abhijñānaśakuntalā*'s second act; see Venugopalan 2007, 128.

35. These edits reduced the previous threefold recitation of lines, eliminated most preplay and postplay rituals, and edited and shortened the content of plays. Nair (1994a, 31) credits Mani Madhava Chakyar with the idea of shortening performances to three hours and of avoiding repetition.

36. Jones studied Kathakali at Kalamandalam in the 1950s, researched koothambalam architecture in the early 1960s, encouraged (with Killimangalam Vasudevan Namboodiripad) Kalamandalam to open a Kutiyattam department, organized the first Kutiyattam conference in 1966, and designed and built the koothambalam stage at the original Kalamandalam campus for his film *Kutiyattam: Sanskrit Drama in the Temples of Kerala* (27 min., 16mm color/sound). For a conference description, see Jones 1977, 10–11; for the conference program and V. Raghavan's paper, see Gopalakrishnan 2016c.

37. This is made from the dried sheath of an areca tree. For more, see Daugherty 1996, 2016; Rajagopalan 1997.

38. The former evidences a headpiece rimmed with thin gold, and the latter, pancake makeup ending at the jawline. Films made in the 1970s at Kalamandalam evidence a costume in transition, showing actresses with the new headpiece and uncovered stomachs; see *Painkulam* (Viswanathan n.d.); *Kutiyattam* (Jones and Jones 1974); *Kutiyattam* (Thakkar Enros 1973); SNA 1995b.

39. Moser (2011, 2013a) characterizes this as a shift from women's immobility to mobility onstage. For an example of immobile temple performance, see Moser 1996. For an example of mobile public performance, see Margi Usha's performance at Kalam News Online 2020.

40. As Daugherty (2016, 103) notes, the Nangiar's facial makeup is called *paḻukkatēkkuka,* meaning "spreading to the color of a ripe fruit." Nirmala Paniker (1992, 29) attributes the name to the makeup color's resemblance to that of a ripe areca nut.

41. This happened after 1987, as a 1987 film in the SNA (1995b) archives features Shylaja performing Nangiarkoothu with a visible stomach.

42. A 1905 photo of Kutiyattam performers evidences this, see Moser 2008; Paulose 2006. For more on changes in Kerala women's dress, see Devika 2007a; Thomas 2018.

43. According to P. K. Narayanan Nambiar, the *pottu* marks for different characters also varied among families.

44. Dr. C. K. Jayanthi recounted that her grandfather, Guru Mani, ordered a durable *chooti* beard made out of copper and attached by rice paste that he regularly used in performance.

45. Kalamandalam Ram Mohan also shared that, for improved aesthetics, he changed the shape of one part of the men's headpiece, the *pāṇakeṭṭa,* to better align with the shape of the *vasikam,* which curves along the forehead. It was previously mismatched, with a more oval than circular shape.

46. Additional changes to men's costumes include: Kalamandalam Ram Mohan making a new wooden model to replace the conch shell headdress (*piriśamkhumāla*)—originally made out of real conch shells—in *Mantrankam* performance; adding a second padded bump to the Chakyarkoothu headdress (*kuṭuma*), meant to resemble the hair tuft of Namboodiri Brahmins, upon the recommendation of Guru Painkulam for aesthetic reasons; and changing the headdress for Pathakam, the Nambiar solo verbal performance meant to inspire bhakthi. According to Ram Mohan-ashan, while Pathakam performers previously only tied a red cloth around their head, Usha Nangiar's father Krishnan Nambiar changed it to resemble Chakyarkoothu's *kuṭuma,* leading to a permanent innovation that is the standard today. In an interview with Richard Schechner, Guru Painkulam notes what seem to be changes made before Kalamandalam to the costume of the demoness Shurpanakha, stating that in "earlier days" her headdress was made of grass and her breasts were constructed from palm leaves (Chakyar 1976).

47. He leads an institution now funded via Kutiyattam Kendra, Koppu Nirmanakendram in Vellinezhi, where he has taught his sons and other students the art of making wooden ornaments for Kutiyattam, Kathakali, and a number of Kerala's traditional art forms.

48. According to Kalamandalam Unnikrishnan Nambiar, the kurunkuzhal is still used at a few temples today, including Triprayar, Karivellur, and Madayikavu.

49. Guru Painkulam included the kurunkuzhal in performances, but, according to Kalamandalam Unnikrishnan Nambiar, it disappeared from the Kalamandalam stage by the 1980s.

50. For a firsthand description, see Sowle 1982. To view this on film, see *Kutiyattam* (Jones and Jones 1974).

51. For an in-depth examination of *kriyas* and their relation to dramatic action onstage, see Johan 2017a.

52. While he is widely credited with the innovation of the form, Guru Narayanan Nambiar describes learning the form from his own guru, Kochampilly Raman Nambiar. He clarifies his contribution: "I was the first to present a Mizhavil Thayabaka recital. I composed new patterns of playing in it, three forms of playing" (Bindu 2016, 409; see also Bindu 2013, 112). The performance begins with the soloist playing a slow *cempaṭa* beat and gradually increasing speed with *kuru, edanila,* and *irikita* beats (Kalamandalam Easwaranunni 2001, 75). For more on mizhavu *tayambaka,* see Nambiar 1994.

53. The number of mizhavu players varies from two to five. The number of soloists can likewise vary, although they are always supported by two mizhavus.

54. As Kalamandalam Sajith Vijayan clarified, while this combination of supporting instruments was common twenty years ago, the main instruments used today are the bass chenda and the *ilathalam* cymbal.

55. For trailers of these productions, see Abel 2014 and Prime Video India 2018.

56. See Casassas 2012; Daugherty 2011; Moser 2011, 2013a; and Oberlin 2016 for more about this revival.

57. Guru Ammannur undertook a parallel effort to create a manual and revive Nangiarkoothu performance at the Ammannur gurukulam around the same period, see Paniker 1992.

58. These include *Narasiṃhāvatāram, Keralolpatti, Pulinjimokṣam,* and *Gajendramokṣam.*

59. For parallel cases of reinvention in Kerala, see Gerety 2017; Lemos 2022.

60. I was told this began during Kalamandalam's first tour abroad, when actresses had to perform even during their menses.

61. Due to diabetes-related complications exacerbated by his poor diet in Europe.

62. She was finally offered a permanent position in January 2025, after nearly fifteen years.

63. In Kerala, this means Nair and above.

64. There are some exceptions to the rule. The Sangeet Natak Akademi has organized occasional performances by nonhereditary performers in the Harippad koothambalam since the 1990s.

65. Despite this trend, there are plenty of individuals, most notably Painkulam Narayana Chakyar, who are extremely open-minded and actively encourage non-hereditary male students.

66. Gopalakrishnan (2016b, 50) confirms that performance space is limited for non-Chakyar actors.

67. As Gopalakrishnan observes about Kalamandalam, "recruiting people based on political considerations over the past few decades has *politicised* the institution" (2016a, 126).

68. The art superintendent of Kalamandalam, Killimangalam Vasudevan Namboodiripad, was previously on the editorial board of two communist newspapers—*Deshabhimani* and *Republic*.

69. Diane Daugherty once asked Kalamandalam Rama Chakyar if his great-uncle, Guru Painkulam, had been a Communist, and he said no (personal communication, 2023). As "being a Communist" in Kerala refers to being a party member, which the guru was not, these views are not incompatible.

70. Heller (2005) confirms that neither Communist nor Congress-led state government has ever reversed any major public service or redistributive program, despite often precarious finances and declining central financial support.

71. See also Damodaran 2022, 153. Nair likewise designed the theater at Kalakshetra.

72. As Jussy (2005, 36) notes, "The left movement spawned a host of cultural organizations that served as extensions of the political struggle."

73. By comparison, senior gurus at Kutiyattam Kendra–administered institutions receive Rs. 14,000 per month.

74. Conversation with J. Devika, February 6, 2020. As Devika elaborated, this individualist model has also led to the cutting of institutional and event funding amid the financial crisis, citing the cancellation of funding for the 2020 international film festival in Thrissur. It also led to cuts at Margi in 2020–2021. Rather than getting the 5 lakh funding increase they were told to expect, Margi's state government funding was cut by 5 lakhs.

75. After routing state taxes through the Indian national government, it refused to refund Kerala's state government the promised amount, sparking the crisis.

76. While I have been writing of the Kutiyattam body in the singular, Kutiyattam in actuality came to have two bodies—the hereditary, ritualized temple body and the democratized, secular public body reflecting the temple sphere and the open public sphere, respectively. It is the latter body that changed most drastically, along with Kerala's rapidly changing social and political bodies.

77. For more details, see Moser and Younger 2013.

78. Personal conversation, February 6, 2020.

79. This references Deleuze and Guattari's (1987, 21) definition of the rhizome as a nonlinear, nonhierarchical network that "connects any point to any other point."

80. This likely reflects the phenomenon that, as Gupta (2006, xx) has observed, "the Left in India is still heavily dominated by the spirit of Stalinism."

81. For example, see Banerji 2019 (Odissi); Chakravorty 2008 (Kathak); O'Shea 2007 (Bharatanatyam).

6

CLAIMING A COSMOPOLIS

Sanskritic Culture and Indian National Heritage

Figure 42. Kalamandalam Sajith Vijayan on mizhavu. Photo by author.

Munching on fried cumin-flavored snacks and sipping dark, milky chai—a bite of one and simultaneous swig of the other—the flavors mix pleasantly in my mouth as the chai tempers the sharply knotted crunch of the *murukku* snack. This combination of snacks and chai is one of my favorite parts of social home visiting in India, and I have made many such visits during my fieldwork, often bringing along a box of sweets or bag of fruit for my perpetually gracious hosts. I am snacking now in the home of Dr. M. D. Muthukumaraswamy—Muthu for short—a well-respected folklorist who is active both locally and nationally. He is endlessly cheerful, always ready to smile or laugh at a moment's notice. I have come to discuss his experience with and opinion of Kutiyattam's inscription as a United Nations Educational, Scientific and Cultural Organization's

(UNESCO) Intangible Cultural Heritage (ICH). He tells me that in 2000, he and a group of folklorists from around the country submitted a list to the Indian Ministry of Culture with nearly three thousand art forms they recommended for ICH inscription. With at least one paragraph of description for each, this submission amounted to thousands of pages and untold hours of work. "But," Muthu said, sighing, "they ignored them, because Sanskrit is all they want."

Raising his eyebrows, he continued, "Kutiyattam getting the recognition created a lot of debate. India is a country with one billion people, and our administrative borders divide it into states that otherwise would have been considered separate countries. There is *sooo* much intangible heritage available, so how was it that only the Sanskrit theater gets recognized as an Indian heritage? Because Sanskrit is seen as a kind of hegemonic language which has power over the rest of the Indian languages, and it is being favored by the government—powerful elite North Indians." Muthu chuckled. "This gives a kind of condescending recognition to the South Indian form, but because it happens to be in Sanskrit, that is why it got the recognition is the general understanding."

"You mean the general understanding among folklorists?" I interjected.

"Among folklorists, scholars and also generally people all over India," he replied.

> You see, all over India it becomes an issue. How is it that Kutiyattam became the only form in India to be selected and then to make it to the privileged list of the nineteen of the world, and the rest of the things are excluded? This created a big debate, but not a very powerful debate. Scholars and practitioners of art do not have any power to influence the decisions of the government. . . . The case of Kutiyattam very clearly demonstrates how power works in India. It is the Keralite lobby, which is very powerful in the national culture sector, joining with the fact that it is a Sanskrit theater finding favor with the North Indian decision-makers. All of them joined together and made Kutiyattam the only privileged intangible heritage of India. It is Brahmin, Keralite, plus Sanskrit; a language, a region, plus the elite, intellectual group which controls the culture sector. The second item that made it to the list was Vedic Chanting . . .

Here Muthu let out such a hearty laugh that it took him a minute to recover before he continued, "which again clearly showed how the alliance of power works. Most people didn't even know that it was an oral tradition!"

While underlying cultural and identity politics were rarely expressed so openly during my fieldwork, they formed the invisible yet solid foundation of the larger narrative at work. As Muthu aptly summarized, "How art forms from around the world came into the privileged list of intangible heritage reveals the process of power working in the cultural sector, how power operates in the world to reach the world's prestigious body—nothing more, nothing less."

~

As Muthu's reflections underscore, UNESCO ICH is primarily about power and privilege, and Kutiyattam's 2001 ICH inscription was ultimately rooted in power structures and cultural politics at the Indian national level. The fact that the Indian Ministry of Culture selected the Sanskritic, upper-caste Hindu art to represent India's national culture on a global scale reveals much about how the Indian government conceptualizes and curates the country's national heritage. This process of selecting the few and excluding the many follows Benedict Anderson's (1983) classic formulation of heritage as an important element of the "imagined community" of the nation. Alongside the map and census, Anderson (1983, 184) proposes that cultural institutions such as museums are implicated in a politics of inclusion and exclusion whereby symbols become part of a "totalizing classificatory grid" of the nation, and peoples, regions, religions, traditions, languages, and monuments are either included or excluded from the national imaginary. Muthu pointed out that Kutiyattam represents a language (Sanskrit), a region (Kerala), and an elite group of people (Brahmins) that together align with how decision-makers in Delhi imagine and construct Indian national heritage.[1] To this list, I add that the temple art also represents a religion—Hinduism—which the Indian government has increasingly privileged over time.

Heritage is firmly rooted in the context of nationalism and a universalizing modernity. Barbara Kirshenblatt-Gimblett (2006, 4) theorizes heritage as an "instrument of modernization and mark of modernity" for the nation-state, while Richard Handler (1988, 142) proposes that it constitutes "crucial proof of national existence." The consensus among heritage scholars is that heritage is essential to nation-building and mobilized as proof of a national past to legitimize a nation-state's present-day existence. After all, what is a modern nation-state without its supposedly premodern past?

In this chapter, I consider how Kutiyattam, as traditional Sanskrit theater, fits an idealized narrative of Indian national heritage as Sanskritic, Hindu, and upper caste since the earliest days of a newly independent India. This nationalist narrative reframed the multireligious Sanskrit cosmopolis as Hindu and claimed it as part of a specifically Indian national past, even though the Sanskrit cosmopolis spanned a geographic area now occupied by multiple nation-states. As part of this exploration, I trace the transformation of Kutiyattam into Indian national heritage in the mid- to late twentieth century, preceding its UNESCO inscription. In so doing, I highlight the role of Guru Mani Madhava Chakyar in bringing the art to a wider national arena. My overall aim is to show that Kutiyattam's case exemplifies a wider process of Indian nation-building that was and continues to be ultimately rooted in Orientalist constructions of an Indian national past that has both nationalized and Hinduized the diverse Sanskrit cosmopolis.

Indian National Heritage and the Sanskrit Cosmopolis

Orientalist Legacies

Indian nationalism is deeply rooted in the colonial legacy, particularly in Orientalist ideas about Indian history and culture. The first of several colonialist approaches to Indian society, Orientalists legitimized the colonialist enterprise as a "civilizing mission," depicting an India in need of civilizing via European post-Enlightenment values (Chatterjee 1989). As part of their colonizing agenda, colonial Orientalists denounced present-day India as inferior while praising its ancient past. Folklorist Sadhana Naithani (2001b, 67) describes a typical colonialist account of India: "The land is marvelous, but the inhabitants are not; the history of this land is old and in ancient times it has seen many philosopher-kings, but at present it is enveloped in darkness; the folklore is abundant, ancient, and well-preserved, but its carriers and creators are stupid and ignorant." Orientalists notably valorized ancient Sanskrit texts, as Sanskrit was discovered to be a progenitor of Indo-European languages and thus connected India to Europe (O'Shea 2007). They viewed these texts as evidence of an ancient Hindu age of glory and by doing so framed contemporary residents of India as degenerates of a former golden age (Cohn 1987). Colonial Orientalists therefore conceptualized Indian civilization and culture as located not in the present but in an ancient, Sanskritic past.

As O'Shea (2007, 32) writes: "Formed through an unequal but dialogic exchange between Brahman informants and English and German scholars, Orientalist writings privileged the voices of elites, their cultural and literary products, and their ritual practices." They saw their role as introducing the Hindu elite to their own ancient lore and in the process "endowing" them with a history (Chakravarti 1989). As part of favoring an elite past over a diverse present, colonial Orientalist views of Indian society privileged ancient Sanskrit texts over contemporary customs and behavior, wrongly assuming the hegemony of Brahmins and Brahminical religious texts over all domains of Indian life. Despite conflicting with the complex realities of power and divergent caste norms at the time, the British codified these views into law, thereby imposing a single set of Brahminic rules on the wider population that disrupted and reconfigured local hierarchies (Dirks 2001).[2] This wide-scale application of Brahminic law in British administration resulted in the destruction of numerous local social systems and constituted both an appropriation and reconstruction of the caste system that ignored more fluid social organization throughout India, both past and present.[3]

Orientalist knowledge production created a number of racialized identities that continue to influence conceptions of Indian nationalism—of who belongs to the nation and who does not. As part of their divide-and-conquer agenda, colonialists defined a North Indian, Hindu-Aryan racial identity in opposition to both South Indian "Dravidians" and "foreign" Muslims, with the three groups seen as racially and biologically distinct from one another (Dalmia 1997). The first of these distinctions is rooted in geography, pitting North and South Indians against one another. The Orientalists constructed a Hindu-Aryan identity that conceptualized a biological link between North Indians and Europeans based on Indo-European linguistic similarities and the related Aryan invasion settlement theory of India (1997).[4] The issue of caste added further nuance to this supposed biological relationship, with Brahmins considered closely related to Europeans and lower-caste groups further removed. This racialized distinction between North and South Indians persists and forms the basis of widespread discrimination today, fitting neatly into existing conceptions of caste-based biological differences.[5] It even continues to influence certain academic studies, such as biological anthropology and population genetics. At an Indian national anthropology conference, a biological anthropologist surprised me by casually describing the clearly racialized morphological differences between North and South Indians—light versus dark skin, thin versus broad noses, and straight versus curly hair, among others.[6] Population genetics studies of South Asia still seek genetic differences between castes based on an erroneous assumption of a static, all-Indian four-varna system that cultural anthropologists and historians have long discounted.[7]

As chapter 5 described, the Orientalist construction of a racialized, South Indian "Dravidian" Other sparked the Dravidian nationalist movement in Kerala's neighboring state of Tamil Nadu. In addition to revolting against British colonial oppression, Dravidian nationalists rebelled against what they saw as North Indian, Brahminical hegemony imposed on them by a Hindu Brahmin "invasion" of South India in the first millennium CE. This event is widely viewed as having brought the caste system to formerly Buddhist, egalitarian South India. Equating Indo-European and Dravidian linguistic differences with North/South Indian racial differences, the non-Brahmin Dravidian nationalist movement used the Orientalist notion of a Dravidian racial identity to argue for greater South Indian unity (Barnett 1976). As we saw in the last chapter, Dravidian nationalism provoked a counterreaction by Kerala's Communist Party, whose upper-caste leaders actively embraced Brahmins as part of a unified, distinctly Keralan regional identity.

Another Orientalist-constructed racialized identity, directly tied to ongoing violence and discrimination in India today, is rooted in religion. Orientalist thinkers dramatically framed Hindus as the original inhabitants of India. In so doing, they characterized Indian Muslims, the majority being Indian natives who had converted historically, as foreign invaders (Ludden 2005). As part of this paradigm, colonialists blamed Indian Muslims for the Mughal Empire, claiming it marked the end of a purportedly Hindu golden age and led to India's subsequent decline. In this way, colonial Orientalists equated local Muslim populations with Muslim Mughal rulers who had arrived from central Asia to establish a religiously tolerant imperial rule across much of the Indian subcontinent from the sixteenth to eighteenth centuries CE. The British thereby denied the Mughal Empire's importance to the history of India while denigrating Indian Muslims as a way to bolster their own image. As Metcalf (1995, 953) observes, "Muslims served as a foil against which the British defined themselves: by saying that Muslims were oppressive, incompetent, lascivious, and given to self-indulgence, the colonial British could define precisely what they imagined themselves to be, namely, enlightened, competent, disciplined, and judicious." The British codified the Orientalist conception of Hindus and Muslims as biologically distinct populations into law, and this eventually formed the ideological basis for the partition of British India into Pakistan and India (Ludden 2005). The largest mass migration in human history, the partition left millions dead and nearly fifteen million displaced.[8] Dividing ethnicity and culture along religious lines, violent echoes of this Hindu/Muslim opposition persist in present-day India, especially with the rise to power of the Bharatiya Janata Party (BJP) Hindu nationalist party and ongoing communalist clashes in recent decades. Similar reverberations can likewise be found in the population genetics literature of India, in which some scientists premise their work on the erroneous assumption that Muslims are genetically distinct Others.[9]

The anticolonialist, middle-class Indian nationalist movement embraced a national history created by colonialists by adopting the Orientalist script of the Hindu golden age (Chatterjee 1993). They used this script not to argue for continued colonial oppression but to advocate for independence. In response to the loss of middle-class self-esteem following the British conquest, anticolonial nationalists adopted a self-image of reconstructed Hindu-Aryan greatness that starkly juxtaposed the glory of the past against a humiliating, subjugated present (Chatterjee 1989). By so doing, nationalists fostered dichotomies such as Indian/Western, spiritual/material, tradition/modernity, private/public, and female/male to produce a nationalist identity that could be both separate and superior to the West (1989). Despite this effort to establish a nationalism in opposition to the West, Chatterjee (1986, 38) emphasized that Indian nationalist thought was really a derivative discourse that, instead of being emancipatory, operated "within a framework of knowledge whose representational structure corresponds to the very structure of power (it) seeks to repudiate." Thus, even as Indian nationalism challenged colonial domination, it participated in the very discourse on which colonial domination was based.

Indian Heritage Discourse

Reminiscent of Muthu's comments made fifty years later, Milton Singer (1958, 191) aptly described India's early consolidation of cultural heritage.

> The movement of modern nationalism in India, as in most other countries, has always shown a strong interest in the recovery or reinterpretation of India's traditional culture. With the achievement of national independence, this interest has received an official definition. Language, national history, archeological monuments, folk arts and crafts, classical music, dance and drama have become symbols of a modern Indian identity alongside the national emblem, Five Year Plans, parliamentary institutions, and atomic installations. The definition is selective and creative. A traditional culture, notably that of India, is far too varied and rich a growth to be adequately displayed in Republic Day celebrations. And not all cultural traditions will be thought suitable for display; some are perhaps thought best left to grow or wither in provincial obscurity. Those cultural traditions that become symbols of national identity undergo, by virtue of their new role, a sea change; they take on a life of their own, quite different from their life as regional and local traditions. They have become the chosen representatives of a national tradition. Theoretically, any element of traditional culture is a potential candidate for selection, but in fact only a small number are so chosen at any given time.

One of Singer's ideas is worth repeating: only a small number of India's cultural traditions are ever chosen to become symbols of national identity. What do these "chosen ones" have in common? As this section details, their commonality is generally upper-caste Hinduism. Heritage discourse in India adopts the Orientalist division of culture along religious lines and in the process constructs the Indian nation, despite its secular founding ideals, as culturally Hindu. According to folklorist Roger Abrahams (1993, 9), the standard legend of national formation entails a process of historical purification, whereby "an old culture [is] resuscitated, [and] the intervening forms . . . swept away, along with the alien powers that conquered the land and put their culture into the place of the old traditions." Closely following this model, Indian nationalists engaged in resuscitating what they perceived as an ancient Hindu culture purportedly swept away by Muslim Mughal conquerors. Instead of considering all periods of history equal contributors to contemporary Indian culture, nationalists embraced periods dominated by "native" Hindus and rejected those by "foreign" Muslims.

Heritage is central to the imagined community of the Indian nation, and as Singer observed, it undergirds the nation-building process as in other countries worldwide. Vasudha Dalmia (1997) charts how nineteenth-century Indian nationalists appropriated Orientalist discourse in a "nationalization" of Hindu traditions (language, religion, and culture). Nationalists legitimized these traditions through references to ancient Sanskrit literature, which they took as evidence of a national past. Dalmia (1997, 338) characterizes this period as "almost obsessed with the antiquity of tradition and its textual fixation as accessible in Sanskrit". She describes a joint Orientalist-nationalist reconstruction of religion and culture that was not only clearly Hindu but also clearly high caste. Both Dalmia (1997) and Bhatti (2005) have noted how Hindus and Muslims sought the "authentic" source of their culture in the depths of history, thereby equating their religious differences with cultural differences. Still evident today, the postcolonial period of Indian state formation has been fraught with tensions between constitutional utopia and social reality where, as Bhatti (2005, 125) emphasizes, "instead of having a national post-colonial cultural heritage, one has a heritage whose claims of ownership are made by a particular religious group."[10]

Mary Hancock (1998) examines how Dr. V. Raghavan played a key role in promoting a dominant Sanskrit-based national culture as a means of fostering unity both nationally and internationally. A renowned Sanskrit scholar, Raghavan defined India as "the product of textualized Hindu values" and played a significant role in formulating and disseminating elite nationalism both in India and abroad (1998, 348). As the head of the national Sanskrit Commission, Raghavan promoted an official nationalism that viewed Sanskrit as the key to producing a "tradition-infused, modern citizen" through the teaching of Sanskrit at secondary schools nationwide, the mass mediation of Sanskrit, and government support of Sanskrit scholars (1998, 364). Inspired by anthropologist M. N. Srinivas's (1952) notion of an all-India Sanskritic Hinduism associated with the *Ramayana* and *Mahabharata* epics, Raghavan imagined a national Indian culture centered around Hinduism as a unifying force and Sanskrit, as the language of Hinduism, as the avenue for forging its new national subject. His view of Sanskritic Hinduism as the vehicle of Indian national culture heavily influenced not only national cultural policy and institutions within India but also the national and international study of India more broadly.[11]

As Anita Cherian (2009, 34) argues, the idea of a singular pan-Indian culture rooted in Sanskritic Hinduism forms the "imagined foundation of a social solidarity that makes the modern State possible." Bhatti (2005, 118) poignantly observes that Sanskrit traditions have nationally been "delegated to the highest rung of cultural value," with all others devalued.[12] Several Indian anthologies of Indian theater history explicitly posit "notions of cultural purity and impurity contingent on the deployment of Sanskrit," resulting in what Hansen (2001) terms a "communalization of knowledge" whereby Parsis and Muslims in particular are excluded (Nicholson 2019, 208). Lelyveld (1994) describes the nation-building efforts at All India Radio that set out to create a "national music" by privileging Hindu over Muslim music and musicians and meticulously balancing northern Hindustani and southern Carnatic styles. Cherian (2009, 34) similarly highlights how national institutions like the Sangeet Natak Akademi (SNA)—the Indian national academy for dance, drama, and music discussed throughout this chapter—imagine India's shared heritage as a "sovereign and pan-Indian space of an ancient culture and aesthetics rooted in a vocabulary of (Hindu) spirituality." Entrusted with the task of establishing the cultural canon of the new nation by linking the national center with its regions, the SNA set out to bring "art forms and institutions into a unified national framework," thereby critically subordinating the regional in a period of competing claims to regional nationhood (SNA 1953/1958, 57).[13] The Indian government thereby took on the project of solidifying a national culture in an effort to, at least discursively, construct something like the imagined Hindu golden age of the past. Dalmia (2006, 170) has noted how, from its founding in 1953, the SNA conceptualized performing arts across India as "rural derivations of and deviations from the all-encompassing Sanskritic tradition from which they had emanated and into which they could, under the new dispensation, flow again." Implicated in a process of inclusion and exclusion, this imagining favors a single, exclusionary narrative while discounting India's vast cultural and religious diversity that, as Singer mentioned above, the nation might not deem "suitable for display."

India's performative cultural solidarity thus came to be based on an Orientalist conception of Indian culture as essentially Hindu, Sanskritic, and upper caste, resulting in the widespread exclusion of the nation's many Others. As this chapter explores, the SNA's long-term sponsorship of Kutiyattam reinforces this colonialist-cum-national projection of Indian culture. I argue that this identification of Sanskritic culture as specifically Hindu and Indian constitutes a national claiming of the Sanskrit cosmopolis. As we saw in chapter 3, while long confined to use within Hindu religious practice, Sanskrit was reinvented near the beginning of the Common Era as a mode of artistic and particularly literary expression. This signaled the beginning of the Sanskrit cosmopolis, a cosmopolitan imaginary of incredible cultural, religious, and geographical diversity characterized by voluntary affiliation with Sanskrit literary culture that spanned South and Southeast Asia (Pollock 2006). As part of the discourse of Indian heritage, the Indian state claims Sanskritic cultural production—the hallmark of the Sanskrit cosmopolis—as part of an Indian and specifically Hindu past. In so doing, it misrepresents Sanskritic culture as exclusively Hindu, when much of it was unassociated with any particular religious viewpoint. It also falsely asserts state ownership of a cosmopolitan cultural phenomenon that is in fact the heritage of numerous contemporary nation-states across South and Southeast Asia.

Engaging the National: Guru Mani Madhava Chakyar

The story of how Kutiyattam first came to national, and to some extent international, attention starts with Padmasree Guru Mani Madhava Chakyar, the art's first nationally recognized "star." Although he is today less publicly acknowledged than Guru Painkulam Rama Chakyar, he was equally important in the development of contemporary Kutiyattam. Beginning as early as the 1930s, Guru Mani was the first to welcome people of other castes and creeds into the fold of Kutiyattam, as both audience members and performers. In his bold stance, he radically defied the conservatism of his fellow Chakyars, leading to the latter's repeated retribution against him over several decades. In his commitment to inclusivity, the guru was vocal in his early support of temple entry for all castes, which entailed a dramatic democratization of Kutiyattam audiences. He also trained the art's first nonhereditary actors, both non-Chakyar and foreign, and took Kutiyattam on tour outside of Kerala for the first time, bringing the art to wider national audiences. Guru Mani was similarly the first

Figure 43. Guru Mani Madhava Chakyar as Kapali with wife Kunjimalu Nangiaramma and son PKG Nambiar. Photo courtesy of Padmasree Mani Madhava Chakyar Smaraka Gurukulam collection.

Kutiyattam artist to win the national Sangeet Natak Akademi Award and the prestigious Padma Shri Award, and he participated extensively in early national SNA documentation and training schemes. In this section, I explore the fundamental role that Guru Mani played in bringing Kutiyattam to wider national attention, ultimately catalyzing the art's transformation into national heritage.

Born in 1899, Guru Mani was the eldest of Kutiyattam's three prominent gurus of the twentieth century—Mani Madhava Chakyar (1899–1990), Painkulam Rama Chakyar (1905–1980), and Ammannur Madhava Chakyar (1917–2008). He was celebrated for the expressiveness of his eyes (*netrabhinaya*), as is evident in Chandrahasan's (1989) description: "It is only when one sees him perform that one realizes how powerful the eyes are to express, to suggest and to communicate emotions and even to convey whole packages of ideas." Guru Mani was also an accomplished Sanskrit scholar. He studied the *Nyāyaśāstra*, *Alaṅkāraśāstra*, and *Nāṭyaśāstra* under the king of Cochin—Rama Varma Parikshith Thampuran—and refused a job offer as a Sanskrit professor to continue in Kutiyattam (Sreekanth 2013). This strong legacy of

Sanskrit persists in his family today, with several of his children and grandchildren Sanskrit teachers or professors. His daughter, my friend Amminikutty Nangiaramma, loves to recite Sanskrit *shlokas* during my visits, asking me to recite what I learned during my Kutiyattam training in return. Guru Mani was also an author, choreographer, and celebrated actor who received awards and accolades from numerous kings and, later, the Indian nation.[14] He authored an important book-length treatise on Kutiyattam training and performance, *Nāṭyakalpadrumam* (1974), which won the Kerala Sahitya Akademi award.[15] Of the three gurus, Guru Mani and Guru Painkulam were socially progressive and forward-thinking from very early on, while Guru Ammannur remained socially conservative and caste-exclusionary for most of his career. Guru Mani is the father of mizhavu guru P. K. Narayanan Nambiar, and, as detailed in chapter 4, his early progressiveness was evident in his personal life. While fathers in Kerala's matrilineal kinship system did not live with their wives or play a prominent role in raising their children, Guru Mani did both.[16]

In the 1930s and 1940s, Guru Mani radically embraced the new audiences that came with temple entry proclamations across Kerala. Issued in Travancore in 1936 and Cochin and Malabar in 1947, these proclamations threw open temple doors to lower castes for the first time in history. As we saw in the last chapter, temples had previously only permitted entry to upper castes (Nair and above), with lower-caste individuals unable to even use the roads surrounding temples. Many Chakyars opposed temple entry, and some even boycotted temples that had opened their doors to all.[17] Renowned actor Ammannur Chachu Chakyar famously stopped performing in protest after temple entry, sending his students Ammannur Madhava Chakyar and Ammannur Parameswara Chakyar in his stead.[18]

Guru Mani, however, was different; he publicly supported temple entry for people of all caste backgrounds, despite the consequences that would befall him as a result. This stance led to upper-caste owners of private temples banning him from performance, which caused a significant loss of income. As his son, P. K. Govindan Nambiar, known as P. K. G., told me, "My father, when he said that everyone [i.e., all Hindus] should be allowed in the temples, many people objected, especially private temples. After temple entry came, Father was banned from performing Koothu at these temples. They didn't allow him to perform because of that, many temples wouldn't give him programs." He clarified that, because Guru Mani performed in government temples that allowed entry for all, private temples "said that if you perform *there*, you cannot perform *here*. So to survive, as he had a lot of children, he went to teach *abhinaya* [acting] to Kathakali students at Kalamandalam. Kelu Nair, Krishnan Nair, Guru Gopinath are very famous, they are all father's disciplines."[19] In teaching Kathakali students the *nētrābhinaya* and *rasābhinaya* (eye and facial expressions) for which he was famous, Guru Mani defied conservativism even further by ignoring a general prohibition in the Kutiyattam community against watching and interacting with the closely allied form of Kathakali. This made a lasting impact, and he became known as "the master who gave eyes to Kathakali" (Gopalakrishnan 2016a, 143; Sreekanth 2013, 9).

Guru Mani's embrace of temple entry had another consequence—other Chakyar families began to shun him, refusing to perform with him onstage. At the time, there were no other Chakyars in the Mani family to perform Kutiyattam roles alongside him. The refusal by other Chakyars to perform with Guru Mani—including not assisting with his performances and not inviting him to perform with them—meant that he could no longer perform the Kutiyattam acting for which he was famous.[20] A newspaper article details an elderly spectator reminiscing on the powers of the guru's acting: "'The tiles of the koothambalam used to shake with the power of Mani Chakyar's voice,' recalls Nair. 'You could hear him in any corner of the village.' In those decades, only Brahmins, and only men, could sit inside the theatre temple. Nair, like many others, had to be content watching through the wooden slats of the windows in the hall. 'But it didn't really matter—I could still see the entire drama unfold just in his eyes'" (Nair 2016). Guru Mani was unable to perform Kutiyattam for nearly ten years because his fellow Chakyars shunned him for his liberal stance on temple entry. As P. K. G. noted, "Then afterward, everyone became the same—caste rules all disappeared, *janmi* landowners all disappeared, everyone became one. Then it was rectified that Father did the right thing. He was a great man."

Being banned from Kutiyattam multicharacter performance by the wider Chakyar community became the primary impetus behind Guru Mani's decision to train two of his Nambiar drummer sons—P. K. Narayanan Nambiar and P. K. G. Nambiar—in Kutiyattam acting roles so they could perform alongside him onstage.[21] The two made their public debut in the roles of Arjuna and the *vidushaka* of *Subhadradhananjaya* at a local school in Killikkurishimangalam in 1955. Despite being sons of a Chakyar, they were nonhereditary performers of Kutiyattam's male acting roles. While several Chakyars today train their non-Chakyar and non-Nangiar children in acting, Guru Mani was condemned by the community for doing so at the time. Other Chakyars purportedly demanded that he stop teaching his sons and formally apologize for his "mistake." Upon his refusal, some even sought his permanent banishment from temple performance altogether.[22]

This performance outside of the temple was also a bold move at the time. The guru had already performed Chakyarkoothu for All India Radio in 1949 and had embraced performance opportunities outside of the temple since

(Sreekanth 2013). As Gopalakrishnan (2013, 29) writes, Guru Mani "pioneered today's practice of presenting only an episode or a *shloka* in minute detail during a short performance." D. Appukuttan Nair (1994a, 31–32) outlines the guru's suggestions for modifying Kutiyattam for modern stages, including condensing performances of one act to three hours, avoiding repetition in abhinaya, shortening *nirvahana* and the *purusharthas,* and translating Nambiar Tamil into Malayalam as a scene-by-scene account. In an SNA film, the guru reflected on all of these efforts, commenting, "I desired that this art should survive the test of time. That was precisely why I ventured outside the temple."[23]

Guru Mani continued his progressive stance that Kutiyattam should be accessible to all by teaching the first foreign student of Kutiyattam, M. Krzysztof Byrski of Poland, in 1963. This began an important trend of foreign students training in the art that continues today, with me as only one of several recent examples. When Byrski—a Sanskrit PhD student in Varanasi (Benares), India, at the time—traveled to Kerala to interview Mani Madhava Chakyar, the guru offered to train him in Kutiyattam and invited him to stay as long as he wanted. As Dr. Byrski told me, "He simply said that if I really want to know what it is all about, I have to participate in it."[24] Describing his subsequent three-month stay with the guru, he recounted,

> I was treated almost like his sons. Mani Madhava was very kind, very demanding as far as the exercises go. That was not an easy-going thing, I had to work hard to satisfy him. My training was partly in Sanskrit, partly Hindi, with the help of his son (P. K. G.) who speaks fluent Hindi. We also got along with my very limited Sanskrit to communicate, we talked a lot, but I managed, especially as I was treated like a member of the family or rather like a traditional *shishya* [student]. I lived with his sons in the bachelors' house, we ate together, I was absolutely part of the family. Every day almost at 3 o'clock I had to get up, and we started with eye training. He had a spot painted on his palm, moving it in front of my eyes, and I had to train my eyes so they would be very expressive. And of course hand gestures, and then steps, with Narayanan Nambiar playing the rhythm. It was from the early morning until noon, this is what I remember.

During his stay, Byrski learned the complete abhinaya (acting) and text of the character of Udayana from the Svapnankam act of Bhasa's *Svapnavāsavadattā*. Living and eating with the family during one's studies was a progressive gesture at the time for a family of the "half-Brahmin" Chakyar and Nambiar temple castes with strict rules of bodily purity and pollution. In a written account of his experience, Byrski (2009, 50) describes a dramatic event that nearly put a stop to his training. When the local Namboodiri (Kerala Brahmin) community discovered that Guru Mani was teaching Kutiyattam to someone who "not only was not a Chakyar by birth but was not even a Hindu and on top of it was a foreigner," they insisted he be dismissed immediately. As Byrski (2009, 50) recounts, "For the first time I saw (Guruji) really very sad, when he told me about the ultimatum of his patrons." Before he could be sent away, however, a journalist from the Communist newspaper *Toḻilāḷi* (*Worker*) came to interview him, interested in the fact that he came from a Communist country himself. As Byrski told me, when asked about his interest in Kutiyattam and theater, he replied, "Well, [my interest in Kutiyattam is] because I am coming from a family like that in Poland, from a Chakyar family, my parents are involved in theater." Byrski's parents were in fact well-known Polish theater figures and close friends with the famed Polish director Jerzy Grotowski. As he explained, "I already knew that the Namboodiris were critical that Mani Madhava Chakyar decided to instruct me, but I did not think about it, this [telling the newspaper I was a Polish Chakyar] was not a strategy." In a surprising turn of events, upon reading the published article, the Namboodiris returned to tell Guru Mani that since Byrski came from "the Chakyar family of Poland," he had their permission to continue his studies. As Byrski (2009, 50) writes of the experience, "We all heaved a sigh of relief and I continued my training."

Near the end of my conversation with him, Dr. Byrski reflected, "I'm very grateful to Mani Madhava Chakyar and to his family for adopting me as one of their sons and for teaching me, because that was an experience I remember very much even today. As I told you, I still remember that verse." He then launched into a Sanskrit shloka with gusto, his voice modulating in Kutiyattam's singsong recitation of a famous verse in which the hero Udayana remembers the daughter of the king of Avanti, "*smarāmy avantyādhipateḥ sutāyāḥ prasthānakāle svajanaṃ smarantyāḥ | bāṣpaṃ pravṛttam. nayanāntalagnaṃ snehān mamaivorasi pātayantyāḥ* ||."[25] He continued wistfully, "When we parted, [Guru Mani] said that if I could stay another three months, he would allow me to perform in *vesham* [costume] as Udayana, with all of the paraphernalia, but I couldn't stay. Unhappily, I had to return to Benares for my studies." Byrski would not return to Kerala until thirty years later, after Guru Mani's death, as the Polish ambassador to India.

A year before Byrski's training, Guru Mani had taken Kutiyattam outside Kerala's borders for the first time, establishing an important trend of expanding Kutiyattam's recognition to the national level. Dr. V. Raghavan, mentioned earlier for his role in promoting an elite, Sanskrit-based nationalism, invited Mani Madhava Chakyar and his troupe to perform at the Samskrita Ranga

Figure 44. Guru Mani Madhava Chakyar and troupe at Samskrita Ranga in Chennai, 1962. Photo courtesy of Padmasree Mani Madhava Chakyar Smaraka Gurukulam collection.

in Madras (now Chennai) in 1962.[26] A few years later in 1964, Byrski was responsible for the invitation that brought Kutiyattam to North India for the first time. As he told me, "What I'm really proud of is that I managed to invite them to Benares [Varanasi]. And it was not so much my invitation, but it was Benares. When they learned that they can come to Benares, they treated it as a *tīrtthayātra*, a pilgrimage to the holy place." Guru Mani and his troupe first performed in Delhi at the American Paderewski Foundation and the National School of Drama, and in Benares at Benares Hindu University, the Sanskrit University, and the Maharaja's Ramnagar Palace. Mani Madhava Chakyar, as both a Sanskrit scholar and Kutiyattam actor, was a fitting first ambassador for the art form to the Hindi-speaking North, as he was fluent in spoken Sanskrit and could reportedly communicate concepts to the audience with relative ease. His son, P. K. G. Nambiar, played the vidushaka jester figure by replacing the Malayalam portions with Hindi. He thus bridged the linguistic divide by making the form as intelligible to audiences in the North as it was to those in Kerala, which no other actor has done. Dr. Byrski (2009, 51) gives a personal account, well encrusted with a patina of romanticism, of Guru Mani's 1964 performance of *Abhiṣekanāṭaka* in the courtyard of the Maharaja's Ramnagar

Figure 45. Guru Mani Madhava Chakyar and daughter Amminikutty Nangiaramma on tour to North India, 1964. Photo courtesy of P. K. Amminikutty Nangiaramma.

Palace in Varanasi: "The impressive courtyard surrounded by the flight of his column-supported arches made a perfect koothambalam [temple theater]. I sat next to His Highness, the Maharaja and explained to him the intricacies of Chakyar's abhinaya [acting]. It was precisely at that very moment that I had an overwhelming feeling of my dream coming true. There I sat next to the ruler of the oldest kingdom on earth and watched a theatre performance that could claim an unbroken tradition of almost two and a half millennia. Could there be a more fantastic experience?!"

Shortly thereafter, then-president of India, philosopher Sarvepalli Radhakrishnan, personally requested a Kutiyattam performance at the presidential palace. Byrski considers this event the greatest achievement of his efforts and those of his friend Eberhard Büser, who helped finance the tour.[27] The same year, Mani Madhava Chakyar became the first Kutiyattam artist to receive national artistic recognition in the form of the Sangeet Natak Akademi Award (1964) as well as the later Padma Shri Award (1974) and the Sangeet Natak Fellowship (1982), adding to awards he had already been given by Kerala kings in the days before independence.[28]

Guru Mani's actions significantly paved the way for Kutiyattam's sustained engagement at the national level as national heritage. He also used this platform to express concerns about the future of Kutiyattam to influential national figures. G. Venu (2002) writes of assisting Kapila Vatsyayan in the 1970s on a Kerala trip. Upon meeting with Guru Mani, the guru emphasized that they needed to prepare a blueprint to sustain Kutiyattam. Venu notes that it was because of Guru Mani's suggestion that the SNA funded the training of higher studies in Kutiyattam a few years later—Guru Mani training Ammannur (Moozhikkulam) Kochukuttan Chakyar and Guru Ammannur training Ammannur Kuttan Chakyar (2002, 19). Menon (1990, 27) writes of a similar visit that Rukmini Devi Arundale made to Guru Mani a year before his death, wherein he reportedly lamented, "At least Bharatanatyam is now world famous, with thousands of new votaries. What about Koodiyattam? . . . I have done what I can. It has not been easy. One has to sacrifice a lot to learn Koodiyattam. How many persons will be ready for it these days? Will there be an audience capable of imbibing it?"

As we've seen here, Guru Mani Madhava Chakyar was an early visionary, the first Kutiyattam artist to actively welcome people of other castes into the fold of Kutiyattam as spectators and performers. "He was kind. I used to call him *muttacchan* [grandfather]," Usha-teacher told me of her encounters with him while visiting his granddaughter, her childhood friend Vasanthi Nangiar. Despite facing personal criticism, Guru Mani worked hard to expand Kutiyattam's horizons in the early days of temple entry battles as well as the postindependence period. As the first to bring Kutiyattam outside of Kerala to reach wider national audiences, he facilitated its incorporation into national structures of heritage. The impact of his first performance in Delhi—the seat of the national government and home to a thriving, powerful national arts scene, still resonates today. At the time, Kutiyattam's exposure to national institutions was part of a wider process, as I describe in the next section, of transforming regional expressive culture into national heritage. Guru Mani's early willingness to teach the art's first foreign student, a democratization of the art as a bodily practice, similarly led to a broadening of Kutiyattam's international horizons, as his student would later cosponsor Kutiyattam's first foreign tour to Europe in 1980, where the art initially came to UNESCO's attention. Guru Mani's efforts significantly forged the national and, to some extent, international connections that have made Kutiyattam what it is today, leading to a formalized, sustained interest in the art by the national SNA.

Becoming National Heritage: Kutiyattam, V. Raghavan, and the Sangeet Natak Akademi

The transformation of Kutiyattam into national heritage occurred over time and was accomplished through several strategies—national documentation and archiving projects, recognition through the SNA awards system, the showcasing of the art at a national level, and incorporation into national funding schemes. Kutiyattam thus became one of the privileged few representatives of a national tradition that tied India's cultural modernity to a past embodied in ancient Sanskritic texts. This section examines the influential roles of Dr. V. Raghavan and the SNA in transforming Kutiyattam into Indian national heritage.

Dr. V. Raghavan of Madras University, mentioned previously for his pivotal role in promoting a Sanskritized national culture, played an important role in bringing an early national spotlight to Kutiyattam. His goal in so doing was to inform and promote Sanskritic nationalism as well as the creation of a national theater. Kutiyattam's first national exposure occurred only seven years after it was first performed in 1949 outside the temple context when Raghavan highlighted the art in his paper "Sanskrit Drama and Performance" at the first national Drama Seminar organized in Delhi in 1956 (SNA 1953/1958). As a programming consultant for All India Radio at the time, Raghavan persuaded the director general of All India Radio to organize a public performance of Kutiyattam before an invited audience at the Zamorin's royal palace in Calicut the same year (Raghavan 2016).[29] According to Raghavan (2016), this performance was organized and broadcast over the radio "to make [Kutiyattam] better known." A member of the general council of the SNA a few years later, he was also instrumental in first bringing Kutiyattam outside of Kerala. As we saw earlier this chapter, Raghavan invited Mani Madhava Chakyar and his troupe to perform at the Samskrita Ranga in Chennai in 1962 with funds obtained by the Central Sanskrit Board. The venue and source of funding for this performance strongly indicate that Raghavan viewed Kutiyattam as part of his national vision of Sanskritization.

Raghavan also helped connect several foreign researchers with Kutiyattam: Clifford R. Jones and M. Kryzstof Byrksi, both of whom went on to have a lasting impact on the art. Raghavan served as the academic adviser of American art history and dance scholar Clifford Reis Jones during Jones's year as a

Fulbright scholar at the Madras Music Academy in 1959, where he studied to be a *nattuvanar* (Bharatanatyam teacher and cymbal player) with K. Ganesan, son of famed dancer Balasaraswati's teacher Kandappa. Jones told me that he first became aware of Kutiyattam from a reference in *The Arts and Crafts of Travancore* (1948), a book cowritten by his future doctoral adviser Stella Kramrisch. It was Raghavan, however, who facilitated Jones's first contact with Kutiyattam in Kerala. Clifford Jones (1967) went on to become the first foreign scholar to write a PhD dissertation on Kutiyattam.[30] As described in the last chapter, he also played a fundamental role in the art's reinvention at Kerala Kalamandalam, organized the first academic seminar on Kutiyattam in 1966, and created an early film about the art.[31]

Raghavan likewise introduced Polish Sanskrit scholar M. Kryzstof Byrski to Kutiyattam. As mentioned in the last section, Byrski trained under Mani Madhava Chakyar and was instrumental in inviting Kutiyattam artists to North India and international stages for the first time.[32] With a scholarship from the Polish American Paderewski Foundation, Byrski undertook Sanskrit PhD studies in Varanasi (Benares), India, from 1961 to 1966. Dr. Raghavan was an examiner of his PhD thesis on Sanskrit drama, and when Byrski personally carried his thesis to Chennai (Madras) for Raghavan's review, the latter told him about Kutiyattam. Byrski told me of his initial interest in the art: "My main purpose was I wanted to check whether the whole tradition, the gestures, as you know the mudras are very precise, whether they're a strait jacket, or whether they help the actor to be more expressive, to communicate with the audience in a more intense way. And I must say that I am convinced this is so. It is not a strait jacket, it does not bind or limit your expression, it helps you to be much more 'vocal,' not only with the voice but with the entire body." When Raghavan told him about Guru Mani's upcoming public performance in Thrissur, Byrski seized the opportunity to watch Kutiyattam and introduce himself to the guru.[33] Sharing his thoughts on seeing the art for the first time, he recounted, "It impressed me, it's much more expressive than anything you can see in European Western theater; the actor's entire body is engaged in the contact with the audience, and especially the face, so that fascinated me."

In my interviews with Dr. Jones and Dr. Byrski, both mentioned that Raghavan held a slightly dismissive attitude toward Kutiyattam, describing it as similar to a "folk tradition." Byrski contextualized this, explaining that he came to understand Raghavan's perspective after seeing a Sanskrit play Raghavan had directed with his students, *Malati-Madhava*, with his daughter in the leading role. He reflected, "I'll tell you what made me understand the attitude of Raghavan toward Kutiyattam. You see, one verse in *Malati-Madhava* is about the moon rising in the sky. Now, there was a box covered with somewhat transparent paper with a bulb inside, and from backstage it was pulled up on a string while the actor was reciting the verse." He paused his storytelling to laugh, "Now, that was simply a horror, because this shouldn't have been shown. It should be shown with gestures, eyes, the expressions, and you should imagine it." He laughed again, this time more heartily. "You are not supposed to see this box with a bulb inside, you know! So then I understood, yes, Kutiyattam is not going to be of special interest to Professor Raghavan, when I saw the way he organized that scene." He finally concluded, "I think it was the fact that they used Sanskrit texts, this is what probably attracted Raghavan to the form. But then he had some different idea of what it might have been long ago during Bharata Muni's time." He laughed again, saying, "And that moon, you know, told me the rest."

At around the same time, both Indian and foreign scholars began researching Kutiyattam as a window into the past of pan-Indian Sanskrit theater production. The so-called Trivandrum Bhasa plays were "discovered" in Kerala in 1912, attributed to the Sanskrit playwright Bhasa, whose works were thought long lost.[34] When the plays were found in performance among the Kutiyattam community, the art became conceptualized as a marginal survival of a long-lost Indian past. Before this, scholars considered Sanskrit dramas to be literary conventions that were never actually staged, and their performance onstage in Kerala sparked a paradigm shift in the study of Sanskrit drama. After this early attention died down, a few articles mentioned the art form in the 1930s, including one by Raja (1934) that referred to Kutiyattam as an "Aryan institution" and an early article by Raghavan (1933) asserting that Kutiyattam acting is based on Bharata's *Natyashastra*.[35] Academic interest in Kutiyattam largely waned until the early 1960s, when it rapidly increased amid nation-building efforts with the arts. Raghavan (2016, 77) attributes this renewed interest both to his efforts and to the performances of Mani Madhava Chakyar across the country, writing that "from Madras to Delhi and elsewhere, Sri [Mani] Madhava Chakyar's tours and performances have proved an eye-opener to all those interested in theatre and the traditions of Sanskrit play-production."

Like Dr. Raghavan, many scholars were not interested in Kutiyattam itself but in its value as a resource for understanding ancient pan-Indian Sanskrit production and informing the creation of an Indian national theater. Clifford Jones confirmed this wider lack of interest in the art itself, telling me that when he visited the translators of the Bhasa plays in Pune, they were not interested in actually seeing Kutiyattam; they only wanted to see the manuscript texts. Regarding Kutiyattam viewed as a resource, Panchal (1968, 30) stressed the need for Kutiyattam and its koothambalam theater to be "rediscovered and rejuvenated for the sake of a true understanding of our traditional Sanskrit theatre." In this way, he called for contemporary theater practitioners to study the art to discover "the inspiration to create a new dramatic vision" (1968, 30). Warrier (1971) sought to pan-Indianize Kutiyattam by drawing parallels between it and Kashmiri Sanskrit drama production as described in the ninth-century CE poem *Kuṭṭanīmatam*. And Byrski's (1967) iconic article "Is Kudiyattam a Museumpiece?" advocates for Kutiyattam on both points. He writes, "It is a store-house of the practical knowledge of the actual practice of the classical Indian theatre. Since, as I do believe, only classical Indian theatre can give a necessary impulse for the creation of the truly national theatre, therefore, the importance of the Kudiyattam as completing our so far limited knowledge of the ancient Indian theatre drawn exclusively from literary sources, with the reliable information concerning its practice, cannot be overstressed" (1967, 53–54). Raghavan (2016, 79) concurred, describing Kutiyattam as "the only living source from which the authentic traditional Sanskrit play production could be reconstructed . . . [which,] aided by the imagination and knowledge of the Sanskrit *Natya Sastra*, could help one in visualizing how it would have all been done in the heyday of the classical Sanskrit stage." He further called for "greater integration of the Indian theatre with its past and its surviving traditional forms . . . [through] increased study and production of Sanskrit plays" in order to build a truly national theater and, in the process, reduce India's reliance on Western theater models (Raghavan 1993b).

It was this flurry of academic excitement about Kutiyattam's potential to both illuminate the past and inform the future of a national Indian theater that sparked the SNA's interest in the art. The SNA was founded by the newly established Indian government to facilitate national patronage for the arts, "symboliz[ing] the new awakening and cultural resurgence that was to take place in the country under a new system of patronage hitherto unknown to Indian Arts" (SNA 1953/1958). The government explicitly acknowledged its responsibility of "filling the vacuum" left behind by crumbled systems of royal patronage of the arts (1953/1958). The SNA, like the scholars of the time, viewed Kutiyattam as a survival of classical Sanskrit drama, an approach that persists today. This depiction is evident in the SNA's description of Guru Mani's first trip to North India: "The Akademi in association with the Paderewski Foundation of Poland organized a performance of Kutiyattam by Shri Mani Madhava Chakiar [*sic*] and Party at the National School of Drama and Asian Theatre Institute, and at the Azad Bhavan (on the 17th), New Delhi. Kutiyattam, the only surviving traditional form of classical Sanskrit Drama was thus presented in North India for the first time" (SNA 1964/1965).

This first trip to Delhi also marked the beginning of Kutiyattam's documentation and incorporation into the SNA's national archives of performing arts. The Indian state invested in recording Kutiyattam's repertoire for the national archives, starting with audio and video documentation of Guru Mani that grew more extensive over time. Antonnen (2005) compares the establishment of national archives to the institutionalization of museums as repositories and manifestations of national identity and cultural achievement. He suggests that national archives house "material" manifestations of the Herderian "spirit of a nation," making them contested spaces in processes of national inclusion and exclusion. Lilja (1996) similarly compares folklore archives to museums, noting their parallel function as watchdogs "guarding the purity of national tradition," while others such as García Canclini (1995) have actively questioned the political consequences of collecting, archiving, and representing cultural heritage.[36] Firmly rooting Kutiyattam in the contested space of the national body, the initial SNA documentation and archiving of Kutiyattam began a longer process of consigning the art's repertoire to the national archive that continues today.

The SNA's Akademi Awards system for individual artistic recognition also incorporated Kutiyattam into a national framework of both award recognition and festival showcasing. Guru Mani's national Sangeet Natak Akademi Award (1964) was accompanied by his performance in a showcase of national award winners that would later come to be known as the Akademi Festival of Arts. Cherian (2005, 120) notes that these national awards allowed the SNA to firmly center the discourse of tradition within the sphere of the state, thereby "naturalizing" the nation-state and "conferring it an indigenous and ancient vintage." As a case in point, former president of India, Sri Venkataraman, once compared state recognition of artists to life-giving sustenance, proclaiming that "the recognition of talent is to art as what sunshine is to flowers" (SNA 1988/1989). In so doing, he discursively naturalized the nation-state as a life-giver to the arts.

Kutiyattam's inclusion in the Akademi Festival of Arts marked a transition from independent performances at the national level to a newly emerging trend of national performing arts festivals, whereby the art was showcased alongside several other "Indian" arts in a performance of the national slogan "unity in diversity."[37] This exhibition of regional forms as representatives of Indian national tradition served to forge national heritage on the festival stage, transforming them from embodied repertoire to archive through extensive videographic documentation destined for the national archives. Cantwell (1993) distinguishes these types of festivals from museums and archives through their engagement of the body in "some immediate exhibitory way." He emphasizes that this form of exhibition serves to identify a participant's living presence with their artistic performance in a process that brings both into the possession of the festival and, I argue, into the possession of the sponsoring institution and nation-state as well.

The national performing arts festival trend in India began with the first national music, dance, and drama festivals in the early 1950s (SNA 1953/1958). While the Akademi of Arts Festival began in 1954, the SNA did not initiate other annual performance festivals on a national scale until the early 1980s, when it started several to support the work of young performing artists nationwide. Kutiyattam's incorporation into these national performance festivals was first facilitated through the newly reinvented female solo Nangiarkoothu in 1986, performed by Kalamandalam Girija at the Yuva Utsav festival in Madras (SNA 1986/1987). Nangiarkoothu's easily condensable female solo performance, which fits more easily into a larger dance framework than the multicharacter Kutiyattam drama, has remained by far the most commonly performed form within the Kutiyattam complex featured in SNA-sponsored national showcase festivals. The predominantly male *nirvahanam* solo element of Kutiyattam has also been featured but on a much smaller scale.[38] The fact that Kutiyattam has predominantly been showcased in dance festivals is indicative of a larger ambiguity surrounding Kutiyattam's classification at the national level. Despite the fluidity of genric classification of performing arts in India, Kutiyattam artists predominantly categorize their art as drama or theater. Within the frame of the Akademi Awards, the SNA has classified Kutiyattam in different ways, with a general progression over time from traditional dance to, in recent years, traditional/folk/tribal dance/music/theater/puppetry or other major traditions of dance or dance theater.

The high point of Kutiyattam's national performance festival participation was the 1995 Kutiyattam Mahotsavam (Kutiyattam Grand Festival), organized in recognition of what the SNA termed the art's "unique and . . . exalted place . . . among the traditional forms of Indian theatre . . . (as) our only surviving link with the ancient Sanskrit theatre" (SNA 1995a). The six-day festival in Delhi was devoted exclusively to performances, lecture demonstrations, interviews of prominent artists and scholars, and discussions of Kutiyattam, bringing artists from all institutions together with scholars and administrators for the first time. The SNA (1995a) video documented the entire festival, with certain performances even "planned exclusively for archival recording during the festival days." The SNA's academic journal,

Sangeet Natak, also published a special issue on Kutiyattam for the occasion (Paniker and Gopalakrishnan 1994). With approximately forty Kutiyattam artists participating from all major training and performance institutions at the time, artists assembled in far-off Delhi as they had never before assembled in Kerala, marking the first instance of interinstitutional collaboration on such a grand scale. The Kutiyattam Mahotsavam festival reflected the art's nationally privileged position as well as its greater integration into India's national performing arts canon.

The final strategy of national heritage translation I discuss here is Kutiyattam's incorporation into national funding schemes. Beginning in the 1970s, the SNA initiated intermittent, individualized funding of Kutiyattam through research and documentation projects, higher study stipends for students and teachers, artist pensions, and lecture demonstrations.[39] Due to Guru Mani's suggestions to Kapila Vatsyayan mentioned previously, the SNA (1976/1977) began the scheme "Promotion and Preservation of Rare Forms of Traditional Performing Arts" in 1976, established "with a view to reviving and supporting [endangered arts] by making [them] better known among the people." Kutiyattam was one of the earliest beneficiaries of this scheme, which sought to ensure the continuation of art forms "threatened with extinction" by providing financial assistance for gurus to train students, thereby ensuring the continuity of tradition. In 1991, the SNA significantly offered longer-term support of Kutiyattam through a similar scheme, likewise aimed to "preserve performing arts traditions threatened by a changing socio-economic environment" (SNA 1991/1992). Kutiyattam was the sole beneficiary of the scheme, titled "National Centres for Specialised Training in Music and Dance," until the addition of Chhau dance in 1993. Describing Kutiyattam as "the only Sanskrit theatre tradition now surviving," the program set out to provide a "total-care plan" for Kutiyattam (1991/1992). In addition to ensuring the "systematic transmission of the art from aging gurus to the younger generation of artists," the plan sponsored regular year-round performances "in order to provide economic sustenance to artists and to create a better understanding of and an appreciative audience for the art" (1991/1992). This "total care" came in the form of financial remuneration to teachers, fellowships and stipends to students, and performance subsidies to three Kutiyattam institutions, excluding the Kerala state–funded Kalamandalam. Whereas all dependable state support had formerly been concentrated at Kalamandalam, this scheme was the first to provide regular support to the art across several institutions, giving alternative training centers regular access to state financial support. This funding scheme continued through 2007 when, as a direct result of Kutiyattam's UNESCO inscription, it was upgraded to establish a national center for Kutiyattam in Trivandrum—Kutiyattam Kendra—that marked Kutiyattam's inclusion in a small, elite group of what Cherian (2009, 41) has termed "model institutions" of arts funded longer term by the SNA.

Implications

The SNA's funding of Kutiyattam, which incorporated the art into a system of national patronage, significantly offered Kutiyattam artists opportunities to both teach and perform Kutiyattam outside of the limited confines of Kerala Kalamandalam. It also facilitated the founding of several new Kutiyattam institutions, thereby ensuring the continuation of diverse performance styles. Greater artist participation in the national arts scene also resulted in greater exposure to many other Indian performing arts and contemporary theater groups, which led to greater creativity and cooperation with other art forms and artists, and infused Kutiyattam with the cultural capital of national prestige. SNA sponsorship perhaps unintentionally promoted a wider regionally based artistic identity among professional Kutiyattam artists. The 1995 Kutiyattam Mahotsavam festival was a crowning event, constructing a unified, professionalized Kutiyattam as national heritage. While early funding schemes provided assistance to individual gurus to train their students, the 1991 scheme aimed to benefit a community of professional artists attached to institutions. This redefined Kutiyattam as a cohesive community of professionalized, institutionally affiliated artists and, in the process, excluded hereditary, nonprofessional Kutiyattam artists from national funding structures they previously had greater access to.

The SNA's increased attention to Kutiyattam notably occurred during a period of increased nationwide consolidation of Hindu identity. In the late 1980s, the state-sponsored national television channel Doordarshan began to widely project representations of a monolithic Hindu cultural identity. This has been considered both "a culminating point in the effort to create an all-India national culture" (Dalmia and Stietencron 1995) and complicit in state acts of violence against India's minority citizens (Mankekar 1999). The 1990s in India was a period dominated by widespread economic liberalization and the increasing "Hinduization" of consumer markets and, by association, communities of consumption (Rajagopal 2001). Finally, the 1999 rise of the BJP as the leading party in a national democratic alliance significantly marked the move of Hindu nationalism from the margins to the mainstream in Indian society (Ludden 2005). The BJP and its Hindu nationalism have remained mainstream ever since, first leading the nation in 1999–2004 and again from 2014 through the present day.[40]

In 2001, the SNA celebrated Kutiyattam's inscription as a UNESCO Masterpiece of the Oral and Intangible Heritage of Humanity as the culmination of its "years of intensive work under the Kutiyattam project," details of which have been discussed here (SNA 2004/2005). Hafstein (2004, vi) argues that UNESCO ICH inscription inevitably restructures cultural practices, "bringing them within the sphere of government and integrating vernacular culture into official administrative structures." As we have seen with Kutiyattam, however, the art's inscription as a UNESCO ICH represented the culmination of years of national heritage consolidation. Instead of signaling the beginning of the art's integration into official administrative structures, it marked an intensification of its preexisting national heritage integration. I argue that if art forms have made it to official UNESCO nomination, they likely are already integrated into official administrative structures.[41] As the next chapter explores, UNESCO inscription served to further entrench Kutiyattam in national structures of patronage, with the SNA's 2007 establishment of the Kutiyattam Kendra institution in Trivandrum providing a longer-term, nationally administered funding base for the art for the first time. Somewhat paradoxically, UNESCO's recognition thus represented a hypernationalization of Kutiyattam.[42]

Conclusion: Muthu's Critique

Returning to Muthu's critique at the beginning of the chapter, his evaluation of the political implications of Kutiyattam's UNESCO ICH inscription similarly applies to the art's longer history of inclusion as Indian national heritage. Muthu articulates a hegemonic notion of Indian culture as elite, upper caste (Hindu), and Sanskritic that is carefully curated by its largely North Indian gatekeepers. He points out that Kutiyattam, as an upper-caste, Sanskrit theater tradition, fits the mold that those in power use to shape Indian national culture. This is apparent in the way the SNA has engaged the art over the years. The national perception that Kutiyattam embodies ancient, Sanskritic culture is particularly evident in the terminology the SNA has used to describe the art in its annual reports. From the 1960s through the present day, typical descriptors of the art in annual reports have included "the only surviving traditional form of classical Sanskrit Drama," "the oldest form of Sanskrit drama tradition," and "the only Sanskrit theatre tradition now surviving in Kerala."[43] We also find the oversimplified description of Kutiyattam as a "form of theatre which is being staged as per the tenets of the Natya Sastra."[44] This explicit connection between the art and ancient Sanskrit drama as well as to the *Natyashastra*, the two-thousand-year-old (200 BC–200 CE) Sanskrit treatise on Indian performing arts, clearly conveys the symbolic capital Kutiyattam represents for the Indian nation.

Muthu partially attributes Kutiyattam's UNESCO success to a powerful Keralite lobby in the national arts scene. Kerala has held a seat at the national performing arts table since the SNA's founding in 1953, preceding Kerala state's 1956 formation. Kerala's early stake at the national level is evidenced by the inclusion of Kathakali, Kerala's all-male dance drama, as one of only four dance forms originally recognized as classical that were showcased in the first National Dance Festival in 1955. In a system where classical recognition by the SNA became "a space where demands for regional recognition were played out," Kerala, as the only state with three recognized classical forms—Kathakali, Mohiniyattam, and Kutiyattam—has maintained a long-standing prominence on the national stage (Cherian 2009, 49).[45] The region's early national clout is evident in the fact that Prime Minister Jawaharlal Nehru attended Kerala Kalamandalam's silver jubilee celebration in 1955 and donated Rs. 1 lakh (approximately $21,000), which helped to purchase the land where its campus is currently located.[46] Notably, the national claiming of Kutiyattam by the SNA through structures of recognition, archiving, and showcasing began before similar processes in Kerala, which started with the 1965 opening of a Kutiyattam department at Kerala Kalamandalam.

Kerala's power in the national cultural sector is undoubtedly related to its wider reputation for preserving marginal survivals of pan-Indian, classical (i.e., Brahminical, Sanskritic) traditions. This reputation is bolstered by Kerala's strong tradition of Kutiyattam and Vedic Chanting, as well as the occasional surfacing of previously unknown Sanskrit manuscripts in dusty corners of crumbling upper-caste homes, similar to those attributed to Bhasa that first brought Kutiyattam to wider attention a century ago. Connecting the dots, Byrski (1967, 46) stresses, "It is certainly not by chance that the unique manuscript of the *Abhinavabharati*, i.e., the only available commentary on the *Natya Sastra* of Bharata written by Abhinavagupta, a Kashmirian, has been preserved in Malabar. . . . It is also not by chance that the *santarasa* portion of Chapter VI of the *Natya Sastra* has been found only in the Malabar manuscript of this treatise, while Kudiyattam performers to this day stage the *Nagananda* of Harshavardhana which is a *santarasa* drama composed most probably as an illustration to the theory enunciated in the *Natya Sastra*." In fact, Cherian (2005, 311) describes Kerala's function in cultural nationalist discourse as "a metaphor for the idealized nation, a space which had developed the essence of India, that is, its Sanskritic civilization."

Given this background, Muthu's statement about Kerala's power in the national cultural sector influencing Kutiyattam's nomination is not surprising. What is the story behind Kutiyattam's selection as India's first candidate for UNESCO ICH inscription? All of the previously noted cultural politics certainly played a role in the process, but Kutiyattam did not win any type of organized, nationwide competition. The story I heard about Kutiyattam's nomination involved national and international connections as well as a certain degree of serendipity. Of course, serendipity is always facilitated through favorable constellations of power.

Dr. Sudha Gopalakrishnan, a successful longtime administrator in India's national cultural sector and Margi's vice president in the period preceding Kutiyattam's UNESCO inscription, authored the art's successful candidature file. Sudha located the origins of the art's inscription not in India but in Paris, with French dancer Milena Salvini, director of the Centre Mandapa for the promotion of South Asian performing arts. During my interview with Milena in Paris, she told me that, after studying Kathakali at Kalamandalam in 1965, she received funding from UNESCO to travel to Kerala to research Kathakali and prepare the Kalamandalam troupe for its first international tour (1967), which she organized. As we saw earlier, she also later organized Kutiyattam's first international tour (1980) with M. Krzysztof Byrski, by then a professor at the University of Warsaw. Milena maintained what she called a "very close personal connection with UNESCO" over the years, working on a UNESCO research assignment in 1969 on the three forms of Chhau in India and receiving a loan from UNESCO to open the Centre Mandapa. Milena described what happened when she first heard about UNESCO's ICH program about ten years before it began accepting applications.

> I wrote to UNESCO and said there is something absolutely extraordinary, Kutiyattam, which is the oldest living art form, and something should be done. At the time I was asking them to give me a grant to go with my husband to make a film and do some research work with Kutiyattam, that's how I attracted their interest. Then when the program was open, I said somebody has to present Kutiyattam, and it cannot come from a foreigner, it has to come from an Indian who is concerned with the subject. I knew Sudha Gopalakrishnan when we were working with Margi for their tour, and I thought she's the person who can do it, because she has the knowledge, she has everything, and she's quite a powerful person

> in her own field. We told her, we have to present Kutiyattam, and only you can do it. Yes, sure, I will do it, she said, and she prepared a network, a program, everything, and she submitted Kutiyattam to UNESCO.

Sudha Gopalakrishnan filled out the story, describing how Milena wrote a letter to Margi in 1997 inviting its Kutiyattam troupe to tour Paris. In that letter, Milena mentioned a new UNESCO program, expressing her hope that Kutiyattam could participate. On the subsequent 1999 tour, the Margi Kutiyattam troupe conducted all-night performances to rapt Parisian audiences. As Sudha told me,

> Noriko Aikawa, the director of intangible heritage at UNESCO, she happened to come for this performance, and she was mesmerized. She said, "Why don't you meet me in my office tomorrow or the next day if you are free." Then I remember that Milena dropped me to UNESCO, saying that "I'm sure something great is going to happen." Then [Norika Aikawa] said that "we are starting this big program at UNESCO—until now we've only looked at landscapes and built heritage, so now we are looking at the intangible which is more important perhaps. We are trying to develop a stream called the oral and intangible heritage of humanity, the masterpieces program, and I think this really fits the bill. Why don't you apply, but you have only two months. You have to go home and do such and such procedures, we have already sent the form to your culture ministry." So when I came back, I rushed to Delhi, to the culture ministry, and they could not find it. Actually my husband had come with me, he's in the IAS [Indian Administrative Service], and he somehow also wielded his power.

After several hours of searching, someone at the Ministry of Culture in Delhi finally found the application for her. Discovering that it also required a documentary film, Sudha set out to find a filmmaker, write the extensive application, and, with the help of Margi's program chief Ram Iyer, assemble the Kutiyattam community to discuss moving forward.[47] After gaining the blessing of the wider Kutiyattam community, Sudha took time off work to write the candidature file and action plan, telling me that if she had not already been writing a book on Kutiyattam, she never would have been able to finish in time.[48] She also found a filmmaker, one of the most renowned in India—Adoor Gopalakrishnan, a longtime supporter of Margi—to make the application video. With a very short timeline, Adoor shot a documentary film at the Kidangur temple theater, one of the most beautiful koothambalams in Kerala, with a cast of both hereditary and nonhereditary artists.[49] This was the nonhereditary artists' first time performing on a traditional koothambalam stage, and it meant a great deal to them. The crew initially ran into a problem—a local angry mob of religious conservatives threatened violence if they filmed inside the koothambalam, saying it would displease the *yakṣi* (demoness) who guarded the theater. A late-night call to the district superintendent of police resulted in police protection, and filming began.

After the filming concluded, Adoor and Sudha traveled to Chennai to begin five days of intense work to edit ten hours of film down to three. They flew back to Trivandrum to screen the film for Noriko Aikawa, who was visiting from UNESCO, before sending it to Paris for further editing by Milena and her filmmaker husband. The application required a crisp, subtitled film sequence of fifteen minutes, which took Milena and her husband a full week to create. After innumerable hours of work, the documentary film sequence and application were finally finished, and Sudha sent Kutiyattam's candidature file to the Indian Ministry of Culture, which forwarded it to UNESCO as India's only submission for UNESCO's first list of ICH Masterpieces.

When I asked Sudha about Muthu's meticulous, thousand-page document, she had not heard of it. It probably ended up on a bureaucrat's desk at the Ministry of Culture, where it likely remains to this day under the piles of thousands of neatly bundled, yellowing documents that suffocate the ministry's offices. But this does not mean that Muthu's assessment was mistaken or misguided. The true significance of Kutiyattam's UNESCO ICH inscription lies in the politics that others read into the art's elevation to the apex of Indian national heritage, and in underlying processes, both conscious and unconscious, of power, cultural representation, and privilege. Several people I spoke with drew connections between Kutiyattam's success as a UNESCO ICH and India's Hindu nationalist BJP, which made a staggeringly successful bid for the governmental majority in the 1999 general election. Diane, a foreign scholar working with Kutiyattam for over thirty years, candidly told me, "It's no coincidence that Kutiyattam's recognition came when the BJP was in power." Kalamandalam Rama Chakyar, one of the art's senior-most gurus today, similarly recognized Kutiyattam's potential synergy with the agenda of the BJP. Telling a tale of waylaid hope that made him throw his hands up in the air, he revealed, "I thought that when the BJP came to power Kutiyattam would get a lot of benefit, but they didn't do anything for us."

M. V. Narayanan (2006) derides what he calls the neocolonialist discourse that he accuses several Western scholars of using in their writings on Kutiyattam, which emphasize the art's ritualistic over aesthetic qualities. Outlining the danger he considers this discourse holding for the art's appropriation by

Hindu nationalism, he writes, "Even more importantly, and perhaps much more dangerously, this discourse, through its emphasis on ritual mysteries and its attempts to establish Vedic roots for kutiyattam, may open the door for kutiyattam's appropriation into revivalist, right-wing Hindu discourses that promote the recreation in contemporary life of a 'glorious Hindu past'" (2006, 151). Narayanan is fully justified in his concern, more so today than ever before, although no concrete connections between Kutiyattam and the BJP have, to my knowledge, yet been forged. In placing the blame for this discourse on a few Western scholars, however, Narayanan ignores the art's longer history of depiction by Indian scholars and officials involved in postcolonial nation-building as a direct link to a Sanskritic national past.[50] Artists regularly claim Kutiyattam to be two thousand years old, thereby tying it to the pan-Indian performance of Sanskrit drama. Muthu, for his part, did not connect Kutiyattam or Vedic Chanting to Hindu nationalism or the BJP. Instead, he associated the political party with India's third UNESCO Masterpiece, recognized in 2005 one year after the BJP lost its national majority—Ramlila, a festival/folk drama performed across North India that celebrates the life of Lord Rama, the hero of the BJP and the subject of the iconic BJP-led Ayodhya communalist clashes of 1992 that left thousands dead.

After the success of Kutiyattam's candidature file, the Indian Ministry of Culture invited Sudha Gopalakrishnan to prepare their 2003 and 2005 UNESCO ICH candidature files as well. These subsequent processes were less haphazard than Kutiyattam's application but equally nontransparent. Sudha and the culture secretary at the time, N. Gopalaswami, personally chose the next expressive forms that India would submit to UNESCO. Gopalaswami, himself a Tamil Brahmin, asked Sudha to bring a short list of potential art forms to her meeting with him. "We can't send another from Kerala," he mused when she suggested Theyyam. After reviewing the rest of the list, he chose Vedic Chanting, an insular Brahminical tradition. Sudha then set about preparing another labor-intensive candidature file—this time for Vedic Chanting—communities of which exist across several states nationwide, including Kerala. The same process was repeated in 2005 with the Ramlila, a drama whose main roles are enacted primarily by Brahmin boys and is associated with a Hindu religious festival celebrated throughout North India. There was never a nationwide call for applications. Given the opaque and circuitous nature of Indian bureaucracy, folklorists like Muthu, though nationally connected, never stood a chance of getting their recommendations considered without insider information or powerful connections.

As this chapter has shown, Kutiyattam's heritagization contributes to a national imagining of India as ancient, Hindu, and Sanskritic that claims the

Sanskrit cosmopolis as its own.[51] The art's increasing recognition, patronage, documentation, and showcasing by the SNA constituted a process of national heritage creation that established a new "metacultural relationship to what was once just habitus" (Kirshenblatt-Gimblett 2006, 161). An art that was once exclusively part of everyday life thereby transformed into a symbol of the nation. In this period of national consolidation, the newly established Indian state sought legitimation through a connection with an imagined glorious national past that Kutiyattam offered as "the only surviving traditional form of classical Sanskrit drama in India" (SNA 1964/1965). And with Kutiyattam's 2001 inscription as a UNESCO Masterpiece of the Oral and Intangible Heritage of Humanity, followed by the later 2003 and 2005 inscriptions of Vedic Chanting and Ramlila, India projected a carefully curated imagining of itself as Hindu, upper caste, and Sanskritic on a global scale.

Notes

1. Chakyars are not Brahmin but half-Brahmin, although an argument can be made for their Brahminic status from a national perspective. Nambiars/Nangiars belong to elite temple castes but are not Brahmin.

2. For example, the British outlawing widow remarriage was detrimental to non-Brahmin women across India.

3. For more on the destruction of local social systems, see Arunima 2003; Barnett 1976; Devika 2007a; Sangari and Vaid 1989. British practices like census-taking created caste as a fixed social category, cementing otherwise fluid local *jati* caste systems (Appadurai 1996).

4. Cultural anthropology, history, and archaeology all consider the Indo-Aryan invasion theory unfounded (Boivin 2007). Historian Romila Thapar (2003, 105) opposes the association of Indo-European and Indo-Aryan as racial rather than language labels and concludes that "the theory of an Aryan invasion no longer has credence."

5. See Thomas 2018; 2021 for more details.

6. Kennedy (2003) has observed the race concept persisting in much of the work of contemporary South Asian biological anthropologists through the continued polytypic sorting of ancient and living peoples.

7. See Egorova 2009.

8. See the 1947 Partition Archive for firsthand narratives of the Partition, https://www.1947partitionarchive.org/.

9. See Aarzoo and Afzal 2005; Balgir 2003.

10. Translated from German by author.

11. Through his work with Milton Singer, Raghavan impacted how India came to be studied in the US (Hancock 1998).

12. Translated from German by author.

13. Alongside the Sahitya Akademi and Lalit Kala Akademi.

14. He choreographed a number of new performances, such as acts from Kalidasa's *Abhijñānaśakuntalā, Vikramōrvaśīya and Mālavikāgnimitra,* Bhasa's *Svapnavasāvadattā* and *Pañcaratna,* and Harsha's *Nāgānanda.* For a list of his awards, see Sreekanth 2013, 11–12, 18.

15. For translated portions, see Chakyar 1994a, 1994b, 2013a, 2013b. Madhavan (2010) refers to this work as the *Kerala Natyashastra.*

16. With his wife Kunjimalu Nangiaramma. Guru Painkulam did the same.

17. Daugherty (2000) writes that some families refused to perform in Travancore temples after the 1936 temple entry. Private temples remained unaffected.

18. Usha Nangiar, a disciple of Ammannur Madhava Chakyar, confirmed this historical detail for me.

19. See also Sreekanth 2013. Kalamandalam Krishnan Nair became a famous Kathakali actor and Guru Gopinath an influential modern dancer. Government temples here means those governed by a regional Devaswom Board.

20. He nevertheless continued performing his *adiyanthirakoothu* ritualistic performance duties like *Mattavilasam, Anguliyankam,* or *Mantrankam,* or solo programs, but was unable to perform in multicharacter Kutiyattam dramas for entertainment (i.e., *kazhchekoothu*).

21. His Nangiar daughters were destined for Kutiyattam acting and trained predominantly with their father and/or elder brothers, as their mother was overburdened with household duties. This, however, was not controversial.

22. Daugherty (2019, 591) notes that as "punishment," Guru Mani was not invited to perform in Vadakkumnathan's temple theater.

23. *Mani Madhava Chakyar: The Master at Work.*

24. At Benares Hindu University.

25. Translation: I remember, still, how the princess of Avantī affectionately spilled tears on my chest, that had welled up in the corners of her eyes, as she remembered what her family looked like at the time she was leaving home (act 5, verse 5 of *Svapnavāsavadattā*).

26. For the program, see Raghavan 2016, 68–73. For a description of Guru Mani's acting in a subsequent performance, see Rajagopalan 1990.

27. Eberhard Büser, a German teacher at Benares Hindu University, played a fundamental role in bringing the artists to Benares, financed by special funds from a German foundation. The Paderewski Foundation and SNA funded the tour's Delhi performance.

28. Guru Mani received the coveted *veerashrinkala* (golden bracelet award) from several Kerala kings, although his most prized award was a small gold ring

from Godavarma Battan Thampuran of the Kodungallur royal family (Chandrahasan 1989). As Guru Mani explained,

> This was presented to me by Sri Godavarama Battan Thampuran of the Kodungallur (Cranganore) Palace years ago. I was only 22 then. Those were days when Kodungallur used to witness the best assembly of scholars in Sanskrit and the sasthras. Present on that day were several highly learned men and women. The stage was in front of Sringapuram temple. I presented Bhagavad Dooth Prabhatham Koothu. My interpretation of one of the *shlokas* was a little more elaborate than and different from the custom-worn treatment. The audience liked it. In appreciation, Bhattan Thampuran removed this ring from his finger and put it on mine. The spontaneous gesture in recognition of my art naturally is the most precious to me. (1989)

29. According to Guru Mani's family, All India Radio first invited him to perform, since he previously performed for them earlier and the Zamorin was his primary patron, but he became ill and recommended Guru Painkulam instead.

30. His art history dissertation at the University of Pennsylvania was on the art's koothambalam temple theater.

31. Funded by the American Institute for Indian Studies, this seminar took place at Kerala Kalamandalam. Raghavan was present alongside several Kutiyattam scholars and artists.

32. Byrski later became the Polish ambassador to India. He trained with Guru Mani for three months in 1963. See Byrski 2009 for a personal account of his experience.

33. As Jimuthavahana in Harsha's *Nagananda*.

34. The debate regarding the Trivandrum plays' authorship is known as the "Bhasa Problem"; see Unni 2001.

35. See also Keith 1924; Pisharoti 1932/1934.

36. Translated from Swedish by author.

37. See also Lowthorp 2013b.

38. Margi Madhu performed *nirvahanam* at the 1990 Sangeet Nritah Samaroh festival in Delhi; see SNA 1990/1991.

39. In 1971, the SNA began funding the training of higher-level Kutiyattam students under the scheme "Fellowship for Specialised Training in Music, Dance, & Drama," and in 1976, additional scholarships were granted for both Kutiyattam acting and mizhavu percussion students.

40. As of 2024.

41. For other examples, see Foster 2015b; Hardwick 2020; Konagaya 2020; Yun 2015.

42. See also Lowthorp 2013b, 2020.

43. This characterization is most prominent from the 1960s to 1980s and again post-UNESCO inscription.

44. See chapter 3 for how Kutiyattam both follows and diverges from the *Natyashastra*.

45. For more on the distinction between classical and folk in India, see Lowthorp 2017; Korom and Lowthorp 2019.

46. Based on a historical exchange rate in 1955 of Indian Rs. 4.79 per US dollar; see http://intl.econ.cuhk.edu.hk/exchange_rate_regime/index.php?cid=15. The current exchange rate hovers around Rs. 86 per dollar.

47. These activities were funded with UNESCO funds Gopalakrishnan acquired for the application.

48. For more, see Gopalakrishnan 2000, 2011a.

49. This was controversial. Guru Ammannur was invited to participate but replied he was unable due to a schedule conflict. This led to accusations from the Ammannur gurukulam that Margi excluded them from the application process, prompting Noriko Aikawa to visit India to investigate. This is why she was in India for the documentary screening described below.

50. Narayanan takes particular issue with Western scholars describing Kutiyattam as a *chakshusha yajña* (visual sacrifice), without acknowledging that artists like Guru Mani and several Indian scholars have similarly described the art.

51. The term *heritagization* is an Anglicization of the German *Heritage-ifizierung* (see Bendix 2007) and French *patrimonialisation* (see Giguère 2010).

7

KUTIYATTAM AS UNESCO INTANGIBLE CULTURAL HERITAGE

Politics, Aftermath, and Community Perspectives

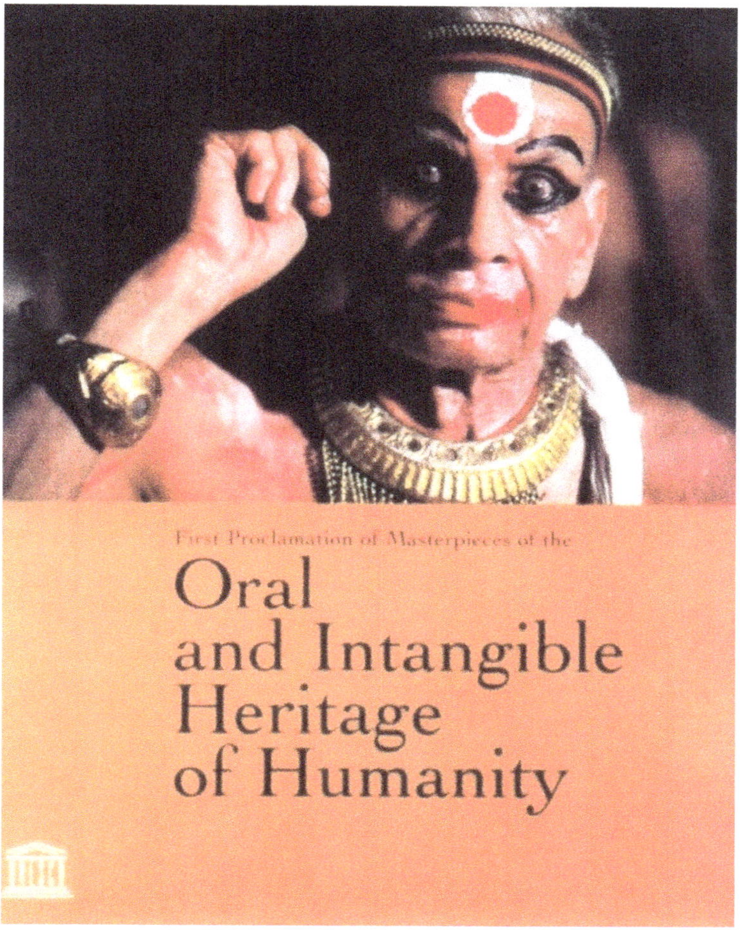

Figure 46. Guru Ammannur Madhava Chakyar on the cover of UNESCO's First Proclamation of Masterpieces. Photo courtesy of Sangeet Natak Akademi.

On May 18, 2001, the director general of the United Nations Educational, Scientific and Cultural Organization (UNESCO), Koïchira Matsuura, declared the first nineteen Masterpieces of the Oral and Intangible Heritage of Humanity. In so doing, UNESCO (2001a) proclaimed expressive forms and cultural spaces from around the world—from India's Kutiyattam Sanskrit theater to Georgian polyphonic singing to China's Kunqu Opera—as endangered "masterpieces of human creative genius" representing the cultural diversity of humankind. Milena Salvini, a Parisian arts administrator central to Kutiyattam's inscription, told me, "Kutiyattam was number one in the selection, with unanimous approval from all members of the jury. There was the Princess of Jordan, she said she had never seen anything like this in her life." Kutiyattam artists were invited to perform at UNESCO headquarters for a celebration of the proclamation that showcased six masterpieces—Gelede ritual from Benin, Nogaku theater from Japan, Kunqu Opera from China, the cultural space of the Jemaa el-Fna marketplace from Morocco, and Kutiyattam theater from India.[1]

Usha-teacher was one of the twelve Kutiyattam artists who performed in Paris. One warm Kerala night, I asked about her experience. The power has just gone out, right on schedule at 7:00 p.m. While just a moment ago the roar of the fans competed with her voice, it is now completely silent, a lone cricket chirping outside as we sit across from each other on the floor in the darkness. Usha-teacher breaks the silence with a laugh and gets up to light a candle. Returning to sit with me, she enthusiastically begins telling her story, her face framed by the glow of candlelight.

> When we did the program in Paris, everyone came together from different countries. I saw art forms from Africa and many places, and spoke with others about their traditional things. Sathi-chechi and I were in a room with a large mirror, so when you saw our costumes in the mirror they looked really fantastic. Many were peeking in and saying, "Wow wow wow!"; they thought that Kutiyattam costumes were especially attractive. When people came over to us I showed them mudras, it was really wonderful. There were many types of people from all over the world. Even if we couldn't speak directly to each other, we could communicate through mudras and facial expressions.

"Wow, what an experience," I interject.

She smiles and continues:

> Yes! And onstage it was wondrous, there were so many people in the audience. First, Ammannur-ashan did a *navarasa* demonstration [facial expressions] for ten to fifteen minutes projected onto a large screen for everyone to see. Then we performed the act of Shurpanakha. I was Sita, but I wasn't actually supposed to play a role. I went to Paris to play the cymbals but brought my costume just in case. Shivan-ashan was planning

> to perform Sita as Rama pretending to listen to and then repeating (*kēṭṭāṭuka*) her lines, but once there Shivan-ashan, Nambiar-ashan, and Eashwaran-ashan decided that it would be more beautiful if I came onstage in costume. Venuji played Shurpanakha, Sajeev was Lakshmanan, Shivan-ashan was Shri Rama, I was Sita, and Sathi-chechi was Lalitha, with Rajeev, Hariharan, Nambiar-ashan, and Eashwaran-ashan on mizhavu.[2] It was only thirty minutes, everyone was happy to see it.

Later in our conversation, Usha-teacher reflects, "Out of all of these art forms, we got first place. We didn't expect it, but I was really happy about it, because it's our traditional art. When UNESCO recognized us, other countries were interested in knowing more about it and some people came to do research. UNESCO brought a symbolic status for Kutiyattam everywhere, and more people began to want to see it. Before when people heard the word *Kutiyattam*, they reacted, 'Oh, ay (tsk),'" as she frowns and waves her hand. "But now in every place, in schools, colleges, they have begun to know about it, and some are coming to study and do research. Like you!" She laughs her infectious laugh, her eyes dancing in the candlelight.

~

I have heard Kutiyattam introduced as a UNESCO Oral and Intangible Heritage of Humanity in venues large and small, urban and rural, to public audiences and those composed mainly of friends and family across Kerala, India, and the United States. The symbolic capital of Kutiyattam's UNESCO recognition carries weight far and wide and has become an essential part of how the art is imagined today. In this chapter, I consider Kutiyattam's 2001 recognition as a UNESCO Intangible Cultural Heritage (ICH) one and two decades after its inscription. I begin by mapping out the results of this recognition, from immediate outcomes through subsequent funding initiatives. In so doing, I consider how strategies of cultural recognition and conservation are negotiated among local, national, and supranational bodies in postcolonial India through an examination of the contested terrain of Kutiyattam's UNESCO project implementation. By presenting the viewpoints of Kutiyattam artists about how UNESCO inscription has affected their lives and art, I critically explore how the intangible cultural heritage enterprise in India has created new forms of cultural authority and agency, as well as how it has both transformed and mirrored wider transformations in cultural practice across India. Due to the sensitive nature of the critiques and discussions presented in this chapter, I have anonymized all artists interviewed.

The United Nations system was founded on the principles of Immanuel Kant's cosmopolitan philosophy. Kant ([1795] 1917) envisioned a lasting world peace created by an alliance of states. He thought of cosmopolitan world citizens as members of a single moral economy while still being primarily citizens of their respective states. As Appiah (2009, 82) has noted, "UNESCO, like all UN bodies, is a creature of the system of nations," and, speaking of its World Heritage sites and by association ICH, "it is nevertheless bound to conceive them as ultimately at the disposal of nations. Because what it unites are nations, not human beings." The implementation of the ICH program is based on UNESCO's foundational Kantian model, which privileges state actors. As discussed previously, this has led some to argue that UNESCO's entire project of world heritage has been co-opted by its member states to reinforce "ethical-nationalist," rather than universalist, values (Alonso-González 2013). Others have argued that it simply legitimizes the appropriation of heritage into national narratives of identity in a competitive, global political economy of prestige (Isar 2011; Kurin 2022). Barbara Kirshenblatt-Gimblett (2006) brings attention to the paradox of the ICH program's attempts to "disconnect" citizenship from nationality while preserving global cultural diversity, thereby working simultaneously to both eliminate and celebrate cultural differences worldwide.

From Temple to Global Horizons: Guru Ammannur Madhava Chakyar

Figure 47. Guru Ammannur Madhava Chakyar. Photo courtesy of Natana Kairali.

Padmabhushan Guru Ammannur Madhava Chakyar was the poster child for the first UNESCO Proclamation of Masterpieces of the Oral and Intangible Heritage of Humanity. His image is featured prominently on the cover, steel-gray eyes staring piercingly into the camera. The Kerala media announced Kutiyattam's UNESCO inscription on the day of Guru Ammannur's eighty-fourth birthday celebration, a special milestone marking one's completion of a thousand full moons. Born in 1917, Guru Ammannur was the youngest of the art's three prominent twentieth-century gurus, outliving the others by several decades. While initially the most conservative among them—openly defiant of the changes introduced by both Mani Madhava Chakyar and Painkulam Rama Chakyar—it was he who, after finally venturing outside of the temple in his sixties, became the primary international ambassador of Kutiyattam.

Ammannur Madhava Chakyar trained under the same guru as Painkulam Rama Chakyar—Ammannur Chachu Chakyar, who we saw sharply critique the abdicated king of Cochin in chapter 4. Like Mani Madhava Chakyar, Guru Ammannur also undertook higher studies with a king—in this case, with Bhagavatar Kunjunny Thampuran, the king of Kodungaloor and exponent of the *Natyashastra* (Chakyar 1994). The king taught him the relationship between the breath and facial expressions and, most famously, how to enact death by using the three sequential forms of breathing that a dying person experiences. Guru Ammannur became renowned for his enactment of the death of Bali in *Balivadham*, which led British theater critic Kenneth Rae to write of a London performance: "One of the bravest and most outrageous pieces of acting I have ever seen. Who else would dare take 15 minutes to die onstage and get away with it?" (quoted in Venu 2002, 31).

The guru's late foray into the wider world would not have been possible without the encouragement and support of Gopal Venu (more famously known as Venuji)—a performer, researcher, and arts administrator already prominent in national and international circles when he approached Guru Ammannur in the late 1970s.[3] Enchanted with the guru's acting, Venuji gave up a good job to fulfill his dream of sustaining the Ammannur Kutiyattam tradition.[4] He promoted Guru Ammannur on stages all over India and the world, from Europe to Japan, encountering influential figures in the Indian national arts scene as well as international luminaries of contemporary performance like Peter Brook and Pina Bausch (Venu 2002). It was only because of Venuji's efforts that Guru Ammannur ventured onto national and international stages, leading to wider acclaim and recognition of his talent.

Venuji also successfully revived the defunct Ammannur *gurukulam* (center of learning), securing funding and attracting a new generation of students, all with little to no compensation.[5] He trained as a Kutiyattam artist in the process, accompanying the guru on stages around the world. It was only after encountering Venuji that Guru Ammannur departed from his strict stance against training students from other castes in Kutiyattam. He began intensively training nonhereditary students at the gurukulam and conducted shorter-term training sessions for university students from across India in association with the organization Spic Macay. During this period, Guru Ammannur also taught briefly at Kalamandalam and for several years at Margi as a visiting senior guru. As discussed in chapter 2, he wrote new manuals for several choreographies that had disappeared from the stage, which Margi produced in the 1990s. In a parallel effort to Kalamandalam, he played an important role in the revival of Nangiarkoothu, choreographing and instructing Usha Nangiar from an attaprakaram he created.[6] Guru Ammannur became increasingly renowned internationally as spectators from around the world began attending the annual Kutiyattam festival in Irinjalakuda founded by Venuji in 1982. Over time, international students increasingly came to train with him. Walter Pfaff (1997, 156), part of a Swiss theater group that trained with Guru Ammannur in the early 1990s, recorded some of the guru's reflections on the learning process.

> Look at the ant on the stone! The ant is so light, and the stone is so heavy and hard. But when the ant walks across the stone over and over, then it can cut a lasting path in the stone. It happens very naturally, not through effort. Learning happens very naturally, not through effort. Only through repetition. Repetition creates a spirit without doubt, without confusion, increasingly sure of itself. Then everything will be a part of your body. Then every action will become a natural body reflex. It lives in the body and comes out without effort. In our work we train all the elements individually—face muscles, bhavas, eyes, mudras, and voice—but in the end they must become one: the whole body in motion. After daily training over a long period of time, these movements will become as natural for a performer as an organic movement of the body.

After Guru Ammannur became unable to tour with age, Venuji continued the gurukulam's international legacy by taking its students to perform around the world and participate in international collaborations like the World Theater Project (Venu 2002). Venuji became a celebrated choreographer, renowned for his nine-hour Kutiyattam production of Shakuntala, which was performed in venues around the world. He later served as a cultural consultant for several UNESCO meetings, including those working toward developing the ICH Convention. When he and Guru Ammannur performed at UNESCO headquarters to celebrate Kutiyattam's ICH inscription, therefore, it was not the first time the art had gained global attention. Rather, this marked the culmination of decades-long work together on stages around the globe and the pinnacle of Guru Ammannur's role as an international ambassador of Kutiyattam.

UNESCO Postinscription Timeline

UNESCO Features reported on Kutiyattam's first international tour in Paris in 1980, funded in part by UNESCO's International Fund for the Promotion of Culture (Kinnane 1980). When Kutiyattam toured Paris again in 1999, a UNESCO representative attended the performance and encouraged Kutiyattam to apply for a new UNESCO program. Margi's troupe leader, Dr. Sudha Gopalakrishnan, seized the opportunity for Kutiyattam. Granted UNESCO funds for the application, she recruited renowned film director Adoor Gopalakrishnan to make the application's documentary film.[7] When UNESCO announced the first Proclamation of Masterpieces of the Oral and Intangible Heritage of Humanity in 2001, Kutiyattam became India's first intangible heritage of humanity. This section charts the official initiatives that resulted from Kutiyattam's UNESCO inscription, drawing from UNESCO, Sangeet Natak Akademi (SNA), and Indian Ministry of Culture documents, as well as from interviews with key figures in the recognition and implementation processes.[8]

UNESCO/Japan Funds-in-Trust

After inscription, Dr. Gopalakrishnan applied for UNESCO funds to facilitate Kutiyattam's action plan. This resulted in the 2004–2007 UNESCO/Japan-Funds-in-Trust (JFIT) project that issued $129,000 to seven Kutiyattam institutions (UNESCO 2007).[9] The funds supported meetings of a newly founded Kutiyattam network (*Kutiyattam parishath*) of senior artists and administrators, student training and stipends, public awareness–raising workshops and performances, academic seminars, publications, the revival of plays, the production of ten documentaries, a cultural journalism course aimed at improving arts coverage in the Kerala media, and a workshop on basic conservation techniques for palm-leaf manuscripts. Several of the originally planned projects—two academic seminars; several national performance festivals; and, most importantly, the creation of three academic resource centers and a centralized library and archive—never came to fruition. They were considered to be either redundant or too expensive.

National Funding Schemes: Ministry of Culture and National ICH

Around the same time as the UNESCO/JFIT project, the Indian Ministry of Culture began a pilot scheme allotting Rs. 0.15 crore (approximately $30,000) for the "preservation and promotion of intangible heritage of humanity" (Ministry of Culture n.d.).[10] This amount was available from 2003/2004 to 2005/2006 for India's UNESCO Masterpieces—Kutiyattam (2001), Vedic Chanting (2003), and Ramlila (2005). The scheme supported the enhancement of Kutiyattam study and performance facilities, the revival of old choreographic texts and productions, pension payments for retired artists, and performance opportunities whereby organizations received funds to host a Kutiyattam performance (UNESCO 2004a).[11] This contributed to a postinscription atmosphere that for many artists felt like anyone could secure money for Kutiyattam. The critique that funds often bypassed artists also recognized that the UNESCO/JFIT project funded academic books and documentaries that provided artists with little or no compensation.[12]

Sudha Gopalakrishnan included the creation of a national Kutiyattam Fund in the art's action plan. After the success of Kutiyattam's application, she accepted invitations to author both of India's subsequent UNESCO Masterpiece candidature files as well. She then lobbied for the creation of a fund for all of India's UNESCO Masterpieces. In 2006, the year after India signed UNESCO's Convention for the Safeguarding of the Intangible Cultural Heritage, Gopalakrishnan's work came to fruition when the Indian government created a special Rs. 50 million provision in its national budget (approximately $1,000,000) for the country's three UNESCO Masterpieces: Kutiyattam, Vedic Chanting, and Ramlila.[13] This sparked the creation of a national scheme supporting India's UNESCO Masterpieces. It was meant to begin the same year, but after the Ministry of Culture discontinued the pilot scheme, the new scheme's funding was delayed for two years (Ministry of Culture n.d.). In 2010, I spoke with retired artists who received pensions from the pilot scheme. They expressed concern that their pensions had been cut off in 2006 and never resumed.

The newfound financial stakes of ICH in India sparked a fight between two major national institutions for control of the project. The SNA argued for control of the project based on its long-standing project with Kutiyattam, while the Indira Gandhi National Center for the Arts argued the same based on its long-standing project with Vedic Chanting (Ministry of Culture n.d.).[14] The SNA eventually emerged victorious and decided to establish a national center in Kerala's capital city of Trivandrum. With the resultant May 2007 opening of the Kutiyattam Kendra, the SNA included Kutiyattam in a small, elite group of the SNA's arts institutions.[15]

Kutiyattam Kendra: National Center for Kutiyattam

Kutiyattam Kendra, the national center for Kutiyattam in Trivandrum, Kerala, represents the most lasting form of Kutiyattam's post-UNESCO project implementation continuing through the present day. The fact that it remained under the purview of the SNA constituted a continuity of state policy in both discourse and practice. The founding of Kutiyattam Kendra represented a significant enhancement, in both funding and scope, of the SNA's previous scheme for Kutiyattam. Prioritizing the art's transmission, the institution began distributing increased student and teacher stipends to three existing and four new institutions, becoming the main source of income for most artists in Kerala.[16] While most existing institutions were established and run by nonartists, the new institutions were all founded and run by Kutiyattam artists.[17] The center is governed by an advisory committee composed of the SNA secretary, Kerala's secretary of culture, two members of the SNA executive board, one scholar of the art, and two artists—initially specified as "one Chakyar" and "one Nambiar"—for a term of five years. This setup problematically favors male hereditary artists as stewards of the art while ignoring those who represent the majority of artists today—female artists, both hereditary and nonhereditary, and male nonhereditary artists.

The Kendra significantly funded the only carpenter in Kerala who makes costumes for Kutiyattam and other Kerala arts, Ramankutty Kothavil, who we met briefly in chapter 5.[18] This allowed him to work full time on costume carpentry for the first time in his career and also attracted students through a student stipend. Because he was the only carpenter of traditional performing arts in Kerala, this led to a continuity of knowledge in costume construction techniques for several other Kerala art forms as well, including Kathakali, Otan Thullal, Krishnanattam, and a variety of folk forms. Kutiyattam Kendra prioritized the art's public promotion, funding monthly lecture demonstrations and performances at universities, schools, cultural institutions, temple trusts, and other organizations across Kerala and, to a lesser extent, India. It began sponsoring an annual performance festival that brought artists from all institutions together, as well as various specialized seminars and workshops throughout the year. In 2008, Kutiyattam was incorporated into the Representative List of the Intangible Cultural Heritage of Humanity according to the terms of UNESCO's 2003 Convention, remaining under state patronage through Kutiyattam Kendra.

On-the-Ground Perspectives: Mediatization, Social Status, Differential Inclusion, and the Rise of the Institution

A young artist once described his understanding of UNESCO to me, asking, "What is UNESCO exactly? We don't know. UNESCO doesn't do anything directly, so for us artists there is no UNESCO. . . . To our knowledge, it is only the Indian government that is doing something." Along with a few artists who openly admitted that they did not know what UNESCO was or what to expect when it recognized Kutiyattam, most artists viewed UNESCO as a distant international organization whose interventions were indirectly facilitated through national and local bodies. Some had directly interacted with the organization—the twelve artists who performed at UNESCO's thirty-first General Conference, for example—but even among the institutions that received direct funding from UNESCO/JFIT, contact was facilitated by their largely nonartist institutional leadership.

Drawing on interviews with over sixty Kutiyattam actors, actresses, and musicians from nine institutions throughout Kerala, this section explores diverse community perspectives regarding Kutiyattam's 2001 inscription as a UNESCO Masterpiece of the Oral and Intangible Heritage of Humanity approximately one decade after its inscription.[19] I consider how inscription impacted their daily lives, their art form, and their place in Kerala society. Among the spectrum of sentiments expressed, I focus on the topics most often raised—Kutiyattam's increased societal recognition and the rise to dominance of the institutional model.

There was a wide range of perspectives surrounding the post-UNESCO project formulation and implementation that reflects the diversity of the contemporary Kutiyattam community. Several artists expressed that they did not feel they had much of a voice in the process, as it was dominated by local and national nonartist institutional leadership, however well meaning, with meetings sometimes held in languages they largely did not understand (English and Hindi) when SNA or UNESCO representatives attended. Other artists described a problematic trend where their fellow artists did not feel comfortable assuming an authoritative voice at such meetings and so remained silent.

While most agreed that UNESCO recognition was good for the art, opinions varied over exactly to what extent. Some attributed to UNESCO a minimal role, having provided "only money" or "only recognition, like an award." Others ascribed a more pivotal role to the recognition, saying that if not for UNESCO, Kutiyattam "would have died out in ten or twenty years since no one would come to study it." Most artists fell somewhere in between, recognizing UNESCO's ephemeral role—as one artist put it, "UNESCO is like a rain that comes and goes suddenly, but doesn't stay"—as well as the lasting impact that its recognition has had on both Kutiyattam's general social standing and position vis-à-vis the Indian government.

UNESCO's recognition of Kutiyattam brought a flurry of media attention. As Kerala has both the highest literacy and media exposure rates in India, this attention made a noticeable impact on Kerala's public imagination. When an artist is asked about their profession nowadays, the reply is no longer met with a blank stare. Kutiyattam's greater media presence has led to increased societal recognition but has not translated into greater audiences as many had hoped. As one artist noted, "Kutiyattam spread out superficially, like smoke. People have come to recognize the name and costume but don't come to watch performances." The smoky tendrils of greater Kutiyattam awareness spread throughout Kerala, India, and the world on the winds of UNESCO. In Kerala, however, the recognition carried the wider misconception that artists received a great deal of UNESCO money and should thus perform without pay—festival organizers eager to include Kutiyattam for its advertising value were often not ready to pay for it. Despite the overall greater media attention and general interest in the art since its UNESCO inscription, more popular art forms like Kathakali and Mohiniyattam, seen as icons of Kerala culture, still dominate Kerala's arts media and wider performance arenas.

The greatest impact of this wider social recognition is on the way many artists relate to their art. As one artist poignantly expressed, "The greatest effect was that working artists had an awakening, they found a belief in themselves. That was the *greatest*. Now we're really proud to be in Kutiyattam. It has gained value. When we go to programs we are happy, because everyone doesn't see us as unimportant anymore. They see us and treat us with respect." Several former students of Kerala Kalamandalam painfully recounted past experiences of being made fun of by students of other art forms, who would mock Kutiyattam's singsong method of text recitation and taunt that they were studying "for nothing" and would never find a job. Narrating the stark juxtaposition of the recent past, they explained, "But nowadays this doesn't happen. Our respect grew. That's the power of UNESCO and the government of India."

The impact most often noted by artists was their newfound ability to make a living as Kutiyattam performers due to an increase in institutions and funding, indicative of a postinscription rise of the institution. The process of institutionalization made the art more visible to the state, leading to its deeper integration into existing national structures of heritage and state patronage. The art's postinscription institutionalization, however, differed from the previous period in one significant way. While earlier institutions were primarily established and run by nonartists able to successfully navigate the structures of state funding, postinscription institutions were founded and run exclusively by artists, thereby disrupting existing structures of authority and giving artists greater self-determination.

Nearly all artists agreed that the Indian government founded the Kutiyattam Kendra and increased the art's funding levels as a direct result of its UNESCO inscription. This was unanimously viewed as a positive aspect of a complex issue with both positive and negative ramifications for the art form. With the 2007 establishment of Kutiyattam Kendra, many artists received a living wage for the first time in their lives. Before this, many had to supplement their income through other means or leave the art altogether. The number of institutions receiving SNA grants more than doubled, adding a large number of artists to the ranks of "normal" wage earners in Kerala.[20]

This increase in funding has consequently had a profound effect on the artists and their lives. While providing peace of mind and the increased confidence that comes with a steady income, it has also contributed to increased social status, greater social mobility, and improved marriageability of young male artists. Lukose (2009) notes that the framework of modern masculinity in Kerala devalues men engaged in traditional economic roles who do not seek greater economic advancement in the public realm. Many young male artists hoping to marry were previously devalued within this framework, spurred to abandon their art for more lucrative employment in the Gulf countries. By 2010, the situation had changed. As one artist reflected, "Support for performance came, standards came, and identity and power came with it. Kutiyattam became a profession with a salary-base. After getting a salary here, Ramesh was able to marry, because he could say he works here. That's a real social change."[21] This change has given the current generation of students, already encouraged by the introduction of a generous stipend, greater confidence in the art and the hope that they, too, may one day be able to make their "life's path" (*jīvita mārgam*) through Kutiyattam.

As noted earlier, the effect that UNESCO inscription has had on Kutiyattam is viewed as a complex issue with both positive and negative aspects. One of the main critiques from artists about this recognition concerns the unequal access to and distribution of funding. In Kutiyattam Kendra's institutional funding model, as one artist put it, "the institution is important, not the individual." Reflecting this, the model privileges institutional seniority over artistic seniority, with senior institutions receiving much higher grants and income allotments for individual artists than those of junior institutions. Consequently, junior artists employed at senior institutions are paid nearly twice as much as more experienced artists at junior institutions, a situation almost everyone finds unjust.[22] Additionally, although Kutiyattam has been undergoing a process of institutionalization since the 1960s, within most previous funding structures there had been room for independent artists. In contrast, the initial UNESCO/JFIT project was implemented solely through institutions and left many feeling that it was mostly the well-known artists who benefited, excluding lesser-known institutionally affiliated artists and noninstitutionally affiliated artists.[23] Furthermore, with Kutiyattam Kendra, the SNA introduced an institution-centric model that left no room for its previous funding of both Kerala Kalamandalam and independent artists. This was the first time that Kalamandalam had been excluded from an SNA scheme involving Kutiyattam. Given the small total number of Kutiyattam artists, many were disappointed to see that, as they phrased it, "only institutions benefited." As one artist asserted, "If UNESCO wanted to save Kutiyattam, it should have saved everyone, not just certain people."[24]

Tensions arose in opinions between safeguarding everyone and only those artists perceived as maintaining a certain performance standard. Most artists agreed that post-UNESCO funding should help everyone, even though it had excluded many to date. As one artist thoughtfully reflected: "This safeguarding is not safeguarding for myself or my institution, but for Kutiyattam as a whole. All artists should be included. Because Kutiyattam has very few members, less than one hundred, this amount was enough for everyone. If it had been divided between everyone, everyone would have gotten enough for their needs. But some didn't get anything, some didn't even know about it." Similar to the pay gaps between junior and senior institutions just mentioned, artists noted other safeguarding inequities as well. Despite the positive development that all new institutions were founded and run by artists, several nonhereditary artists pointed out that these were all "given" to Chakyars, thus privileging male hereditary leadership over others.[25] They related tales of new institutions founded by nonhereditary artists whose applications for recognition and funding by Kutiyattam Kendra were rejected. As we saw earlier, Kutiyattam Kendra also privileged male hereditary artists as members of the Kutiyattam committee, thus institutionalizing and solidifying their power in the arena of contemporary Kutiyattam in ways that may not otherwise have happened.

This discourse of inclusion and exclusion, of safeguarding some people over others or some more than others, parallels the larger inclusion/exclusion discourse of heritage as a whole. Several artists applied this critique not only to *who* is being safeguarded in the post-UNESCO world of Kutiyattam but also to *what* is being safeguarded, particularly in terms of repertoire. The institution-centric model dominating Kutiyattam in the postinscription period is widely viewed as safeguarding only repertoire associated with institutions—that of a highly edited Kutiyattam for the public stage—to the detriment of the art's unedited, temple-bound repertoire.[26] Dramatic pieces essential to Kutiyattam temple performance, such as *Anguliyankam* and *Mantrankam*—known as the encyclopedias of Kutiyattam for acting and verbal prowess, respectively—are not being taught to younger, institutionally trained generations.[27] Consequently, some view the knowledge of this repertoire as being in urgent need of safeguarding.[28]

Some critics of the pay model pointed out that artists receive a stipend instead of a governmental salary, leaving them without benefits such as vacation time, health insurance, cost of living adjustments, or a retirement pension. This is especially problematic with a mandatory retirement age in Kerala of fifty-five. Many lamented the pay schedule as well. As one senior artist told me, "We can't depend on getting our salary regularly; that is a problem. Now it comes quarterly, but once it didn't come for six months. This makes it difficult to pay rent, so we have to supplement our income with private programs." A few Kalamandalam instructors, who receive regular monthly salaries from the Kerala government, also commented on the situation, saying, "We've heard payments often don't come for months at a time. How are you supposed to pay your monthly bills?"

There was also a widespread sentiment that with the increase in funding, both devotion to and quality of the art have decreased. This sentiment encapsulates two fears: the fear of favoring the pursuit of money and fame over the art, and the fear of artistic stagnation through financial security. The latter fear was generally portrayed as a danger to be avoided in the future; one artist stressed, "Artists should have some poverty, otherwise they will not honor Kutiyattam. If you have luxuries, you cannot live as an artist; you will think, why do I have to suffer? With your body, with your mind, with the traveling, with the bitter experiences with the organizers, it's really tough. A luxury man cannot tolerate all of this."

The former fear, however, was rooted in the present, often expressed through a discussion of the postinscription explosion of new choreographies. As one young artist explained, "You can't only do the old pieces, because the world we are seeing is new, so an actor has to do new things. If there hadn't been experiments like that in the past, Kutiyattam wouldn't exist today. Great actors are improvising changes to the art each generation; otherwise, it would not survive." While artists view innovation as a vital constituent of an ever-changing art, most assert it should ultimately be made for the greater good of the art while maintaining its "frame." The majority of earlier twentieth-century choreographic innovations were undertaken by senior gurus and tended to constitute revivals of group pieces previously existing in Kutiyattam's repertoire. While these types of choreographies have continued, the current trend is characterized by the prevalence of new, solo pieces many artists consider inspired by government funding initiatives. Composed by all levels of artists, they are generally accompanied by a sense of personal ownership, competition, and ephemerality, performed expressly by their composers usually only a few times in total. In contrast with the standard repertoire, which tends to be collaborative and is performed by everyone again and again, the newer choreographies are viewed by many as motivated by the pursuit of money and personal fame rather than the greater good of Kutiyattam.

Taking a different perspective, new choreographies today also serve as a way to challenge the monopoly on performance texts held by hereditary Kutiyattam families. Generally, only hereditary performers have access to existing performance manuals for purposes such as reviving group pieces that have fallen out of performance. Traditional palm-leaf manuscripts tend to be jealously guarded by Chakyar and Nambiar families, as evidenced by the testimony of a member of the national manuscript preservation team belonging to the UNESCO/JFIT project mentioned above. He told me that, as a non-Malayalam speaker, he was selected to work with the manuscripts because he could not read them and therefore could not divulge their contents. Nonhereditary artists interested in creating anything new, therefore, must both choreograph new pieces and write new performance manuals from scratch. With UNESCO/JFIT funding, Margi published the complete performance manuals in Malayalam for the entire *Ascharyachoodamani* play, available for the first time to all.[29] However, many artists remain disappointed that in a post-UNESCO environment, all existing performance manuals are still not publicly available.

Concern about prioritizing the pursuit of money over the art was also expressed through generational difference in comments such as "This generation uses the art for living; they aren't living for the art." Commentary often centered around the issue of paying students stipends to study Kutiyattam. Some artists were critical of stipends, believing that the money leads to a lack of sincerity on the part of students and their parents. The general consensus, however, was that stipends are necessary to encourage children to study the art and to give them more confidence in their future as artists. Most artists agreed on the socioeconomic necessity of stipends, as the majority of full-time students of the arts in Kerala have lower socioeconomic backgrounds these days. Kutiyattam student stipends became widespread after the art's recognition by UNESCO, administered first by UNESCO/JFIT and then by Kutiyattam Kendra. These mirrored what had been happening at Kerala Kalamandalam more generally for decades. As a Kalamandalam teacher explained, "Children with parents who have a good financial situation aren't coming to Kalamandalam, because they want their kids to be doctors, engineers, scientists, do English medium studies, and then have more work opportunities. So poor people with no money, they are coming. They don't want to, but they are coming."

The final critique centers around the appropriateness of an institutional model for Kutiyattam. Although already widely institutionalized at the time of UNESCO inscription, the establishment of an institution-centric Kutiyattam Kendra and the stricter regulations that came with it brought this issue into greater focus for many artists. While the previous model left day-to-day practices largely unregulated, artists became required to reside at their institution for six days per week, to formally request time off (thereby reducing their salary), to take attendance for both students and artists, and to submit paperwork detailing their monthly activities. One artist observed that, despite these strict regulations, artist-run institutions tended to give artists more informal flexibility than nonartist-run institutions. Artists fundamentally shared the idea that art requires flexibility and freedom to develop, continuing to hold up the unregulated gurukulam model as the ideal environment for Kutiyattam. Using rich metaphor, one artist reflected, "If we put a plant in our garden and restrain it in a strict way, it won't develop. But if we take it to the forest, it will develop into a majestic tree. Artists need a forest atmosphere, not a garden atmosphere. An institution is like a garden, with a fixed place, a fixed height, a fixed color, . . . but a forest is natural. The best development for Kutiyattam is always a natural development." While salaries were viewed positively by everyone and regulations were considered a necessity to a certain degree, many perceived Kutiyattam Kendra's increasing regulations as a loss of freedom. As one artist commented, "We were totally free with our programs but now that has all been regulated. Now we have a condition of normal working people. It is good for an office but bad for art."

Discussion: Liberalization, State Patronage, and Dynamic Safeguarding

The range of these artists' reactions to Kutiyattam's UNESCO inscription and its legacy evidences tensions surrounding a liberalizing Kutiyattam. Liberalization as a term is generally preferred to globalization in the Indian context to describe both the opening of its economy in the 1990s to global market forces and the profound impact this had on its political, economic, and cultural landscapes.[30] In Kerala, intense economic liberalization and heightened levels of nonelite Gulf migration have led to conspicuous consumption practices that assume key roles in social distinction and identity fashioning through the present day (Osella and Osella 2003). Comments about young artists using the art to live rather than living for the art index an Indian generation known as "liberalization's children," characterized as technology savvy, admiring capitalism, desiring wealth, preferring jobs in the private sector, and consuming guiltlessly (Lukose 2009). Before UNESCO's recognition, the act of choosing Kutiyattam as a profession clearly signified artistic dedication, as it meant foregoing more profitable employment. But now that Kutiyattam has become a way for artists to make a decent—though still meager—living, these boundaries have become blurred. Many artists were steadfast in their assertion that "if you start thinking about money, Kutiyattam will be lost. You need money to live, but you can't live for money."

These statements became commentaries on contemporary Kerala society and its changing values, particularly surrounding work, money, and time. As one artist commented, "Nowadays there is the thought, 'Work, money, work, money,' and if you think like this, our traditional things will go." Others made comparisons to earlier times, before the introduction of capitalism to Kerala. As one artist emphasized, "Earlier if a family didn't have money, they would be given food and people would give them a lot of help. Now society isn't like that. In today's age, you need money to live; everything is expensive, so if an art doesn't make money, you can't live by it. Even if you have the desire, thinking, 'This is God's art,' you are not able to continue in it. What can you do?" Related to this focus on work and money, many described a fast-paced world in today's Kerala where people no longer have the time or attention span to watch Kutiyattam. One artist reflected, "The whole world today with cinema and television, after watching something quickly people leave. They don't have the time to watch and understand an art form. Everyone has no time and moves fast, fast, fast, running after the bus, or when you order something they make your copies fast, fast, fast, like this. People don't have the time to sit, watch, and enjoy." This lack of time was even perceived to be affecting children. One artist described children in Kerala losing the leisure of childhood: "The reason people don't have any time nowadays is because the kids go to school, then to after-school tuition, then to another subject until eight or nine o'clock at night. The kids don't have any time to relax. It's not the children studying, it's their mothers, because my child should be better than the others. . . . So they don't have time for Kutiyattam, they don't give it importance; studying and education only. But when they come to know about India's culture, even if their education is lacking, they will have knowledge." These characterizations conceptualize the social present as profoundly different from the past—obsessed with money and associated social status, selfish and individualistic, competitive, and fast-paced, with no time for an art like Kutiyattam.

The view that money is necessary to survive but art should not pursue it was complicated by the introduction of salaries, the rise in demand for performances, and the art's increased social status following its UNESCO inscription. While everyone genuinely viewed these as positive developments, an underlying aversion toward art as a commodity manifested in fears about the future and a rising mistrust of the motivations behind both younger artists and the proliferation of new choreographies. As one artist insisted, however, Kutiyattam still represents the choice of artistic dedication and market eschewal: "If a boy is not intelligent, he cannot study Kutiyattam, because he has to remember so many things, he has to study the grammar of *both* Malayalam and Sanskrit. If he is that intelligent, he can go to study BTech or CA and earn three or four times as much."[31] This artist argued that while the basic economic level of Kutiyattam had increased, in light of the changing demands of society, the scale of what artists gave up for the art had actually remained the same.

In what might seem like a contradiction, despite fears that Kutiyattam's greater social and economic success signals its impending surrender to the market economy, artists fundamentally agree that Kutiyattam needs patronage to survive. Statements such as "art needs patronage" and "a Kutiyattam artist cannot make a living only through performance since it has never been that kind of commercial art," place the art squarely *outside* of a neoliberal frame that "seeks to bring all human action into the domain of the market" (Harvey 2005, 3). As chapter 6 discussed, with the founding of the SNA in 1953, the newly established Indian government explicitly acknowledged its responsibility of "filling the vacuum" left by crumbled systems of royal arts patronage, heralding a "new awakening and cultural resurgence . . . to take place in the country under a new system of patronage hitherto unknown to Indian Arts" (SNA 1953/1958). By 2010, this approach had largely been maintained despite its conflict with the nation's wider liberalization policies, and artists generally continue to view patronage as the "duty" of the state.

While the SNA provided low levels of funding to Kutiyattam over the years, its opening of Kutiyattam Kendra in 2007 symbolized to artists that the art would be patronized indefinitely, albeit through a controlled institutional form. The coupling of the acknowledgment that Kutiyattam cannot survive in the marketplace with the assertion that it will, indeed, survive through state patronage, represents a mode of resistance to market tyranny that continues to value the economically unsustainable as a public good (Bourdieu 1998). Through its ICH program, UNESCO, a champion of modernity, frames postmodernity as the enemy in its struggle against a globalization (i.e., neoliberalism) seen to threaten global cultural diversity.[32] As evident in the Masterpieces program, which expressly recognized arts that "risk disappearing" and framed tourism—often one of the only options for economic sustainability—as a threat, UNESCO vilified the cultural commodification feared by Kutiyattam artists as a result of inscription (UNESCO 2001a). It simultaneously idealized a model that the Indian state had long followed and simply intensified for Kutiyattam postinscription, that of the state as patron-ad-infinitum. It raises the question of whether this economically unsustainable model, that of the state as patron, is the only acceptable path forward offered by UNESCO within the boundaries of its modernist limits.

This concept of infinite patronage was also deeply implicated in the way artists conceived of the concept of "safeguarding" (*samrakṣaṇam*), namely, as the financial support of artists. This was shown through questions like "Without safeguarding the artists, how will you safeguard the art?"[33] This equation of safeguarding with steady patronage shaped artists' concerns for the future, particularly for the next generation, with some questioning: "Our generation has been safeguarded, but what about the future generation? When our students finish, where will they work? Will they be able to continue in the art?"[34] As a process facilitating the continuity of artists rather than a strictly defined form, this is a dynamic safeguarding based on a concept of art as inherently changing and adapting to contemporary audiences. Many emphasize that they as artists are contemporary individuals who live and think according to the times in which they live, and that art, as a dynamic creative endeavor, *is meant to change.* In the words of Guru P. K. Narayanan Nambiar, "Art will never disappear, but the shape of its performance, what persists, will continually change." Tied to assertions made by several artists that "Kutiyattam is not a museum piece," this perspective was institutionalized in the very founding of the SNA, inaugurated with the words "Nowhere is it truer than in the field of art that to sustain means to create. Traditions cannot be preserved but can only be created afresh" (SNA 1953/1958).[35]

UNESCO's definition of intangible cultural heritage as "constantly recreated" resonates with the conception of Kutiyattam artists and the Indian arts establishment of art as ever-changing (UNESCO 2003b, 2). UNESCO's recognition of Kutiyattam, therefore, represents a continuity with decades of existing heritage discourse and practice in India. As previously discussed, the ICH program was developed to counter a hegemonic Western heritage discourse that privileges material forms and assumes safeguarding to be a static process, one that locates "authenticity" in *urforms* (original forms) rather than in the moment of change itself. While the program offers dynamic safeguarding (i.e., acknowledging cultural change) as a "new" tool, UNESCO's toolbox itself has remained the same. Forged by the European Enlightenment, it replays "the oldest modernist angst, 'the specter of difference vanishing'" (Comaroff and Comaroff 2009, 23). It refashions the "saved-from-the-fire" narrative of salvage anthropology and folkloristics, pitting "endangered" culture against a new enemy—globalization (Abrahams 1993).[36] The UNESCO ICH program is, as Kirshenblatt-Gimblett (2006, 58–59) has argued, "caught between freezing the practice and addressing the inherently processual nature of culture." UNESCO's modernist toolbox is thus filled with both static and dynamic safeguarding tools to be used at the discretion of each nation-state, making it essential to examine the processes whereby this toolbox is differentially utilized and differentially impacts constituent communities around the world.[37]

Conclusion

Chosen to represent the cultural face of a national India on a global scale, Kutiyattam's inscription as a UNESCO ICH marked the pinnacle of ongoing efforts to recognize the art as Indian national heritage. This served to construct the art as both a cosmopolitan heritage of humanity and Indian national heritage. As I noted earlier, the ICH program is implemented on a national-particular scale rather than a universalist one, with implementation clearly defined by UNESCO as the responsibility of each nation-state. This hypernationalization can be equated with the hyperinstitutionalization that occurred in the wake of Kutiyattam's inscription. As a process that renders art forms visible to the state, in the national-cum-global cosmopolitanism of post-UNESCO project implementation, the Indian state simply accelerated the processes of Kutiyattam's existing institutionalization. Within the framework of UNESCO's nation-centric Kantian cosmopolitanism, institutionalization becomes a necessary process for rendering these forms cosmopolitan by first making them visible to the state.

Many of the criticisms made by Kutiyattam artists here focus on processes of inclusion and exclusion, revealing the contested negotiation of cultural recognition and safeguarding among local, national, and supranational bodies in the wake of the art's inscription by UNESCO. These concerns reveal how UNESCO's intangible cultural heritage enterprise in India has shifted the terrain of cultural authority and agency in Kutiyattam through the creation of new

Figure 48. Kutiyattam Kendra–sponsored performance of *Naganantham* with (*left to right*) Aparna Nangiar, T. R. Saritha, Ammannur Rajaneesh Chakyar, Kalamandalam Hariharan, Ammannur Kuttan Chakyar, and Sooraj Nambiar. Photo by author.

hierarchies of authority and privilege. These include decentering the power of both nonartist leadership and Kerala Kalamandalam, favoring male hereditary artists in structures of institutional leadership and decision-making, introducing salaries and thereby increasing artists' social standing within Kerala, privileging institutionalized artists over noninstitutionalized artists, and democratizing the monopoly of hereditary artists over new artistic productions. Studies of the impact of UNESCO ICH inscription on expressive cultural forms in other countries have noted its potential to disrupt local hierarchies and processes of cultural negotiation.[38] As Valdimar Hafstein (2018, 49) has provocatively asked, "When is protection not a means of dispossession?"[39] In the case of Kutiyattam, as we have seen here, some individuals or institutions lost a degree of power, while others made substantial gains, and due to the increased administrative control by Kutiyatam Kendra, the lives of all involved changed significantly.

Hafstein's (2018) reflections on UNESCO ICH as a tool of intervention are relevant here. When successful, safeguarding "1) *reforms the relationship of subjects with their own practices* (through sentiments such as 'pride'), 2) *reforms the practices* (orienting them toward display through various conventional heritage genres), and ultimately 3) *reforms the relationship of the practicing subjects with themselves* (through social institutions of heritage that formalize informal relations and centralize dispersed responsibilities)" (2018, 128). He observes that Kutiyattam's postinscription outcomes fulfill all three of these points (Hafstein 2015, 148–152). Hafstein's first point is reminiscent of Kirshenblatt-Gimblett's (2006, 171) conclusion that the heritage industry changes the "relationship of practitioners to their art." Foster (2011, 66) has referred to this as the "UNESCO effect" of defamiliarization, or "considering one's own tradition through the eyes of another." As we saw here, recognition of Kutiyattam by a supranational organization like UNESCO, with its accompanying gains in status in Kerala society, changed how artists relate to their art by inspiring a newfound "belief in themselves." To the second point of reforming practices, while Kutiyattam had long been oriented toward display through its inclusion in national-level festivals and performances, these intensified during the post-UNESCO period. This occurred particularly in Kerala, where public awareness programs were instituted on a much larger scale than ever before. Finally, to Hafstein's third point, the move away from a decentralized system of administrative control toward a centralized one with the founding of Kutiyattam Kendra—and all of the benefits and problems that came with it—reformed the relationships of artists with themselves.

Economists Damodaran and Chavin (2019) interviewed Kutiyattam artists, administrators, and local communities in 2014 as part of their analysis of the policy roots of Kutiyattam's ongoing economic precarity, including the limitations of post-UNESCO public policy interventions. They note particularly low morale among young artists dissatisfied with the SNA's low salaries and the unpredictable nature of funds dispersal, especially since 2013. SNA leadership shared with the authors that as more regional forms were incorporated into UNESCO's Representative List, the agency found it increasingly difficult to maintain the desired funding levels for Kutiyattam.[40] Damodaran and Chavin (2019, 414) emphasize that one of the main limitations of Kutiyattam's post-UNESCO policy implementation is the SNA's separation of an artist's creative work from their performance and teaching work. Funding is provided only for the teaching work, making Kutiyattam institutions less appealing to nongovernmental funders. They also criticize the ongoing extraction of Kutiyattam institutions from their "historical landscape/region/place," with Kutiyattam Kendra focused more on bringing the art to new venues and audiences rather than promoting it among local communities. The authors found that, as a result, the majority of local community spectators valued Kutiyattam "more as a globally recognised art form than as a slice of their own heritage," with a low sense of "belongingness" to their local Kutiyattam institution (2019, 413). Thus, one could perhaps add to Hafstein's (2018) characterizations above that UNESCO ICH additionally reforms the relationship of communities with their local practices.

Coda

Now looking back two decades after Kutiyattam's UNESCO inscription, has anything changed? Many agree that UNESCO simply came and went, much like one artist's reflection earlier in this chapter that "UNESCO is like a rain that comes and goes suddenly, but doesn't stay." When I explained to Usha-teacher the shift in my research—from the politics and impact of UNESCO inscription to the much wider scope of Kutiyattam's multiple cosmopolitanisms—she thought it a natural progression now that the art has largely moved beyond UNESCO.

Yet several postinscription concerns have remained the same or worsened. The problem of late salary payments from the SNA has become consistently worse, increasing artists' economic precarity. Paychecks are now regularly issued six to twelve months late. One senior artist told me that, as a result, some artists are pawning their gold jewelry to pay basic living expenses. Some have even confided that they cannot be certain paychecks will arrive at all, as happened some years ago. Since the Bharatiya Janata Party Hindu nationalist party came to power again in 2014, the Indian central government has made a concerted push toward further liberalization with the wide-scale privatization of state-owned enterprises.

In the same spirit, the SNA has moved away from the institution's founding patronage model toward a market model of financial sustainability, measuring success in terms of economic independence.[41] In this period, SNA leadership has increasingly voiced concerns that Kutiyattam institutions have not yet become economically independent, although this was never an explicit goal when founding the center. Kutiyattam Kendra's first five-year funding period ended in 2012, and from that point, the SNA determined it should only be renewed annually. This uncertainty reached crisis proportions halfway through 2015 when the SNA suddenly cut all stipends to Kutiyattam Kendra institutions (SNA 2015/2016). The same artist who told me about the ongoing pawning issue said that, with no warning, artists lost over a year of income as a result. "What happens to your gold at the pawnshop then?" I ask. "You lose it," he replied, then continued. "The money is coming from Delhi, right? The North Indians are making the decisions, according to their own desires. One day they could simply decide they have no more interest and will cancel it, then what would we do? It's the North Indians who make all of the decisions," he emphasized. Stipends to Kutiyattam institutions only resumed after the SNA chair reinstated the previous funding model by the end of 2016.

Newer administrative issues for artists have also arisen. Several institutions lost an entire year of stipend paychecks due to a failure to submit their paperwork on time (SNA 2015/2016). Newer public outreach programs, now open to individual artists and not just institutions, operate on a reimbursement basis, which makes individuals liable for expenses. One artist told me that Kutiyattam Kendra rejected a slightly late reimbursement application, forcing the artist to pay for the outreach program from their limited income. Institutions are also in danger of losing their funding status altogether. The Kutiyattam Kendra advisory committee, which, as we saw, privileges male hereditary artists, has the power to decide if institutions will be cut from the funding scheme, further consolidating their power. Some have even implied that personal vendettas of artists on the committee have led to the defunding of several institutions. Of the original eight institutions funded by Kutiyattam Kendra in 2007, only five remained by 2017 (SNA 2016/2017). By 2019, a further institution was cut, while a previously cut institution was restored (SNA 2018/2019). And more recent pressures to attract new, specifically male students have others fearing their institution is in danger of being cut as well, and once cut, it will not likely be restored.

Initially meant to be a resource center for Kutiyattam artists, the Kutiyattam Kendra's location has also been problematic. The first Kutiyattam Kendra was located in an area of Trivandrum that was very difficult to reach, especially for the majority of artists who must travel by train from other parts of the state. To remedy this, the second director K. K. Gopalakrishnan moved the office to a central location not far from the train station, with an open-door policy for artists to visit whenever they like. The third director moved the office to an even more inconvenient location than the first and changed the open-door policy to a closed-door one, with a security guard often turning artists without appointments away at the gate.

As with decisions about location, Kutiyattam Kendra's programs are highly dependent on the director, who generally serves a five-year term. Notably, there have been several positive developments in this arena in the past decade. Directors have exponentially increased the number of public outreach programs, expanding their scope across the state to areas with little exposure to Kutiyattam, to schools and colleges, and to areas of India that had never seen Kutiyattam, such as the Northeast.[42] A special effort was made to provide performance opportunities for young, nonhereditary artists (SNA 2012/2013). "Now there are many more opportunities for the younger generation to perform, which is good," one artist observed. Criticisms of Kutiyattam Kendra's exclusion of important temple repertoire were addressed through a program to revive the play act *Mantrankam* in Peruvanam temple in 2016. An attempt was made that year to address the issue of nonhereditary artists being excluded from temple *koothambalam* performance by establishing a monthly program at the Harippad koothambalam in Alappuzha for all artists (SNA 2015/2016).[43] Another positive development was that pension payments (*gurudakṣiṇa*) to several elderly hereditary artists, which had been stopped in 2006, resumed (SNA 2011/2012).

Despite all of this, Kerala audiences are still a hard nut to crack. As Ushateacher joked, "Foreigners watch Kutiyattam sitting, while Malayalis watch it walking [i.e., passing by]." Kutiyattam Kendra's extensive public outreach efforts in the past decade, combined with UNESCO's initial recognition of the art, have made a positive impact on Kutiyattam's public recognition in Kerala today.[44] Because of these institutions, there are more performance opportunities, greater numbers of interested students, and more Kutiyattam institutions now than ever before. With the increasing instability of SNA funding, however, the art's financial future is more uncertain than ever. The UNESCO inscription unfortunately did not bring the stability of dependable state patronage that artists had hoped for. Returning to community conceptions of safeguarding (*samrakshanam*) as the financial support of artists, I end with a question from the Kutiyattam community: "Without safeguarding the artists, how will you safeguard the art?"

Notes

1. At UNESCO's thirty-first General Conference from October 16 to November 3, 2001; see Venu 2002.

2. Performers were Ammannur Madhava Chakyar, P. K. Narayanan Nambiar, Kalamandalam Shivan Namboothiri, Gopalan Venu, Margi Usha, Margi Sathi, Margi Sajeev Narayana Chakyar, Kalamandalam Eashwaranunni, Kalamandalam Rajeev, Kalamandalam Hariharan, Margi Subrahmanian Potti (*edakka*), and Kalamandalam Shivaraman (*chooti*).

3. See Venu 2020 for his career retrospective.

4. See Venu 2002 for a personal account.

5. The first batch included Usha Nangiar and Margi Raman Chakyar, and the second, Kapila Venu, Ammannur Rajaneesh Chakyar, Sooraj Nambiar, Aparna Nangiar, Pothiyil Renjith Chakyar, and T. R. Saritha.

6. According to Diane Daugherty, Guru Ammannur had a different source manuscript than P. K. Narayanan Nambiar, from the Viluvattattu Nambiar/Nangiar family (email communication, 2023).

7. For obstacles encountered during the application and filming process, see Lowthorp 2013a, 205–221.

8. For more details, see Lowthorp 2013a, 232–247, 303–309.

9. Included institutions were Margi, Kerala Kalamandalam, Ammannur Chachu Chakyar Smaraka Gurukulam, Padmasree Mani Madhava Chakyar Smaraka Gurukulam, International Centre for Kutiyattam, Center for the Development of Imaging Technology, and the Department of Ancient Theatre at Shree Shankara Sanskrit University in Kalady.

10. I use an average conversion rate at the time of Rs. 50 per dollar.

11. See also UNESCO 2004b.

12. See Erlewein 2014 for the media's impact on Kutiyattam's transmission toward ICH safeguarding.

13. The full amount was not spent that year because of a failure to disburse funds before the government's fiscal year-end. For more details on the UNESCO recognition and implementation process, see Gopalakrishnan 2011b.

14. See Lowthorp 2013a.

15. Unlike other SNA institutions, Kutiyattam Kendra is a grants-in-aid institution that distributes grants to gurukulams and training institutions.

16. Existant "senior" institutions were Margi, Ammannur Chachu Chakyar Smaraka Gurukulam, and Padmasree Mani Madhava Chakyar Smaraka Gurukulam. New "junior" institutions were Pothiyil Gurukulam, Nepathya, Painkulam Ramachakyar Smaraka Kalapeedom, and Krishnan Nambiar Mizhavu Kalari. Senior institutions were given higher salaries and an annual production/materials grant not offered to junior institutions.

17. Mani gurukulam is an exception to the former, exclusively run by artists since its founding in the early 1990s.

18. The Koppa Nirmanakendram institution in Vellinezhi, Palakkad was funded with student/teacher stipends and a materials grant.

19. See also Lowthorp 2015. For an artist's account of the positives and negatives of UNESCO inscription, see Jayanthi 2011.

20. At the time of research (2010), wages were Rs. 7,000 monthly (approximately $145) for the lowest earners at senior institutions and midrange earners at junior institutions.

21. A pseudonym.

22. The junior salary at junior institutions at the time (2010) was an insufficient Rs. 4000 (approximately $80) monthly, forcing artists to regularly pawn their gold jewelry to cover expenses.

23. There was also a noticeable sense that many UNESCO/JFIT funds never reached the artists, spent instead on costly projects like documentaries and the production of scholarly works in English, both remaining inaccessible to most artists.

24. The Malayalam verb used by the artists, *samrakshikan,* means to save, to rescue, to safeguard.

25. Except Krishnan Nambiar Mizhavu Kalari, founded by Usha Nangiar and V. K. K. Hariharan.

26. There are exceptions, like Usha Nangiar's *nirvahanam* for Mandodari in *Aṣōkavanikāṅkam.*

27. See Jayanthi 1993, 1999; Oberlin and Shulman 2019.

28. See Johan 2011b, 2017b.

29. See Venugopalan 2009, although, according to Heike Oberlin, this has several mistakes; in 1967, Pisharoti published an incomplete yet error-free version.

30. For wider discussions of these reforms and their effects, see Deshpande 2003; Mazzarella 2003; Oza 2006.

31. BTech (bachelor's in technology) and CA (certified accountant) are coveted degrees in Kerala.

32. UNESCO's (2003b, 1) 2003 Convention states that "the processes of globalization and social transformation . . . give rise . . . to grave threats of deterioration, disappearance and destruction of the intangible cultural heritage."

33. Ammannur Rajaneesh Chakyar (2011, 9) ends his essay on UNESCO with the quote "To protect an art form, one must protect the artists first."

34. These concerns form part of a sense of perpetual endangerment that has pervaded Kutiyattam for at least half a century (Lowthorp 2011).

35. See also Lowthorp 2017. I argue that this warrants India's inclusion in a "pan-Asian" heritage paradigm (Lowthorp 2020).

36. See also Hafstein 2018.

37. As does Foster and Gilman 2015.

38. See Dutta 2017; Escallón 2023; Gilman 2022; Hardwick 2020; Kapchan 2014; Kuutma 2007; Ranwa 2021; Tauschek 2010.

39. See *The Flight of the Condor.*

40. Another complication they observe is Kutiyattam's national funding hailing from 'plan' (rather than 'non-plan') sources, making it more susceptible to budget cuts.

41. In the same period, the Indian Ministry of Culture decreased or eliminated grants to several institutions that depended on their annual renewal.

42. See SNA 2012/2013–2018/2019. For more on the second director's activities, see Daugherty 2019, 602–604.

43. Organized by Kalamandalam Jishnu Prathap's Kutiyattam institution Rangadhwani.

44. As has the Kerala state school youth festival and the International Centre for Kutiyattam in Thrippunithura, since before UNESCO inscription.

EPILOGUE

Figure 49. Swathi Nangiar playing *thalam* cymbals. Photo by author.

It has now been fifteen years—the time required for the making of a Kutiyattam artist—since my training with Usha-teacher. She and I still talk regularly. I have visited Kerala several times since, and much has changed. Two of Margi's then-youngest students, Margi Vishishta and Margi Mahesh, are now members of Margi's teaching and performing staff. Of the nine Margi artists we met in chapter 2, only three remain—Usha-teacher, Sajeev-ashan, and Sajikumar, now a grown man with a family of his own. Sathi-teacher sadly passed away in 2015. Sindhu-chechi left for a better salary as a temporary teaching staff member at Kalamandalam, although she misses the performance and training opportunities at Margi. Ravi-ashan left Kutiyattam long ago, hoping to return to modern theater. Ramanunni-chetan left as well, moving to join his family in Tamil Nadu where he works as a security guard. Unni-ashan, Raman-ashan, and Mohanan-ashan all have retired, and no one has come to take their place.

The Kutiyattam positions that Margi advertises nowadays tend to remain unfilled. During one of our phone calls, Usha-teacher explained that young artists these days are not willing to settle for the same conditions—relatively low pay without much freedom to make extra income through private programs, as had been possible before the art's inscription by the United Nations Educational, Scientific and Cultural Organization (UNESCO). For the past several years, Margi has been unable to attract male acting students—many parents of boys in Kerala do not want them to study Kutiyattam, hoping that they will instead pursue high-paying IT or government jobs.[1] As a result, Kutiyattam Kendra has threatened to cut Margi's funding, although many Kutiyattam institutions struggle with the same issue. What does this all mean for the future of Kutiyattam?

When I asked the usually jocular Unni-ashan if he thinks Kutiyattam is in danger of disappearing someday, he sharply replied,

> It won't ever disappear, hey! All those years Kutiyattam didn't have all of these recognitions, artists lived in poverty, and it didn't disappear, right? New castes came to study and the government recognized it. This is all because the art was still there, right? For thirty years Kutiyattam had a medium level, it was in the hands of the families. It is because of this that UNESCO was able to recognize it. So if one day the government doesn't help anymore and there are no new choreographies, after twenty or thirty years it will go back to a medium position. The families are still there.

Defying UNESCO's discourse of endangerment, Unni-ashan and other Kutiyattam artists maintain that while its circumstances may change, the art will never disappear. While seeking additional financial support, many artists have emphasized that Kutiyattam needs safeguarding (*samrakshanam*), as the art is economically unsustainable in a capitalist system.[2] Notably absent among these safeguarding assertions, however, is a colonialist discourse of endangerment that assumes that without intervention, the art will disappear. For Kutiyattam artists, their art has never been endangered in this sense. Kutiyattam has persisted and developed over nearly one thousand years, supported by those willing to endure immense hardship to ensure its continued existence. Artists insist that the art will always be part of the world in some form or another, because there will always be someone to carry it forward. For them, a world without Kutiyattam is unfathomable.

~

In this book, I have explored how the *longue durée* of Kutiyattam's deep cosmopolitanism unsettles the endangered-local to safeguarded-global trajectory undergirding UNESCO's Intangible Cultural Heritage (ICH) program. When UNESCO first encountered Kutiyattam, the art needed financial support to flourish, but it was not on the brink of extinction in the face of globalization, as UNESCO assumed it to be. It was not a parochial form whose only hope of survival was through conversion to a cosmopolitan UNESCO ICH. Instead, Kutiyattam had its own cosmopolitan origins as part of a premodern South Asian cosmopolis. The art's UNESCO inscription was only the most recent installment of a rich history filled with varied cosmopolitan engagements, from the Sanskrit cosmopolis to border crossings and encounters with cultural Others, international communism, and cosmopolitan cultural space claimed by the Indian nation. In charting Kutiyattam's multiple cosmopolitanisms over time, *Deep Cosmopolitanism* tells the story of a UNESCO ICH form on its own terms, outside the framework of colonial modernity.

My ethnographic exploration of Kutiyattam's deep cosmopolitanism disentangles cosmopolitanism and tradition from colonial modernity. In so doing, it generates new ways of thinking about these concepts and challenges readers to reconsider their existing assumptions about them. Kutiyattam's thousand years of continuous performance poignantly connect cosmopolitan pasts and presents. Circumventing dominant Kantian conceptions of cosmopolitanism that wed the cosmopolitan with modernity and the nation-state, we have seen Kutiyattam defy this Eurocentric pairing through South Asian cosmopolitan encounters that span premodern and modern periods. In the process, the art challenges conceptions of universal history and time, "provincializing" universalized European genealogies of cosmopolitanism by centering non-Western experiences and histories (Chakrabarty 2000). By exploring Kutiyattam's historical and contemporary cosmopolitanisms, I have shown how cosmopolitan imaginaries have both intersected and coexisted with Kutiyattam's numerous identities and allegiances over its millennial history, thus decentering, pluralizing, and radically expanding the temporal limits of cosmopolitan possibility today. In so doing, *Deep Cosmopolitanism* accomplishes Breckenridge, Bhabha, Pollock, and Chakrabarty's (2002) twofold aim: (1) to "radically rewrite" the history of cosmopolitanism and "redraw its map" by thinking outside the confines of European intellectual history; and (2) to conceive of cosmopolitanism as fundamentally plural and composed of a wide range of practices that open its theorization to new, alternative horizons.

The cosmopolitan encounters of Kutiyattam that I have chronicled here are limited to the context of my research. There are undoubtedly many more lost to memory or simply not shared with me. One facet of Kutiyattam's contemporary cosmopolitanism that I was unable to include here is the global circulation of touring artists, especially throughout Europe, East Asia, and the Middle East. An issue worth exploring in depth, Kutiyattam artists have regularly moved throughout the world since before the art's UNESCO inscription. Many have emphasized how Kutiyattam's emotion-centered acting transcends linguistic and cultural boundaries, facilitating its understanding by audiences worldwide. Recounting his participation in the World Theatre Project alongside actors from China, Sweden, Mozambique, and Italy, Sooraj Nambiar poetically described Kutiyattam as "human expression with no boundaries." As Guru Ammannur once ruminated: "The mind—or the inner substance—is the same for all human beings. When someone feels something, the one opposite him experiences the same feeling. That is what makes an exchange between humans at all possible. . . . That a performer can successfully transmit feelings to the audience, that in the viewer the desired rasa can be aroused, is to this day a wonder to me, and I don't know how I do it" (Pfaff 1997, 145). I heard this conceptualization echoed by many artists. After one of my American friends attended a Margi performance, Sindhu-chechi asked, "Even if she couldn't understand the language, she still understood the expressions, right?"

Returning to the book's disentanglement efforts, *Deep Cosmopolitanism* likewise challenges the colonialist binary of tradition and modernity. Walter Mignolo and Catherine Walsh (2018) emphasize the necessity of laying bare "fictions of modernity" like that of tradition in order to end coloniality. Looking toward decolonial futures, Mignolo (2011) offers a decolonizing road map that decouples tradition from modernity, thereby freeing tradition from its conceptual constraints as the precursor of modernity.

> One of the intellectual tasks for imagining and doing toward communal futures . . . is to undo the colonial difference and the contribution of "time" to it. Thinking in terms of "transmodernity," instead of modernity and tradition, and thinking in terms of Pachamama or Gaia as a living system, instead of nature and culture, may open our imaginary to the restitution of suppressed epistemologies—epistemologies inscribed in languages such as Mandarin, Arabic, or Aymara, which were relegated, precisely, to the realm of tradition or almost nature from the perspective of a conception of time and of culture. (2011, 174)

The perspective of time and culture that Mignolo refers to here is that of the modern/colonial world that considers the tradition/modernity binary to be universal. Dominated by hegemonic conceptions of linear time and progress, Mignolo (2011) articulates how colonialist paradigms map the world into racialized regions designated as modern or premodern. Rooted in white supremacy, colonial orders of Otherness were created and reproduced through the temporal paradigm of tradition. This paradigm denied the nonwhite peoples of the world coevality, the recognition that they, too, lived in the modern moment, and this denial of modernity was used to justify their often brutal colonialization.

Folklorists Richard Bauman and Charles Briggs (2003) acknowledge inequality as a "cornerstone of modernity." They trace how European thought on language and tradition became universalized over time, in the process creating and legitimizing schemes of social inequality based on race, gender, class, and nationality that persist today. Bauman and Briggs (2003, 306) note that tradition, characterized as dying for more than three hundred years, "continues to provide useful means of producing and legitimizing new modernist projects, sets of legislators, and schemes of social inequality." As we have seen here, one such modernist project is UNESCO ICH. Bauman and Briggs (2003, 307) observe that, through its early efforts to create the ICH program, UNESCO sought to "preserve the tradition/modernity opposition and use it to legitimize structures of authority."[3]

As I have contended here, the scheme of social inequality that UNESCO legitimizes through its ICH program, however unintentionally, is white supremacy. In conceptualizing expressive culture primarily from the Global South as endangered by globalization, UNESCO denies the coevality of the world's nonwhite peoples through the trope of tradition. The concept of the nonmodern is key to this fiction of coexisting temporalities (Mignolo and Walsh 2018). As Mignolo and Walsh emphasize (2018, 117), the nonmodern is "necessary for the invention, in the present, of underdeveloped, uncivilized people: all that has to catch up to become modern or postmodern." UNESCO's ICH program creates a troubling spatiotemporal map of the world that equates the nonwhite Global South with the nonmodern, thereby perpetuating colonialist cultural hierarchies rooted in racist paradigms. While the move toward recognizing intangible cultural heritage was a significant step decades ago, it is insufficient to characterize UNESCO ICH as a decolonizing project today.

Returning to Mignolo's (2011) decolonizing road map, is decoupling tradition from modernity one strategy to decolonize UNESCO ICH? Alivizatou (2024) describes a recent shift in UNESCO's ICH program away from "safeguarding anxiety" toward sustainable development.[4] Rather than transcending its modernist paradigm, however, UNESCO thereby maintains the same structures of inequality. As Bauman and Briggs (2003, 308) note, the discourse of development is a "classic othering device of modernity." The narrative of sustainable development applied only to certain communities is a thinly veiled refashioning of the narrative of the "undeveloped" Global South needing to catch up with the "developed" North. With its Masterpieces program, UNESCO (2001a) initially framed tourism, often one of the only options for economic sustainability, as a threat. With no mention of sustainable development at the time, the organization idealized a model of the state as patron. This newest shift demanding that ICH create global capital highlights the increasing neoliberalization of UNESCO.[5] As discussed in chapter 7, a similar shift of economic burden from the state to the expressive forms themselves characterizes the Indian state's most recent approach to Kutiyattam. Unfortunately, I do not have a solution for how to extricate tradition from the problematic temporalizing practices of modernity, particularly at the deeply modernist institution of UNESCO. However, Bauman and Briggs's (2003, 317) advice resonates: "Never let constructions of language and tradition masquerade as cartographies of the real."

Kutiyattam itself provides a provocative model for decolonizing modernity. Its artists operate with a fundamental assumption of change and adaptation as core elements of artistic continuity. Rather than assuming tradition as static, they recognize its intrinsic dynamism. In this model, art as tradition-in-performance maintains its relevance by adapting to the changing tastes of audiences over time. Tradition thus conceived never participated in the temporal inequalities of colonial modernity but has always been contemporary in its own right. Scholar and hereditary artist Dr. C. K. Jayanthi once explained to me, "You can't say this theater tradition is old. It is not old or new. When we enact it, it is new. When an actor uses it, it is contemporary." Offering a poetic simile, she continued, "Kutiyattam is like a river. We bathe ourselves in only one small corner of the river, so how can we know the whole river? We enter the river to bathe, just that. Where does the river come from? We don't know. The river of Kutiyattam has flowed for one, two thousand years. I've been in this river for only thirty years in one small corner, so how can I know where the river will flow from here? Maybe it will flow into an ocean; it should go its own way."

In reflecting on these issues, I have come to view my own field in a new light. Often criticized for a lack of rigorous theory, folkloristics is in fact partially aligned with decolonial approaches seen as the cutting edge of theory today. Through our dynamic definition of tradition as "the creation of the future out of the past," our commitment to devalued epistemologies and theory from below, and our discarding of the concept of authenticity as an analytical tool, we have already made concrete steps toward decolonizing modernity, in Mignolo's sense, that deserve more recognition outside of the field (Glassie 2003, 176).[6] Yet much remains to be done. Building on Naithani's (2010) study of colonial folkloristics, Charles Briggs and Sadhana Naithani (2012) suggest that one way to decolonize the field is through a "multi-genealogical" practice that recognizes the central role that colonialism has always played in shaping folkloristics. And as folklorist Rachel González-Martin (2021, 36) poignantly observes, "Tradition is a racialized tool. The academic concept of tradition is an organizational device that undervalues racialized communities in our contemporary Western, White supremacist society, where Whiteness is synonymous with 'unmarked' and tradition is part of a validation of a community's capacity to historicize its existence in place and time."

Coda

I opened this book with an image of the lighting of the *nilavilakku* lamp, signaling a Kutiyattam performance about to begin. I close it with an image of *mudiakkita,* the ceremonial extinguishing of the lamp's flame that marks the performance's end.

Figure 50. Pothiyil Renjith Chakyar performing *mudiakkita*. Photo by author.

Notes

1. See Damodaran and Chavin 2019, 409.

2. The complicated art does not draw big audiences, nor is there a model of ticket sales for traditional arts in Kerala.

3. Referring to UNESCO and WIPO 1985 and UNESCO 1989.

4. See Bortolotto and Skounti 2024 for more details.

5. UNESCO's neoliberalization is apparent in other arenas, such as the connection between UNESCO ICH and "neoliberal nationalism" (Scher 2010) and the "neoliberal logics" that pervade the UNESCO ICH application process (Chocano 2020, 2023).

6. See also Noyes 2016 and Bendix 1997, respectively.

GLOSSARY

abhinaya—acting

adiyanthirakoothu—Kutiyattam's hereditary, annual temple performance

aithihyam—narratives told as true stories about individuals from the past, often equated with legend

aramandalam—basic stance of Kutiyattam

arangettam—onstage debut initiating a performer into an art form

ashan—term of respect for male guru

attaprakaram—Kutiyattam stage manual of the dramatic text and acting techniques

bhava—facial expressions representing the nine basic emotional states

Chakyar—hereditary male actor of Kutiyattam

Chakyarkoothu—male solo verbal performance part of the Kutiyattam complex

chechi—"big sister," term of respect used for addressing older women fairly close in age

chetan—"big brother," term of respect used for addressing older men fairly close in age

Guru—teacher/mentor

guru-shishya—teacher-student relationship

gurukulam—a center of learning where students, usually living nearby or at the center, learn from the guru in everyday life as well as in more formalized settings *kalaripayattu*—martial art of Kerala

Kathakali—all-male classical dance drama of Kerala

koothambalam—Kutiyattam's temple theater

kramadeepika—Kutiyattam stage manual of stage logistics

lokadharmi—realistic acting

Maharaja—king

marumakkathayam—kinship system of matrilineal descent in Kerala

mizhavu—pot-shaped drum played to accompany Kutiyattam

Mohiniyattam—all-female classical dance of Kerala

mudras—symbolic hand gesture alphabet used in classical dance across India

Nambiar—hereditary male drummer of Kutiyattam

Namboodiri—Kerala Brahmin

Nangiar/Nangiaramma—hereditary female actor of Kutiyattam

Nangiarkoothu—female solo dramatic performance part of the Kutiyattam complex

natyadharmi—stylized acting

netrabhinaya—acting technique that conveys emotion through the eyes

nityakriya—first item of repertoire learned by Kutiyattam students

pakarnnattam—a technique whereby the solo actor or actress switches back and forth seamlessly between various roles as an omniscient storyteller

Pathakam—solo narrative form performed traditionally by Nambiars

purushavesham—male costume/role

rasa—facial expressions representing the nine basic emotional states

shishya—student

shloka—Sanskrit verse, chanted in singsong manner in Kutiyattam

shyli—style

streevesham—female costume/role

Teacher—term of respect for female guru

thalam/kuzhithalam—small cymbals used to accompany Kutiyattam

vesham—costume; acting

vidushaka—jester figure and companion to the hero in Sanskrit drama

Zamorin—king of Malabar region of Kerala

BIBLIOGRAPHY

Aarzoo, S. Shabana, and Mohammad Afzal. 2005. "Gene Diversity in Some Muslim Populations of North India." *Human Biology* 77 (3): 343–353.

Abel, Roysten. 2014. "The Kitchen by Roysten Abel. Trailer by Gyan Dev." YouTube video, January 1. 1:09. https://www.youtube.com/watch?v=uznsHHg6m14.

Abrahams, Roger D. 1987. "An American Vocabulary of Celebrations." In *Time Out of Time: Voices of the Festival*, edited by Alessandro Falassi, 173–183. Albuquerque: University of New Mexico Press.

———. 1993. "Phantoms of Romantic Nationalism in Folkloristics." *Journal of American Folklore* 106:3–37.

Aikawa-Faure, Noriko. 2009. "From the Proclamation of Masterpieces to the Convention for the Safeguarding of Intangible Cultural Heritage." In *Intangible Cultural Heritage*, edited by Laurajane Smith and Natsuko Akagawa, 13–44. London: Routledge.

Aiyer, V. Nagam. 1906. *Travancore State Manual*, vol. 1. Trivandrum: Travancore Government Press. https://archive.org/details/travancorestateooaiyagoog/page/n11/mode/2up.

Ajayan, T. 2017. "Midterm Election in Kerala in 1960 and the American Government." *History and Sociology of South Asia* 11 (2): 212–220.

Alam, Muzaffar, and Sanjay Subrahmanyam. 2007. *Indo-Persian Travels in the Age of Discoveries, 1400–1800*. Cambridge: Cambridge University Press.

Alivizatou, Marilena. 2024. "Repurposing Intangible Heritage—Convergence, Creativity and Community Empowerment Post Covid-19." *Critical Studies in Cultural Heritage* 4 (1): 1–20.

Alonso-González, Pablo. 2013. "The Heritage Machine: A Heritage Ethnography in Maragatería." PhD diss., Universidad de León.

Anderson, Benedict. 1983. *Imagined Communities: Reflections on the Origin and Spread of Nationalism*. London: Verso.

Antonnen, Pertti. 2005. *Tradition through Modernity: Postmodernism and the Nation-State in Folklore Scholarship*. Helsinki: Finnish Literature Society.

Appadurai, Arjun. 1996. *Modernity At Large*. Minneapolis: University of Minnesota Press.

Appiah, Kwame A. 2009. "Whose Culture Is It?" In *Whose Culture? The Promise of Museums and the Debate over Antiquities*, edited by J. Cuno, 71–86. Princeton, NJ: Princeton University Press.

Arunima, G. 2003. *There Comes Papa: Colonialism and the Transformation of Matriliny in Kerala, Malabar, c. 1950–1940*. New Delhi: Orient Longman.

———. 2006. "Who Is a Malayali Anyway? Language, Community, and Identity in Precolonial Kerala." In *Assertive Religious Identities: India and Europe*, edited by Satish Saberwal and Mushirul Hasan, 33–57. Delhi: Manohar.

Ayyar, Krishna K. V. 1938. *The Zamorins of Calicut: From the Earliest Times Down to AD 1806*. Calicut: K. V. Krishna Ayyar. https://archive.org/details/in.gov.ignca.3379/page/n3/mode/2up.

Balakrishnan, Pulapre. 2019. "The 'Kerala Model' Is Unsustainable." *The Hindu*, August 22. https://www.thehindu.com/opinion/op-ed/the-kerala-model-is-unsustainable/article29213883.ece.

Balgir, R. S. 2003. "Morphological and Regional Variations in Body Dimensions of the Gujjars of Different Localities in North-Western India." *Human Biology* 77:343–353.

Banerji, Arunima. 2019. *Dancing Odissi: Paratopic Performances of Gender and State*. New York: Seagull Books.

Barbosa, Duarte. 1812. *A Description of the Coasts of East Africa and Malabar in the Beginning of the Sixteenth Century*. Translated by Henry E. J. Stanley. London: Hakluyt Society. https://www.gutenberg.org/files/38253/38253-h/38253-h.htm.

Barnett, Marguerite Ross. 1976. *The Politics of Cultural Nationalism in South India*. Princeton, NJ: Princeton University Press.

Bar-On Cohen, Einat. 2024. *Awakening a Living World on a Kūṭiyāṭṭam Stage*. Albany: State University of New York Press.

Bauman, Richard, and Charles L. Briggs. 1990. "Poetics and Performance as Critical Perspectives on Language and Social Life." *Annual Review of Anthropology* 19:59–88.

———. 2003. *Voices of Modernity: Language Ideologies and the Politics of Inequality*. Cambridge: Cambridge University Press.

Bayly, Christopher Alan. 1998. *Origins of Nationality in South Asia: Patriotism and Ethical Government in the Making of Modern India*. Delhi: Oxford University Press.

Bayly, Susan. 1984. "Hindu Kingship and the Origin of Community: Religion, State and Society in Kerala, 1750–1850." *Modern Asian Studies* 18 (2): 177–213.

Beazley, Olwen, and Harriet Deacon. 2007. "Safeguarding Intangible Heritage Values under the World Heritage Convention: Auschwitz, Hiroshima, and Robben

Island." In *Safeguarding Intangible Cultural Heritage: Challenges and Approaches,* edited by Janet Blake, 93–107. Builth Wells: Institute of Art and Law.

Ben-Amos, Dan. 1969. "Analytical Categories and Ethnic Genres." *Genre* 2 (3): 275–301.

Bendix, Regina. 1997. *In Search of Authenticity: The Formation of Folklore Studies.* Madison: University of Wisconsin Press.

———. 2007. "Kulturelles Erbe zwischen Wirtschaft und Politik: ein Ausblick." In *Prädikat 'Heritage': Perspektiven auf Wertschöpfungen aus Kultur,* edited by Dorothee Hemme, Regina Bendix, and Markus Tauschek, 337–356. Münster: Lit.

Bendix, Regina, Aditya Eggert, and Arnika Peselmann. 2013. "Introduction: Heritage Regimes and the State." In *Heritage Regimes and the State,* edited by Regina Bendix, Aditya Eggert, and Arnika Peselmann, 11–20. Göttingen: Universitätsverlag Göttingen.

Bhadra, P. K. M., and B. Rajneesh. 2019. "Aṅgulīyāṅkam: The Nāṭyaveda of Kūṭ iyāṭṭam." In *Kūṭiyāṭṭam: Mantrāṅkam and Aṅgulīyāṅkam,* edited by Heike Oberlin and David Shulman, 225–229. New Delhi: Oxford University Press.

Bharata-Muni. 1951. *The Nāṭyaśāstra,* 2 vols. Translated and edited by Manomohan Ghosh. Calcutta: Asiatic Society of Bengal.

———. 1996. *The Nāṭyaśāstra.* Translated and edited by Adya Rangacharya. New Delhi: Munshiram Manoharlal.

Bhargavinilayam, Das. 1999. *Māṇimādhavīyam.* Trivandrum: Government of Kerala.

Bhatti, Anil. 2005. "Der koloniale Diskurs und Orte des Gedächtnisses." In *Kulturerbe als soziokulturelle Praxis,* edited by Moritz Csáky and Monika Sommer, 115–128. Innsbruck: Studien.

Bindu, Karin. 2013. *Percussion Art Forms. Aspekte der Produktion und Kommunikation südindischer* Talas *im* Kūṭiyāṭṭam. Vienna: Lit.

———. 2016. "*Miḻāvu*—göttliches Perkussionsinstrument im südindischen Sanskrit-Drama *Kūṭiyāṭṭam.*" *Anthropos* 111 (2): 395–414.

Blake, Janet. 2001. *Developing a New Standard-Setting Instrument for the Safeguarding of Intangible Cultural Heritage: Elements for Consideration.* Paris: UNESCO.

Blau, Herbert. 1992. *To All Appearances: Ideology and Performance.* London: Routledge.

Boivin, Nicole. 2007. "Anthropological, Historical, Archaeological and Genetic Perspectives on the Origins of Caste in South Asia." In *The Evolution and History of Human Populations in South Asia,* edited by M. D. Petraglia and B. Allchin, 341–361. New York: Springer.

Bortolotto, Chiara. 2007. "From Objects to Processes: UNESCO's 'Intangible Cultural Heritage.'" *Journal of Museum Ethnography* 19:21–33.

———. 2015. "UNESCO and Heritage Self-Determination: Negotiating Meaning in the Intergovernmental Committee for the Safeguarding of the ICH." In

Between Imagined Communities of Practice: Participation, Territory and the Making of Heritage, edited by Nicolas Adell, Regina F. Bendix, Chiara Bortolotto, and Markus Tauschek, 249–272. Göttingen: Universitätsverlag Göttingen.

Bortolotto, Chiara, and Ahmed Skounti, eds. 2024. *Intangible Cultural Heritage and Sustainable Development: Inside a UNESCO Convention*. New York: Routledge.

Bose, Satheese Chandra, and Shiju Sam Varughese. 2015. "Introduction: Situating an Unbound Region: Reflections on Kerala Modernity." In *Kerala Modernity: Ideas, Spaces and Practices in Transition*, edited by Satheese Chandra Bose and Shiju Sam Varughese, 1–24. New Delhi: Orient Blackswan.

———, eds. 2015. *Kerala Modernity: Ideas, Spaces and Practices in Transition*. New Delhi: Orient Blackswan.

Bourdieu, Pierre. 1984. *Distinction: A Social Critique of the Judgment of Taste*. Translated by R. Nice. London: Routledge.

———. (1980) 1990. *The Logic of Practice*. Translated by R. Nice. Stanford, CA: Stanford University Press.

———. 1998. *Acts of Resistance: Against the Tyranny of the Market*. New York: New Press.

Brandon, James R. 1993. "Introduction." In *Sanskrit Drama in Performance*, edited by R. van M. Baumer and J. R. Brandon, xvii—xx. Honolulu: University of Hawaii Press.

Breckenridge, Carole A., Homi K. Bhabha, Sheldon Pollock, and Dipesh Chakrabarty, eds. 2002. *Cosmopolitanism*. Durham, NC: Duke University Press.

Briggs, Charles, and Sadhana Naithani. 2012. "The Coloniality of Folklore: Towards a Multi Genealogical Practice of Folkloristics." *Studies in History* 28 (2): 231–270.

Browning, Barbara. 1995. *Samba: Resistance in Motion*. Bloomington: Indiana University Press.

Brückner, Heidrun. 1999/2000. "Manuscripts and Performance Traditions of the So-Called 'Trivandrum-Plays' Ascribed to Bhasa—A Report on Work in Progress." *Bulletin d'Études Indiennes* 17/18:501–550.

Byrski, Maria Krzysztof. 1967. "Is Kudiyattam a Museumpiece?" *Sangeet Natak* 5:45–54.

———. 1973. *Concept of Ancient Indian Theatre*. New Delhi: Munshiram Manoharlal.

———. 1993. "Sanskrit Drama as an Aggregate of Model Situations." In *Sanskrit Drama in Performance*, edited by R. van M. Baumer and J. R. Brandon, 141–166. Honolulu: University of Hawaii Press.

———. 2009. "The Dance Theatre That Braved Time." In *Attendance: The Dance Annual of India, 2008–09*, edited by Ashish Mohan Khokar, 48–51. New Delhi: Ekah-Printways.

———. 2015. "Abhināya Redefined." In *The Nāṭyaśāstra and the Body in Performance*, edited by Sreenath Nair, 63–71. Jefferson, NC: McFarland.

Caldwell, Robert. 1856. *A Comparative Grammar of the Dravidian or South-Indian Family of Languages*. London: Harrison.

Cantwell, Robert. 1993. *Ethnomimesis: Folklife and the Representation of Culture*. Chapel Hill: University of North Carolina Press.

Casassas, Coralie. 2012. "Female Roles and Engagement of Women in the Classical Sanskrit Theatre *Kūṭiyāṭṭam*: A Contemporary Theatre Tradition." *Asian Theatre Journal* 29 (1): 1–30.

Cashman, Ray. 2008. *Storytelling on the Northern Irish Border: Characters and Community*. Bloomington: Indiana University Press.

Cashman, Ray, Tom Mould, and Pravina Shukla, eds. 2011. *The Individual and Tradition: Folkloristic Perspectives*. Bloomington: Indiana University Press.

C-DIT (Center for Development of Imaging Technology). n.d. *Master of Valour: Kalamandalam Sivan Namboothiri*. Film, directed by Viju Varma. C-DIT-UNESCO documentation series. Thiruvananthapuram: C-DIT.

Chakiar, A. M. N. 1999. *The Last Caste Inquisition: A Victim's Reminiscences*. Self-published, Tripunithura: Padma C. Menon.

Chakrabarty, Dipesh. 2000. *Provincializing Europe: Postcolonial Thought and Historical Difference*. Princeton, NJ: Princeton University Press.

Chakravarti, Uma. 1989. "Whatever Happened to the Vedic Dasi? Orientalism, Nationalism, and a Script for the Past." In *Recasting Women: Essays in Colonial History*, edited by Kumkum Sangari and Sudesh Vaid, 27–87. New Delhi: Kali for Women.

Chakravorty, Pallabi. 2008. *Bells of Change: Kathak Dance, Women and Modernity in India*. Calcutta: Seagull Books.

Chakyar, Ammannur Kuttan, and Aparna Nangiar. 2019. "Distinct Conventions in the Staging of *Aṅgulīyāṅkam Kūttu*." In *Kūṭiyāṭṭam: Mantrāṅkam and Aṅgulīyāṅ kam*, edited by Heike Oberlin and David Shulman, 257–270. New Delhi: Oxford University Press.

Chakyar, Ammannur Madhava. 1994. "My Training, My Gurus." Edited by K. Ayyappa Paniker and Sudha Gopalakrishnan. Special issue: Kutiyattam, *Sangeet Natak* 111–114:141–146.

Chakyar, Ammannur Rajaneesh. 2011. "Kutiyattam—An Overview of Ten Years after the Declaration of UNESCO." Edited by Heike Moser. Special Issue: Kutiyattam—10 Years after the UNESCO-Declaration, *Indian Folklife* 38:9.

Chakyar, Madhu. 2019. "My Experience of Performing *Aṅgulīyāṅkam* and *Mantrāṅkam*." In *Kūṭiyāṭṭam: Mantrāṅkam and Aṅgulīyāṅkam*, edited by Heike Oberlin and David Shulman, 271–274. New Delhi: Oxford University Press.

Chakyar, Mani Madhava. 1974. *Nāṭyakalpadrumam*. Cheruthuruthy: Kerala Kalamandalam.

———. 1994a. "The Training Methods of Kūṭiyāṭṭam." Edited by K. Ayyappa Paniker and Sudha Gopalakrishnan. Special issue: Kutiyattam, *Sangeet Natak* 111–114:48–54.

———. 1994b. "Vachikabhinaya." Edited by K. Ayyappa Paniker and Sudha Gopalakrishnan. Special issue: Kutiyattam, *Sangeet Natak* 111–114:74–89.

———. 2013a. "Preface to *Nāṭyakalpadrumam*." Translated by P. K. Madhavan. Special issue: Guru Mani Madhava Chakyar, *Nartanam* 13 (1): 36–43.

———. 2013b. "*Mangalācharanam*: Introductory Verses of Nāṭyakalpadrumam." Translated by P. K. Madhavan. Special issue: Guru Mani Madhava Chakyar, *Nartanam* 13 (1): 7–21.

Chakyar, Margi Madhu. 2015. *Kutiyattam and Kerala Temples*. Translated by L. S. Rajagopalan. Athens: Athens Area Arts Council and Athenshasart! Originally published as *Āṭṭattinṭe Vaḷiyaṭayāḷaṅṅaḷ*. Thripunithura: International Centre for Kutiyattam, 2002.

Chakyar, Painkulam Rama. 1976. "Interview Conducted by Richard Schechner." Richard Schechner Papers and The Drama Review Collection, Princeton University.

———. 1994. "The Chakyar Families." Edited by K. Ayyappa Paniker and Sudha Gopalakrishnan. Special issue: Kutiyattam, *Sangeet Natak* 111–114:125.

Chandrahasan, K. A. 1989. "In Pursuit of Excellence." *The Hindu*, March 26.

Chatterjee, Partha. 1986. *Nationalist Thought and the Colonial World: A Derivative Discourse*. London: Zed Books on behalf of the United Nations University.

———. 1989. "Colonialism, Nationalism, and Colonial Women." *American Ethnologist* 16 (4): 622–633.

———. 1993. *The Nation and Its Fragments: Colonial and Postcolonial Histories*. Princeton, NJ: Princeton University Press.

Cherian, Anita E. 2005. "Fashioning a National Theater: Institutions and Cultural Policy in Post-Independence India." PhD diss., New York University.

———. 2009. "Institutional Maneuvres, Nationalizing Performance, Delineating a Genre: Reading the Sangeet Natak Akademi Reports 1953–1959." *Third Frame: Literature, Culture and Society* 2 (3): 32–60.

Chocano, Rodrigo. 2020. "Heritage is a Struggle: Music, Neoliberal Logics, and the Practice of Intangible Cultural Heritage in Peru." PhD diss., Indiana University.

———. 2023. "Strategic Skepticism: The Politics of Grassroots Participation in an Afro-Andean Nomination to the UNESCO Intangible Cultural Heritage Representative List." *Journal of American Folklore* 136 (541): 249–273.

Cohn, Bernard. 1987. *An Anthropologist among the Historians and Other Essays*. New York: Oxford University Press.

Comaroff, Jean, and John L. Comaroff. 2009. *Ethnicity, Inc.* Chicago: University of Chicago Press.

Culp, Amanda. 2021. "Prakrits in Performance: Theatricality and Multilingual Drama in Premodern India." *Asian Theatre Journal* 38 (2): 561–575.

Dalmia, Vasudha. 1997. *The Nationalization of Hindu Traditions: Bharatendu Harischandra and Nineteenth Century Benaras*. Delhi: Oxford University Press.

———. 2006. *Poetics, Plays and Performances: The Politics of Modern Indian Theater.* Oxford: Oxford University Press.

Dalmia, Vasudha, and Heinrich von Stietencron. 1995. "Introduction." In *Representing Hinduism: The Construction of Religious Traditions and National Identity,* edited by Vasudha Dalmia and Heinrich von Stietencron, 17–32. New Delhi: Sage.

Damodaran, A. 2022. *Managing Art in Times of Pandemics and Beyond.* Oxford: Oxford University Press.

Damodaran, Appukuttan Nair, and Larry Chavin. 2019. "Nurturing UNESCO's 'Aged' Infants in India: Lessons in Heritage Policy." *International Journal of Cultural Policy* 25 (4): 407–422.

Daugherty, Diane. 1996. "The Nangyār: Female Ritual Specialist of Kerala." *Asian Theatre Journal* 13 (1): 54–67.

———. 2000. "Fifty Years On: Arts Funding in Kerala Today." *Asian Theatre Journal* 17 (2): 237–252.

———. 2011. "Subhadra Redux: Reinstating Female Kūṭiyāṭṭam." In *Between Fame and Shame: Performing Women—Women Performers in India,* edited by Heidrum Brückner, Hanne de Bruin, and Heike Moser, 85–98. Wiesbaden: Harrasowitz.

———. 2016. "The Nangyār: Female Ritual Specialist of Kerala." *Nartanam* 16 (3): 89–106.

———. 2019. "Women on the Classical Kerala Stage: The *Kutiyattam* and *Kathakali* Traditions." In *The Palgrave Handbook of the History of Women on Stage,* edited by Jan Sewell and Clare Smout, 585–615. London: Palgrave.

Davis, Donald R., Jr. 2014. "Satire as Apology: The *Puruṣārtthakūttŭ* of Kerala." In *Irreverent History: Essays for M.G.S. Narayanan,* edited by Kesavan Veluthat and Donald R. Davis Jr., 93–109. Delhi: Primus.

Deacon, Harriet, Luvuyo Dondolo, Mbulelo Mrubata, and Sandra Prosalendis. 2004. *The Subtle Power of Intangible Heritage: Legal and Financial Instruments for Safeguarding Intangible Heritage.* Cape Town: Human Sciences Research Council.

Dégh, Linda, and Andrew Vázsonyi. 1976. "Legend and Belief." In *Folklore Genres,* edited by Dan Ben-Amos, 93–123. Austin: University of Texas Press.

de Jong, Ferdinand. 2022. *Decolonizing Heritage: Time to Repair in Senegal.* Cambridge: Cambridge University Press.

De Lannoy, Mark. 1986. "A 'Dutchman' in the Service of the Raja of Travancore: Eustache Benoit de Lannoy (1715–1777)." *Journal of Kerala Studies* 13:1–16.

Deleuze, Gilles, and Félix Guattari. 1987. *A Thousand Plateaus: Capitalism and Schizophrenia.* Minneapolis: Minnesota University Press.

Deshpande, Satish. 2003. *Contemporary India: A Sociological View.* New York: Viking.

Devadevan, Manu V. 2019. "Knowing and Being: Kūṭiyāṭṭam and Its Semantic Universe." In *Two Masterpieces of Kūṭiyāṭṭam: Mantrāṅkam and Aṅgulīyāṅkam,* edited by Heike Oberlin and David Shulman with Elena Mucciarelli, 275–305. London: Oxford University Press.

Devika, J. 2007a. *Engendering Individuals: The Language of Re-Forming in Early Twentieth Century Keralam*. New Delhi: Orient Longman.

———. 2007b. "'A People United in Development': Developmentalism in Modern Malayali Identity." Working Paper 386,Center for Development Studies, Thiruvananthapuram.

———. 2010. "Egalitarian Developmentalism, Communist Mobilization, and the Question of Caste in Kerala State, India." *Journal of Asian Studies* 69 (3): 799–820.

Diamond, Sarah. 1999. "Karagattam: Performance and the Politics of Desire in Tamil Nadu, India." PhD diss., University of Pennsylvania.

Dirks, Nicholas. 2001. *Castes of Mind: Colonialism and the Making of Modern India*. Princeton, NJ: Princeton University Press.

Douglas, Mary. (1970) 1973. *Natural Symbols: Explorations in Cosmology*. New York: Vintage Books.

DuComb, Christian. 2007. "Present-Day Kutiyattam: G. Venu's Radical and Reactionary Sanskrit Theatre." *TDR* 51 (3): 98–117.

Dundes, Alan. 1966. "Metafolklore and Oral Literary Criticism." *Monist* 60:505–516.

———. 1971. "Laughter behind the Iron Curtain: A Sample of Rumanian Political Jokes." *Ukrainian Quarterly* 27:50–59.

———. 1999. *Holy Writ as Oral Lit: The Bible as Folklore*. Lanham, MD: Rowman & Littlefield.

Dutta, Parasmoni. 2017. "Intangible Cultural Heritage in India: Reflections on Selected Forms of Dance." In *The Routledge Companion to Intangible Cultural Heritage*, edited by M. L. Stefano and P. Davis, 230–239. New York: Routledge.

Egorova, Yulia. 2009. "De/geneticizing Caste: Population Genetic Research in South Asia." *Science as Culture* 18 (4): 417–438.

Enros, Pragna Thakkar. 1979. "A Reconstruction of the Style of Producing Plays in the Ancient Indian Theatre." PhD diss., University of Toronto.

"Entering the Kalari: Featuring Kalamandalam Sajith Vijayan." Harmony with A.R. Rahman, season 1, episode 1, August 14, 2018, Amazon Prime India, https://www.amazon.com/Harmony-R-Rahman-Season-1/dp/B07GBGZW55.

Erlewein, Shina-Nancy. 2014. "Screening Intangible Heritage: Media, Heritage and Representation—The Case of Kutiyattam Sanskrit Theatre, India." PhD diss., Brandenburg University of Technology.

Escallón, Maria Fernanda. 2023. *Becoming Heritage: Recognition, Exclusion, and the Politics of Black Cultural Heritage in Colombia*. Cambridge: Cambridge University Press.

Fabian, Johannes. 1983. *Time and the Other: How Anthropology Makes Its Object*. New York: Columbia University Press.

Foster, Michael Dylan. 2011. "The UNESCO Effect: Confidence, Defamiliarization, and a New Element in the Discourse on a Japanese Island." *Journal of Folklore Research* 48 (1): 63–107.

———. 2015a. "UNESCO on the Ground." *Journal of Folklore Research* 52 (2/3): 143–156.

———. 2015b. "Imagined UNESCOs: Interpreting Intangible Cultural Heritage on a Japanese Island." *Journal of Folklore Research* 52 (2/3): 217–232.

Foster, Michael Dylan, and Lisa Gilman, eds. 2015. *UNESCO on the Ground: Local Perspectives on Intangible Cultural Heritage*. Bloomington: Indiana University Press.

Franke, Richard W., and Barbara H. Chasin. 1994. *KERALA: Radical Reform as Development in an Indian State*. Oakland: Institute for Food and Development Policy.

Freeman, Rich. 1998. "Rubies and Coral: The Lapidary Crafting of Language in Kerala." *Journal of Asian Studies* 57 (1): 38–36.

Frenz, Margret. 2000. *Vom Herrscher zum Untertan: Spannungsverhältnis zwischen lokaler Herrschaftsstruktur und der Kolonialverwaltung in Malabar zu Beginn der britischen Herrschaft (1790–1805)*. Stuttgart: Franz Steiner.

Fuller, Christopher. 1976. *The Nayars Today*. Cambridge: Cambridge University Press.

Gamliel, Ophira. 2014. "The Best Snack Ever: On the Jester in God's Own Theater," Guest lecture at the Käte Hamburger Kolleg Ruhr Universität, Bochum, June 23, 2014. https://www.academia.edu/9813892/The_Best_Snack_Ever_The_Jester_in_Koodiyattam.

———. 2018. "Textual Crossroads and Transregional Encounters: Jewish Networks in Kerala 900s–1600s." *Social Orbit* 4 (1): 41–73.

———. 2020. *A Linguistic Survey of the Malayalam Language in Its Own Terms*. Wiesbaden: Harrassowitz.

García Canclini, N. 1995. *Hybrid Cultures: Strategies for Entering and Leaving Postmodernity*. Minneapolis: University of Minnesota Press.

Gerety, Finnian M. M. 2017. "The Amplified Sacrifice: Sound, Technology, and Participation in Modern Vedic Ritual." Edited by Frank J. Korom and Leah Lowthorp. Special issue: South Asian Folklore in the 21st Century, *South Asian History and Culture* 8 (4): 560–578.

Ghosh, Manomohan. 1951. "Introduction." In *The Nāṭyaśāstra Ascribed to Bharata-Muni*, 2 vols. Translated and edited by Manomohan Ghosh, 37–86. Calcutta: Asiatic Society of Bengal.

Gibb, H. A. R., and C. F. Beckingham, trans. 2000. *The Travels of Ibn Battuta, A.D. 1325–1354*, 5 vols. London: Hakluyt.

Giguère, Hélène. 2010. *Viva Jerez! Enjeux esthétiques et politiques de la patrimonialisation de la culture*. Québec: Presses de l'Université Laval.

Gilchriest Hatch, Emily. 1933. *Travancore: A Guide Book for the Visitor*. London: Oxford University Press.

———. 1934. "The Kathakali: The Indigenous Drama of Malabar." PhD diss., Cornell University.

Gilman, Lisa. 2022. "'Our Culture Is Dying': Safeguarding versus Representation in the Implementation of the UNESCO ICH Convention." *International Journal of Intangible Heritage* 17:40–52.
Glassie, Henry. 1994. "Epilogue." In *Swedish Folk Art: All Tradition Is Change*, edited by Barbro Klein and Mats Widbom, 247–255. New York: Harry N. Abrams.
———. 2003. "Tradition." In *Eight Words for the Study of Expressive Culture*, edited by Burt Feintuch, 176–197. Urbana: University of Illinois Press.
González-Martin, Rachel V. 2021. "White Traditioning and Bruja Epistemologies: Rebuilding the House of USAmerican Folklore Studies." In *Theorizing Folklore from the Margins: Critical and Ethical Approaches for the 21st Century*, edited by Solimar Otero and Mintzi Martínez-Rivera, 22–41. Bloomington: Indiana University Press.
Gopalakrishnan, K. K. 2004. "Revolution in Dance." *The Hindu*, July 18.
———. 2013. "The Master with 'Magical Eyes.'" Special issue: Guru Mani Madhava Chakyar, *Nartanam* 13 (1): 22–36.
———. 2016a. *Kathakali Dance-Theatre: A Visual Narrative of Sacred Indian Mime*. New Delhi: Niyogi Books.
———. 2016b. "Kutiyattam: Fifty Years of Transcendence into a Secular Art Form." Edited by K. K. Gopalakrishnan. Special issue: 50 Years of Kutiyattam, *Nartanam* 16 (3): 11–56.
———, ed. 2016c. "Special issue: 50 Years of Kutiyattam." *Nartanam* 16 (3): 7–218.
Gopalakrishnan, Sudha. 1988. "Kūṭiyāṭṭam and Its Correspondence to the Nāṭyaśāstra." *Sangeet Natak* 88:32–38.
———. 1993. *From the Comic to the Comedian: The Traditions of Comedy of Bhasa and Shakespeare*. New Delhi: Sharada.
———. 2000. *Candidature File of Kutiyattam for UNESCO's Proclamation of 'Masterpieces of the Oral and Intangible Heritage of Humanity*. Trivandrum: Margi.
———. 2011a. *Kutiyattam: The Heritage Theatre of India*. New Delhi: Niyogi Books.
———. 2011b. "Kutiyattam: UNESCO Proclamation and the Change in Institutional Model and Patronage." Edited by Heike Moser. Special issue: Kutiyattam—10 Years after the UNESCO-Declaration, *Indian Folklife* 38:4–8.
———. 2019. "*Aṅgulīyāṅkam* and *Mantrāṅkam:* Two Wondrous Crest Jewels of Kūṭiyāṭṭam." In *Kūṭiyāṭṭam: Mantrāṅkam and Aṅgulīyāṅkam*, edited by Heike Oberlin and David Shulman, 3–9. New Delhi: Oxford University Press.
Gopalan, A. K. 1973. *In the Cause of the People: Reminiscences*. New Delhi: Orient Longman.
Goren Arzony, Sivan. 2019. "An Actor in Red and White: The Cākyār Community and the Early Maṇipravālam Corpus." In *Two Masterpieces of Kūṭiyāṭṭam: Mantrāṅkam and Aṅgulīyāṅkam*, edited by Heike Oberlin and David Shulman with Elena Mucciarelli, 305–325. London: Oxford University Press.

Gough, Kathleen. 1955. "Female Initiation Rites on the Malabar Coast." *Journal of the Royal Anthropological Institute* 85:45–80.

———. 1959. "The Nayars and the Definition of Marriage." *Journal of the Royal Anthropological Institute* 89:23–34.

———. 1978. *Dravidian Kinship and Modes of Production*. New Delhi: Indian Council of Social Science Research.

Guha, Sumit. 2019. *History and Collective Memory in South Asia 1200–2000*. Seattle: University of Washington Press.

Gundert, Hermann. 1868. *Kēraḷōlpatti (The Origin of Malabar)*, 2nd ed. Mangalore: Stole & Reuther, Basel Mission Press. https://archive.org/details/1868_Keralolpathi_Hermann_Gundert/page/n5/mode/2up.

Gupta, Akhil, and Jessie Stoolman. 2022. "Decolonizing US Anthropology." *American Anthropologist* 124:778–799.

Gupta, D. N. 2008. *Communism and Nationalism in Colonial India, 1939–45*, SAGE Series in Modern Indian History, vol. 12. New Delhi: Sage.

Gupta, Sobhanlal Datta. 2006. *Comintern and the Destiny of Communism in India: 1919–1943—Dialectics of Real and a Possible History*. South 24 Parganas. Kolkata: Seribaan.

Habermas, Jürgen. 1989. *The New Conservatism*. Cambridge: Polity.

Hafstein, Valdimar Tr. 2004. "The Making of Intangible Cultural Heritage: Tradition and Authenticity, Community and Humanity." PhD diss., University of California, Berkeley.

———. 2015. "Intangible Heritage as Diagnosis, Safeguarding as Treatment." *Journal of Folklore Research* 52 (2/3): 281–298.

———. 2018. *Making Intangible Heritage: El Condor Pasa and Other Stories from UNESCO*. Bloomington: University of Indiana Press.

Halbwachs, Maurice. 1992. *On Collective Memory*. Translated by Lewis A. Coser. Chicago: Chicago University Press.

Hancock, Mary. 1998. "Unmaking the 'Great Tradition': Ethnography, National Culture, and Area Studies." *Identities* 4 (3/4): 343–388.

Handler, Richard. 1988. *Nationalism and the Politics of Culture in Quebec*. Madison: University of Wisconsin Press.

Hansen, Kathryn. 2001. "Parsi Theatre, Urdu Drama, and the Communalization of Knowledge: A Bibliographic Essay." *Annual of Urdu Studies* 16:43–63.

Harder, Hans, Naishat Zaidi, and Thorsten Tschacher. 2023. *The Vernacular: Three Essays on an Ambivalent Concept and Its Uses in South Asia*. New Delhi: Routledge.

Hardwick, Patricia Ann. 2020. "*Mak Yong*, a UNESCO 'Masterpiece': Negotiating the Intangibles of Cultural Heritage and Politicized Islam." Edited by Ziying You and Patricia Hardwick. Special issue: Intangible Heritage in Asia, *Asian Ethnology* 79 (1): 67–90.

Haridas, V. V. 2016. *Zamorins and the Political Culture of Medieval Kerala*. Hyderabad: Orient BlackSwan.

Hariharan, B. 2009. "Paeans to Lord Krishna." *The Hindu*, October 9.

Haring, Lee. 1972. "Performing for the Interviewer: A Study of the Structure of Context." *Southern Folklore Quarterly* 36 (4): 383–398.

Harvey, David. 2005. *A Brief History of Neoliberalism*. London: Oxford University Press.

Heller, P. 2005. "Reinventing Public Power in the Age of Globalization: The Transformation of Movement Politics in Kerala." In *Social Movements in India: Poverty, Power, and Politics*, vol. 7, edited by R. Ray and M. F. Katzenstein, 79–106. Lanham, MD: Rowman & Littlefield.

Hemme, Dorothee, Regina Bendix, and Markus Tauschek, eds. 2007. *Prädikat 'Heritage': Perspektiven auf Wertschöpfungen aus Kultur*. Münster: Lit.

Hobsbawm, Eric. 1983. "Introduction: Inventing Tradition." In *The Invention of Tradition*, edited by Eric Hobsbawm and Terence Ranger, 1–14. Cambridge: Cambridge University Press.

Hufford, Mary. 1994a. "Introduction: Rethinking the Cultural Mission." In *Conserving Culture: A New Discourse on Heritage*, edited by Mary Hufford, 1–14. Urbana: University of Illinois Press.

———ed. 1994b. *Conserving Culture: A New Discourse on Heritage*. Urbana: University of Illinois Press.

Hymes, Dell. (1975) 1981. "Breakthrough into Performance." In *In Vain I Tried to Tell You: Essays in Native American Ethnopoetics*, edited by Dell Hymes, 79–141. Philadelphia: University of Pennsylvania Press.

Inda, Jonathan Xavier, and Renato Rosaldo. 2002. "Introduction: A World in Motion." In *The Anthropology of Globalization: A Reader*, edited by Jonathan Xavier Inda and Renato Rosaldo, 1–34. Oxford: Blackwell.

Isar, Y. R. 2011. "UNESCO and Heritage: Global Doctrine, Global Practice." In *Heritage, Memory & Identity*, edited by H. K. Anheier and Y. R. Isar, 39–52. London: Sage.

Ivy, Marily. 1995. *Discourses of the Vanishing: Modernity, Phantasm, Japan*. Chicago: University of Chicago Press.

Iyer, P. Rama. 1989. *Margi Annual Report and Accounts*. Trivandrum: Margi.

Jayanthi, C. K. 1993. "Mantrāṅkam in Kūṭiyāṭṭam Theatre." M Phil thesis, Calicut University, Dept. of Sanskrit.

———. 1999. "Aṅgulīyāṅka kūṭiyāṭṭaprayōgamārgaḥ samīkṣātmakam adhyayanam—A Critical Study of Aṅgulīyāṅka in Kūṭiyāṭṭam System." PhD diss., Sree Shankaracharya University of Sanskrit.

———. 2011. "Kutiyattam after the UNESCO Recognition." Edited by Heike Moser. Special issue: Kutiyattam—10 Years after the UNESCO-Declaration, *Indian Folklife* 38:18–19.

Jeffrey, Robin. 1976. "Temple-Entry Movement in Travancore, 1860–1940." *Social Scientist* 4 (8): 3–27.

———. 1992. *Politics, Women and Well-Being: How Kerala Became "a Model."* London: Macmillan.

———. 2004. "Legacies of Matriliny: The Place of Women and the 'Kerala Model.'" *Pacific Affairs* 77 (4): 647–664.

Johan, Virginie. 2000. "Kūttu-kūṭiyāṭṭam: Présentation de ces théâtres dans leur context kéralais et recherches sur la transmission du savoir chez les Cakyar," mémoire de DEA, M. de Rougemont, G. Tarabout dir., Institut d'Études Théâtrales, Université Paris III.

———. 2011a. "Actresses on the Temple Stages? The Conception and Performance of Women in Kūṭiyāṭṭam Rāmāyana Plays." In *Between Fame and Shame: Performing Women—Women Performers in India,* edited by Heidrun Brückner, Hanne M. de Bruin, and Heike Moser, 245–274. Wiesbaden: Harrassowitz.

———. 2011b. "The Flower Needs Its Root to Continue to Grow." Edited by Heike Moser. Special issue: Kutiyattam—10 years after the UNESCO-Declaration, *Indian Folklife* 38:20–24.

———. 2014. "Du Je au Jeu de l'Acteur: Ethnoscénologie du Kūṭiyāṭṭam, Théâtre Épique Indien." Thèse de doctorat d'Etudes Théâtrales, M. de Rougemont et G. Tarabout Dir. Université Paris 3.

———. 2017a. "Dancing the Ritual on the Kūṭiyāṭṭam Theatre Stage." *Cracow Indological Studies* 19 (1): 59–89.

———. 2017b. "The Flower Needs Its Root to Continue to Grow." *Nartanam* 17 (1): 35–44.

———. 2019. "Aṅgulīyāṅkam, Rāmāyaṇa-Vēda of the Cākyārs." In *Two Masterpieces of Kūṭiyāṭṭam: Mantrāṅkam and Aṅgulīyāṅkam,* edited by Heike Oberlin and David Shulman, 187–224. New Delhi: Oxford University Press.

John, C. Stanley. 2006. "States' Reorganisation and the United Kerala Movement." *Journal of Kerala Studies* 33:228–249.

Jones, Betty True. 1977. "Kūṭiyāṭṭam Sanskrit Drama: Changing Criteria of Excellence." In *Asian and Pacific Dance: Selected Papers from the 1974 CORD-SEM Conference (Dance Research Annual XIII),* edited by Adrienne L. Kaeppler, Judy Van Zile, and Carl Wolz, 1–17. New York: Committee on Research in Dance.

Jones, Clifford Reis. 1967. "The Temple Theatre of Kerala: Its History and Description." PhD diss., University of Pennsylvania.

———, ed. 1984. *The Wondrous Crest-Jewel in Performance.* Delhi: Oxford University Press.

Jussy, Selvyn. 2005. "A Constitutive and Distributive Economy of Discourse: Left Movement in Kerala and the Commencement of a Literary Moment." *Social Scientist* 33 (11/12): 29–42.

Kalamandalam Easwaranunni. 2001. "Architect of Mizhavu—Music." In *Proud Imprints of Natya Veda: A Tribute to Gurus of Classical Art Traditions,* edited by V. Kaladharan, 70–76. Mumbai: Keli and Prithvi.

Kalam News Online. 2020. "മാർഗി ഉഷയുടെ നങ്ങ്യാർകൂത്ത് | കംസവധം | കളം | Margi Usha | Nangyarkoothu | Kalam Campus." YouTube video, February 19. 15:18 mins. https://www.youtube.com/watch?v=oH5Ah-uwimA.

Kalidasan, Vinod Kottayil. 2015. "A King Lost and Found: Revisiting the Popular and the Tribal Myths of Mahabali from Kerala." *Studies in South Asian Film & Media* 7 (1/2): 103–118.

Kant, Immanuel. (1795) 1917. *A Perpetual Peace: A Philosophical Essay*, trans. M. Campbell Smith. New York: The Macmillan Company.

Kapchan, Deborah. 2014. "Intangible Heritage in Transit: Goytisolo's Rescue and Moroccan Cultural Rights." In *Cultural Heritage in Transit: Intangible Rights as Human Rights*, edited by Deborah Kapchan, 177–194. Philadelphia: University of Pennsylvania Press.

Kaul, Shonaleeka, ed. 2022. *Retelling Time: Alternative Temporalities from Premodern South Asia*. Delhi: Routledge.

Keith, A. Barriedale. 1924. *The Sanskrit Drama in Its Origin, Development, Theory, and Practice*. Oxford: Clarendon.

Kennedy, Kenneth A. R. 2003. "The Uninvited Skeleton at the Archaeological Table: The Crisis of Paleoanthropology in South Asia in the Twenty-First Century." *Asian Perspectives* 42 (2): 352–367.

Kerala Tourism. 2015. "Signature Video Kerala Tourism: Experience Kerala, God's Own Country." YouTube video, December 8. 4:10 mins. https://www.youtube.com/watch?v=R83BlU5nnbs.

Kerala Varma Pazhassi Raja. 2009. Directed by T. Hariharan, Sree Gokulam Release.

Kinnane, D. 1980. "Ancient Dance Theater Makes First Appearance Outside India." *UNESCO Features* 24:1–3.

Kirshenblatt-Gimblett, Barbara. 2006. "World Heritage and Cultural Economics." In *Museum Frictions: Public Cultures/Global Transformations*, edited by I. Karp, C. A. Kratz, L. Szwaja, and T. Ybarra-Frausto, 161–202. Durham, NC: Duke University Press.

Konagaya, Hideyo. 2020. "Heritage Production in National and Global Cultural Policies: Folkloristics, Politics, and Cultural Economy in Ryukyuan/Okinawan Performance." Edited by Ziying You and Patricia Hardwick. Special issue: Intangible Heritage in Asia, *Asian Ethnology* 79 (1): 45–66.

Korom, Frank. 1989. "Inventing Traditions: Folklore and Nationalism in Colonial Bengal." In *Folklore and Historical Process*, edited by Dunja Rihtman-Auguštin and Maja Povrzanović, 57–83. Zagreb: Institute of Folklore Research.

Korom, Frank J., and Leah Lowthorp, eds. 2019. *South Asian Folklore in Transition: Crafting New Horizons*. London: Routledge.

Kramrisch, Stella, J. R. Cousins, and R. Vasudeva Poduval. 1948. *The Arts and Crafts of Travancore*. London: Royal India and Pakistan Society.

Kurien, Elizabeth Mani. 2013. "Kutiyattam: Intangible Heritage and Transnationalism." PhD diss., University of California, Riverside.

Kurin, Richard. 2022. "Recognizing Intangible Cultural Heritage." In *Music, Communities, Sustainability: Developing Policies and Practices*, edited by Huib Schippers and Anthony Seeger, 21–51. New York: Oxford Academic.

Kutiyattam. Directed by Pragna Thakkar Enros, 8mm color/sound, 1973.

Kutiyattam: Sanskrit Drama in the Temples of Kerala. Directed by Clifford Reis Jones and Betty True Jones, 27 min., 16mm color/sound, 1974.

Kuutma, Kristin. 2007. "The Politics of Contested Representation." In *Prädikat "Heritage"— Perspektiven auf Wertschöpfungen aus Kultur*, edited by Dorothee Hemme, Markus Tauschek, and Regina Bendix, 177–195. Münster: Lit.

———. 2016. "From Folklore to Intangible Heritage." In *Companion to Heritage Studies*, edited by William Logan, Máiréad Nic Craith, and Ullrich Kockel, 41–54. West Sussex, UK: Wiley-Blackwell.

Lahiri, Aradhana. 1997. "Currents and Cross-Currents in the Relation between the CPI and the CPI(M) during 1964–85." PhD diss., University of Burdwan.

Lelyveld, David. 1994. "Upon the Subdominant: Administering Music on All-India Radio." *Social Text* 39:111–127.

Lemos, Justine. 2022. *Tradition and Transformation in Mohiniyattam: An Ethnographic History*. Lanham, MD: Rowman & Littlefield.

Lilja, Agneta. 1996. *Föreställningen om den ideala uppteckningen. En studie av idé och praktik vid tradiitonssamlande arkiv—ett eksempel från Uppsala 1914–1945*. Skrifter utgivna genom Dialekt- och folkminnesarkivet I Uppsala, ser. B. 22. Uppsala: Dialekt- och folkminnesarkivet.

Lowthorp, Leah. 2011. "'Post-UNESCO' Kutiyattam: Some Methodological Considerations." Edited by Heike Moser. Special issue: Kutiyattam—10 Years after the UNESCO-Declaration, *Indian Folklife* 38:10–13.

———. 2013a. "Scenarios of Endangered Culture, Shifting Cosmopolitanisms: Kutiyattam and UNESCO Intangible Cultural Heritage in Kerala, India." PhD diss., University of Pennsylvania.

———. 2013b. "The Translation of Kutiyattam into National and World Heritage on the Festival Stage: Some Identity Implications." In *South Asian Festivals on the Move*, edited by Ute Hüsken and Axel Michaels, 193–225. Wiesbaden: Harrassowitz.

———. 2014. "The Irish Kerryman Joke: Culchies, Cute Hoors, and the Emergence of a Late-Modern Fool Region Joke." Edited by Rosemary Lévy Zumwalt and Perin Gürel. Special issue: Dundes Matters, *Western Folklore* 73 (2/3): 297–322.

———. 2015. "Voices on the Ground: Kutiyattam, UNESCO, and the Heritage of Humanity." *Journal of Folklore Research* 52 (2/3): 157–180.

———. 2016. "Freedom in Performance: Actresses and Creative Agency in the *Kutiyattam* Theatre Complex." Edited by Arya Madhavan. Special issue: Women in Indian Theatre, *Samyukta: A Journal of Women's Studies* 16:83–108.

———. 2017. "Folklore, Politics, and the State: Kutiyattam and National/Global Heritage in India." Edited by Frank J. Korom and Leah Lowthorp. Special issue: South Asian Folklore in the 21st Century, *South Asian History and Culture* 8 (4): 542–559.

———. 2020. "Kutiyattam, Heritage, and the Dynamics of Culture: Claiming India's Place within a Global Paradigm Shift." Edited by Ziying You and Patricia Hardwick. Special issue: Intangible Heritage in Asia, *Asian Ethnology* 79 (1): 21–44.

Ludden, David, ed. 2005. *Making India Hindu: Religion, Community, and the Politics of Democracy in India*, 2nd ed. Delhi: Oxford University Press.

Lukose, Ritty. 2006. "Re(casting) the Secular." *Social Analysis* 50 (3): 38–60.

———. 2009. *Liberalization's Children: Gender, Youth, and Consumer Citizenship in Globalizing India*. Durham, NC: Duke University Press.

Madhavan, Arya. 2010. *Kudiyattam: Theatre and the Actor's Consciousness*. Amsterdam: Rodopi.

———. 2015. "Actor's Imagination: *Kūṭiyāṭṭam* and the *Nāṭyaśāstra*." In *The Nāṭyaśāstra and the Body in Performance*, edited by Sreenath Nair, 182–195. Jefferson, NC: McFarland.

Madhu, Margi, and Unnikrishnan Nambiar. 1994. "Directory of Kutiyattam Artists: 20th Century." Edited by K. Ayyappa Paniker and Sudha Gopalakrishnan. Special issue: Kutiyattam, *Sangeet Natak* 111–114:239–243.

Madhukar, Jayanthi. 2013. "Creation of 'God's Own Country.'" *Bangalore Mirror*, August 7. https://bangaloremirror.indiatimes.com/opinion/you/creation-of-gods-own-country/articleshow/22075259.cms.

Māmāṅkam. 2019. Directed by M. Padmakumar, Kavya Film Company.

Mani Madhava Chakyar: The Master at Work. 1994. Directed by K. N. Panikkar, Sangeet Natak Akademi. https://archive.org/details/dni.ncaa.SNA-15-VCD.

Mankekar, Purnima. 1999. *Screening Culture, Viewing Politics: An Ethnography of Television, Womanhood, and Nation in Postcolonial India*. Durham, NC: Duke University Press.

Manmadhan, Ullattil. 2016. "The Legend of Prester John." Maddy's Ramblings: Thoughts, Opinions, and Musings of a Restless Nomad, March 5. https://maddy06.blogspot.com/2016/03/the-legend-of-prester-john.html.

———. 2018. "The Englishman's Tail." Maddy's Ramblings: Thoughts, Opinions, and Musings of a Restless Nomad, July 22. https://maddy06.blogspot.com/2018/07/the-englishmans-tail.html.

———. 2020. "Zamorin—An Etymological Discussion." Historic Alleys: Historic Musings from a Malabar Perspective, November 11. https://historicalleys.blogspot.com/2020/11/zamorin-etymological-discussion.html.

Mannathukkaren, Nissim. 2006. "Communism and the Appropriation of Modernity, Kerala, India: A Critique of the Subaltern Studies and Postcolonial Theory." PhD diss., Queen's University.

Mardsen, Magnus. 2008. "Muslim Cosmopolitans? Transnational Life in Northern Pakistan." *Journal of Asian Studies* 67 (1): 213–237.
Mascia-Lees, Frances E. 2011. "Aesthetic Embodiment and Commodity Capitalism." In *A Companion to the Anthropology of the Body and Embodiment*, edited by Frances E. Mascia-Lees, 3–23. Oxford: Wiley-Blackwell.
Matsuura, Koïchiro. 2006. "Address on the Occasion of the First Session of the Intergovernmental Committee for the Safeguarding of the Intangible Cultural Heritage, Algiers, Algeria, November 18, 2006." Paris: UNESCO.
Mauss, Marcel. 1936. "Les techniques du corps." *Journal de la Psychologie* 32 (3–4): 271–293.
Mazzarella, William. 2003. *Shoveling Smoke: Advertising and Globalization in Contemporary India*. Durham, NC: Duke University Press.
Menon, A. Sreedhara. 2018. *Kerala History and Its Makers*. Kottayam: DC Books.
———. 2019. *A Survey of Kerala History*. Kottayam: DC Books.
Menon, Dilip. 1994. *Caste, Nationalism and Communism in South India: Malabar, 1900–1948*. New York: Cambridge University Press.
———. 1999. "Houses by the Sea: State-Formation Experiments in Malabar, 1760–1800." *Indian Economic and Political Weekly* 34 (29): 1995–2003.
———. 2002. "Being a Brahmin the Marxist Way: E. M. S. Namboodiripad and the Pasts of Kerala." In *Invoking the Pasts: The Uses of History in South Asia*, edited by Daud Ali, 55–88. Delhi: Oxford University Press.
———. 2006. *The Blindness of Insight: Essays on Caste in Modern India*. Pondicherry: Navayana.
———. 2018. "Deep Time and the Colonial Present: A Prologue to the History Writing of 'Kesari' Balakrishna Pillai." In *Clio and Her Descendants: Essays in Honour of Kesavan Veluthat*, edited by Manu V. Devadevan, 54–71. Delhi: Primus Books.
Menon, K. P. S. 1994. "Major Kūṭiyāṭṭam Artists and Families." Edited by K. Ayyappa Paniker and Sudha Gopalakrishnan. Special issue: Kutiyattam, *Sangeet Natak* 111–114:128–140.
Menon, P. T. Narendra. 1990. "Kulapati of Koodiyattam." *Sruti* 71:23–27.
Menon, T. Madhava, trans. 2003. *Gundert: Keralolpatti, Translation into English*. Trivandrum: International School of Dravidian Linguistics.
Merleau-Ponty, Maurice. 1964. *The Primacy of Perception*. Translated by Carleton Dallery. Evanston, IL: Northwestern University Press.
Metcalf, Barbara D. 1995. "Presidential Address—Too Little and Too Much: Reflections on Muslims in the History of India." *Journal of Asian Studies* 54 (4): 951–967.
Meyer-Rath, Anne. 2007. "Zeitnah, weltfern? Das Konzept des immateriellen Kulturerbes und seine Folgen." In *Prädikat "Heritage": Perspektiven auf Wertschöpfungen aus Kultur*, edited by Dorothee Hemme, Regina Bendix, and Markus Tauschek, 147–176. Münster: Lit.

Mignolo, Walter. 2000. *Local Histories/Global Designs: Coloniality, Subaltern Knowledges, and Border Thinking*. Princeton, NJ: Princeton University Press.

———. 2002. "The Many Faces of Cosmo-polis: Border Thinking and Critical Cosmopolitanism." In *Cosmopolitanism*, edited by Carol A. Breckenridge, Homi K. Bhabha, Sheldon Pollock, and Dipesh Chakrabarty, 157–187. Durham, NC: Duke University Press.

———. 2011. *The Darker Side of Western Modernity: Global Futures, Decolonial Options*. Durham, NC: Duke University Press.

Mignolo, Walter, and Catherine E. Walsh. 2018. *On Decoloniality: Concepts, Analytics, Praxis*. Durham, NC: Duke University Press.

Ministry of Culture [India]. 1949/1950–2008/2009. *Annual Report*. New Delhi: Government of India.

Ministry of Culture [India]. n.d. Unpublished Documents Concerning Ministry of Culture's UNESCO-Related Funding of Kutiyattam, in Lowthorp's research collection.

Mohandas, K. P. 2008. "നങ്ങ്യാർ കൂത്ത് - അമേരിക്കൻ വനിതയുടെ (Manorama News) (American Woman's Nangiarkoothu, Manorama News)." YouTube video, September 18. 1:19 mins. https://www.youtube.com/watch?v=HDYZ28crHg8.

Moser, Heike. See Oberlin, Heike.

Moser, Heike. 1996. "Film Clip 1: Ēṭanāṭu Sarōjini Naṅṅyār" [original: Moser Hi8 25.2], https://www.phil.uni-wuerzburg.de/indologie/women-performers/contributors/moser/film-clips/film-clip-1/.

———. 1999/2000. "Mantrāṅkam: The Third Act of Pratijñāyaugandharāyaṇam in Kūṭiyāṭṭam." *Bulletin d'Études Indiennes* 17–18:563–584.

———. 2007. "To Enjoy Playing with Play." In *The Power of Performance*, edited by Heidrun Brückner, Elisabeth Schömbucher, and Philip Zarrilli, 209–234. Delhi: Manohar.

———. 2008. *Naṅṅyār-Kūttu: Ein Teilaspekt des Sanskrittheaterkomplexes Kūṭiyāṭṭam: Historische Entwicklung und performative Textumsetzung*. Wiesbaden: Harrassowitz (Drama und Theater in Südasien 6).

———. 2011. "How Kūṭiyāṭṭam Became Kūṭi-āṭṭam, 'Acting Together' or: The Changing Role of Female Performers in the Naṅṅyār-Kūttu Tradition of Kerala." In *Between Fame and Shame: Performing Women; Women Performers in India*, edited by Heidrun Bruckner, Hanne de Bruin, and Heike Moser, 169–188. Wiesbaden: Harrassowitz.

———. 2013a. "Kūṭiyāṭṭam on the Move: From Temple Theatres to Festival Stages." In *South Asian Festivals on the Move*, edited by Ute Hüsken and Axel Michaels, 245–273. Wiesbaden: Harrassowitz.

———. 2013b. "Tanzende Frauen und spielende Männer: gender crossing und gender bender im indischen Tanz und Theater." In *Frauenbilder /*

Frauenkörper. Inszenierungen des Weiblichen in den Gesellschaften Süd- und Ostasiens, edited by Stephan Köhn and Heike Moser, 353–366. Wiesbaden: Harrassowitz.

Moser, Heike, and Paul Younger. 2013. "Kerala: Plurality and Consensus." In *The Modern Anthropology of India: Ethnography, Themes and Theory*, edited by Peter Berger and Frank Heidemann, 136–156. London: Routledge.

Mucciarelli, Elena, and Adheesh Sathaye. 2024. "Transcreating Sanskrit Humour through Kūṭiyāṭṭam: The Translation and Performance of the Rasasadana Bhāṇa." *Asian Literature and Translation* 11 (1): 16–51.

Munjeri, Dawson. 2004. "Tangible and Intangible Heritage: From Difference to Convergence." *Museum International* 56 (1/2): 12–20. https://doi.org/10.1111/j.1350-0775.2004.00453.x.

———. 2009. "Following the Length and Breadth of the Roots: Some Dimensions of Intangible Heritage." In *Intangible Cultural Heritage*, edited by Laurajane Smith and Natsuko Akagawa, 131–150. London: Routledge.

Nagarajan, Saraswathy. 2009. "Time Traveller." *The Hindu*, June 6.

Nair, Appukuttan D. 1994a. "The Art of Kūṭiyāṭṭam." Edited by K. Ayyappa Paniker and Sudha Gopalakrishnan. Special issue: Kutiyattam, *Sangeet Natak* 111–114:12–32.

———. 1994b. "Abhinaya in Kūṭiyāṭṭam." Edited by K. Ayyappa Paniker and Sudha Gopalakrishnan. Special issue: Kutiyattam, *Sangeet Natak* 111–114:55–57.

———. 1994c. "Purvaranga in Kūṭiyāṭṭam vis-a-vis Natya Sastra." Edited by K. Ayyappa Paniker and Sudha Gopalakrishnan. Special issue: Kutiyattam, *Sangeet Natak* 111–114:58–62.

Nair, Malini. 2016. "Dance Like a King." *The Hindu*, October 15. https://www.thehindu.com/features/magazine/Dance-like-a-king/article16074837.

Naithani, Sadhana. 1997. "The Colonizer-Folklorist." *Journal of Folklore Research* 34 (1): 1–14.

———. 2001a. "An Axis Jump: British Colonialism in the Oral Folk Narratives of Nineteenth-Century India." *Folklore* 112:183–88.

———. 2001b. "Prefaced Space: Tales of the Colonial British Collectors of Indian Folklore." In *Imagined States*, edited by Luisa Del Giudice and Gerald Porter, 64–79. Logan: Utah State University Press.

———. 2002. "To Tell a Tale Untold: Two Folklorists in Colonial India." *Journal of Folklore Research* 39 (2/3): 201–216.

———. 2010. *The Story-Time of the British Empire: Colonial and Postcolonial Folkloristics.* Jackson: University Press of Mississippi.

Nambiar, G. K. 2010. *Anuṣṭhāna Kalōpāsakaḷ* (Ritual Arts). Bangalore: Self-published.

Nambiar, P. K. Narayanan. 1984. *Śrīkṛṣṇacaritam Naṅṅyārammakūttu* (*The Story of Lord Krishna in Nangiarammakoothu*). Kottayam: National Bookstall.

———. 1994. "Rhythm and Music." Edited by Sudha Gopalakrishnan and K. Ayyappa Paniker. Special issue: Kutiyattam, *Sangeet Natak* 111–114:101–112.
———. 2005. *Miḻāvŭ: Nambyāruṭe Kramadeepika* (Mizhavu: The Nambiar's Production Manual). Killimangalam: Padmasree Mani Madhava Chakyar Smaraka Gurukulam.
———, ed. 1980. *Mantrāṅkam*. Thrissur: Kerala Sahitya Akademi.
Namboodiripad, E. M. S. 1944. *Party Sanghādakan* (Party Organizer). Calicut: Deshabhimani.
———. 1952. *The National Question in Kerala*. Bombay: People's Publishing House.
———. 1982. *Selected Writings*, vol. 1. Calcutta: National Book Agency.
———. 1994. *The Communist Party in Kerala: Six Decades of Struggle and Advance*. New Delhi: National Book Centre.
———. (1946) 1999. "Onnēkālkkōti Malayāḷikaḷ" (One and a Quarter Crore Malayalees). In *E.M.S. Sampoornakritikal*, vol. 6, edited by P. Govinda Pillai. Thiruvananthapuram: Chinta.
———. 2010a. *History, Society, and Land Relations: Selected Essays*. New Delhi: LeftWord Books.
———. 2010b. *The Frontline Years: Selected Articles*. New Delhi: LeftWord Books.
———. (1948) 2017. *Kēraḷam, Malayāḷikaḷuṭe Mātṛubhūmi* (*Kerala, the Motherland of the Malayalis*). Thiruvananthapuram: Chintha Publications.
Nangiar, Usha. 2018. *Abhinētri: The Strisaradhi of Natyayana*. Thrissur: Krishnan Nambiar Mizhavu Kalari.
Narayan, Kirin. 1989. *Storytellers, Saints, and Scoundrels: Folk Narrative in Hindu Religious Teaching*. Philadelphia: University of Pennsylvania Press.
Narayanan, Mundoli Vasudevan. 2005. "From Exclusivity to Exposure: The Changing Circumstances of Kutiyattam." *Comparative Culture* 11:31–46.
———. 2006. "Over-Ritualization of Performance: Western Discourses on Kutiyattam." *TDR* 50 (2): 136–153.
———. 2022. *Space, Time, and Ways of Seeing: The Performance Culture in Kutiyattam*. New Delhi: Routledge.
Nicholson, Rashna Darius. 2019. "What's in a Name?: The Performance of Language in the Invention of Colonial and Postcolonial South Asian Theatre History." In *The Methuen Drama Handbook of Theatre History and Historiography*, edited by Claire Cochrane and Joanna Robinson, 199–209. London: Bloomsbury.
Nieuhoff, John. 2003. *Voyages and Travels into Brazil and the East-Indies, 1640–1649*, 2 vols. New Delhi: Asian Educational Institute. https://archive.org/details/voyagetravelsinto2john/page/n9/mode/2up.
Nilayamgode, Devaki. 2011. *Antharjanam: Memoirs of a Namboodiri Woman*. Translated by Indira Menon and Radhika P. Menon. New Delhi: Oxford University Press.
Nossiter, T. J. 1982. *Communism in Kerala: A Study in Political Adaptation*. Berkeley: University of California Press.

Notar, Beth E. 2008. "Producing Cosmopolitanism at the Borderlands: Lonely Planeteers and 'Local' Cosmopolitans in Southwest China." *Anthropological Quarterly* 81 (3): 615–650.

Noyes, Dorothy. 2015. "From Cultural Forms to Policy Objects: Comparison in Scholarship and Practice." *Journal of Folklore Research* 52 (2/3): 299–313.

———. 2016. *Humble Theory: Folklore's Grasp on Social Life*. Bloomington: Indiana University Press.

Oberlin, Heike. 2016. "Nangiar-Kuttu: The Changing Role of Female Performers." *Nartanam* 16 (3): 107–134.

———. 2019. "*Mantrāṅkam*, an Ancient Integration Project? Its Structure and Composition." In *Kūṭiyāṭṭam: Mantrāṅkam and Aṅgulīyāṅkam*, edited by Heike Oberlin and David Shulman, 39–53. New Delhi: Oxford University Press.

Oberlin, Heike, and David Shulman, eds. 2019. *Two Masterpieces of Kūṭiyāṭṭam: Mantrāṅkam and Aṅgulīyāṅkam*. New Delhi: Oxford University Press.

Ollett, Andrew. 2017. *Language of the Snakes: Prakrit, Sanskrit, and the Language Order of Premodern India*. Berkeley: University of California Press.

Oring, Elliott. 1986. *Folk Groups and Folklore Genres: An Introduction*. Logan: Utah State University Press.

———. 2004. "Political Jokes under Repressive Regimes." *Western Folklore* 63 (3): 209–236.

Osella, Filippo, and Caroline Osella. 2000a. *Social Mobility in Kerala: Modernity and Identity in Conflict*. London: Pluto.

———. 2000b. "The Return of King Mahabali: The Politics of Morality in Kerala." In *The Everyday State and Society in Modern India*, edited by Christopher Fuller and Véronique Bénéï, 137–162. New Delhi: Social Science Press.

———. 2003. "Migration and the Commoditization of Ritual: Sacrifice, Spectacle and Contestations in Kerala, India." *Contributions to Indian Sociology* 37 (1/2): 109–139.

———. 2006. "Once Upon a Time in the West? Stories of Migration and Modernity from Kerala, South India." *Journal of the Royal Anthropological Institute* 12:569–588.

O'Shea, Janet. 2007. *At Home in the World: Bharata Natyam on the Global Stage*. Middletown, CT: Wesleyan University Press.

Otero, Solimar, and Mintzi Auanda Martínez-Rivera. 2021. "Introduction: How Does Folklore Find Its Voice in the Twenty-First Century? An Offering/Invitation from the Margins." In *Theorizing Folklore from the Margins: Critical and Ethical Approaches*, edited by Solimar Otero and Mintzi Auanda Martínez-Rivera, 3–21. Bloomington: Indiana University Press.

Oza, Rupal. 2006. *The Making of Neoliberal India: Nationalism, Gender, and the Paradoxes of Globalization*. New York: Routledge.

Painkulam Rama Chakyar, Kootiyattom. n.d. Directed by T. V. Viswanathan, 18 mins.

Panchal, Goverdhan. 1968. "Koottampalam Sanskrit Stage of Kerala." *Sangeet Natak* 8:17–30.

Paniker, K. Ayyappa. 1994. "Introduction: The Aesthetics of Kūṭiyāṭṭam." Edited by K. Ayyappa Paniker and Sudha Gopalakrishnan. Special issue: Kutiyattam, *Sangeet Natak* 111–114:7–11.

Paniker, K. Ayyappa, and Sudha Gopalakrishnan, eds. 1994. Special issue: Kutiyattam, *Sangeet Natak* 111–114:1–243.

Paniker, Nirmala. 1992. *Nangiar Koothu*. Irinjalakuda: Natana Kairali.

Parayil, Govindan, ed. 2000. *Kerala: The Development Experience—Reflections on Sustainability and Replicability*. London: Zed Books.

Paredes, Américo, and Richard Bauman, eds. 1972. *Toward New Perspectives in Folklore*. Austin: University of Texas Press.

Paul, G. S., ed. 2005. *Heritage: Preserving the Age-Old Sanskrit Theatre*. Irinjalakuda: Ammannur Chachu Chakyar Smaraka Gurukulam.

Paulose, K. G., transl. and ed. 1993. *Naṭāṅkuśa: A Critique on Dramaturgy*. Tripunithura: Ravivarma Government Sanskrit College.

———. 2000. *Bhagavadajukkam in Kūṭiyāṭṭam: The Hermit and the Harlot—The Sanskrit Farce in Performance*. Delhi: New Bharathiya Book Corporation.

———. 2003. *Improvisations in Ancient Theatre*. Tripunithura: International Centre for Kutiyattam.

———. 2006. *Kūṭiyāṭṭam Theatre: The Earliest Living Tradition*. Kottayam: DC Books.

———. 2013. *Vyaṅgyavyākhyā: The Aesthetics of Dhvani in Theatre*. New Delhi: Rashtriya Sanskrit Sansthan & DK Printworld.

Peterson, Indira Viswanathan, and Davesh Soneji. 2008a. "Introduction." In *Performing Pasts: Reinventing the Arts in Modern South Asia*, edited by Indira Peterson and Davesh Soneji, 1–40. New Delhi: Oxford University Press.

———, eds. 2008b. *Performing Pasts: Reinventing the Arts in Modern South India*. New Delhi: Oxford University Press.

Pfaff, Walter. 1997. "The Ant and the Stone: Learning Kutiyattam." *TDR* 41 (4): 133–162.

Pillai, Manu S. 2015. *The Ivory Throne: Chronicles of the House of Travancore*. New Delhi: HarperCollins.

Pisharoti, K. P. Narayana, ed. 1967. *Āścaryacūḍāmaṇi: Śaktibhadramahākaviyuṭe Āścaryacūḍāmaṇi nāṭakavum atinṭe abhinayattinuvēṇṭi raciccittuḷḷa kramadīpika, āṭṭaprakāram, tuṭaṅṅiya āṭṭakrama viśadīkaraṇaṅṅaḷum*. Thrissur: Kerala Sangeet Natak Akademi.

Pisharoti, K. Rama. 1932/1934. "Kerala Theatre." *Journal of the Annamalai University* 1 (1): 91–113 (part 1); 3 (2): 141–159 (part 2).

Pollock, Sheldon. 1996. "The Sanskrit Cosmopolis, 300–1300: Transculturation, Vernacularization, and the Question of Ideology." In *Ideology and Status of Sanskrit*, edited by Jan E. M. Houben, 197–247. Leiden: Brill.

———. 2000. "Cosmopolitan and Vernacular in History." *Public Culture* 12 (3): 591–625.

———. 2006. *The Language of the Gods in the World of Men: Sanskrit, Culture and Power in Premodern India*. Berkeley: University of California Press.

———. 2016. *A Rasa Reader: Classical Indian Aesthetics*. New York: Columbia University Press.

Prabhakaran Pillai, P. N. 1974. "Historical Introduction to the Kerala Land Reforms Act and the Working of the Land Tribunals." *Cochin University Law Review* 1 (1): 14–70.

Pradeep, K. 2015. "The Story of a Statue." *The Hindu*, June 19. https://www.thehindu.com/features/metroplus/the-story-of-a-statue/article7333585.ece.

Prange, Sebastian R. 2018. *Monsoon Islam: Trade and Faith on the Medieval Malabar Coast*. Cambridge: Cambridge University Press.

Prasad, Leela. 2020. *The Audacious Raconteur: Sovereignty and Storytelling in Colonial India*. Ithaca, NY: Cornell University Press.

Prickett, Stephen. 2009. *Modernity and the Reinvention of Tradition: Backing into the Future*. Cambridge: Cambridge University Press.

Prime Video India. 2018. "Harmony with A. R Rahman | Mizhavu – Featurette | TV Show | Prime Exclusive | Amazon Prime Video." YouTube video, August 11. 1:08 mins. https://www.youtube.com/watch?v=FVSXR1ewZ5U.

Radhakrishnan, Ratheesh. 2015. "Thiruvithamkoor, Malabar, Kerala: Speculations on the Regions in 'Regional Cinema.'" *BioScope* 6 (2): 126–144.

Raghavan, V. 1933. "Kathakali and Other Forms of Bharata Natya Outside Kerala." *Triveni* 6 (2) (September–October). https://www.wisdomlib.org/history/compilation/triveni-journal/d/doc67509.html

———. 1993a. "Sanskrit Drama in Performance." In *Sanskrit Drama in Performance*, edited by R. van M. Baumer and J. R. Brandon, 9–44. Honolulu: University of Hawaii Press.

———. 1993b. *Sanskrit Drama: Its Aesthetics and Production*. Madras: Self-published.

———. 2016. "Kutiyattam: Its Form and Significance as Sanskrit Drama." Edited by K. K. Gopalakrishnan. Special issue: 50 Years of Kutiyattam, *Nartanam* 16 (3): 57–74 (originally published in 1966/1967, *Samskrita Ranga Annual* 5:77–84).

Raja, K. Kunjunni. 1964. *Kūṭiyāṭṭam: An Introduction*. New Delhi: Sangeet Natak.

———. (1958) 1980. *The Contribution of Kerala to Sanskrit Literature*. Madras: University of Madras.

Raja, K. Rama Varma. 1934. "Chakkiyar-Kuttu of Kerala." *Quarterly Journal of the Mythic Society* 24 (3): 236–244.

Rajagopal, Arvind. 1999. "Thinking through Emerging Markets: Brand Logics and the Cultural Forms of Political Society in India." *Social Text* 17 (3): 131–149.

———. 2001. *Politics after Television: Religious Nationalism and the Reshaping of the Indian Public*. New York: Cambridge University Press.

Rajagopalan, L. S. 1990. "The Wizard of Eyes." *Sruti* 71:17–22.

———. 1994. "Music in Kūṭiyāṭṭam." Edited by K. Ayyappa Paniker and Sudha Gopalakrishnan. Special issue: Kutiyattam, *Sangeet Natak* 111–114:113–122.

———. 1997. *Women's Role in Kūdiyāṭṭam*. Chennai: Kuppuswami Sastry Research Institute.

———. 2000. *Kūdiyāṭṭam: Preliminaries and Performance*. Chennai: Kuppuswami Sastry Research Institute.

Rajendran, Chettiarthodi. 1989. *The Traditional Sanskrit Theatre of Kerala*. Calicut: University of Calicut.

———. 2016. "From Fast to Feast: The Aśana Discourse of the Vidūṣaka in Kerala's Traditional Sanskrit Theatre." In *A World of Nourishment: Reflections on Food in Indian Culture*, edited by Cinzia Pieruccini and Paola M. Rossi, 111–119. Milan: LEDIpublishing.

Rajendu, S. 2012. *Vaḷḷuvanāṭū Caritram: Prāchīnakālam mutal AD 1792 ware (Valluvanadu History: From Prehistoric Times until AD 1792)*. Perintalmanna: K. Sankaranarayanan.

———. 2016. *Āṟaṅṅōṭuswarūpam Granthavari Tirumānāmkunnu Granthavari, A.D. 1484–1874 (Arangode Swaroopam Palm-Leaf Manuscripts Tirumanamkunnu Palm-Leaf Manuscripts, A.D. 1484–1874)*. Edapal: Vallathol Vidyapeetham.

Ramanath, Renu. 1996. "A New Lease of Life for Kerala's Koothambalams." *Sruti* 1996:13–14.

Ramanujan, A. K. 1989. "Where Mirrors Are Windows: Toward an Anthology of Reflections." *History of Religions* 28 (3): 187–216.

Ramavarma, K. T. 1978. "Putiya Vihāraraṅṅall (Old Art, New Pastures)." *Mathrubhumi* 56 (25) (September 3): 6–13; 56 (26) (September 10): 43–48.

———. 1981. *Ammannūr Cāccuccākyār*. Śukapuraṃ: Vaḷḷattōḷ Vidyāpīṭhaṃ.

Ranwa, Rucha. 2021. "Heritage, Community Participation, and the State: Case of the Kalbeliya Dance of India." *International Journal of Heritage Studies* 27 (10): 1038–1050.

Rao, Velcheru Narayana, David Shulman, and Sanjay Subrahmanyam. 2001. *Textures of Time: Writing History in South India 1600–1800*. Delhi: Permanent Black.

Reddington, Helena. 2021. "Performing the Vernacular: The Tuḷḷal Tradition of Kerala." PhD diss., McGill University.

Reddy, Deepa S. 2005. "The Ethnicity of Caste." *Anthropological Quarterly* 78 (3): 543–584.

Ricci, Ronit. 2011. *Islam Translated: Literature, Conversion, and the Arabic Cosmopolis of South and Southeast Asia*. Chicago: University of Chicago Press.

Richmond, Farley P. 1990. "Introduction: The Classical Tradition and Its Predecessors." In *Indian Theatre: Traditions of Performance*, edited by Farley Richmond, Darius Swann, and Phillip Zarilli, 21–24. Honolulu: University of Hawaii Press.

———. 1993. "Suggestions for Directors of Sanskrit Plays." In *Sanskrit Drama in Performance*, eds. R. van M. Baumer and J. R. Brandon, 74–109. Honolulu: University of Hawaii Press.

Richmond, Farley, and Yasmin Richmond. 1985. "The Multiple Dimensions of Time and Space in Kūṭiyāṭṭam: The Sanskrit Theatre of Kerala." *Asian Theatre Journal* 2 (1): 50–60.

Robbins, Bruce. 2012. *Perpetual War: Cosmopolitanism from the Viewpoint of Violence*. Durham, NC: Duke University Press.

Royce, Anya Peterson. 2004. *Anthropology of the Performing Arts: Artistry, Virtuosity, and Interpretation in a Cross-Cultural Perspective*. Oxford: Alta Mira Press.

Salini, V. G. 2021. "The Terrible Beauty on the Stage: Narrative and Performance Aesthetics of *Kutiyattam* Analyzed through the Representation of Shurpanakha." *Asian Theatre Journal* 38 (2): 441–461.

Sangameswaran, A. 2009. "Tribute to Maestros." *The Hindu*, February 6.

Sangari, Kumkum, and Sudesh Vaid. 1989. *Recasting Women: Essays in Colonial History*. New Delhi: Kali for Women.

Sanjeev, S. 2011. "On Castes, Malayalams and Translations." In *Translation in Asia: Theories, Practices, Histories*, edited by Ronit Ricci and Jan van der Putten, 167–180. London: Routledge.

Sankunni, Kottarathil. 2016. *Aitihyamāla: The Great Legends of Kerala*, 3rd ed., vols. 1–3. Translated by Sreekumari Ramachandran. Kozhikode: Mathrubhumi Books.

Sastri, Ganapati T., ed. 1915. *The Svapnavāsavadattā of Bhāsa*. 2nd ed. Bhasa's Work No. 1. Trivandrum: Trivandrum Government Press.

Schechner, Richard. 2001. "Rasaesthetics." *TDR/The Drama Review* 45 (3 [171]): 27–50.

Scheper-Hughes, Nancy, and Margaret Lock. 1987. "The Mindful Body: A Prolegomenon to Future Work in Medical Anthropology." *Medical Anthropology Quarterly* 1 (1): 6–41.

Scher, Philip W. 2010. "UNESCO Conventions and Culture as a Resource." *Journal of Folklore Research* 47 (1/2): 197–202.

Schoepf, B. G. 1992. "AIDS, Sex and Condoms: African Healers and the Reinvention of Tradition in Zaire." *Medical Anthropology* 14 (2–4): 225–242.

Scott, James C. 1987. *Weapons of the Weak: Everyday Forms of Peasant Resistance*. New Haven, CT: Yale University Press.

———. 1990. *Domination and the Arts of Resistance: Hidden Transcripts*. New Haven, CT: Yale University Press.

Seeger, Anthony. 2015. "Understanding UNESCO: A Complex Organization with Many Parts and Many Actors." *Journal of Folklore Research* 52 (2/3): 269–280.

Seitel, P., and J. Early. 2002. "UNESCO Meeting in Rio: Steps toward a Convention." *Smithsonian Talk Story* 21:13.

Seizer, Susan. 2005. *Stigmas of the Tamil Stage: An Ethnography of Special Drama Artists in South India*. Durham, NC: Duke University Press.

Shanmugam, S. V. 2018. *Essays on the History of Malayalam*. Kuppam: Dravidian University.

Sharma, V. S. 1994. "Kūṭiyāṭṭam at Kerala Kalamandalam." Edited by Sudha Gopalakrishnan and K. Ayyappa Paniker. Special issue: Kutiyattam, *Sangeet Natak* 111–114:217–219.

Shulman, David Dean. 1986. *The King and the Clown in South Indian Myth and Poetry*. Princeton, NJ: Princeton University Press.

———. 2022a. *The Rite of Seeing: Essays on Kūṭiyāṭṭam*. Delhi: Primus Books.

———. 2022b. "Proleptic Pasts and Involuted Causalities in Kūṭiyāṭṭam." In *Retelling Time: Alternative Temporalities from Premodern South Asia*, edited by Shonaleeka Kaul, 25–40. London: Routledge.

Singer, Milton. 1958. "From the Guest Editor." Special issue: Traditional India—Structure and Change, *Journal of American Folklore* 71 (281): 191–204.

Singh, Prerna. 2010. "We-Ness and Welfare: A Longitudinal Analysis of Social Development in Kerala, India." *World Development* 39 (2): 282–293.

Sklar, Deidre. 1994. "Can Bodylore Be Brought to Its Senses?" *Journal of American Folklore* 107 (423): 9–22.

———. 2001. *Dancing with the Virgin: Body and Faith in the Fiesta of Tortugas, New Mexico*. Berkeley: University of California Press.

Śliwczyńska, Bożena. 2009. *Tradycja teatru świątynnego* (The Tradition of the Temple Theatre Kūṭiyāṭṭam). Warsaw: Wydawnictwo Akademickie Dialog.

———. 2020. "The *Rāmāyaṇa* Story in the Cākyār Kūttu Format." In *Oral-Written-Performed: The Rāmāyaṇa Narratives in Indian Literature and Art*, edited by Danuta Stasik, 105–112. Heidelberg: CrossAsia eBooks.

Smith, Laurajane. 2006. *Uses of Heritage*. London: Routledge.

SNA (Sangeet Natak Akademi). 1953/1958–2018/2019. *Annual Report*. New Delhi: Sangeet Natak Akademi.

———. 1995a. *Kutiyattam Mahotsavam Booklet*. New Delhi: Sangeet Natak Akademi.

———. 1995b. "Painkulam Rama Chakyar: Kutiyattam film parts 1 and 2, Nangiarkoothu (2 hrs 45 min, copy from Kerala Kalamandalam), Accession: 24-9-1995" (Note: part 1 is *Painkulam*, Viswananthan, n.d., and part 2 is *Kutiyattam*, Jones and Jones, 1974).

———. 2006a. Interview with Ammannur Parameswara Chakyar by P. Venugopalan. April 15–16, 2006. Sangeet Natak Akademi Archives. Video, 1:56:00. Acquisition date April 28, 2006.

———. 2006b. Interview with Thankammu Nangiaramma by P. Venugopalan. April 14–15, 2006. Sangeet Natak Akademi Archives. Video, 1:56:00. Acquisition date April 28, 2006.

Sobhanan, B. 1978. *Dewan Velu Tampi and the British*. Trivandrum: Kerala Historical Society.

Sowle, John Stevens. 1982. "The Traditions, Training, and Performance of Kutiyattam, Sanskrit Drama in South India." PhD diss., University of California, Berkeley. http://www.kaliyuga.com/JohnDissertationPg.htm.

Special Correspondent. 2010. "Army Celebrates Anniversary of Colachel Battle." *The Hindu*, July 31. https://www.thehindu.com/news/cities/Thiruvananthapuram/Army-celebrates-anniversary-of-Colachel-battle/article16217159.ece.

Sreekanth, V. 2013. "The Visionary Virtuoso of Kūṭiyāṭṭam Māni Mādhava Chākyār." Special issue: Guru Mani Madhava Chakyar, *Nartanam* 13 (1): 7–21.

Sreekumar, Sharmila. 2007. "The Land of Gender Paradox: Getting Past the Commonsense of Contemporary Kerala." *Inter-Asia Cultural Studies* 8 (1): 34–54.

Srinivas, M. N. 1952. *Religion and Society among the Coorgs of South India*. Oxford: Oxford University Press.

Stokker, Kathleen. 1995. *Folklore Fights the Nazis: Humor in Occupied Norway, 1940–1945*. Madison, NJ: Farleigh Dickinson University Press.

Stoler Miller, Barbara, ed. 1984. *Theater of Memory: The Plays of Kalidasa*. New York: Columbia University Press.

Sullivan, Bruce M. 1995. "Introduction to the Kūṭiyāṭṭam Tradition." In *The Sun God's Daughter and King Saṃvaraṇa: Tapatī-Saṃvaraṇam and the Kūṭiyāṭṭam Drama Tradition*, edited by N. P. Unni and Bruce Sullivan, 18–32. Delhi: Nag.

———. 1997. "Temple Rites and Temple Servants: Religion's Role in the Survival of Kerala's Kūṭiyāṭṭam Drama Tradition." *International Journal of Hindu Studies* 1 (1): 97–115.

———. 2007. "Dying on the Stage in the *Nāṭyaśāstra* and *Kūṭiyāṭṭam*: Perspectives from the Sanskrit Theatre Tradition." *Asian Theatre Journal* 24 (2): 422–439.

Sutton, Maude Keely. 2015. "In the Forest of Sand: History, Devotion, and Memory in South Asian Muslim Poetry." PhD diss., University of Texas at Austin.

Swann, Darius L. 1993. "Rās Līlā and the Sanskrit Drama." In *Sanskrit Drama in Performance*, edited by R. van M. Baumer and J. R. Brandon, 264–274. Honolulu: University of Hawaii Press.

Tarabout, Gilles. 2005. "Malabar Gods, Nation-Building and World Culture on Perceptions of the Local and the Global." In *Globalizing India: Perspectives from Below*, edited by Jackie Assayag and Christopher J. Fuller, 185–209. London: Anthem.

———. 2009. "The Annamanada Case: A Hundred Years of Conflict over Rights and Territories in Kerala." In *Territory, Soil and Society in South India*, edited by D. Berti and G. Tarabout, 271–309. Delhi: Manohar.

Tauschek, Markus. 2010. *Wertschöpfung aus Kultur: der Karneval von Binche und die Konstituierung kulturellen Erbes*. Berlin: Lit.

Taylor, Christopher. 2014. "Global Circulation as Christian Enclosure: Legend, Empire, and the Nomadic Prester John." *Literature Compass* 11 (7): 445–459.

Taylor, McComas. 2022. "Time Is Born of His Eyelashes: Puranic Measurement and Conceptions of Time." In *Retelling Time: Alternative Temporalities from Premodern South Asia*, edited by Shonaleeka Kaul, 75–88. London: Routledge.

Thapar, Romila. 2003. *Early India: From the Origins until AD 1300*. Berkeley: University of California Press.

The 1947 Partition Archive, Berkeley, CA. https://www.1947partitionarchive.org/.
The Flight of the Condor: A Letter, a Song, and the Story of Intangible Heritage. 2018. Directed by Áslaug Einarsdóttir, performance by Valdimar Tr. Hafstein.
Thomas, Sonja. 2018. *Privileged Minorities: Syrian Christianity, Gender, and Minority Rights in Postcolonial India*. Seattle: University of Washington Press.
———. 2021. "Studying Race in the Field of South Asian Religions." *Religion Compass* 15 (4): 1–9.
Tripathi, Radhavallabh. 2013. "Nāṭyaśāstra and Its Regional Manifestations." In *Vyaṅgyavyākhyā: The Aesthetics of Dhvani in Theatre*, edited by K. G. Paulose, 12–20. New Delhi: Rashtriya Sanskrit Sansthan & DK Printworld.
UNESCO. 1977. *Letter from the Ministry of Foreign Affairs and Religion, Republic of Bolivia, April 24, 1973*. Document FOLK/I/3, Annex. Paris: UNESCO.
———. 1989. *Recommendations on the Safeguarding of Tradition Culture and Folklore*. Paris: UNESCO.
———. 2001a. *First Proclamation of Masterpieces of the Oral and Intangible Heritage of Humanity*. Paris: UNESCO.
———. 2001b. *UNESCO Universal Declaration on Cultural Diversity*. Paris: UNESCO.
———. 2001c. *Proclamation of Masterpieces of the Oral and Intangible Heritage of Humanity. Guide for the Presentation of Candidature Files*. Paris: UNESCO.
———. 2003a. *Second Proclamation of Masterpieces of the Oral and Intangible Heritage of Humanity*. Paris: UNESCO.
———. 2003b. *Convention for the Safeguarding of the Intangible Cultural Heritage*. Paris: UNESCO.
———. 2004a. "Mission Report." (By R. P. Perrera to Cochin/Trivandrum, Kerala, February 6–7, 2004). Unpublished manuscript.
———. 2004b. *UNESCO New Delhi Office Annual Report*. New Delhi: UNESCO.
———. 2007. "UNESCO Japan Funds-in-Trust Terminal Report: Safeguarding and Transmission of the Kutiyattam Sanskrit Theatre." (By Moe Chiba, New Delhi Regional Office). Unpublished manuscript.
UNESCO and WIPO. 1985. *Model Provisions for National Laws on the Protection of Expressions of Folklore against Illicit Exploitation and Other Prejudicial Actions*. Parisand Geneva: UNESCO and WIPO. https://www.wipo.int/edocs/lexdocs/laws/en/unesco/unesco001en.pdf.
Unni, N. P. 1990. "Nāgānanda on the Kerala Stage." *Pūrṅatrayī*, 17 (1): 1–24.
———. 1995. "Kulaśekhara Varman and *Tapatī-Saṃvaraṇam*." In *The Sun God's Daughter and King Saṃvaraṇa: Tapatī-Saṃvaraṇam and the Kūṭiyāṭṭam Drama Tradition*, edited by N. P. Unni and Bruce Sullivan, 1–17. Delhi: Nag.
———. 1998. *Mattavilāsa Prahasana*. New Delhi: Nag.
———, ed. 2001. *Bhasa Afresh: New Problems in Bhasa Plays*. Delhi: Nag.

———. 2013. "Introducing Vyaṅgyavyākhyā." In *Vyaṅgyavyākhyā: The Aesthetics of Dhvani in Theatre,* translated and edited by K. G. Paulose, 22–26. New Delhi: Rashtriya Sanskrit Sansthan & DK Printworld.

Unni, N. P., and Bruce Sullivan, eds. 1995. *The Sun God's Daughter and King Saṃ varaṇa: Tapatī-Saṃvaraṇam and the Kūṭiyāṭṭam Drama Tradition.* Delhi: Nag.

———. 2001. *Wedding of Arjuna and Subhadrā: The Kūṭiyāṭṭam Drama Subhadrā Dhanañjaya.* New Delhi: Nag.

van Zanten, Wim. 2004. "Constructing New Terminology for Intangible Cultural Heritage." *Museum International* 56 (1/2): 36–44. https://doi.org/10.1111/j.1350-0775.2004.00456.x.

Vatsyayan, Kapila. 1980. *Traditional Indian Theatre: Multiple Streams.* New Delhi: National Book Trust.

———. 2001. *Bharata: The Nāṭyaśāstra.* New Delhi: Sahitya Akademi.

Veluthat, Kesavan. 2004a. "The *Kēraḷōlpatti* as History: A Note on Pre-colonial Traditions of Historical Writing in India." In *Culture and Modernity: Historical Explorations,* edited by K. N. Ganesh, 19–38. Calicut: University of Calicut.

———. 2004b. "Evolution of a Regional Identity: Kerala in India." *India: Studies in the History of an India,* edited by Irfan Habib, 82–97. Aligarh: Munshiram Manoharlal.

———. 2009. *The Early Medieval in South India.* New Delhi: Oxford University Press.

———. 2013. *Of Ubiquitous Heroines and Elusive Heroes: The Cultural Milieu of Manipravalam Poetry from Medieval Kerala.* Published lecture. New Delhi: Indian Council of Historical Research, March 18.

———. 2018. "History and Historiography in Constituting a Region: The Case of Kerala." *Studies in People's History* 5 (1): 13–31.

Venu, Gopalan. 1988. "The Kootiyattam Artistes of the Ammannur Family." *National Center for the Performing Arts (NCPA) Quarterly Journal* 17 (1): 12–22. https://www.sahapedia.org/ncpaq-march-1988-vol-xvii-issue-1#lg=1&slide=0.

———. 2002. *Into the World of Kutiyattam with the Legendary Ammannur Madhavachakyar.* Kottayam: DC Press.

———. 2009. "Kutiyattam: Beyond Religion and Ritual Observance." In *Religion, Ritual, Theatre,* edited by Bent Holm, Bent Flemming Nielsen, and Karen Vedel, 121–130. Frankfurt: Peter Lang.

———. 2013. *Rāmāyaṇa Saṁkṣepaṁ: An Āṭṭaprakāraṁ (Acting Manual) for Depicting the Story of Rāmāyaṇa through Mudrās in Kūtiyāṭṭaṁ Theatre.* Irinjalakuda: Natana Kairali.

———. 2020. "Six and a Half Decades on the Stage." *Narthaki,* June 21, 2020. https://narthaki.com/info/prism/prism14.html.

Venugopalan, P. 2007. *Kutiyattam Register.* Thiruvananthapuram: Margi.

———, ed. 2009. *Aścaryacūḍamaṇi: Sampūrṇamāya Āṭṭaprakāravum Kramadīpikayum.* Trivandrum: Margi.

Wacquant, Loïc. 2004. *Body and Soul: Ethnographic Notebooks of an Apprentice-Boxer.* New York: Oxford University Press.

Wadley, Susan S. 1986. "The Kathā of Śakaṭ: Two Tellings." In *Another Harmony: New Essays on the Folklore of India,* edited by Stuart H. Blackburn and A. K. Ramanujan, 195–232. Berkeley: University of California Press.

Wardle, Huon. 2000. *An Ethnography of Cosmopolitanism in Kingston, Jamaica.* Lewiston, NY: Edwin Mellen Press.

Warrier, N. V. Krishna. 1971. "Staging of Sanskrit Plays in the North India in the Seventh and the Ninth Centuries A.D. and Its Relation to Kutiyattam." *Keli* 8 (2): 36–38.

Webb, Adam K. 2015. *Deep Cosmopolis: Rethinking World Politics and Globalisation.* London: Routledge.

Weidman, Amanda. 2006. *Singing the Classical, Voicing the Modern: The Postcolonial Politics of Music in South India.* Durham, NC: Duke University Press.

Wendland, Wend. 2004. "Intangible Heritage and Intellectual Property: Challenges and Future Prospects." *Museum International* 56:97–107. https://doi.org/10.1111/j.1350-0775.2004.00463.x.

Werbner, Pnina, ed. 2008. *Anthropology and the New Cosmopolitanism.* Oxford: Berg.

Wilcox, Emily E. 2018. "Dynamic Inheritance: Representative Works and the Authoring of Tradition in Chinese Dance." *Journal of Folklore Research* 55:77–111.

Young, Katharine G. 1987. *Taleworlds and Storyrealms: The Phenomenology of Narrative.* Dordrecht: Martinus Nijhoff.

Young, Katharine, and Barbara Babcock, eds. 1994. Special issue: Bodylore, *Journal of American Folklore* 107 (423): 1–196.

Yun, Kyoim. 2015. "The Economic Imperative of UNESCO Recognition: A South Korean Shamanic Ritual." *Journal of Folklore Research* 52 (2/3): 181–198.

Zarilli, Phillip. 1984. *The Kathakali Complex: Actor, Performance and Structure.* New Delhi: Abhinav.

———. 1996. *When the Body Becomes All Eyes: Paradigms, Discourses and Practices of Power in Kalarippayattu, a South Indian Martial Art.* Delhi: Oxford University Press.

———. 2000. *Kathakali Dance-Drama: Where Gods and Demons Come to Play.* London: Routledge.

Zerubavel, Eviatar. 2004. *Time Maps: Collective Memory and the Social Shape of the Past.* Chicago: University of Chicago Press.

Websites

Muziris Heritage website: http://www.muzirisheritage.org.

Mrunmaya website: https://mrunmaya.wordpress.com/.

INDEX

Abrahams, Roger, 222
acting (*abhinaya*), 80–81, 84, 102n9, 226, 228, 231; via facial expressions (*sāttvikābhinaya*), 14, 36, 57, 74, 81, 252; via the body (*āṅgikābhinaya*), 74; via the eyes (*nētrābhinaya*), 33, 41, 225, 227; fourfold acting, 84–85; *lokadharmi* (realistic acting), 64, 65, 81, 86, 179; microtraditions of, 62; *natyadharmi* (stylized acting), 65, 81, 86, 179; repetition (*kēṭṭāṭuka*) of lines, 253; Stanislavsky method in Western acting, 81–82
actors [*purushavesham*] (*pūruṣaveṣam*), 48–50, *50*, 202; in Kutiyattam troupe, 45; male students as minority, 198, 200; red thread tied around forehead, 196; remuneration of, 50, 264; in Sanskrit theater, 82. *See also* Chakyar (Cākyār) caste
actresses [*streevesham*] (*strīveṣam*), 46–48, *48*, 59, 101; female students as majority, 197, 198; imaginative freedom among, 87; in Nangiarkoothu, *88*; notions of propriety in female body and dress, 185–86; in Sanskrit theater, 82. *See also* Nangiar (Naṅṅyār) caste
aesthetic embodiment, 178
All India Radio, 173, 223, 227, 233, 249n29
Ammannur Chachu Chakyar Smaraka Gurukalam, 49, 51, 59, 66, 71n4, 71n14, 250n49, 276n16; acting style associated with, 62; annual Kutiyattam festival, 120; embodied cosmopolitanism and, 90; revival of, 255
Ammannur Chakyar family, 63, 138, 144
Ammannur performance style, 62, 64–65, 70
Anderson, Benedict, 217
Anguliyankam [The Act of the Ring]. See *Ascharyachoodamani* [*Aścaryacūḍamaṇi*, Wondrous Crest Jewel]
Anguliyankam/Anguliyankamkoothu (type of solo performance), 71n10, 91, 99, 126, 193, 248n20, 264; Nambiar Tamil recitation in, 91–92
Appadurai, Arjun, 6, 29n7, 247n3
Appiah, Kwame A., 254

Leah Lowthorp is Assistant Professor of Anthropology and Folklore at the University of Oregon. She is editor (with Frank J. Korom) of *South Asian Folklore in Transition: Crafting New Horizons* (Routledge, 2019).

For Indiana University Press
Lesley Bolton, Project Manager/Editor
Allison Chaplin, Acquisitions Editor
Anna Garnai, Production Coordinator
Sophia Hebert, Assistant Acquisitions Editor
Katie Huggins, Production Manager
Alyssa Lucas, Marketing and Publicity Manager
Dan Pyle, Online Publishing Manager
Pamela Rude, Senior Artist and Book Designer

www.ingramcontent.com/pod-product-compliance
Lightning Source LLC
Chambersburg PA
CBHW051435270326
41935CB00019B/1826
9780253073594